# Volume 3

## Ema Toyama

**Translated and adapted by
Alethea Nibley and Athena Nibley**

**Lettered by Paige Pumphrey**

# Missions of Love
## Ema Toyama

# Character

## Shigure Kitami

The ever-popular, yet black-hearted, student body president. He made a game of charming all the girls and making them confess their love to him, then writing it all down in his student notebook, but Yukina discovered his secret!

**Yukina Himuro**
Least favorite food: urchin

## Yukina Himuro

A third-year junior high student who strikes terror in the hearts of all around her with her piercing gaze, feared as the "Absolute Zero Snow Woman." Only Akira knows that she is also the popular cell phone novelist Yupina.

**Shigure Kitami**
Least favorite food: natto/fermented soybeans

## Akira Shimotsuki

Yukina's cousin and fellow student. He loves to eat. As Yukina's confidant, he can always be found nearby, watching over her. There's a good-looking face hiding behind that hair.

**Akira Shimotsuki**
Least favorite food: baked beans

It is time for love.
Secret cell phone novelist vs. the most popular boy in school.
A mission of love for absolute servitude.

## Story

Yukina, who is secretly a cell phone author, has one major concern: her utter lack of romantic experience makes it impossible for her to write love stories. But she happens upon a certain student notebook, which allows her to blackmail Shigure. She decides to learn about love by forcing Shigure into romantic situations--holding her hand, putting his arms around her, kissing her, etc. At first, Shigure was on the lookout for his chance at a counterattack, but as he continues carrying out her missions, their relationship begins to change...?! Then, Akira joins the fray in an attempt to get Yukina back from Shigure. Akira frankly confesses his love to Yukina, and she...

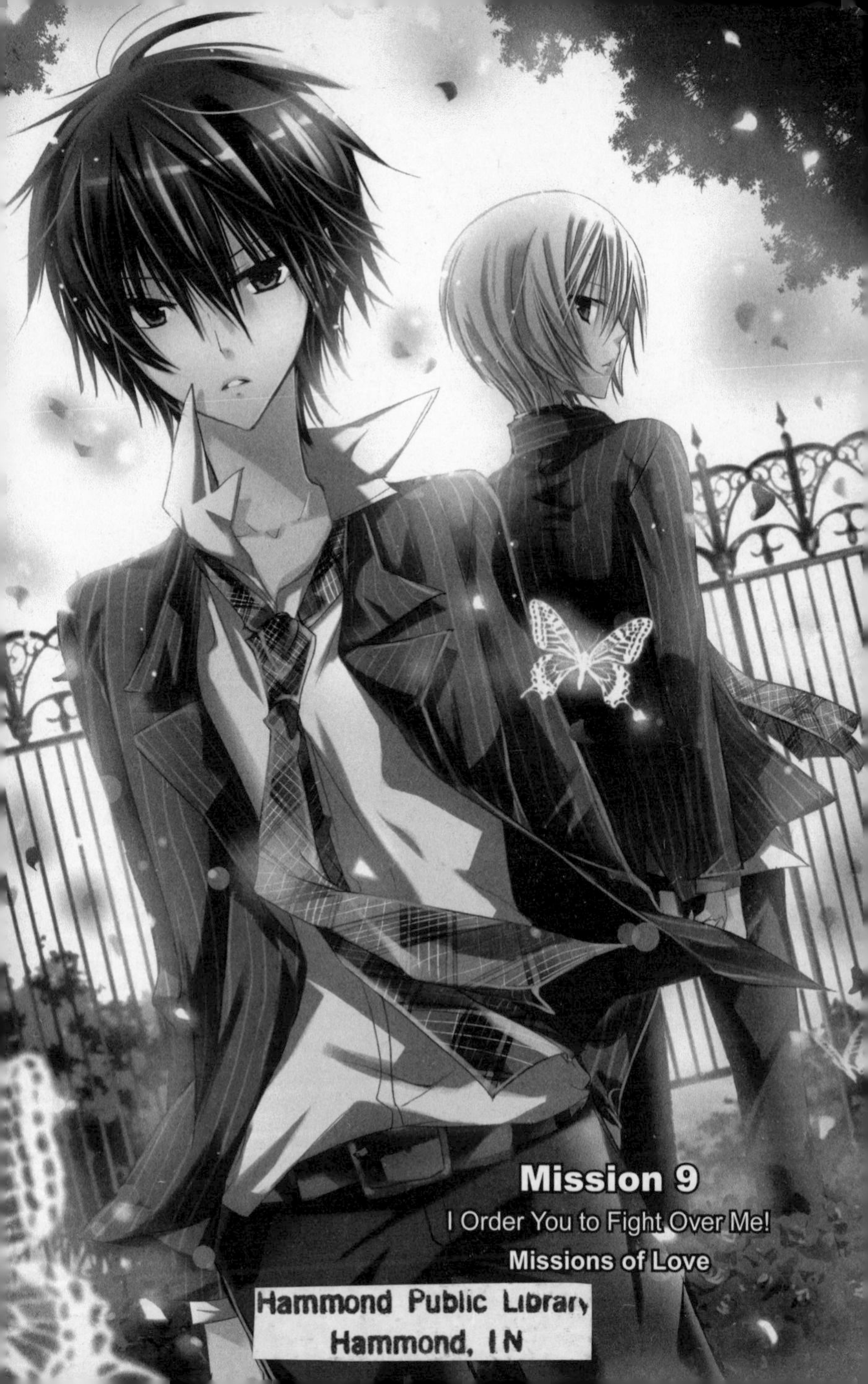
Mission 9
I Order You to Fight Over Me!
Missions of Love

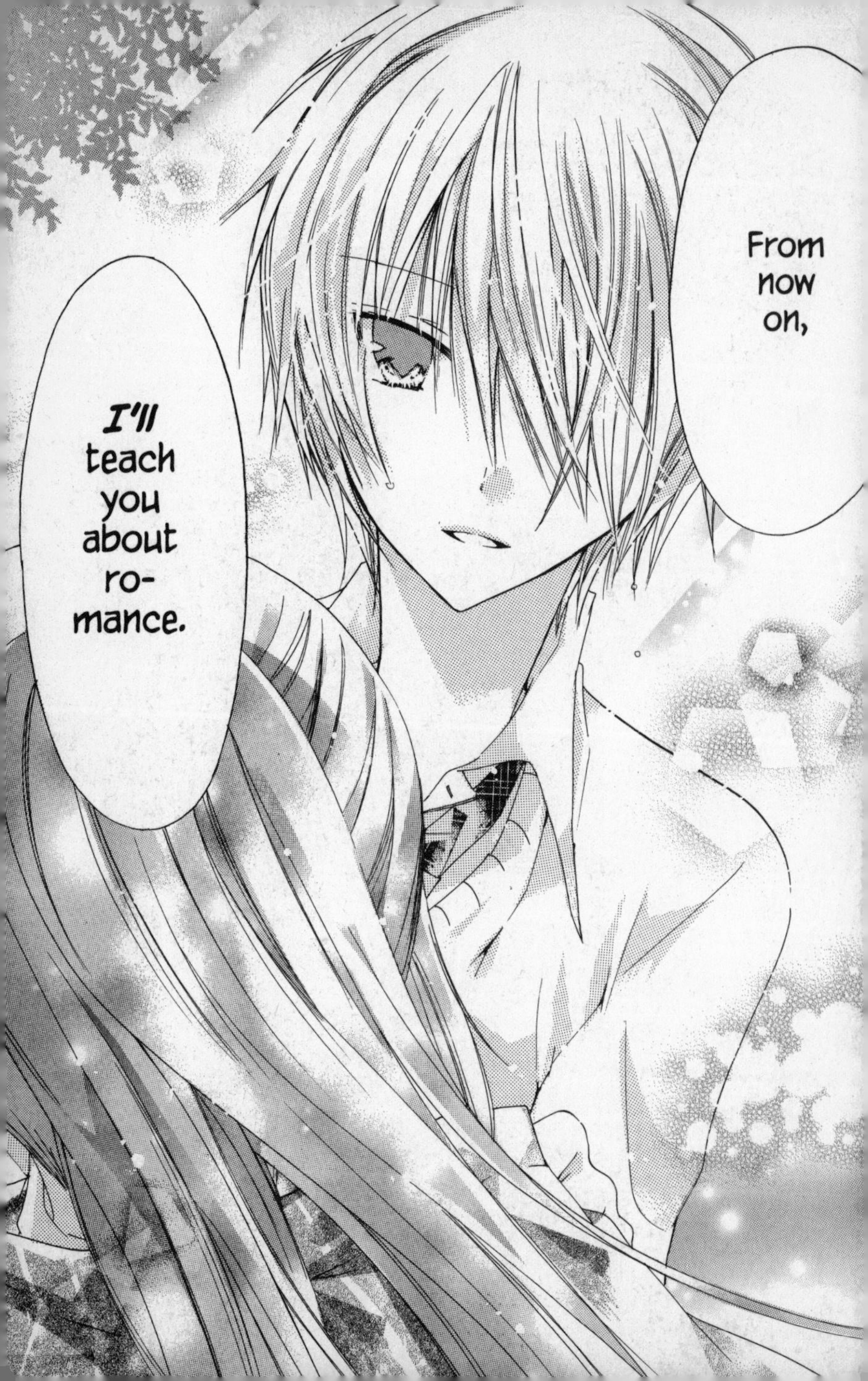
From now on,
I'll teach you about ro-mance.

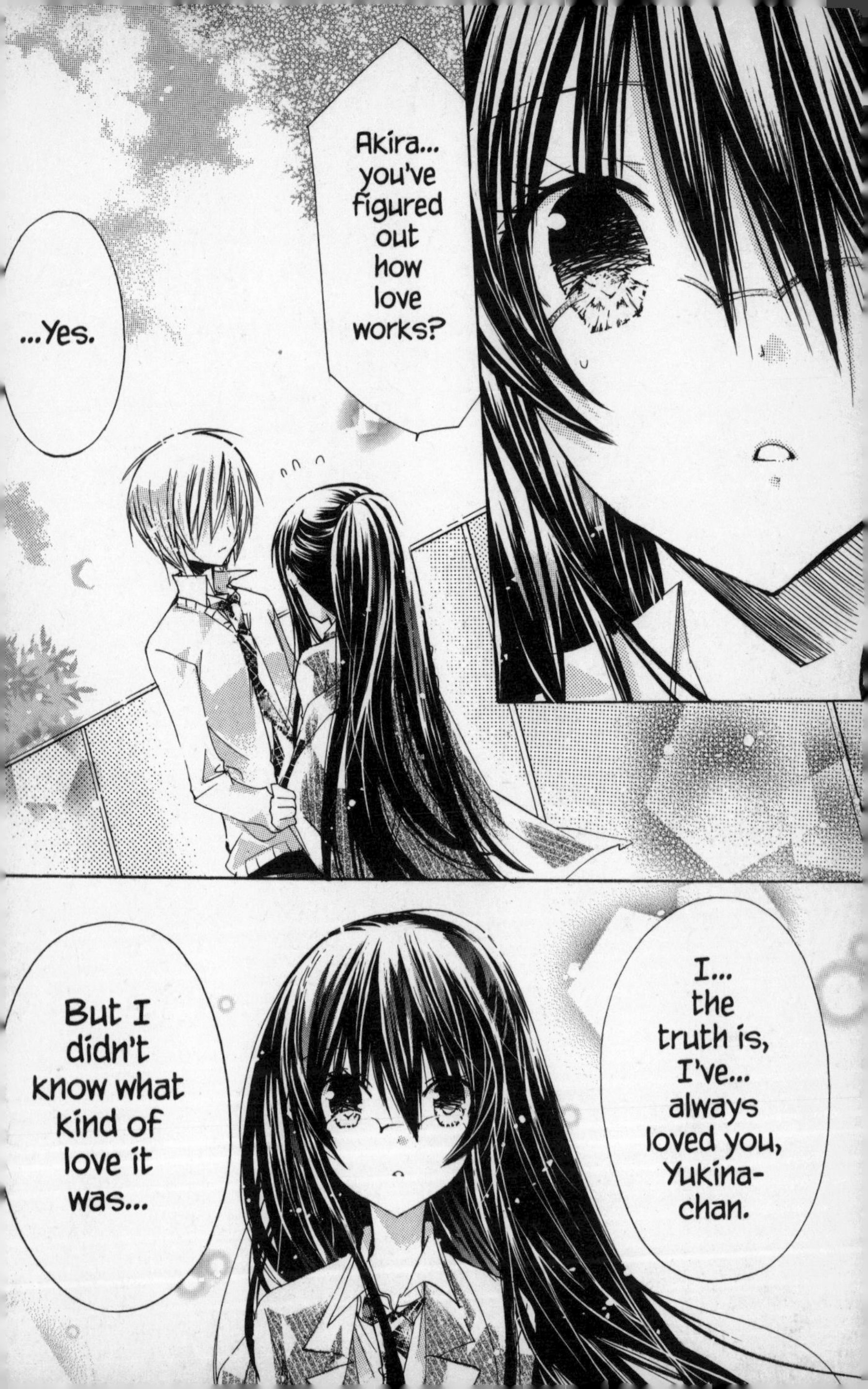
Akira... you've figured out how love works?
...Yes.
I... the truth is, I've... always loved you, Yukina-chan.
But I didn't know what kind of love it was...

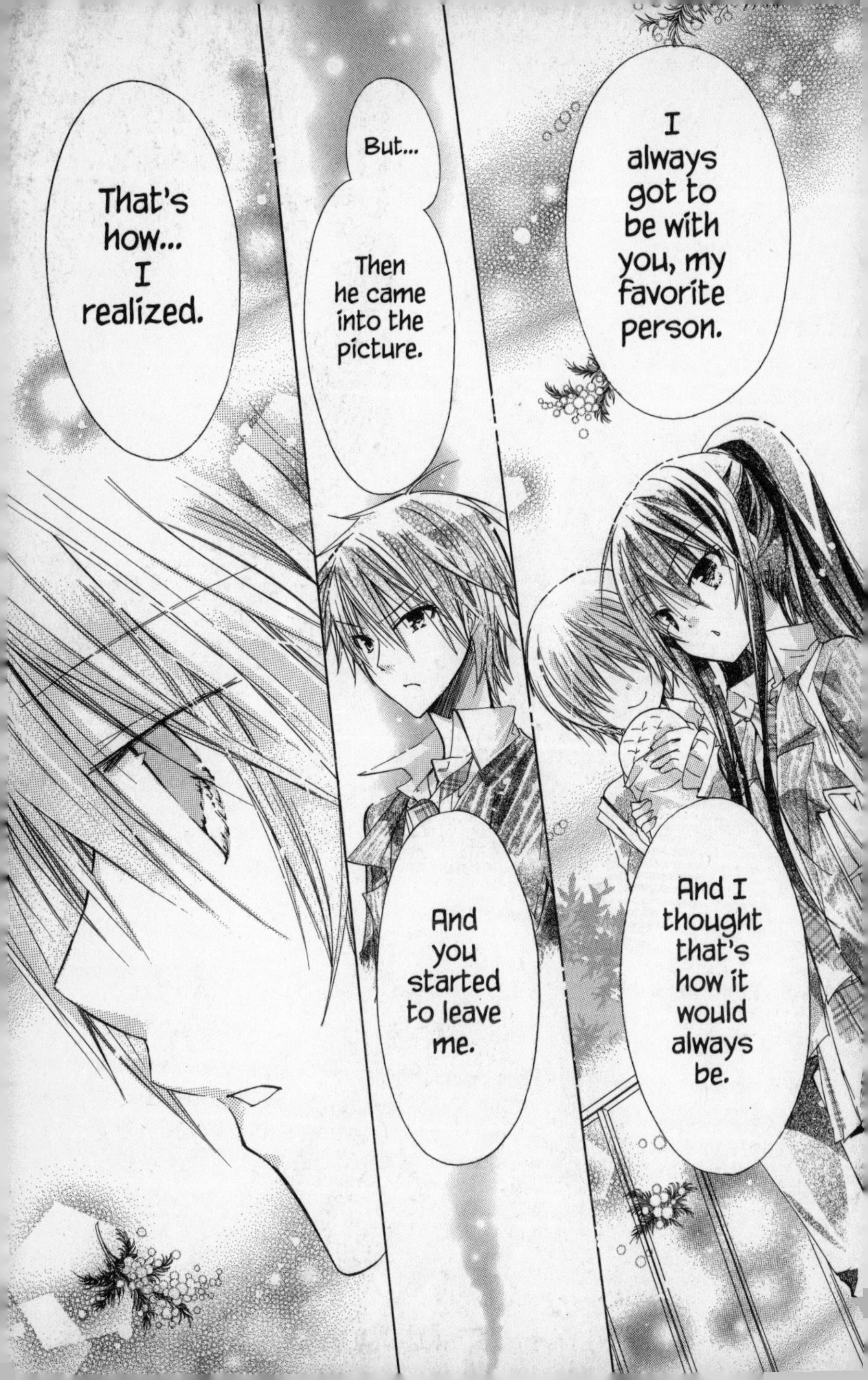
I always got to be with you, my favorite person.
And I thought that's how it would always be.
But...
Then he came into the picture.
And you started to leave me.
That's how... I realized.

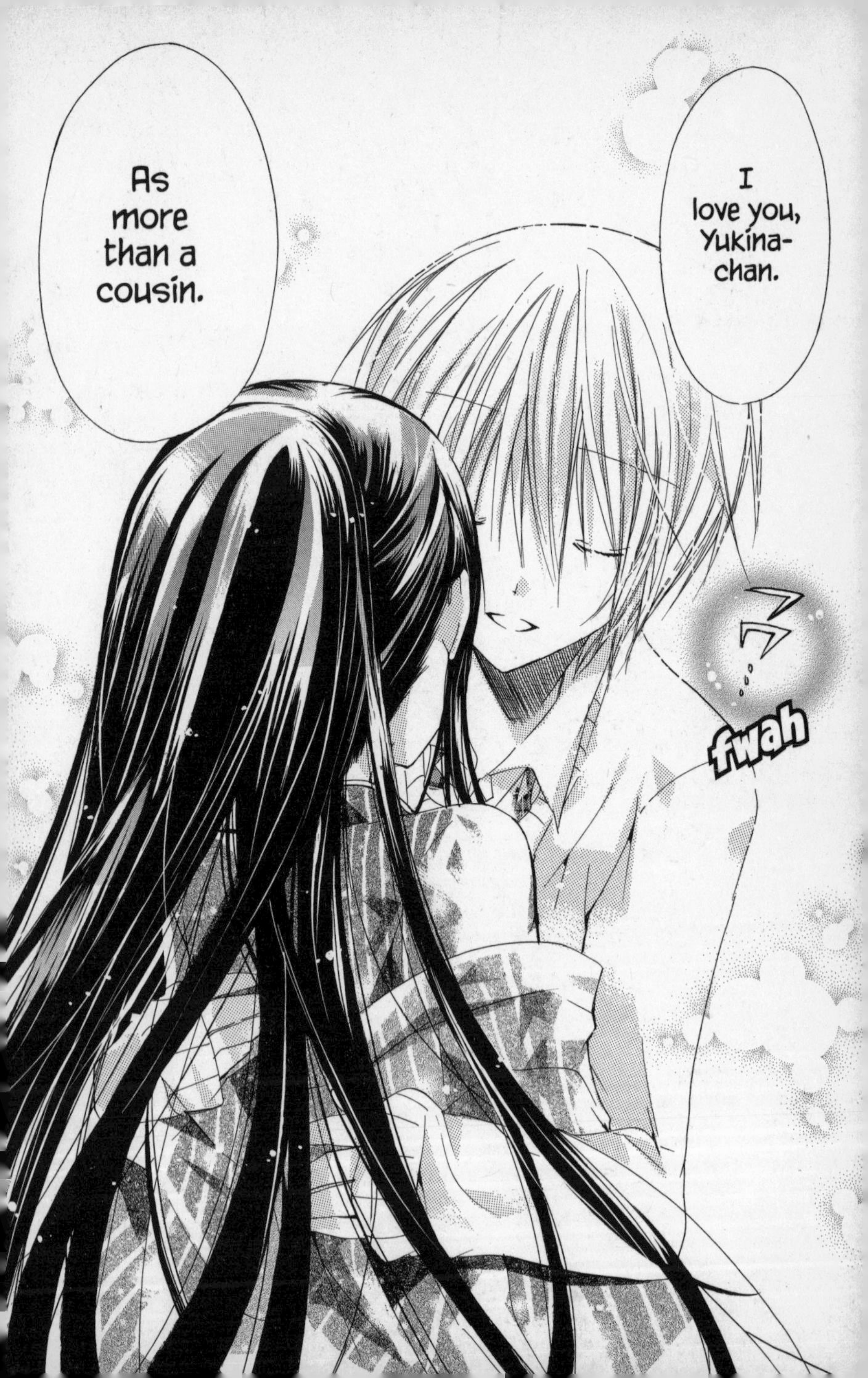
I love you, Yukina-chan.
As more than a cousin.
fwah

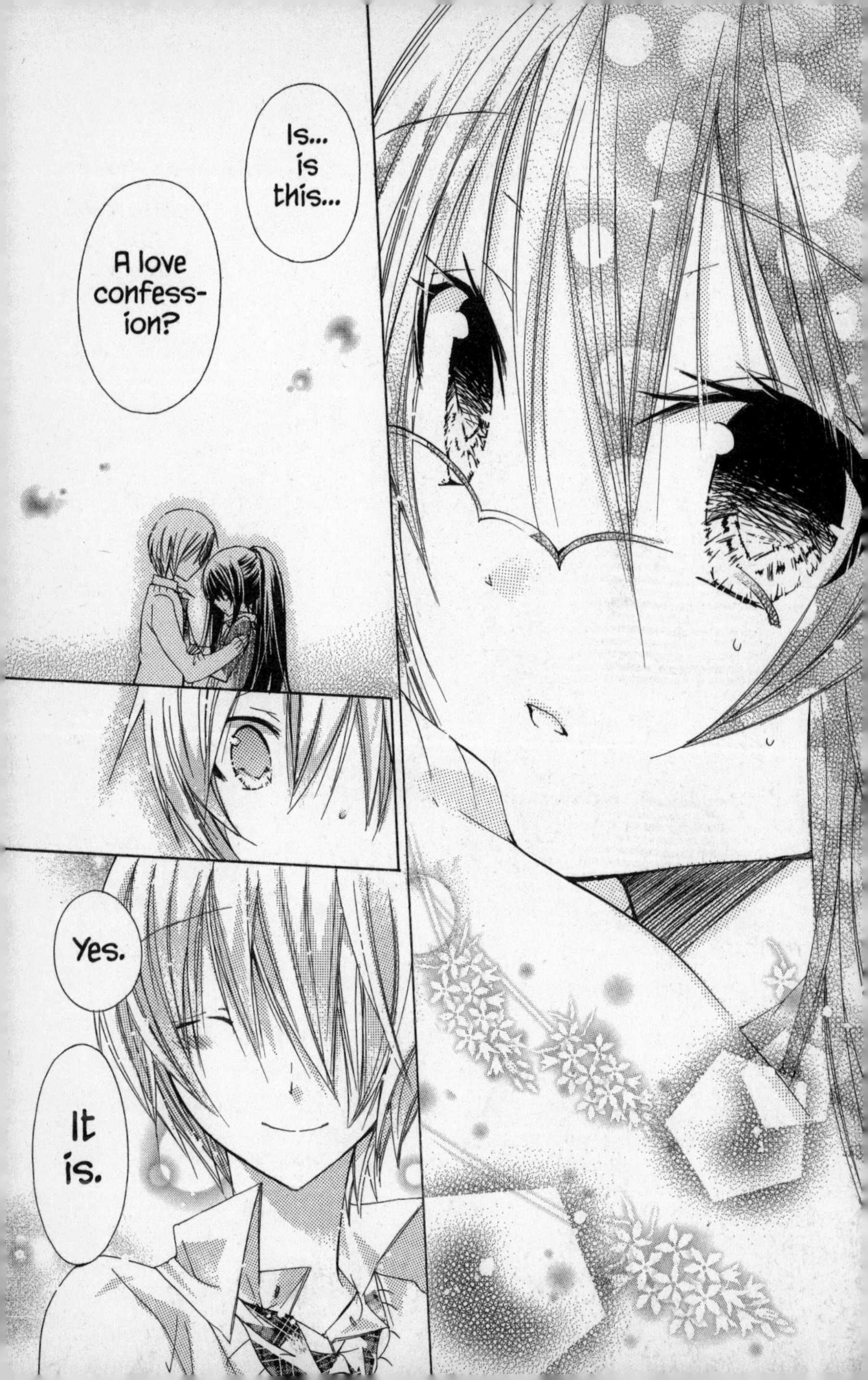
Is... is this...
A love confess-ion?
Yes.
It is.

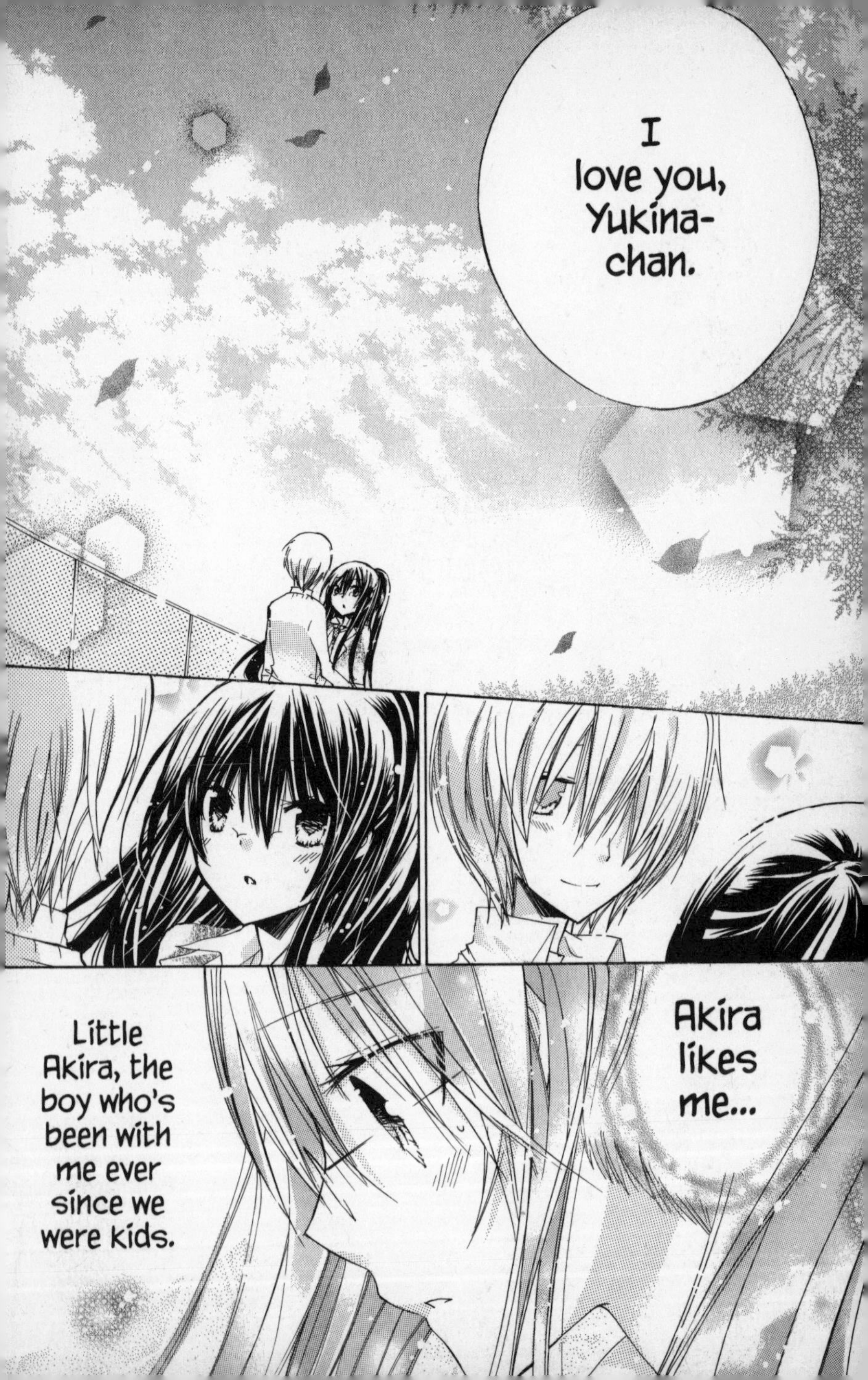
I love you, Yukina-chan.
Akira likes me...
Little Akira, the boy who's been with me ever since we were kids.

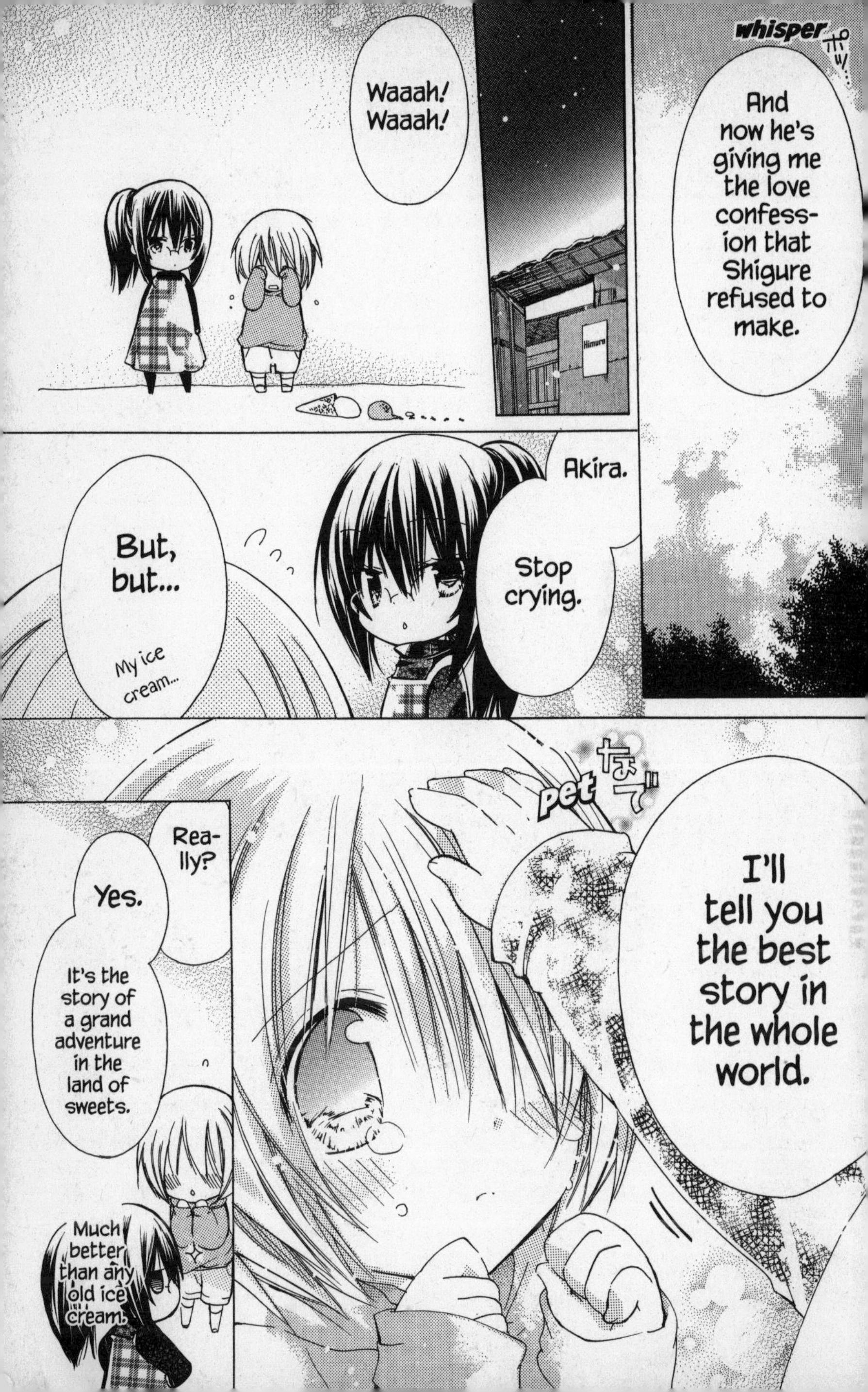
whisper ポツ…
And now he's giving me the love confess-ion that Shigure refused to make.
Himuro
Waaah! Waaah!
Akira.
Stop crying.
But, but...
My ice cream...
pet なで
I'll tell you the best story in the whole world.
Rea-lly?
Yes.
It's the story of a grand adventure in the land of sweets.
Much better than any old ice cream.

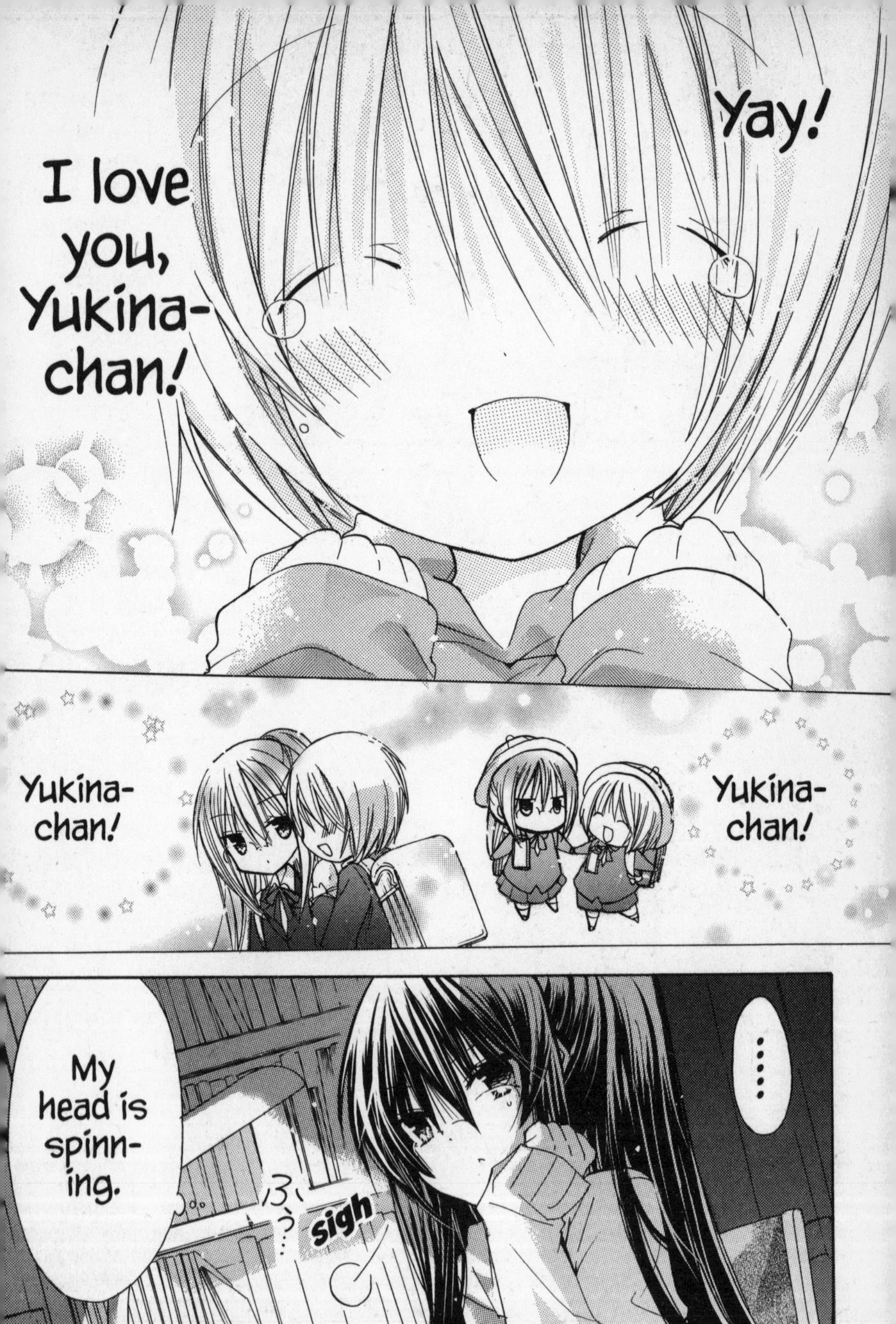
Yay!
I love you, Yukina-chan!
Yukina-chan!
Yukina-chan!
......
My head is spinn-ing.
ふう…
sigh

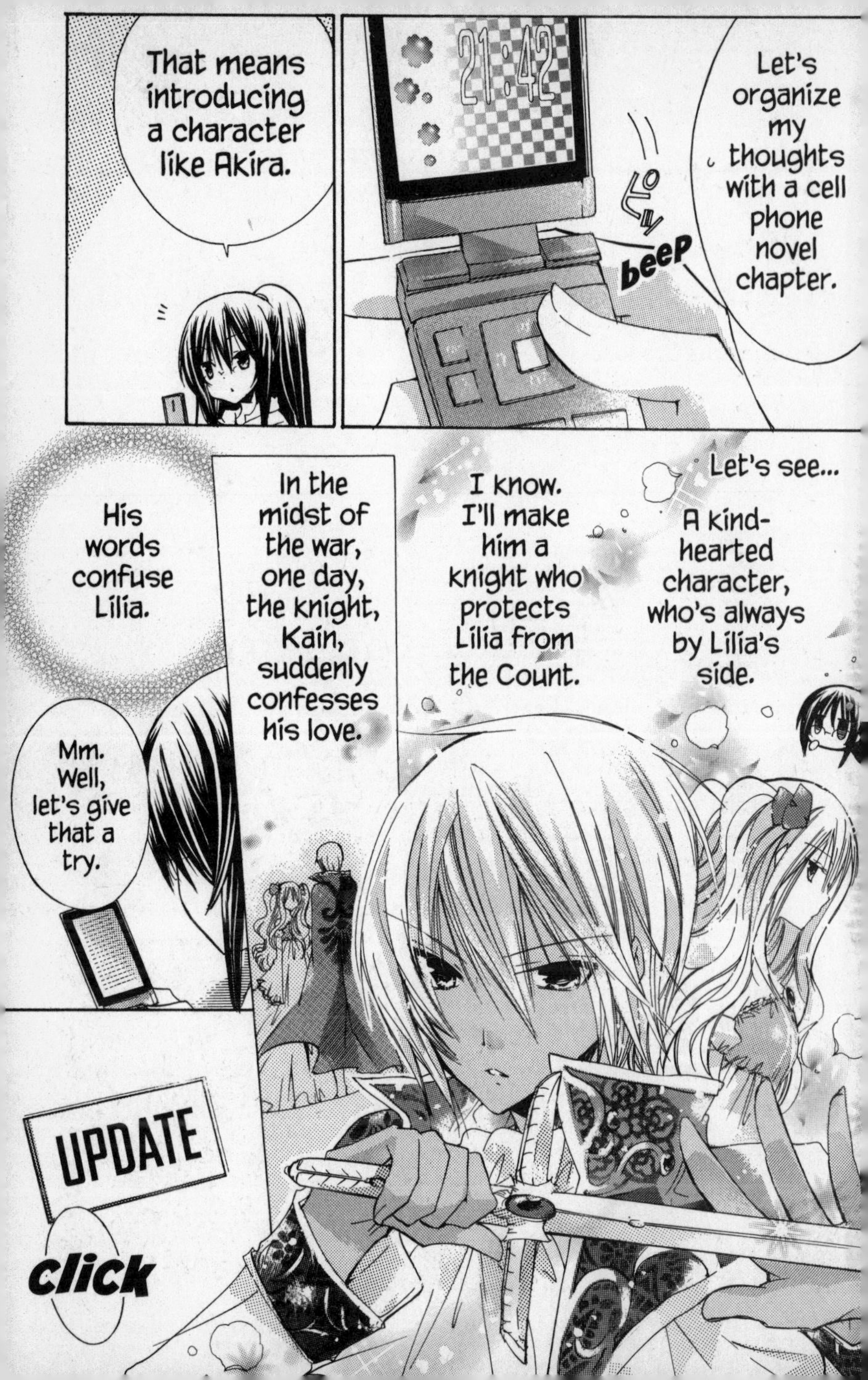
Let's organize my thoughts with a cell phone novel chapter.
beep
That means introducing a character like Akira.
Let's see...
A kind-hearted character, who's always by Lilia's side.
I know. I'll make him a knight who protects Lilia from the Count.
In the midst of the war, one day, the knight, Kain, suddenly confesses his love.
His words confuse Lilia.
Mm. Well, let's give that a try.
UPDATE
click

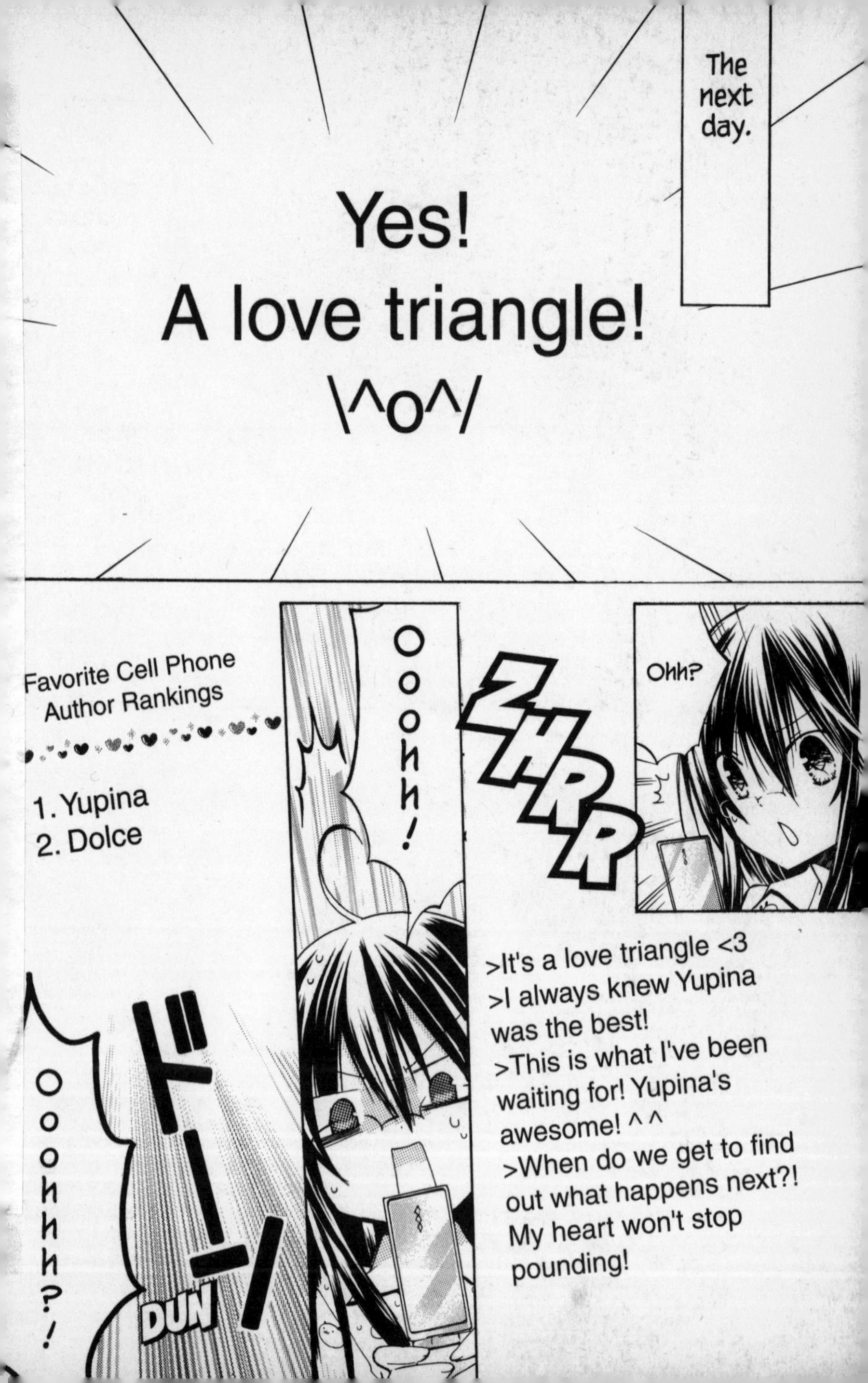
The next day.
Yes! A love triangle! \^o^/
Ohh?
ZHRR
Ooohh!
>It's a love triangle <3
>I always knew Yupina was the best!
>This is what I've been waiting for! Yupina's awesome! ^ ^
>When do we get to find out what happens next?! My heart won't stop pounding!
Favorite Cell Phone Author Rankings
1. Yupina
2. Dolce
Ooohhh?!
DUN

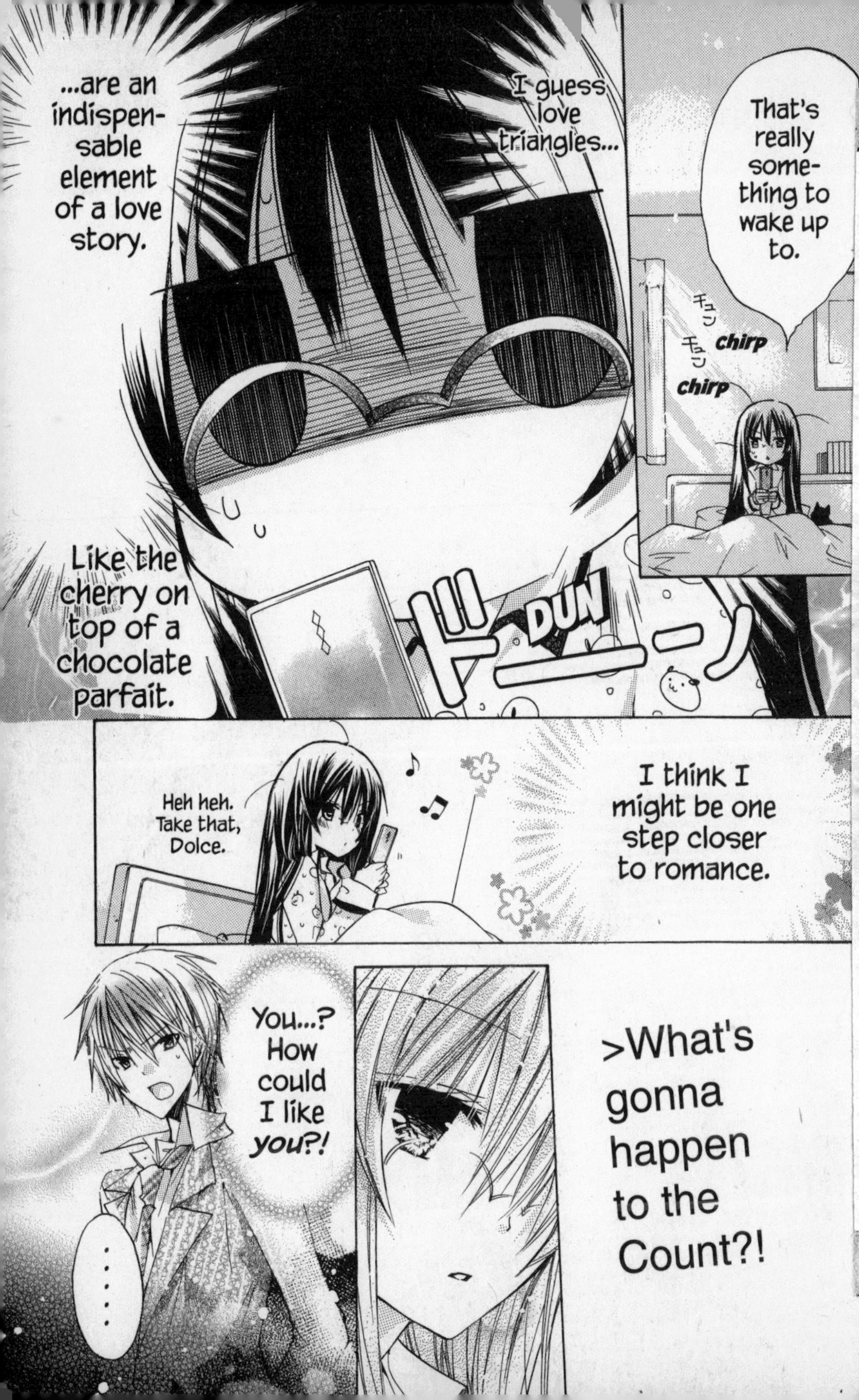
That's really some-thing to wake up to.
チュン
chirp
チュン
chirp
I guess love triangles...
...are an indispen-sable element of a love story.
Like the cherry on top of a chocolate parfait.
ドーン
DUN
I think I might be one step closer to romance.
Heh heh. Take that, Dolce.
>What's gonna happen to the Count?!
You...? How could I like you?!
......

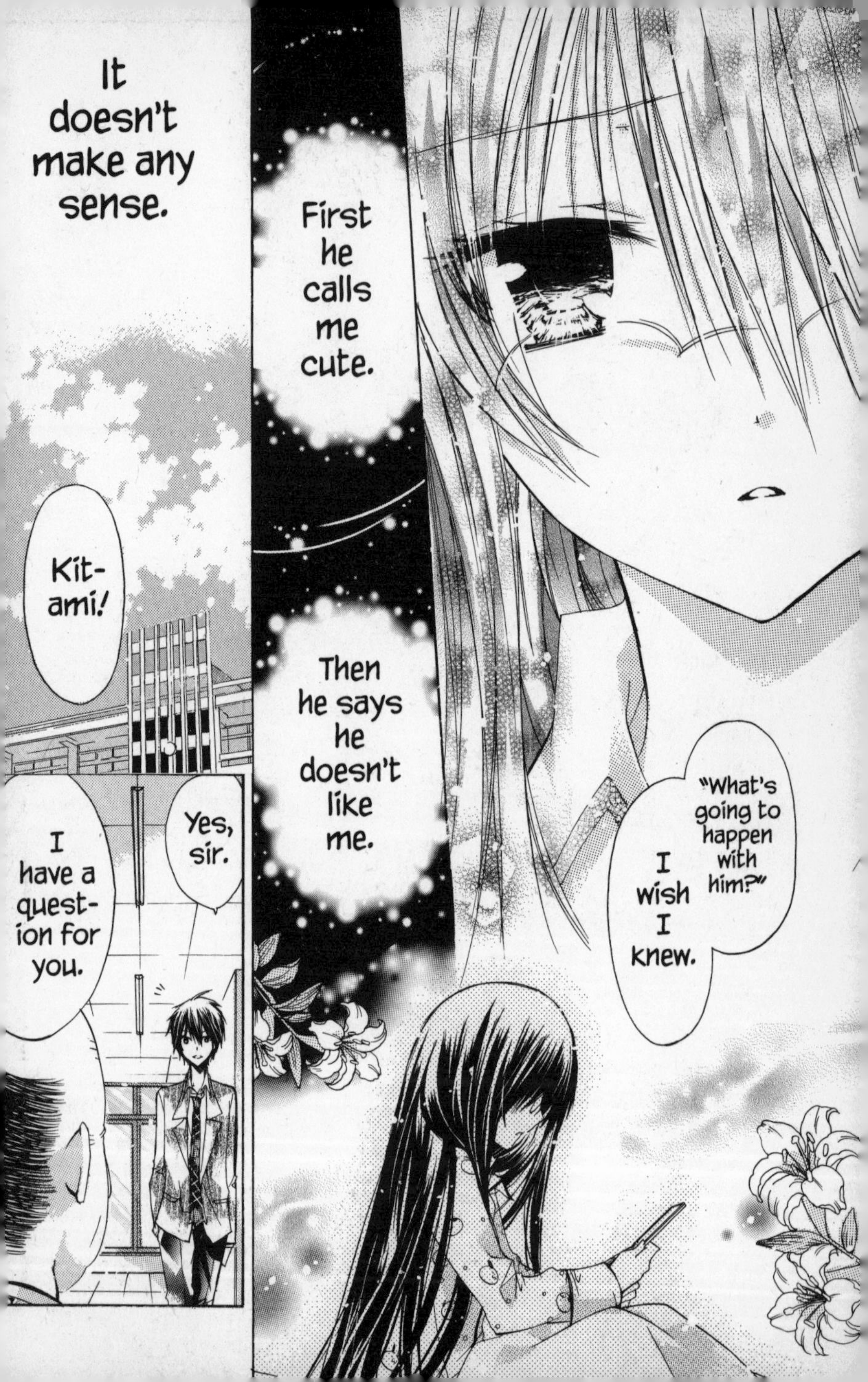
First he calls me cute.
Then he says he doesn't like me.
"What's going to happen with him?"
I wish I knew.
It doesn't make any sense.
Kit-ami!
Yes, sir.
I have a quest-ion for you.

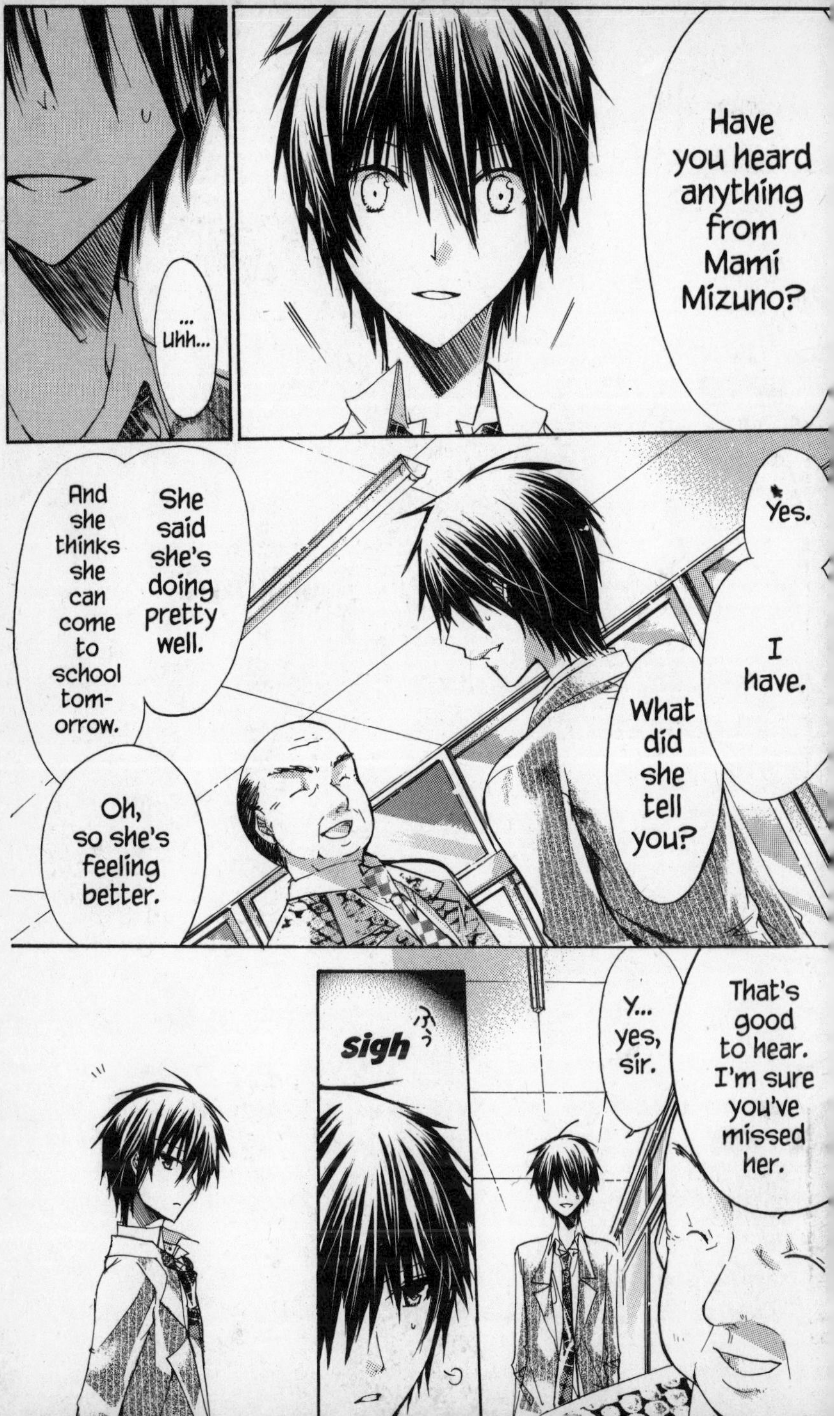
Have you heard anything from Mami Mizuno?
... uhh...
Yes.
I have.
What did she tell you?
She said she's doing pretty well.
And she thinks she can come to school tom-orrow.
Oh, so she's feeling better.
That's good to hear. I'm sure you've missed her.
Y... yes, sir.
ふぅ
sigh

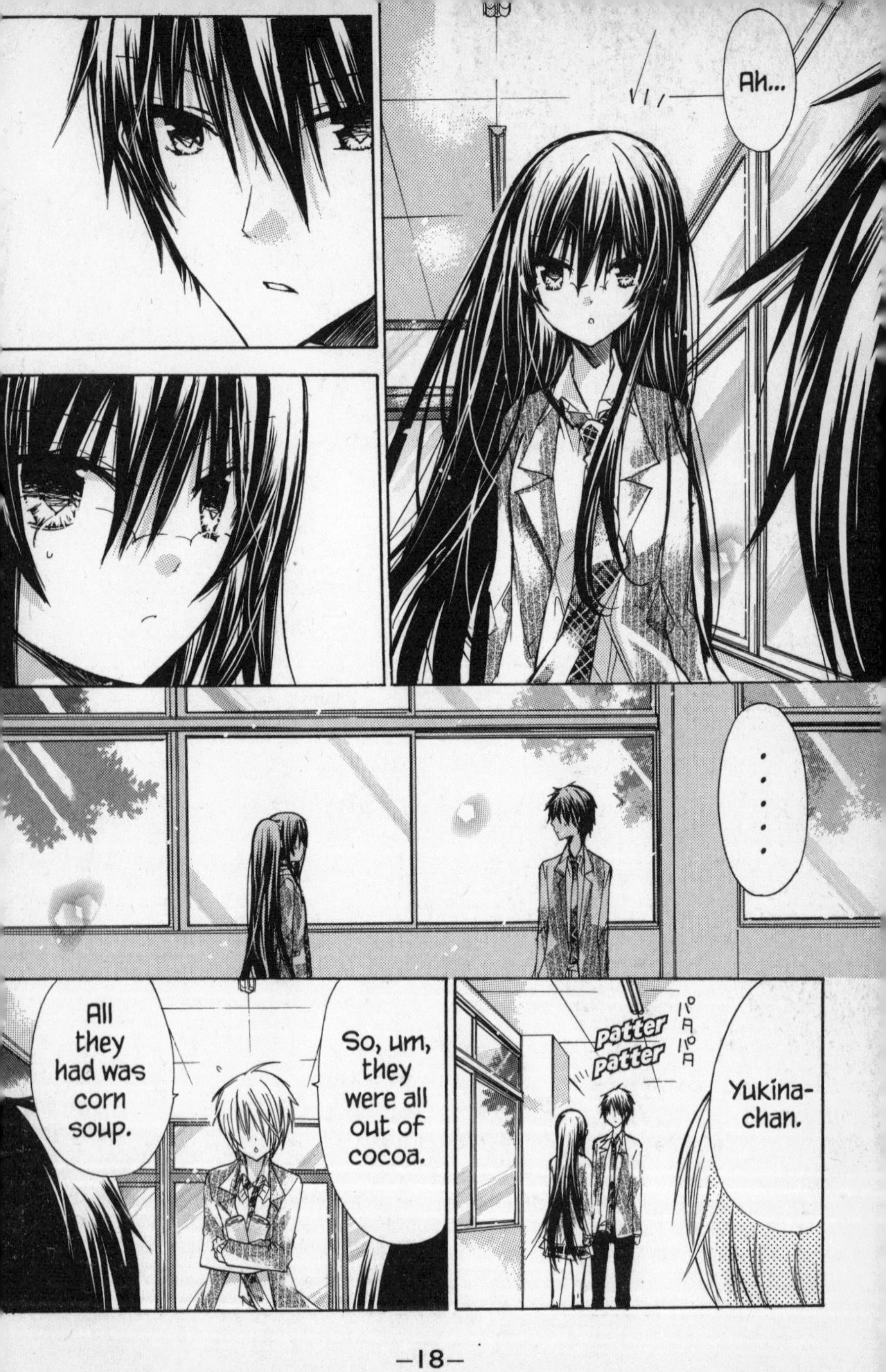
Ah...
......
Patter Patter
パタパタ
Yukina-chan.
So, um, they were all out of cocoa.
All they had was corn soup.

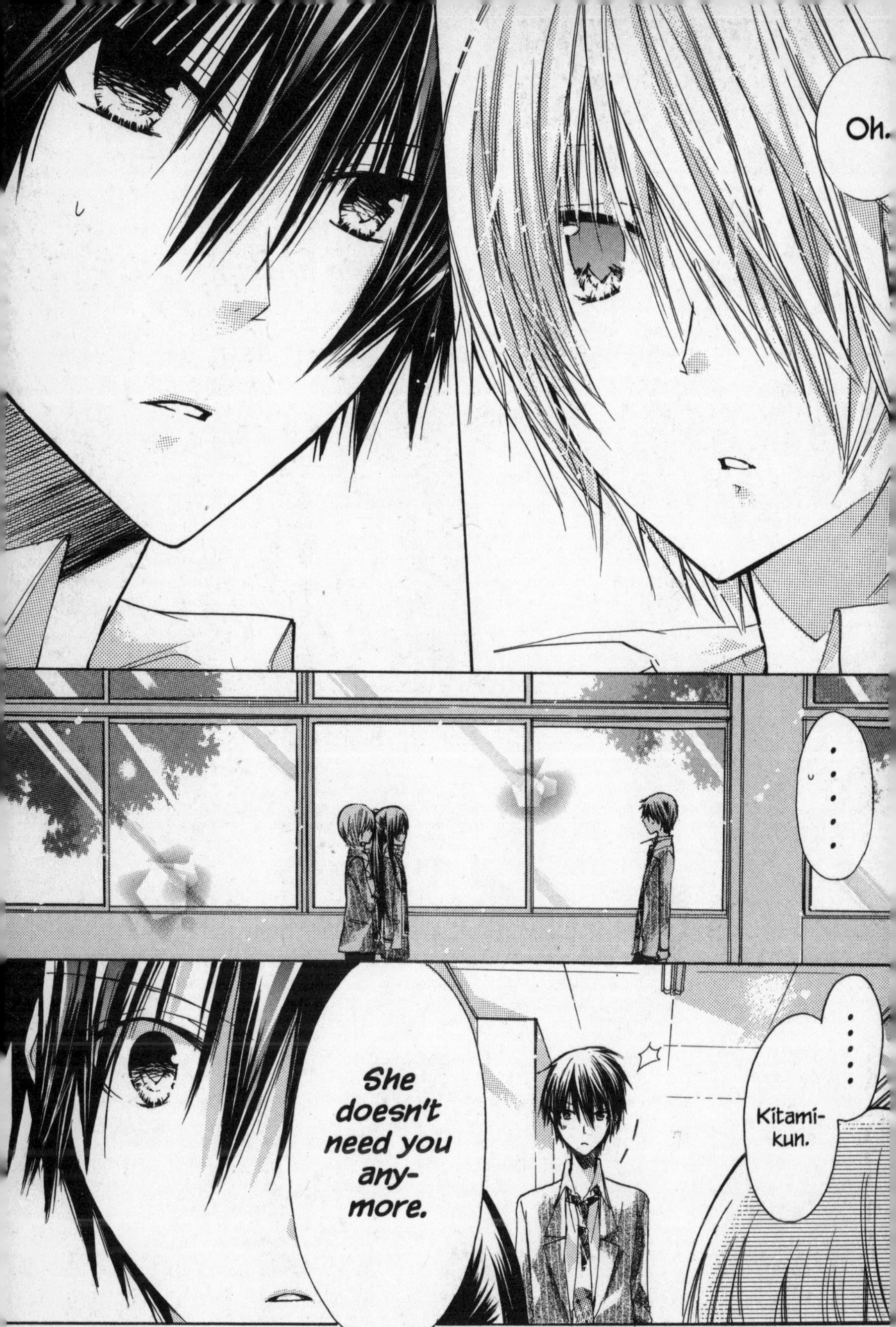
Oh.
......
...... Kitami-kun.
She doesn't need you anymore.

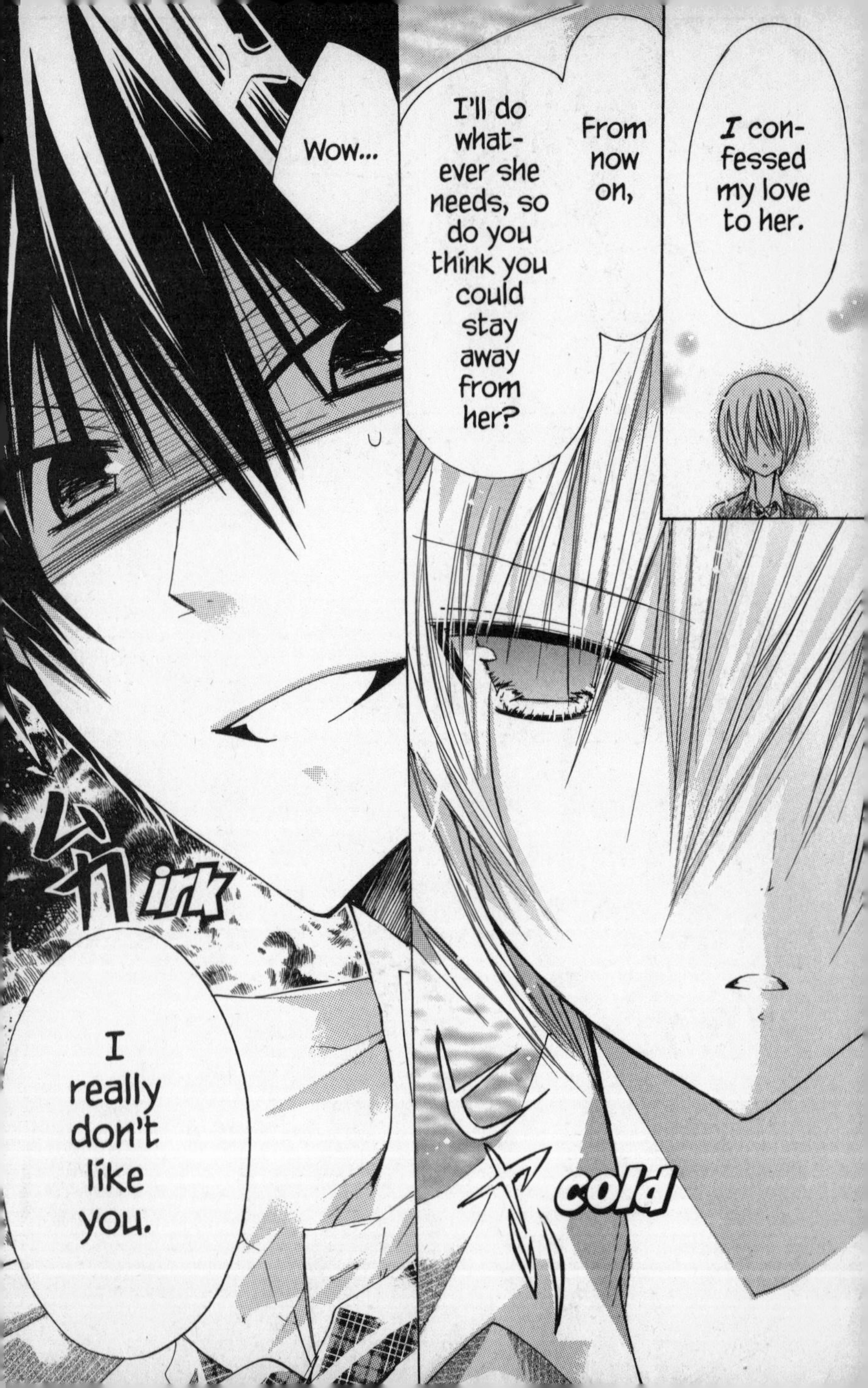
I confessed my love to her.
From now on,
I'll do whatever she needs, so do you think you could stay away from her?
cold
Wow...
irk
I really don't like you.

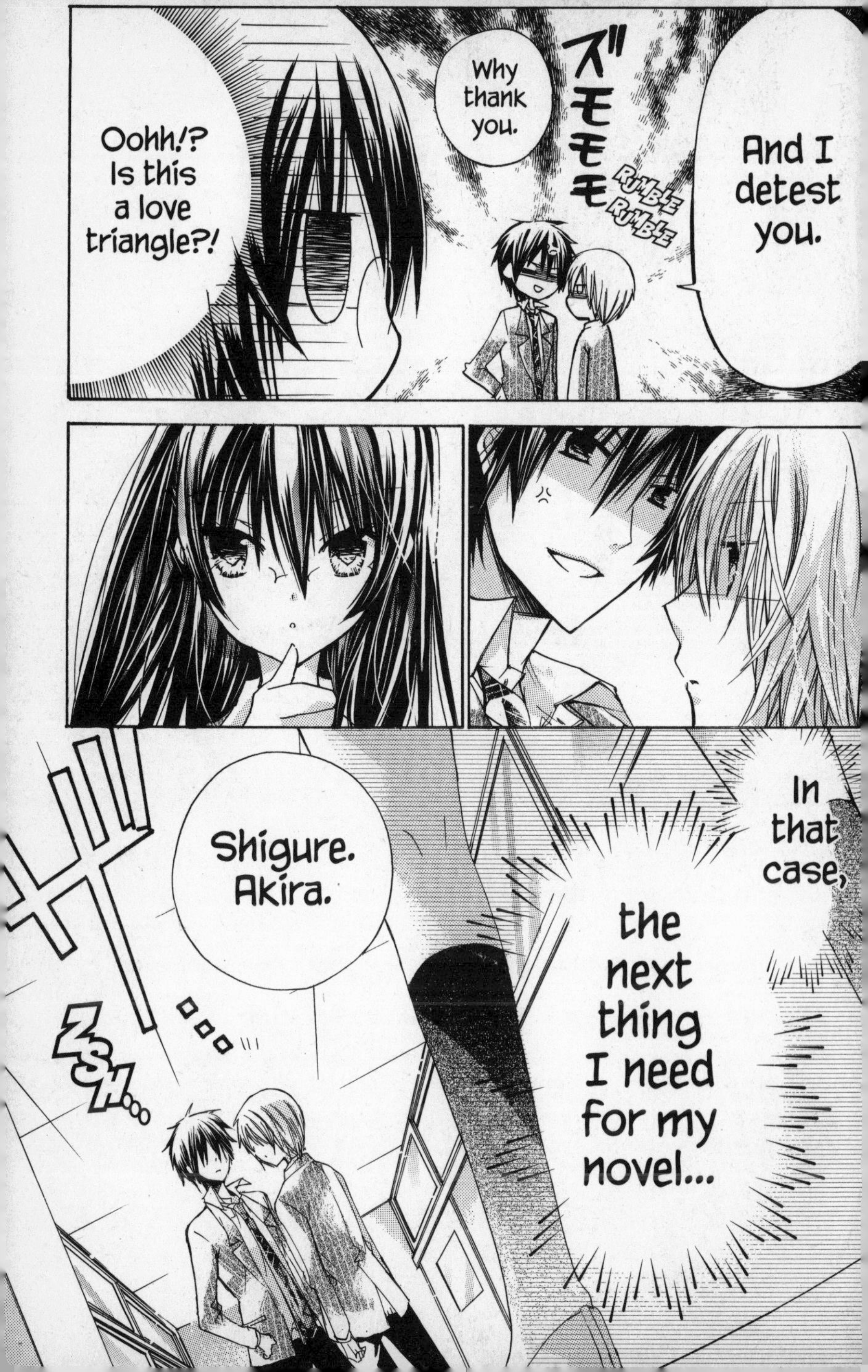
And I detest you.
ズモモモ
RUMBLE RUMBLE
Why thank you.
Oohh!? Is this a love triangle?!
In that case,
the next thing I need for my novel...
Shigure. Akira.
...
ZSH...

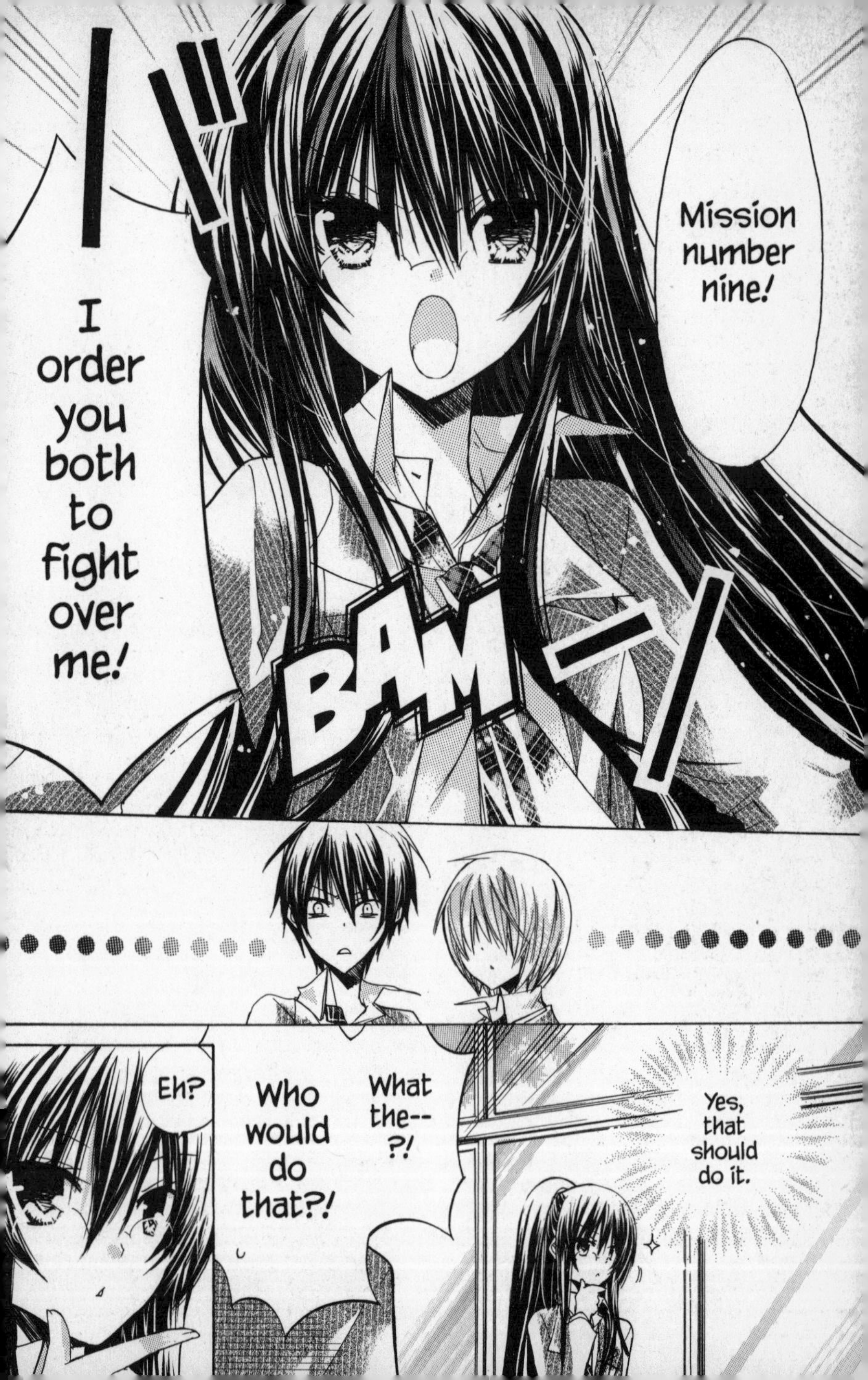
Mission number nine!
I order you both to fight over me!
BAM—
Yes, that should do it.
What the--?!
Who would do that?!
Eh?

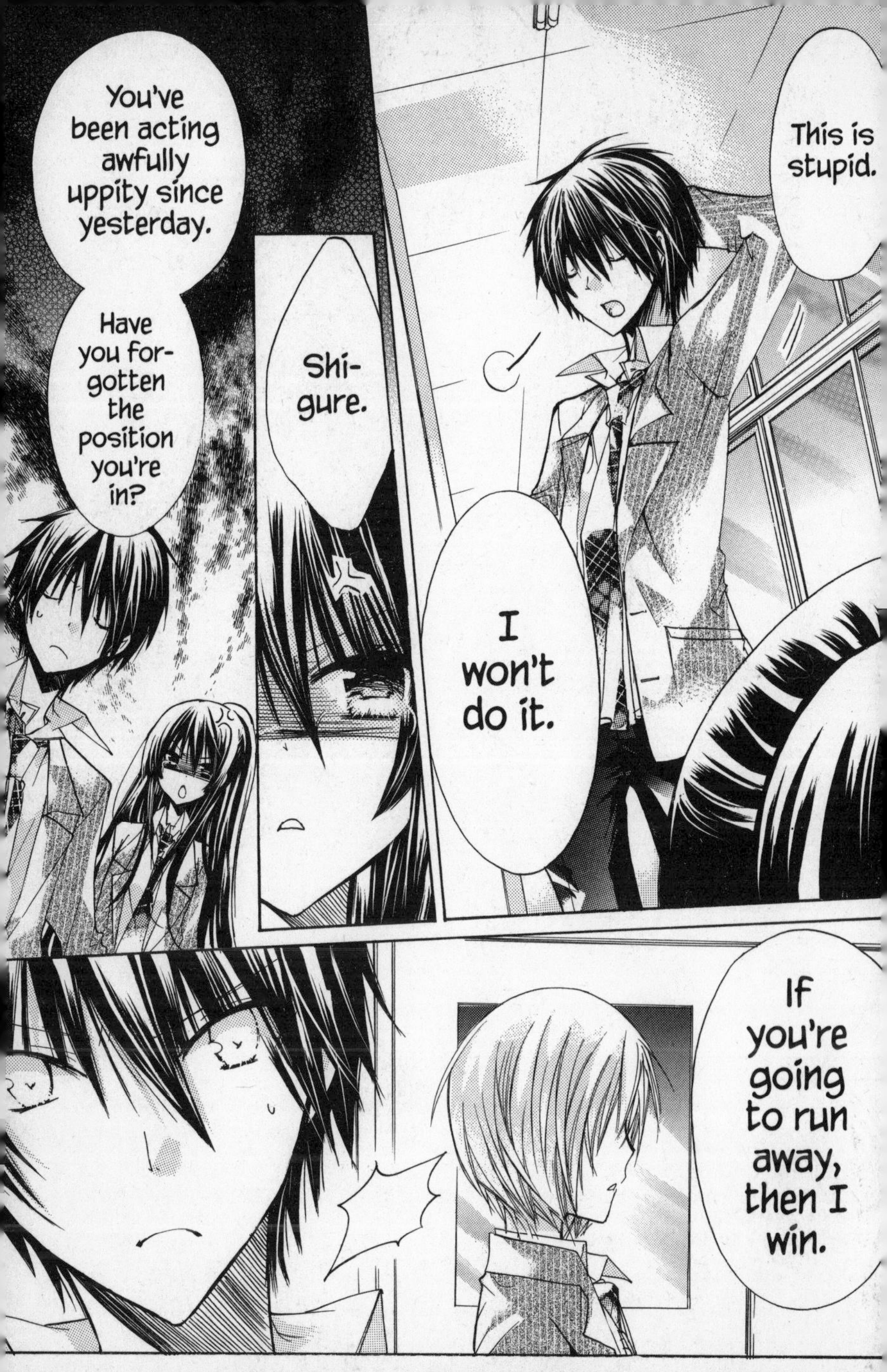
This is stupid.
I won't do it.
Shi-gure.
You've been acting awfully uppity since yesterday.
Have you for-gotten the position you're in?
If you're going to run away, then I win.

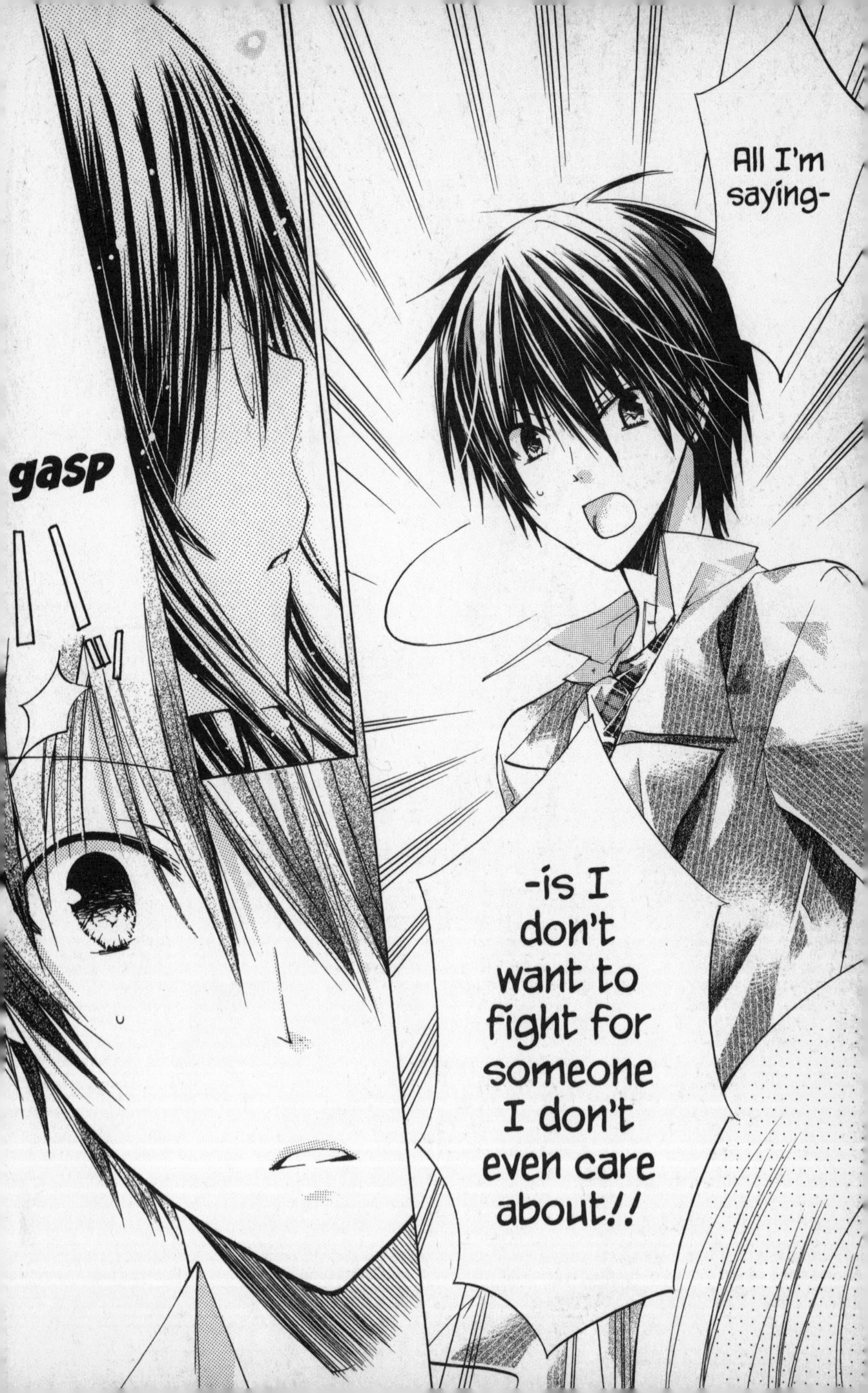
All I'm saying-
-is I don't want to fight for someone I don't even care about!!
gasp

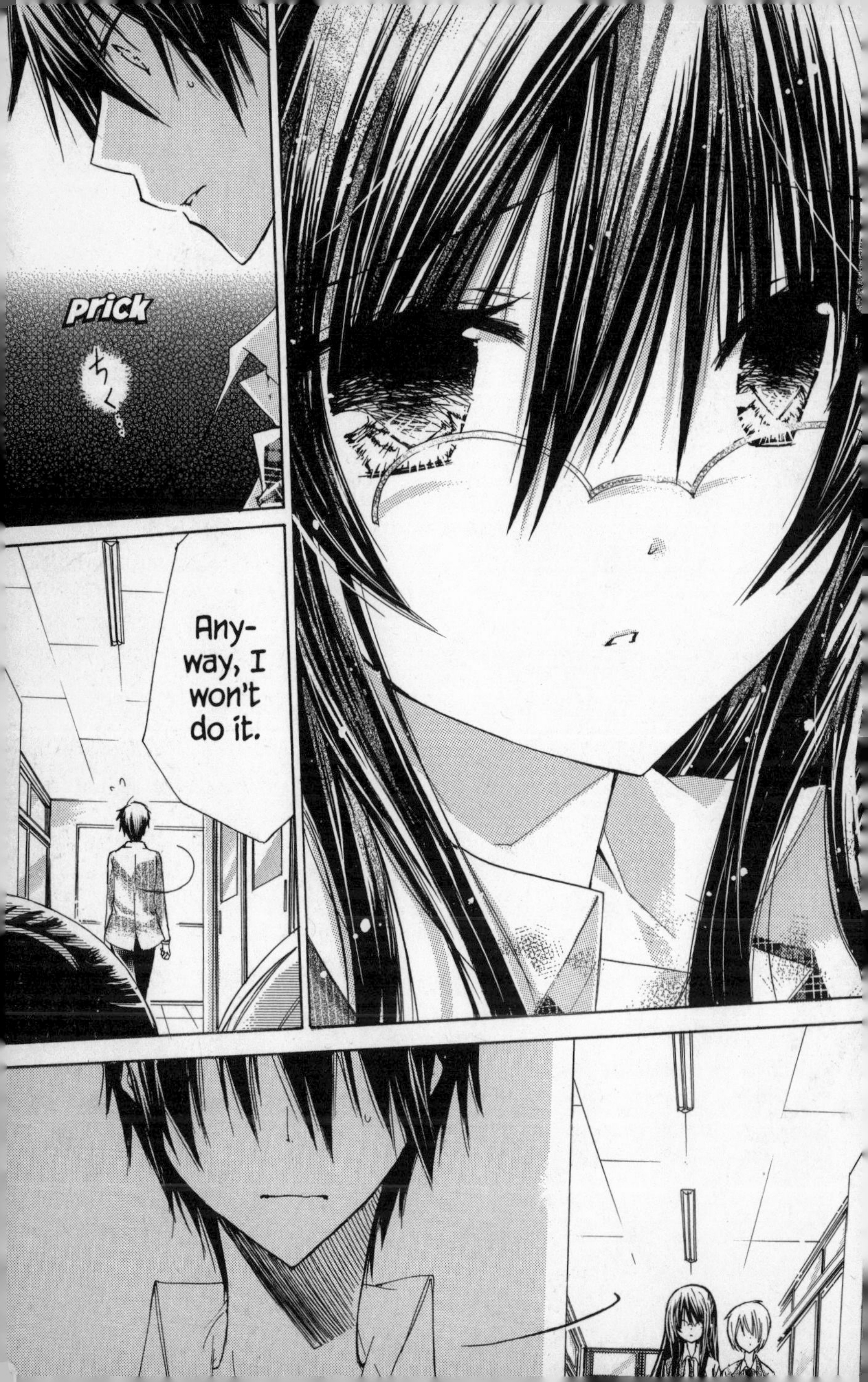
Prick
ちく
Any-way, I won't do it.

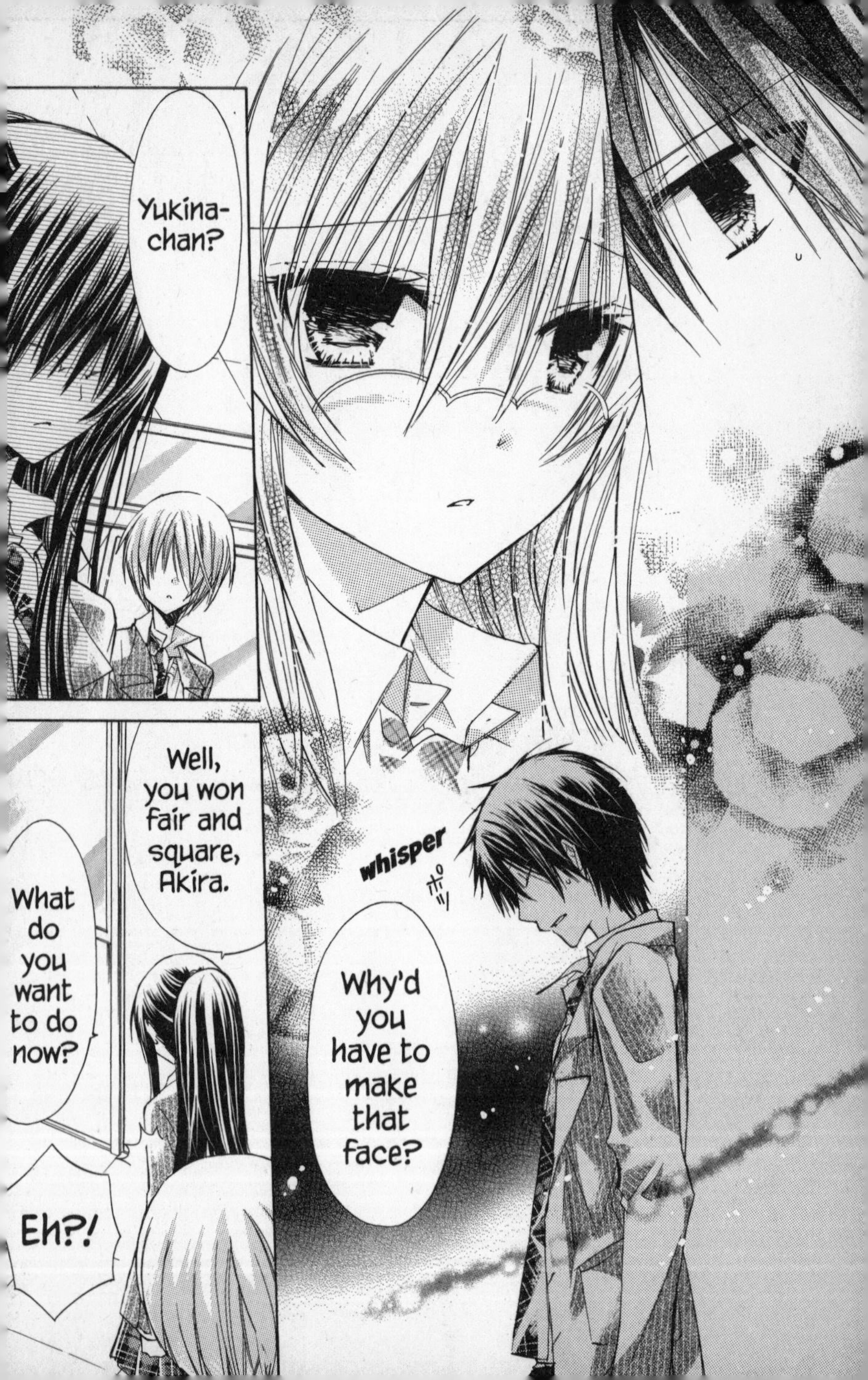
whisper
Why'd you have to make that face?
Yukina-chan?
Well, you won fair and square, Akira.
What do you want to do now?
Eh?!

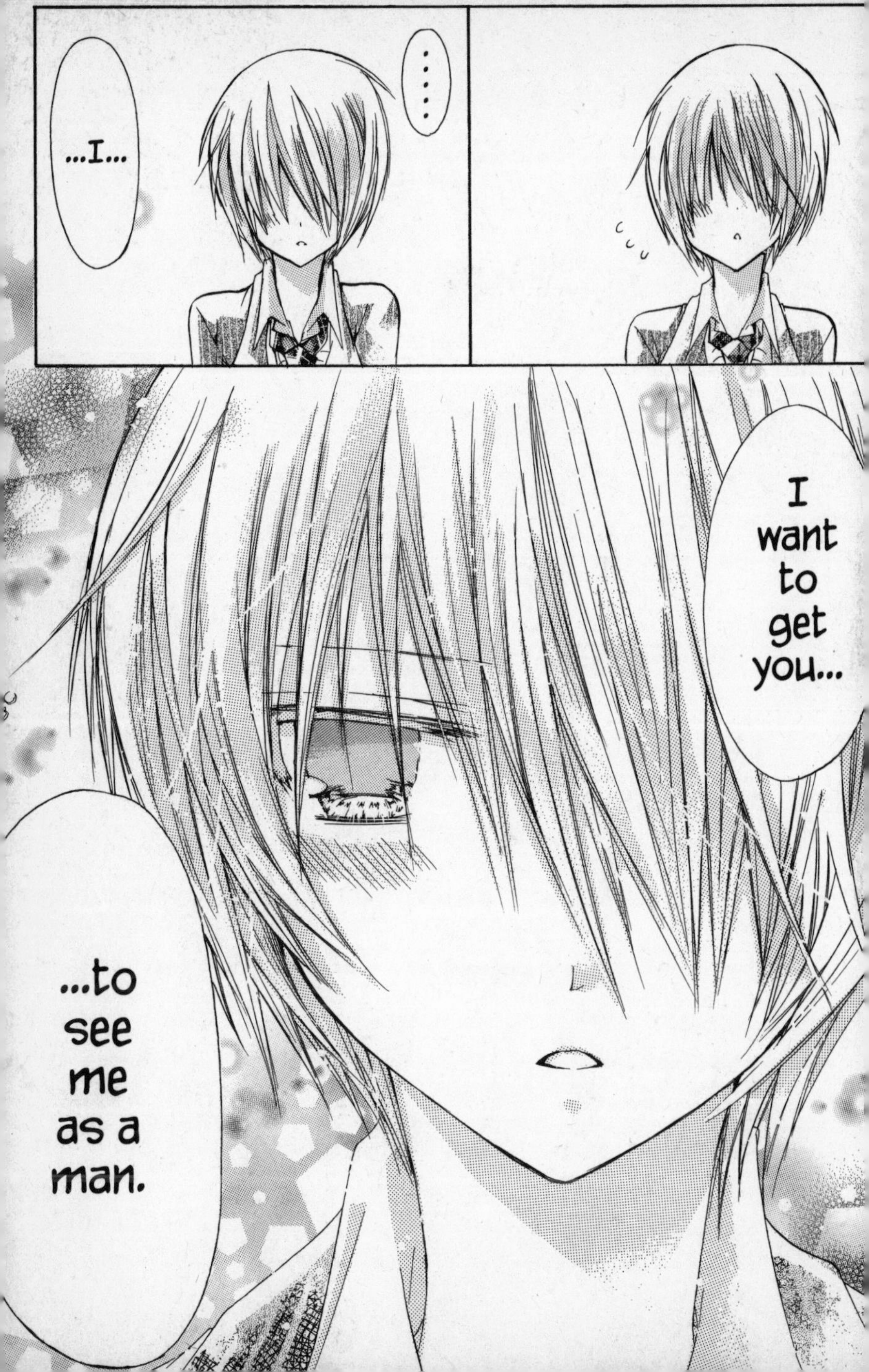
......
...I...
I want to get you...
...to see me as a man.

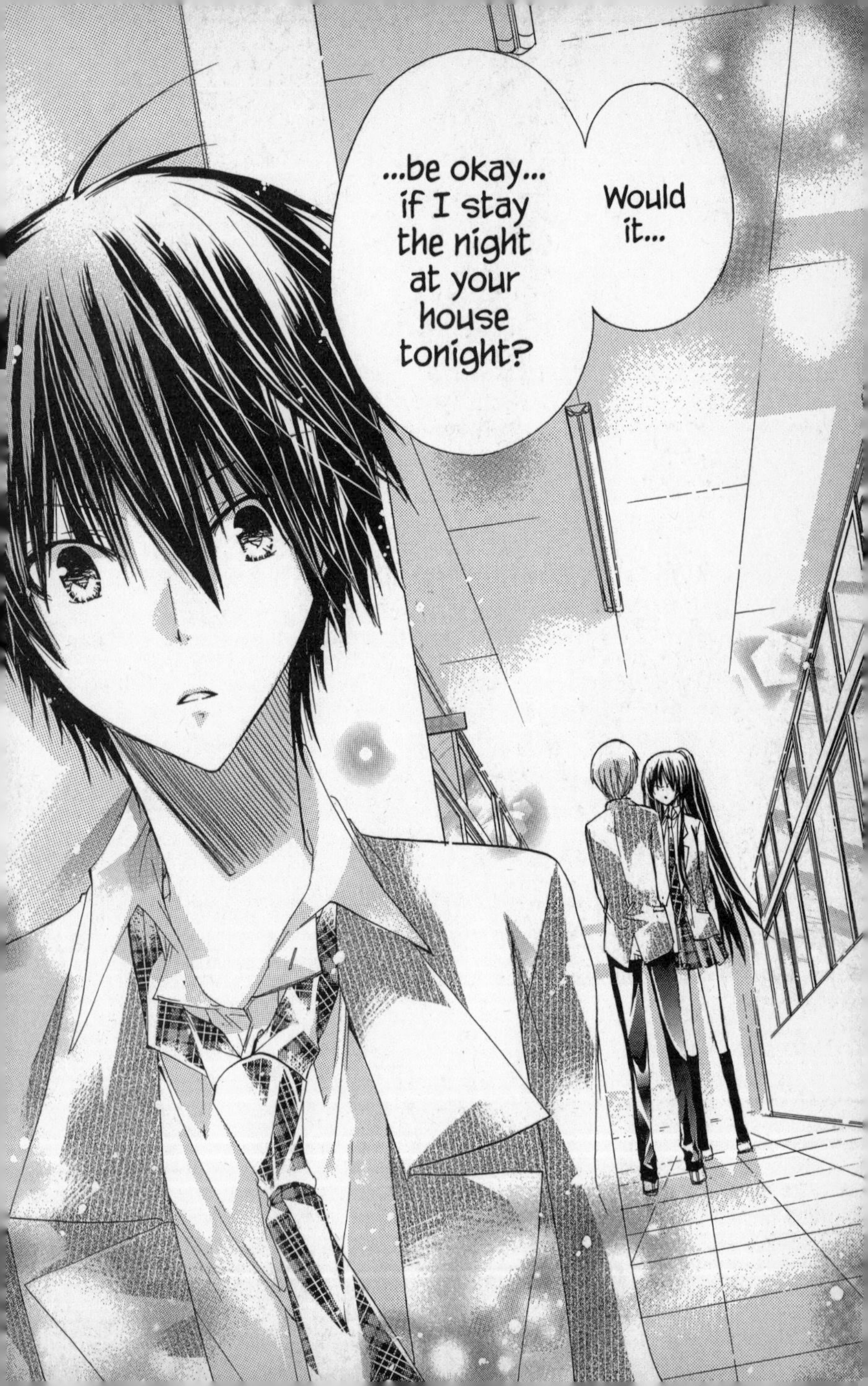
Would it...
...be okay... if I stay the night at your house tonight?

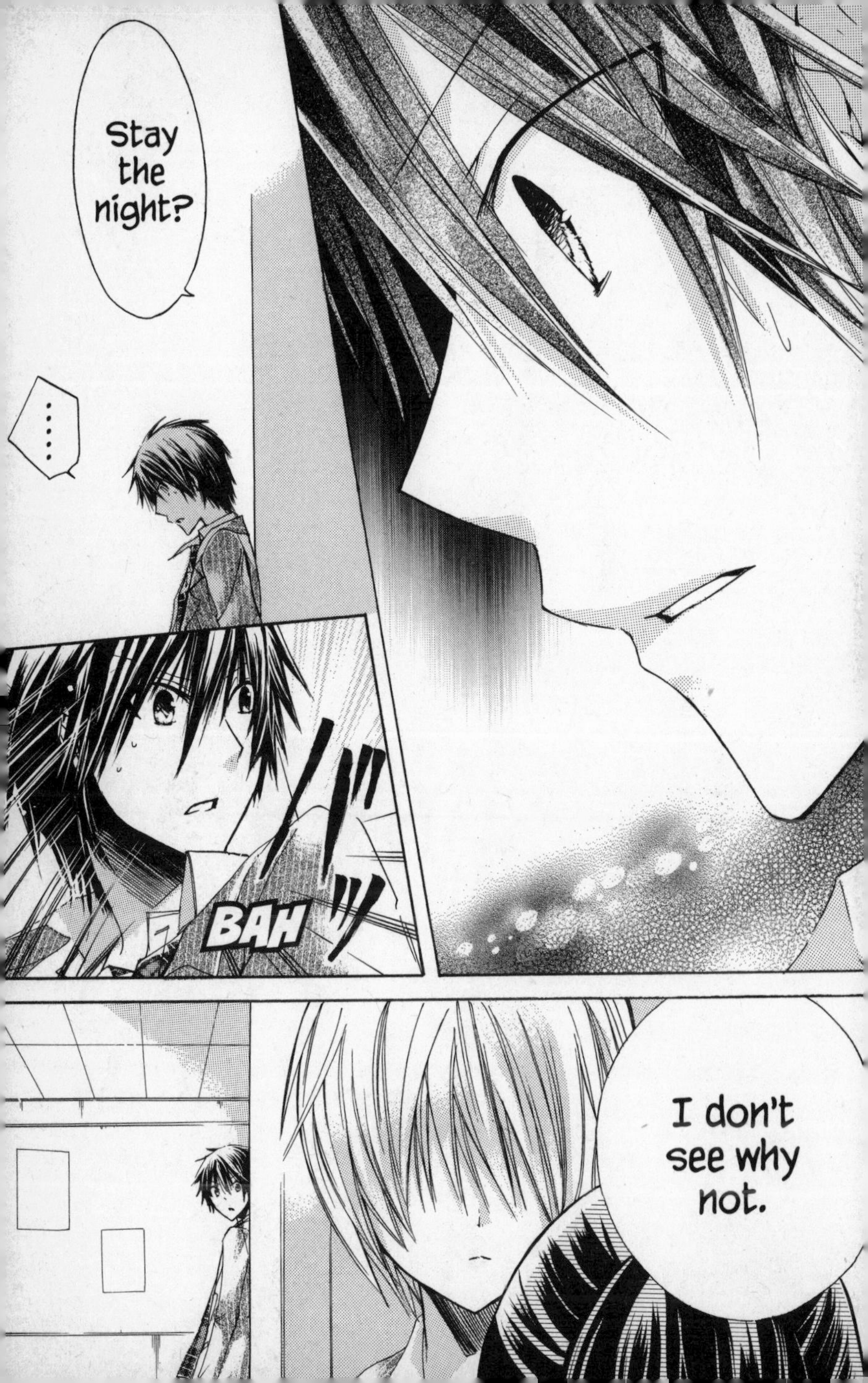
Stay the night?
......
BAH
I don't see why not.

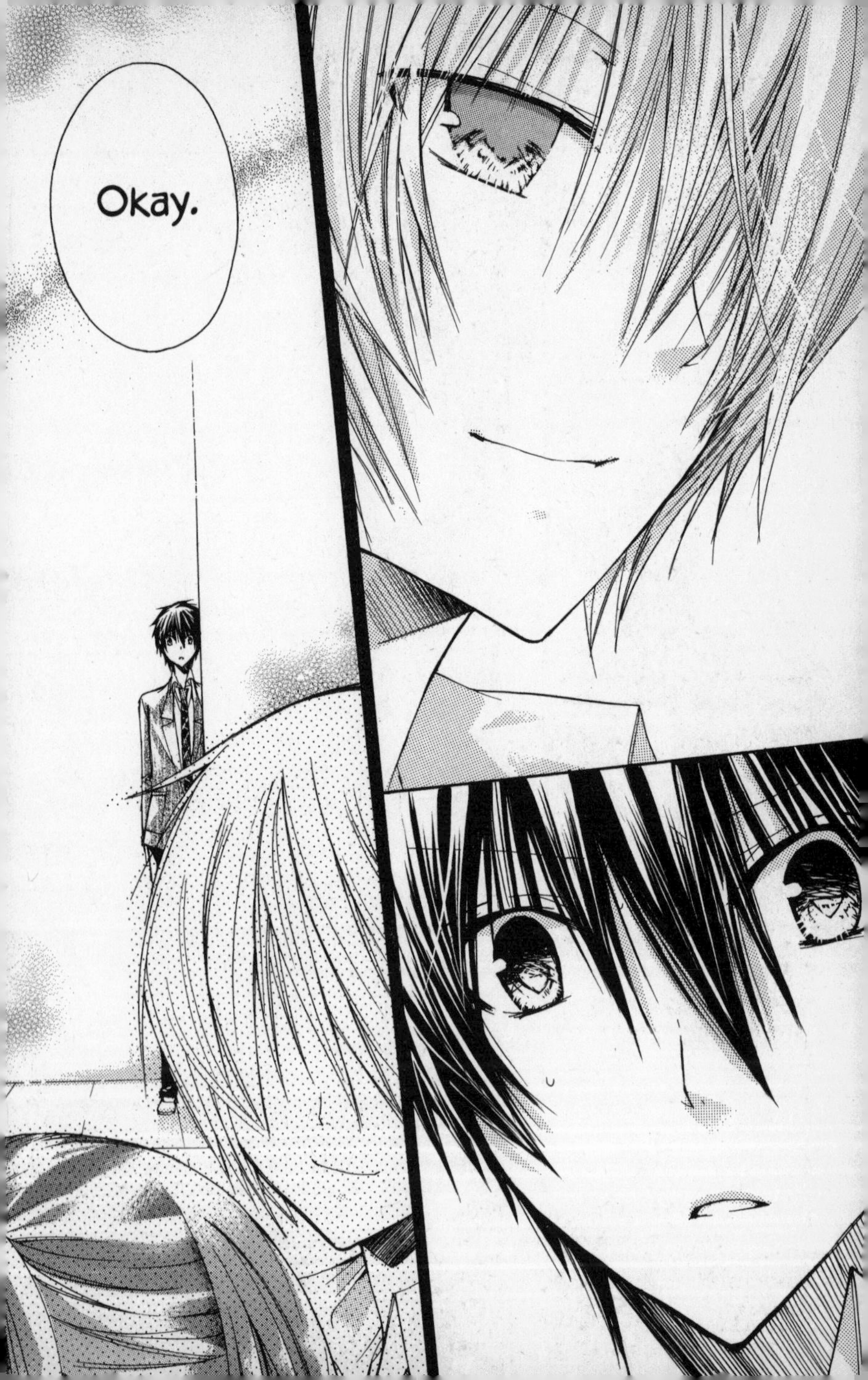
Okay.

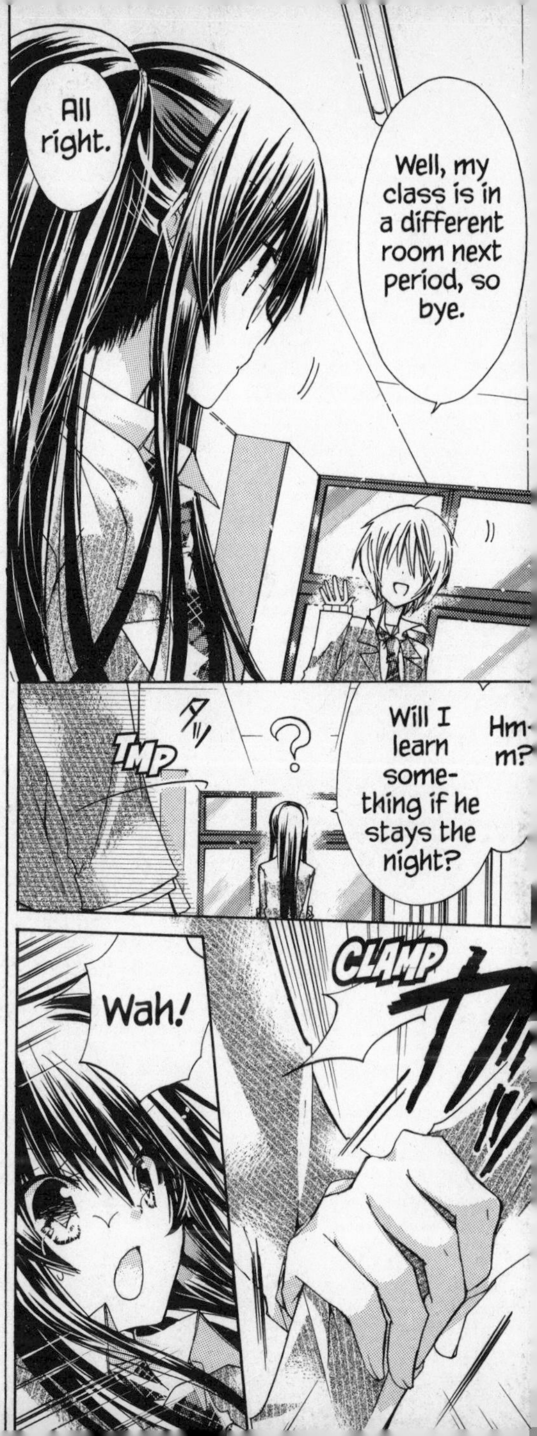
Well, my class is in a different room next period, so bye.
All right.
Hm-m?
Will I learn something if he stays the night?
?
TMP
CLAMP
Wah!

Snow Yukina

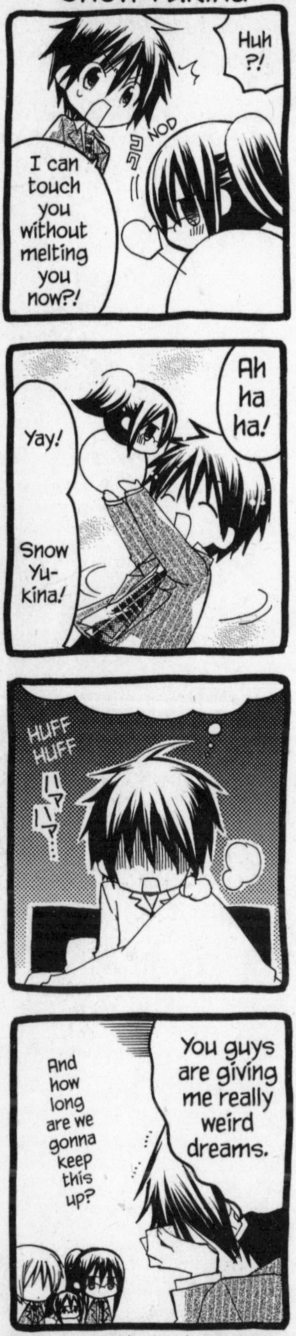
Huh?!
NOD
I can touch you without melting you now?!
Ah ha ha!
Yay!
Snow Yu-kina!
HUFF HUFF
You guys are giving me really weird dreams.
And how long are we gonna keep this up?

Forever, that's how long.

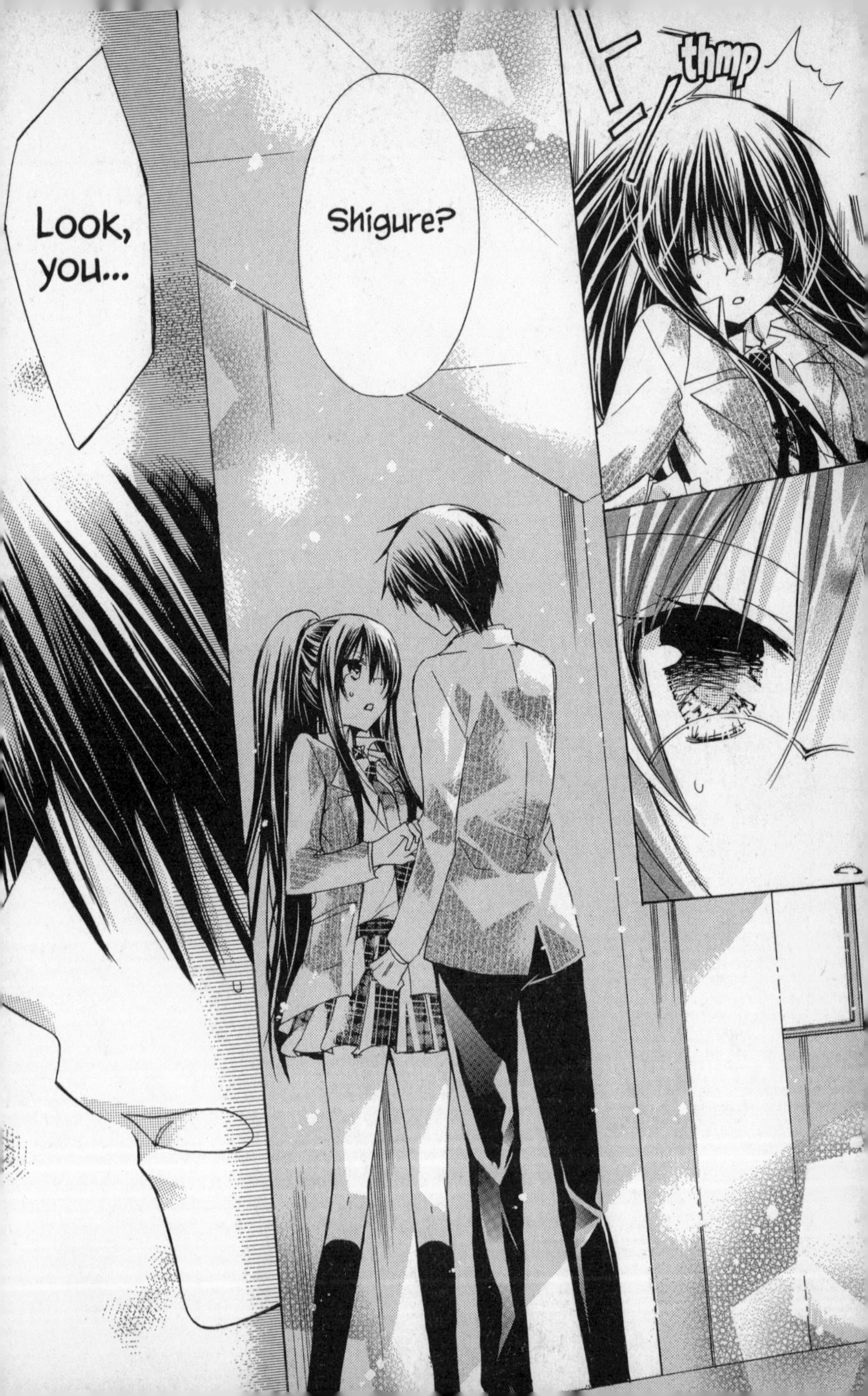
thmp
Shigure?
Look, you...

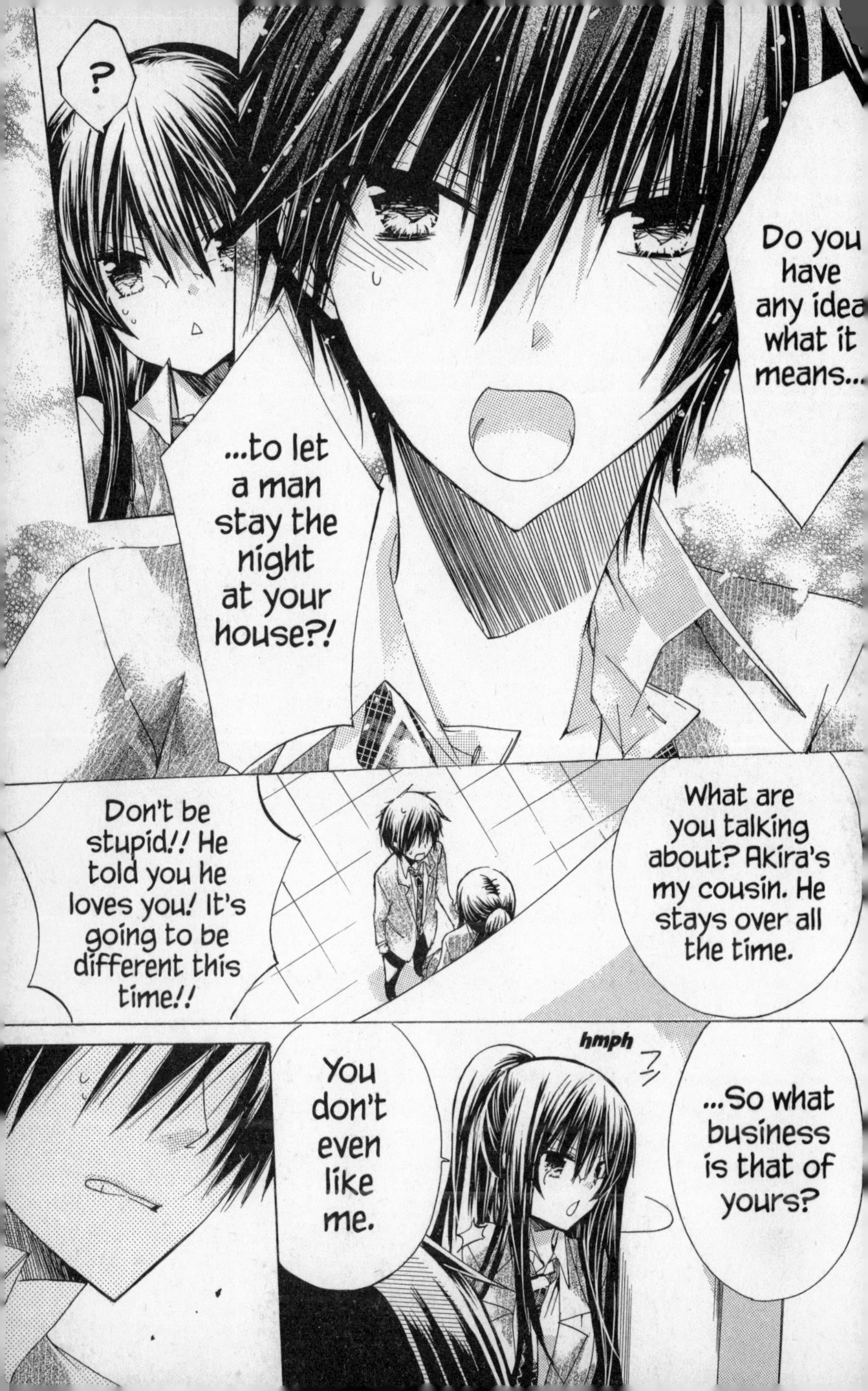
?
Do you have any idea what it means...
...to let a man stay the night at your house?!
What are you talking about? Akira's my cousin. He stays over all the time.
Don't be stupid!! He told you he loves you! It's going to be different this time!!
...So what business is that of yours?
hmph
You don't even like me.

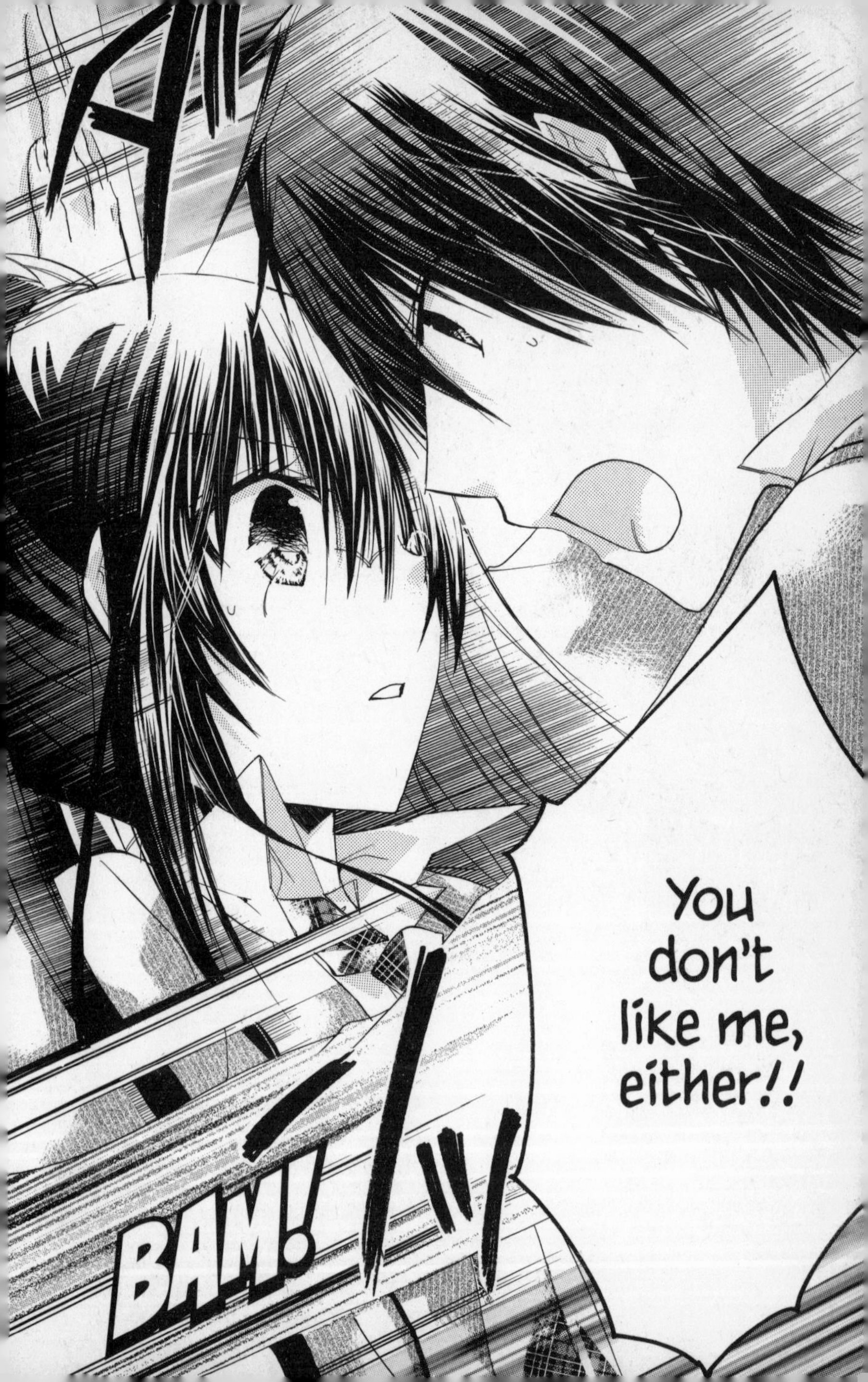
You don't like me, either!!
BAM!

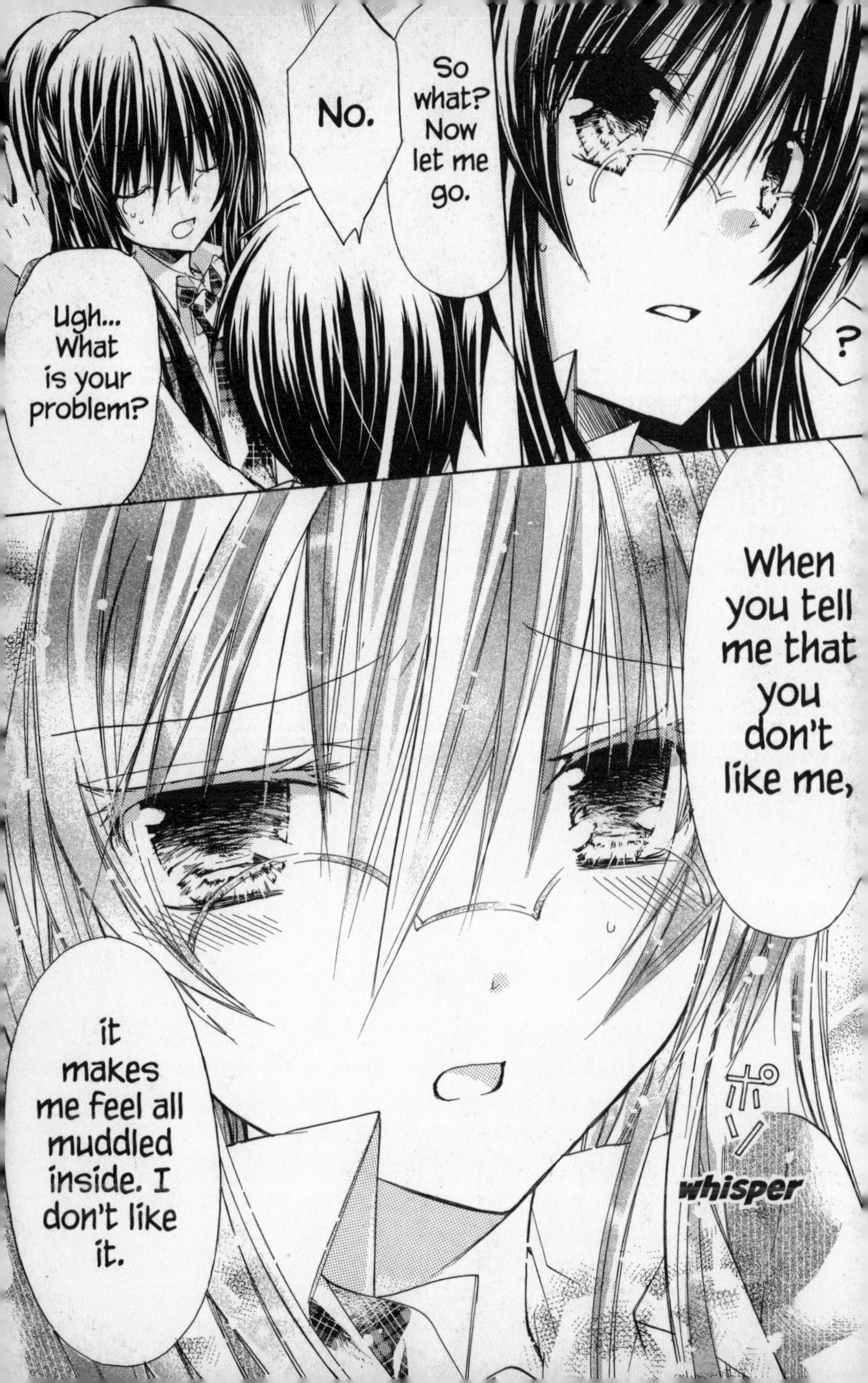
So what? Now let me go.
No.
?
Ugh... What is your problem?
When you tell me that you don't like me,
whisper
it makes me feel all muddled inside. I don't like it.

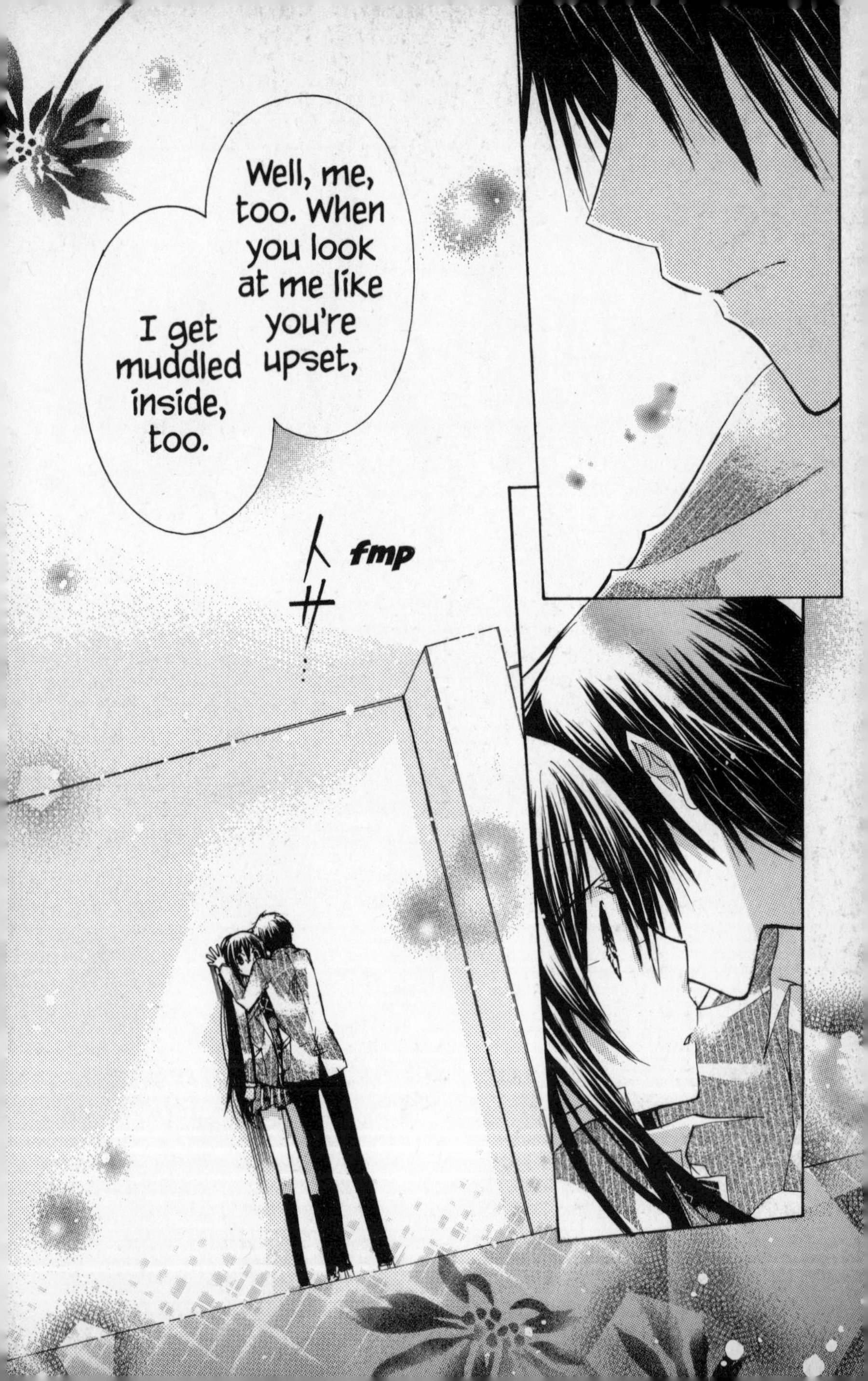
Well, me, too. When you look at me like you're upset, I get muddled inside, too.
fmp

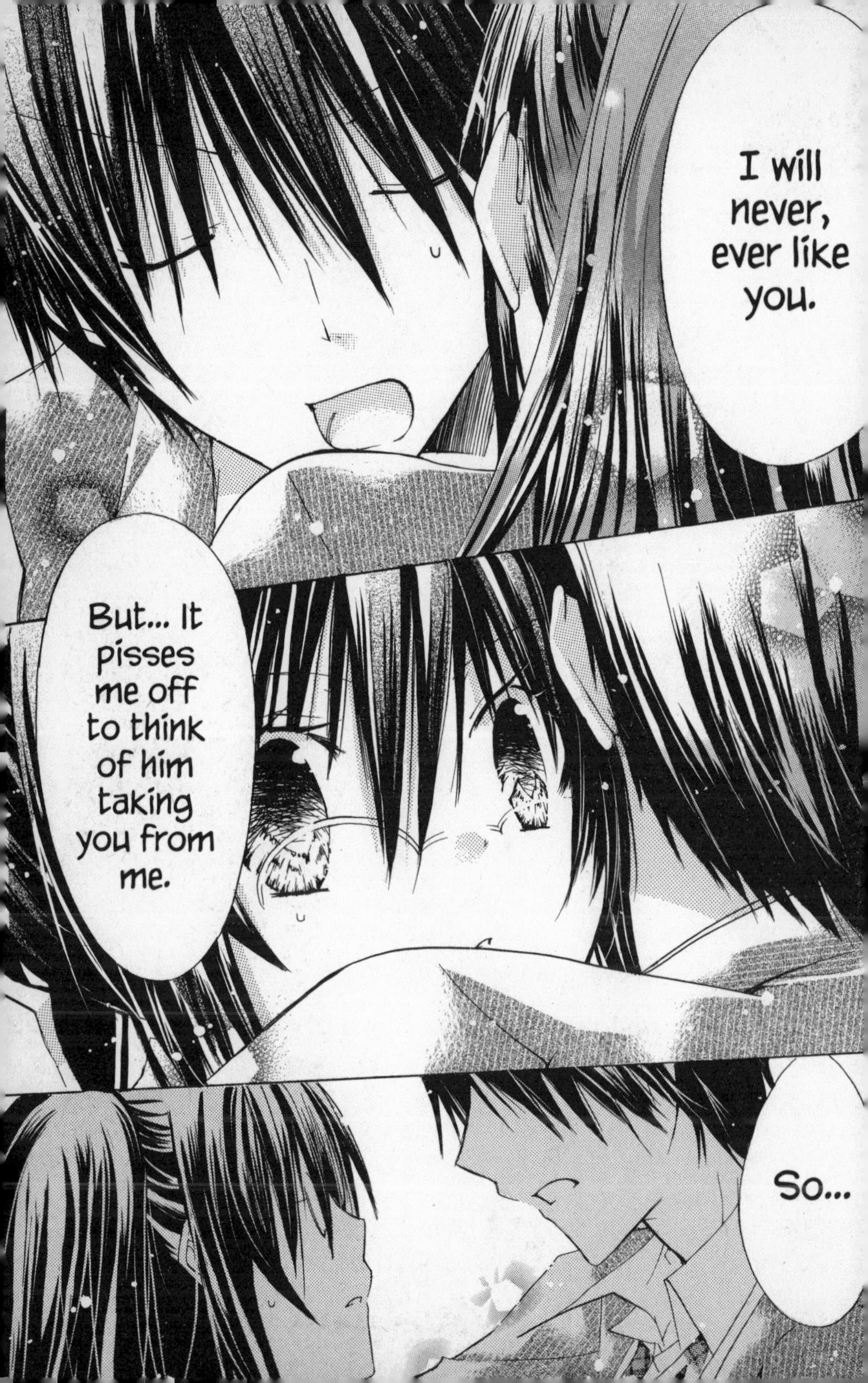
I will never, ever like you.
But... It pisses me off to think of him taking you from me.
So...

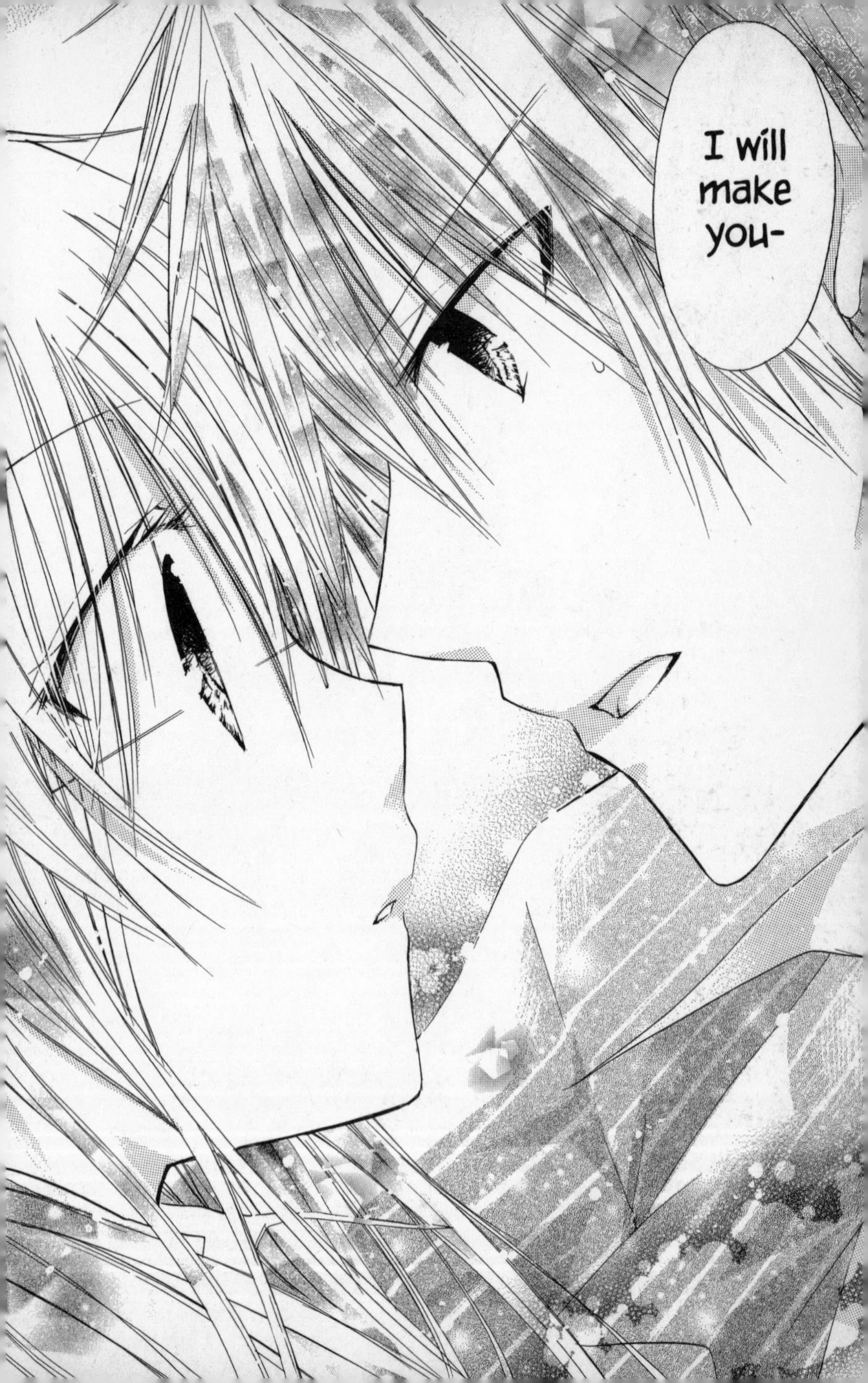
I will make you-

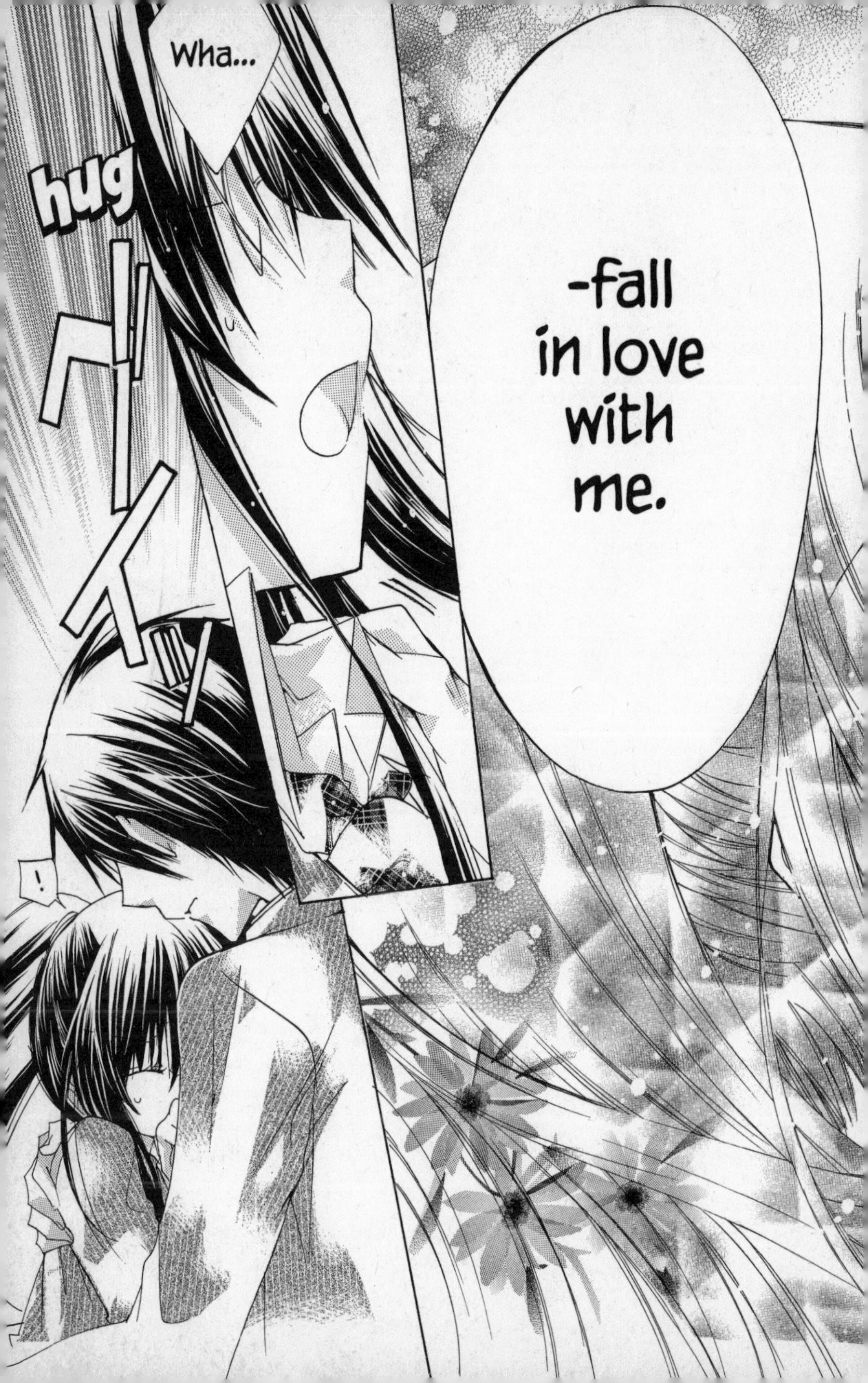
-fall in love with me.
Wha...
hug
!

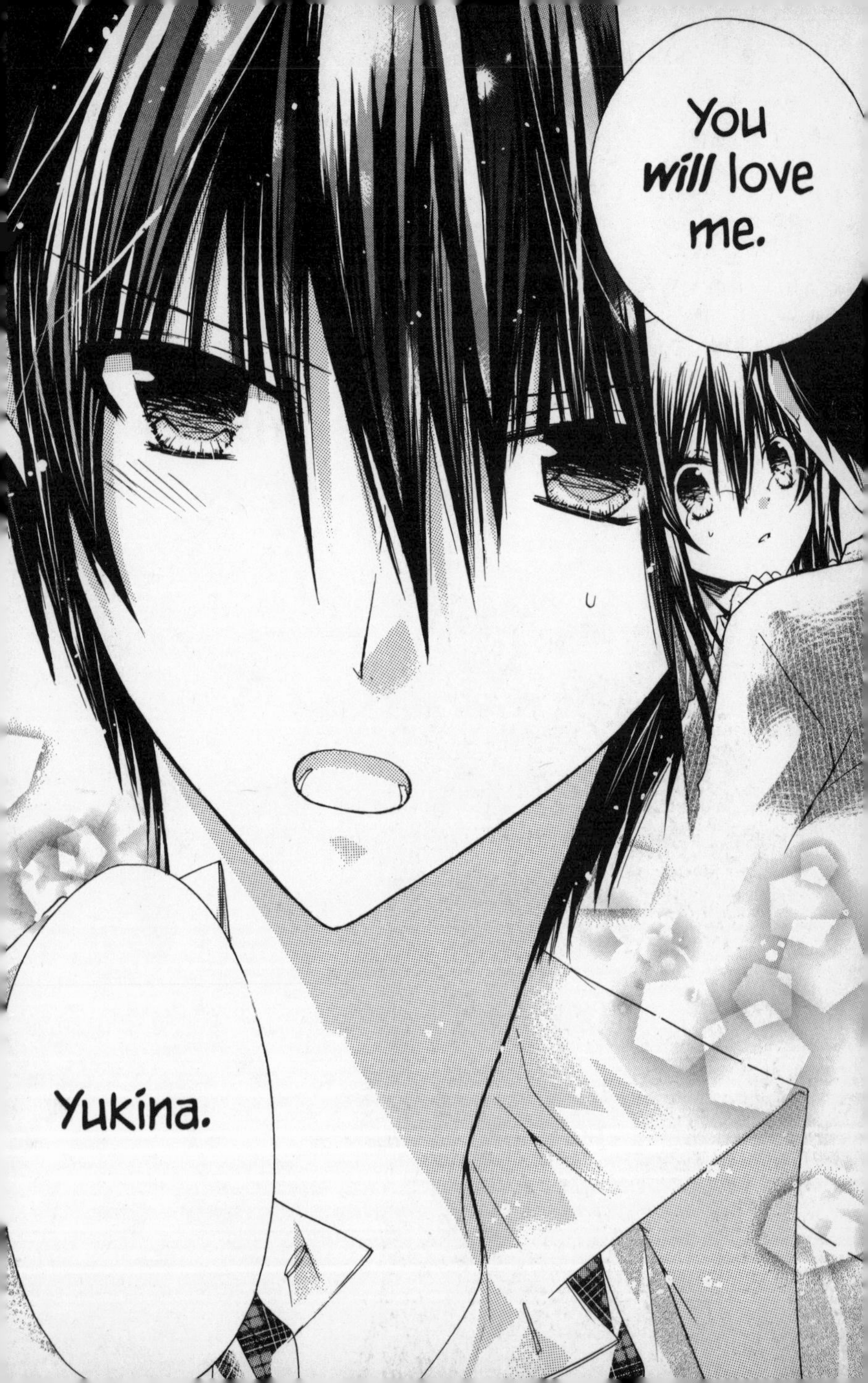
You *will* love me.
Yukina.

# Missions of Love

**It is time for love.
Secret cell phone
novelist vs. the most
popular boy in school.
A mission of love for
absolute servitude.**

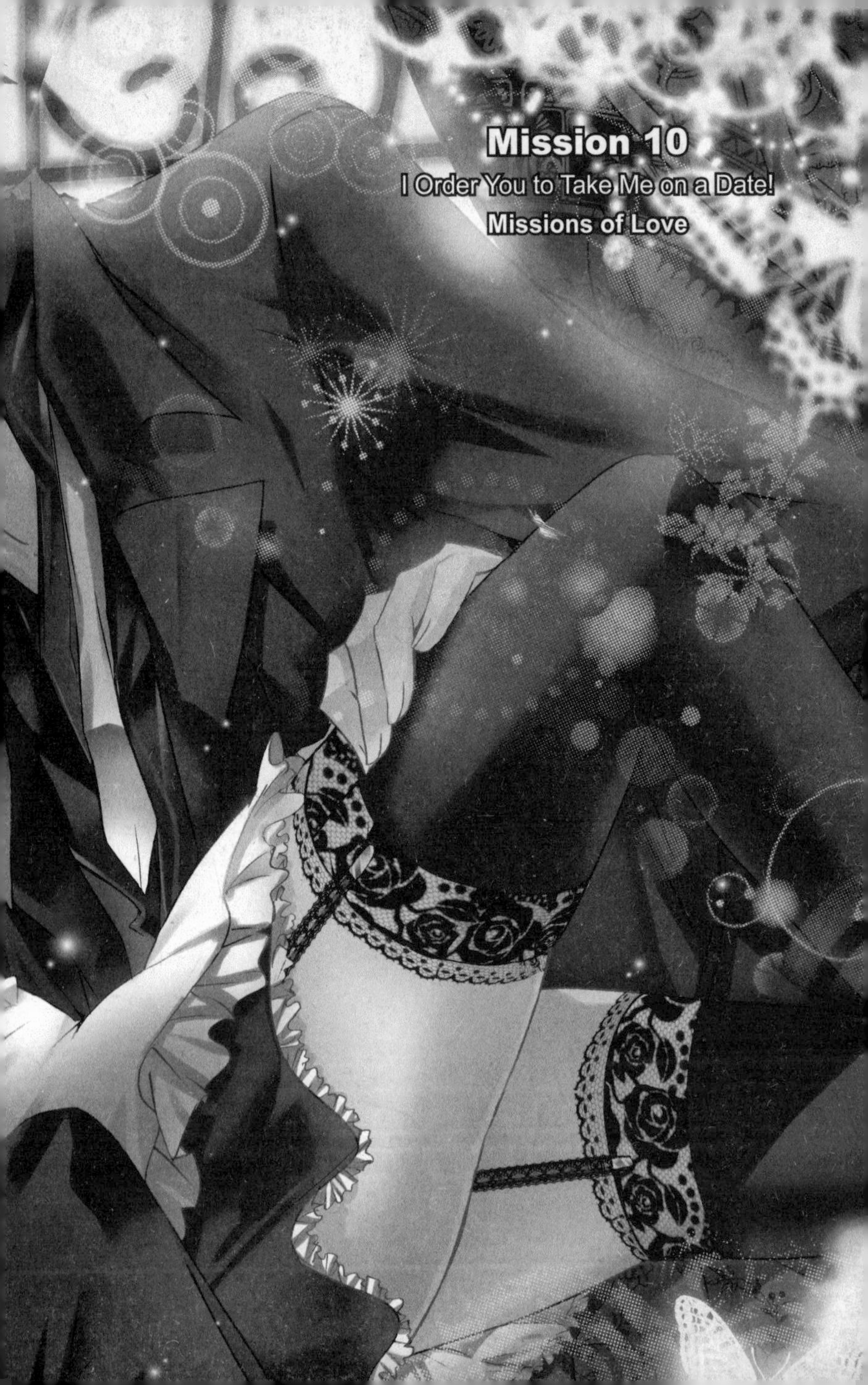
Mission 10
I Order You to Take Me on a Date!
Missions of Love

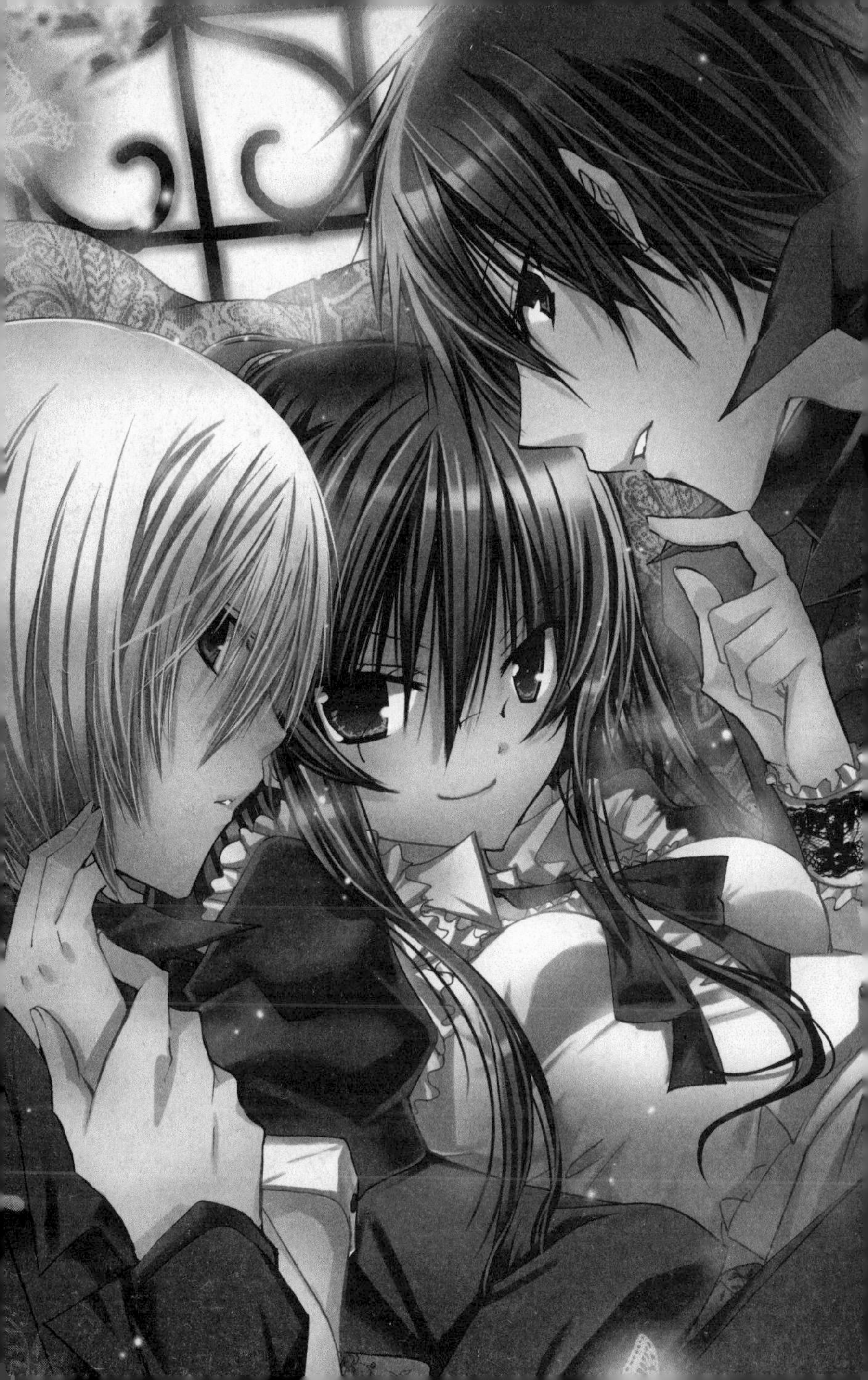

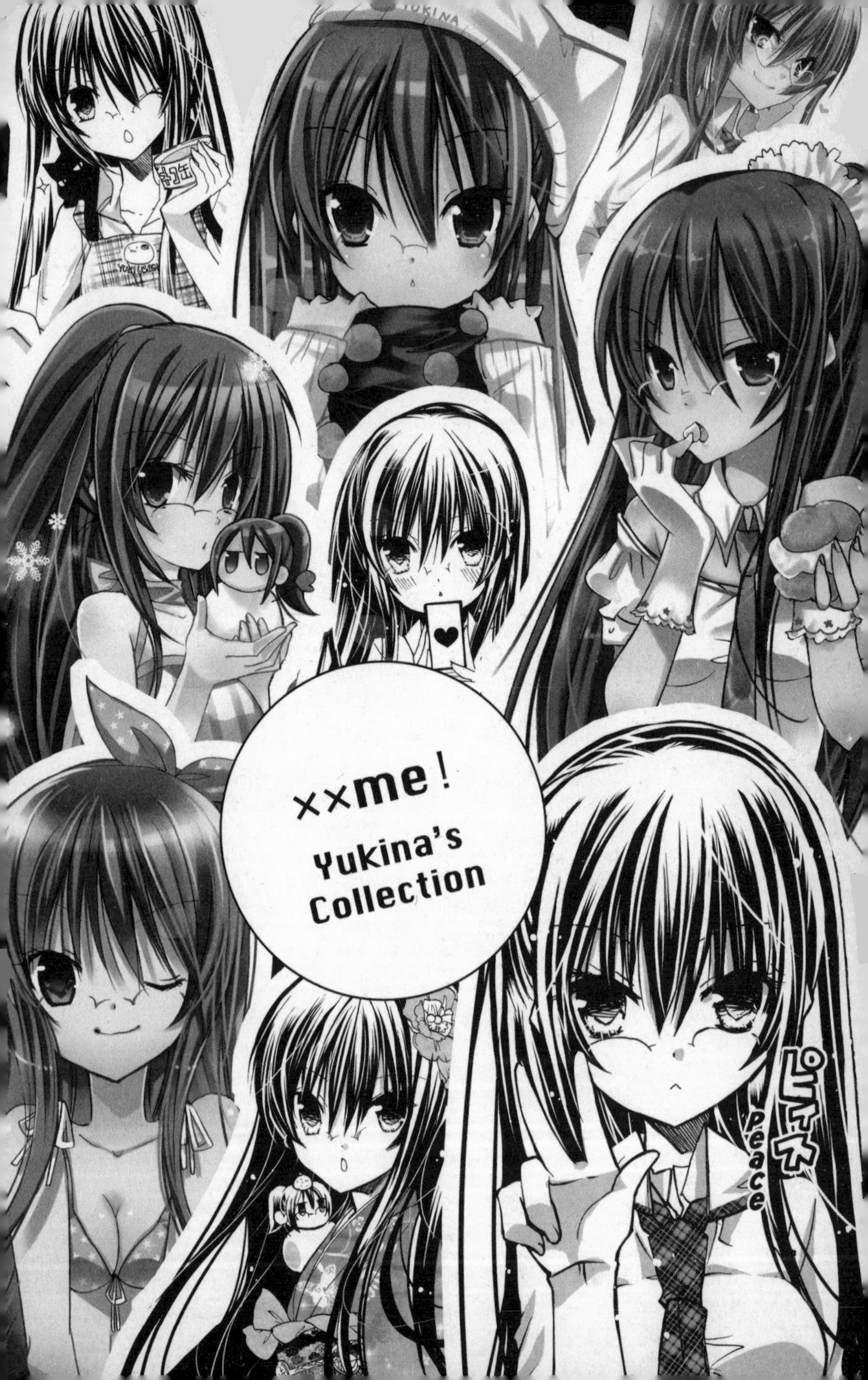
××me!
Yukina's Collection
ピース
peace

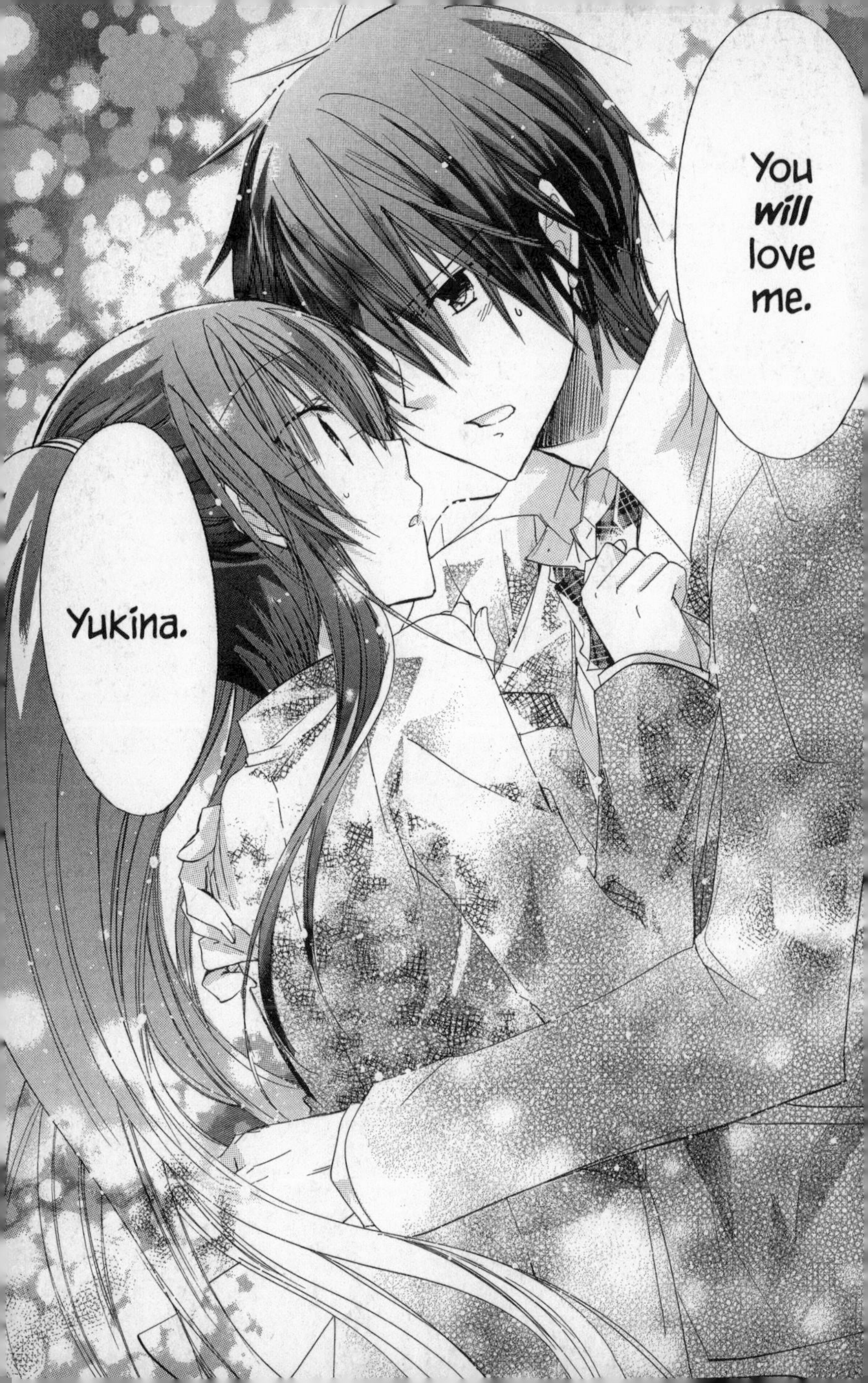
You ***will*** love me.
Yukina.

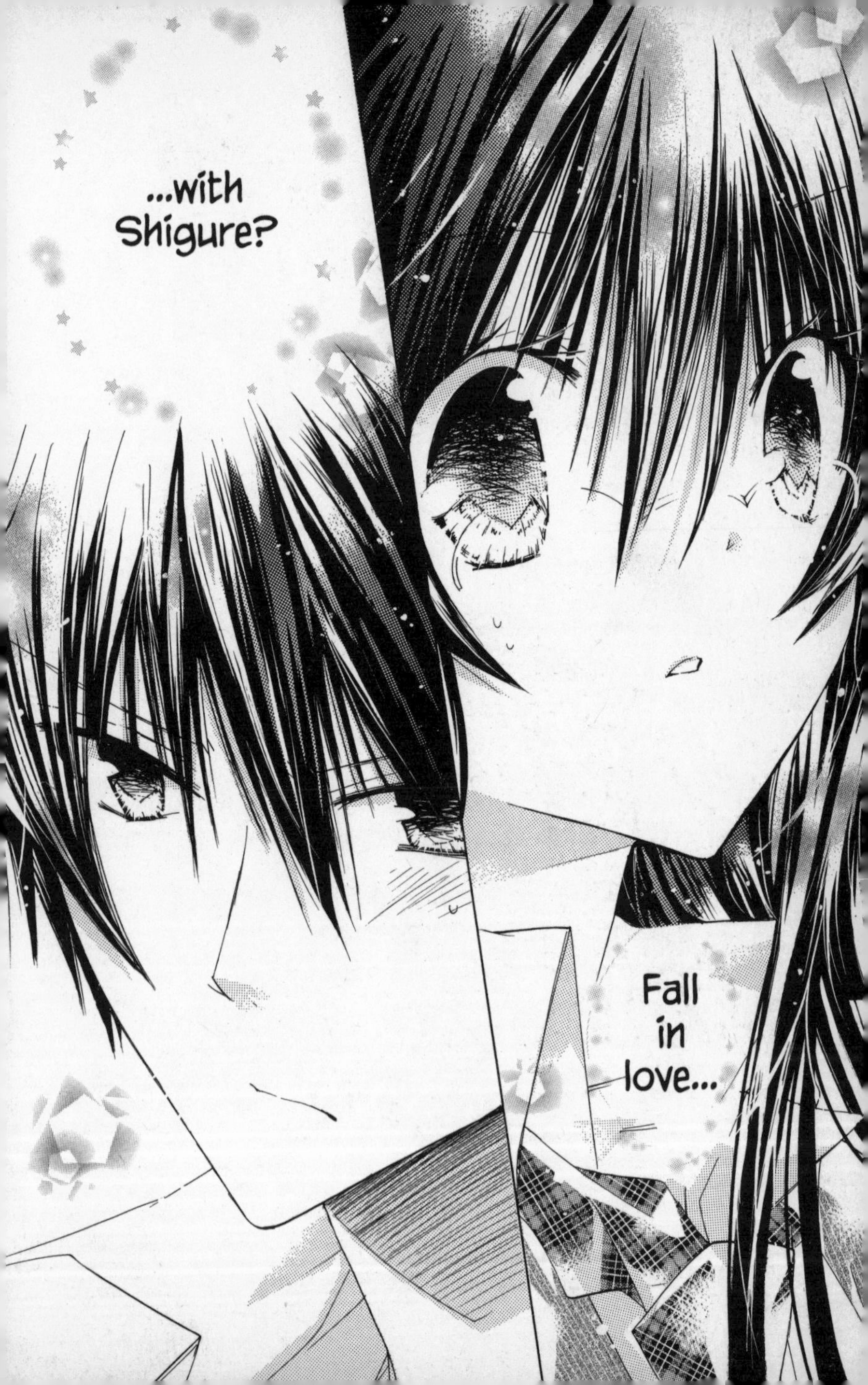
...with Shigure?
Fall in love...

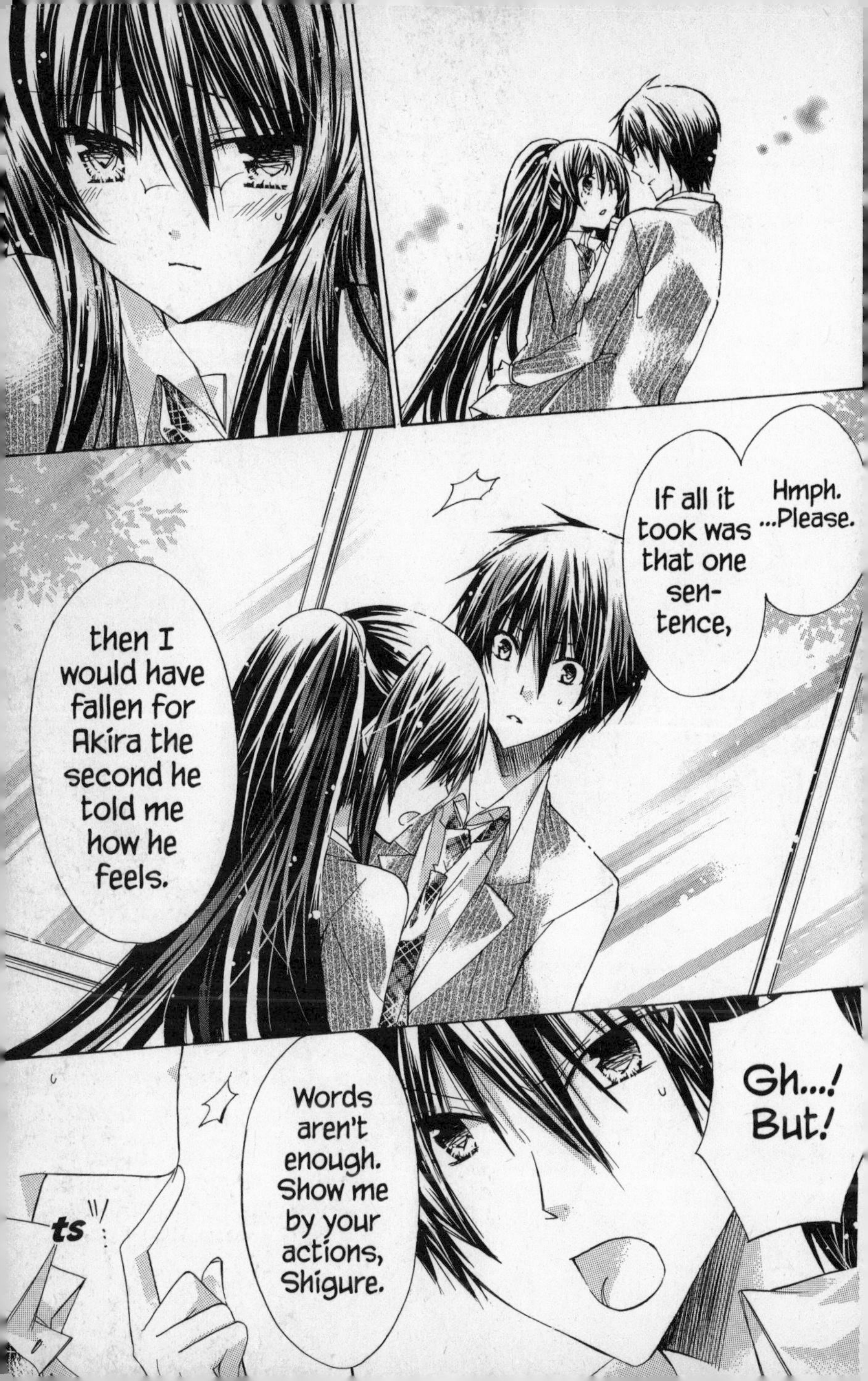
Hmph. ...Please.
If all it took was that one sen-tence,
then I would have fallen for Akira the second he told me how he feels.
Gh...! But!
Words aren't enough. Show me by your actions, Shigure.
ts

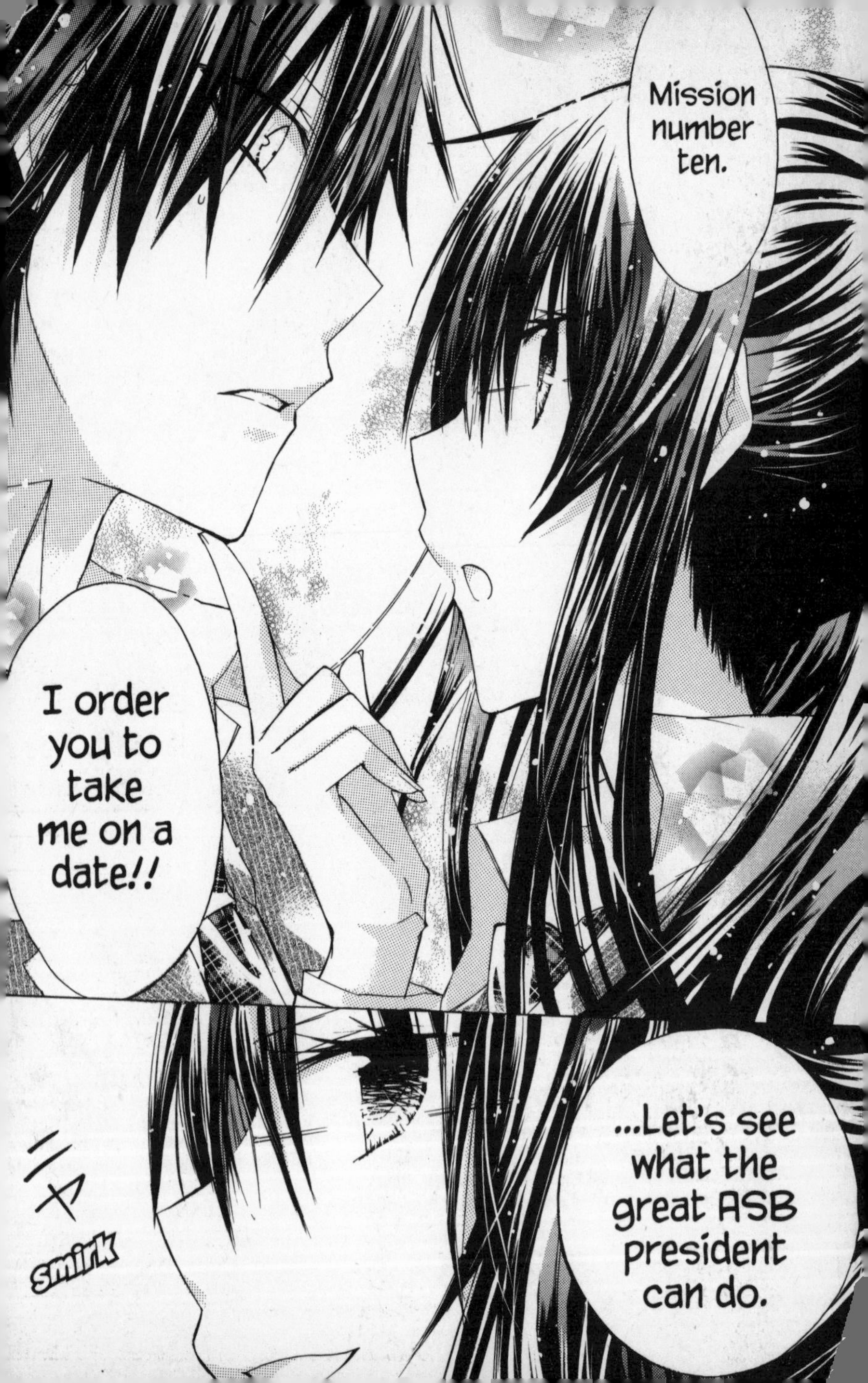
Mission number ten.
I order you to take me on a date!!
...Let's see what the great ASB president can do.
ニヤ
smirk

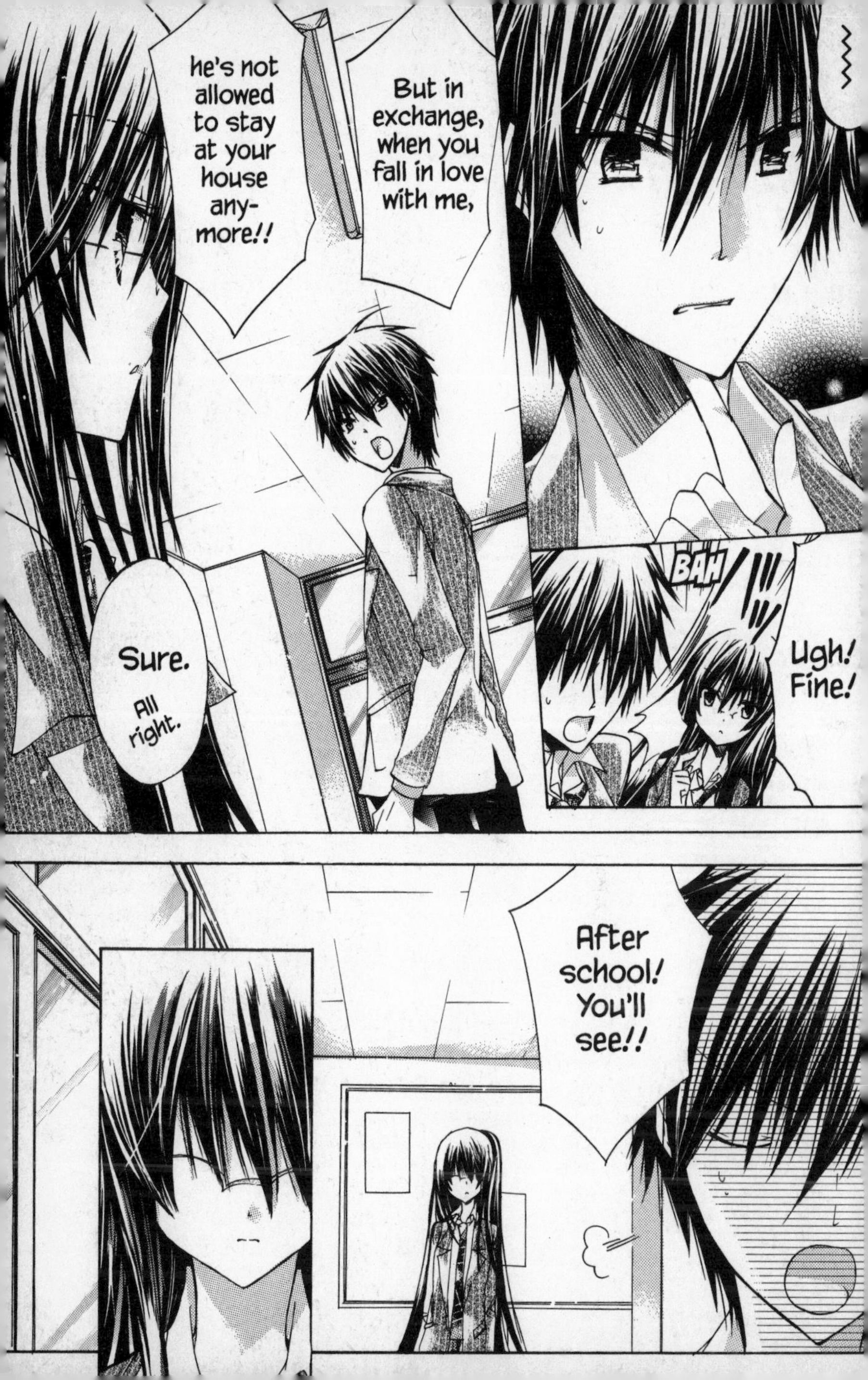
BAH
Ugh! Fine!
But in exchange, when you fall in love with me,
he's not allowed to stay at your house any-more!!
Sure.
All right.
After school! You'll see!!

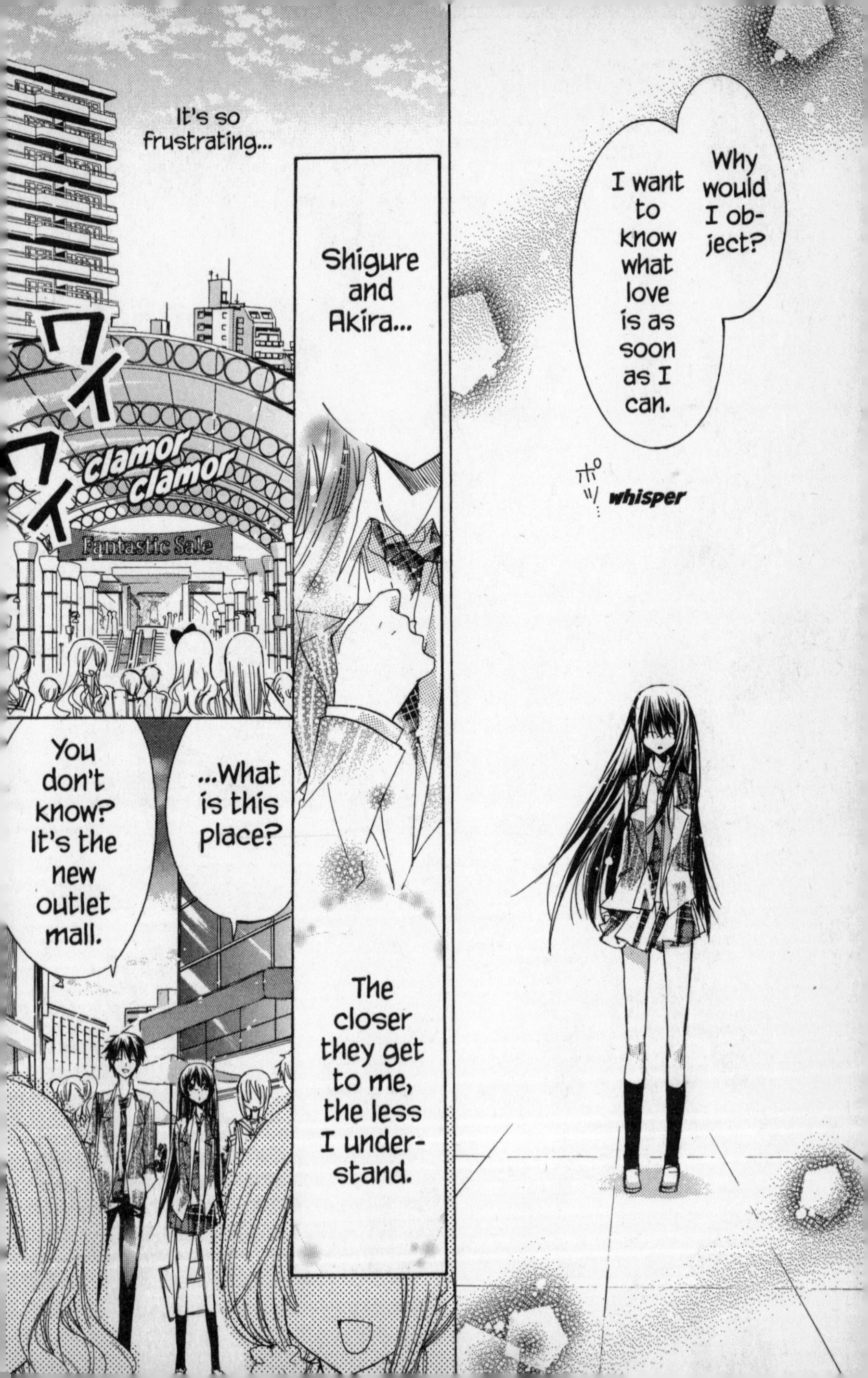
Why would I object?
I want to know what love is as soon as I can.
ポツ
whisper
Shigure and Akira...
The closer they get to me, the less I understand.
It's so frustrating...
ワイワイ
Clamor clamor
Fantastic Sale
...What is this place?
You don't know? It's the new outlet mall.

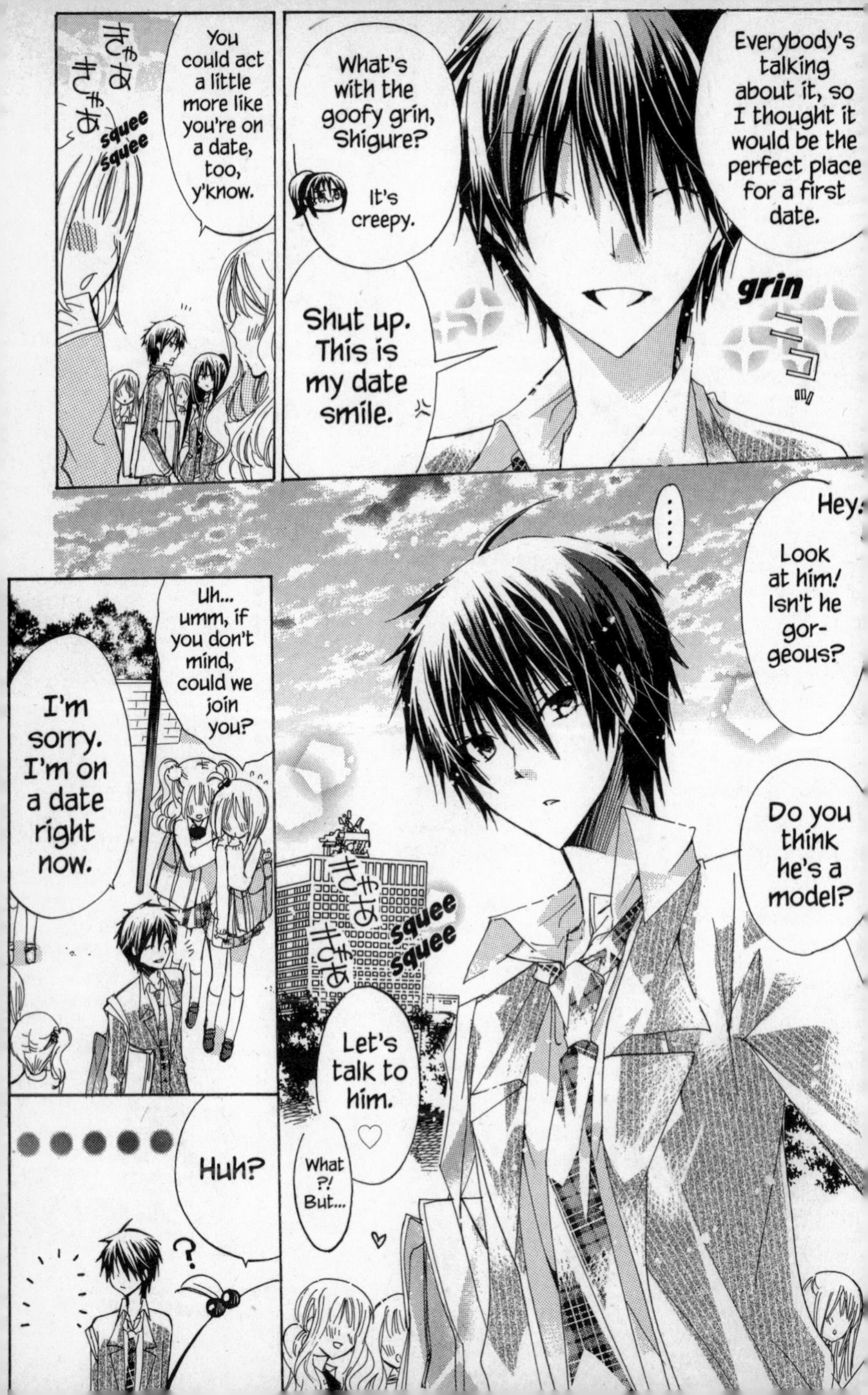

Everybody's talking about it, so I thought it would be the perfect place for a first date.
grin
ニコ
What's with the goofy grin, Shigure?
It's creepy.
Shut up. This is my date smile.
きゃあ きゃあ
squee squee
You could act a little more like you're on a date, too, y'know.
Hey!
Look at him! Isn't he gor-geous?
......
Do you think he's a model?
きゃあ きゃあ
squee squee
Let's talk to him.
What?! But...
Uh... umm, if you don't mind, could we join you?
I'm sorry. I'm on a date right now.
Huh?

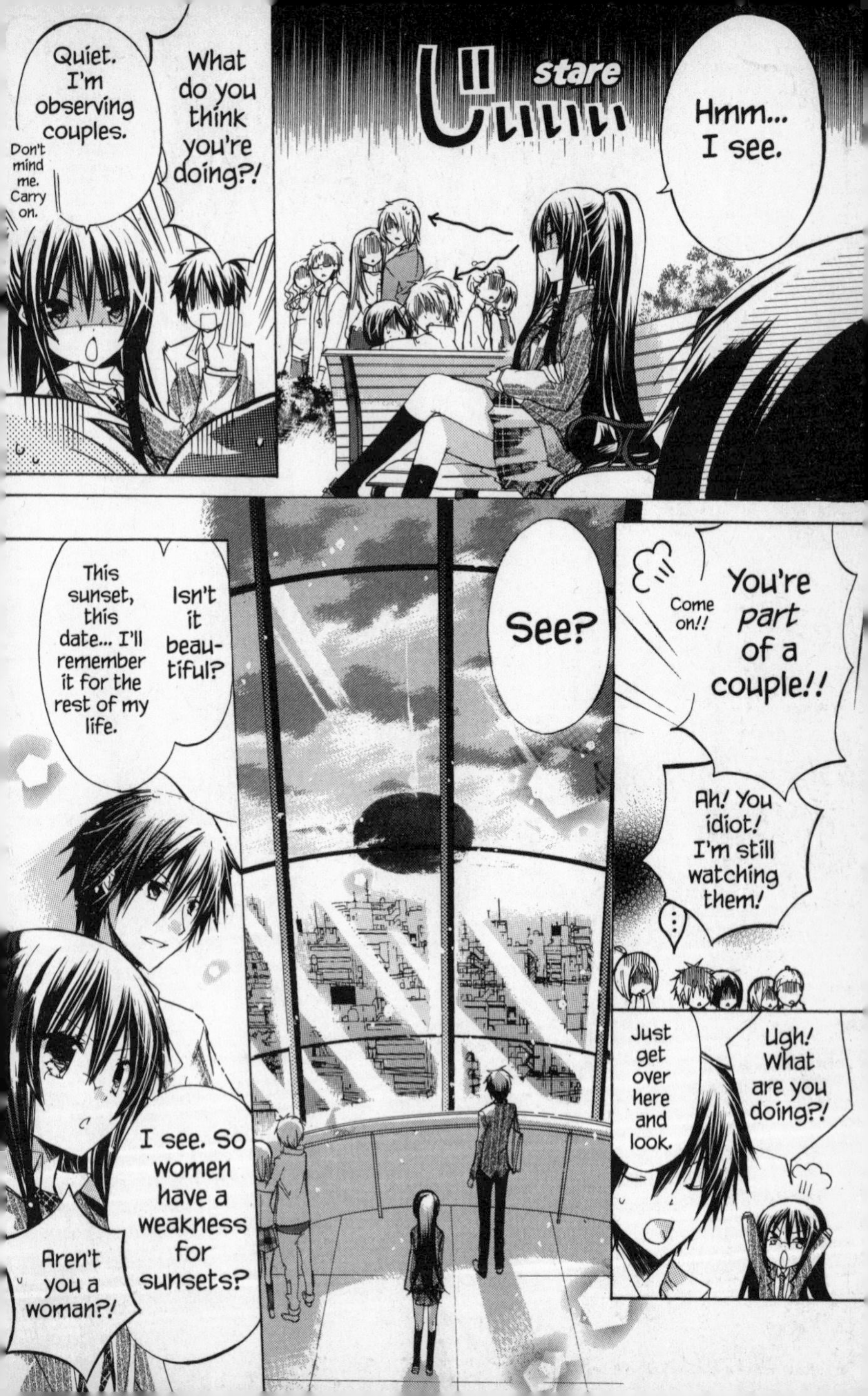
Hmm... I see.
じいいい stare
What do you think you're doing?!
Quiet. I'm observing couples.
Don't mind me. Carry on.
You're *part* of a couple!!
Come on!!
Ah! You idiot! I'm still watching them!
...
Ugh! What are you doing?!
Just get over here and look.
See?
Isn't it beautiful?
This sunset, this date... I'll remember it for the rest of my life.
I see. So women have a weakness for sunsets?
Aren't you a woman?!

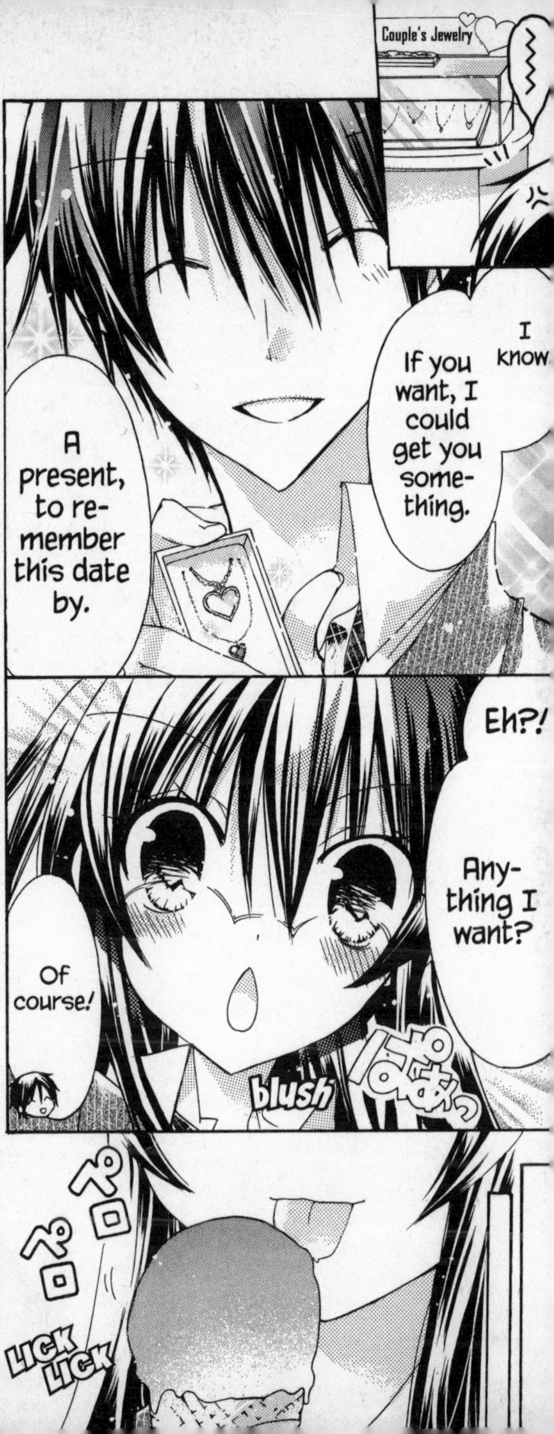
Couple's Jewelry
I know.
If you want, I could get you some-thing.
A present, to re-member this date by.
Eh?!
Any-thing I want?
Of course!
blush
LICK LICK

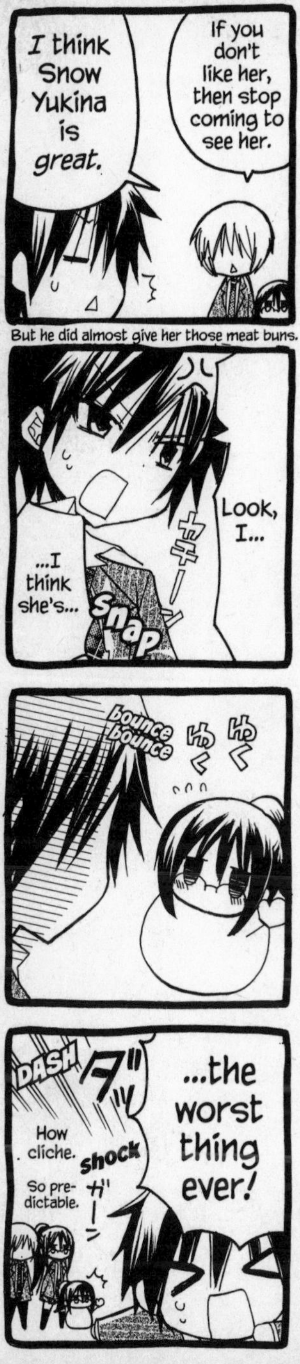
If you don't like her, then stop coming to see her.
I think Snow Yukina is great.
But he did almost give her those meat buns.
Look, I...
...I think she's...
Snap
bounce bounce
DASH
...the worst thing ever!
shock
How cliche.
So pre-dictable.

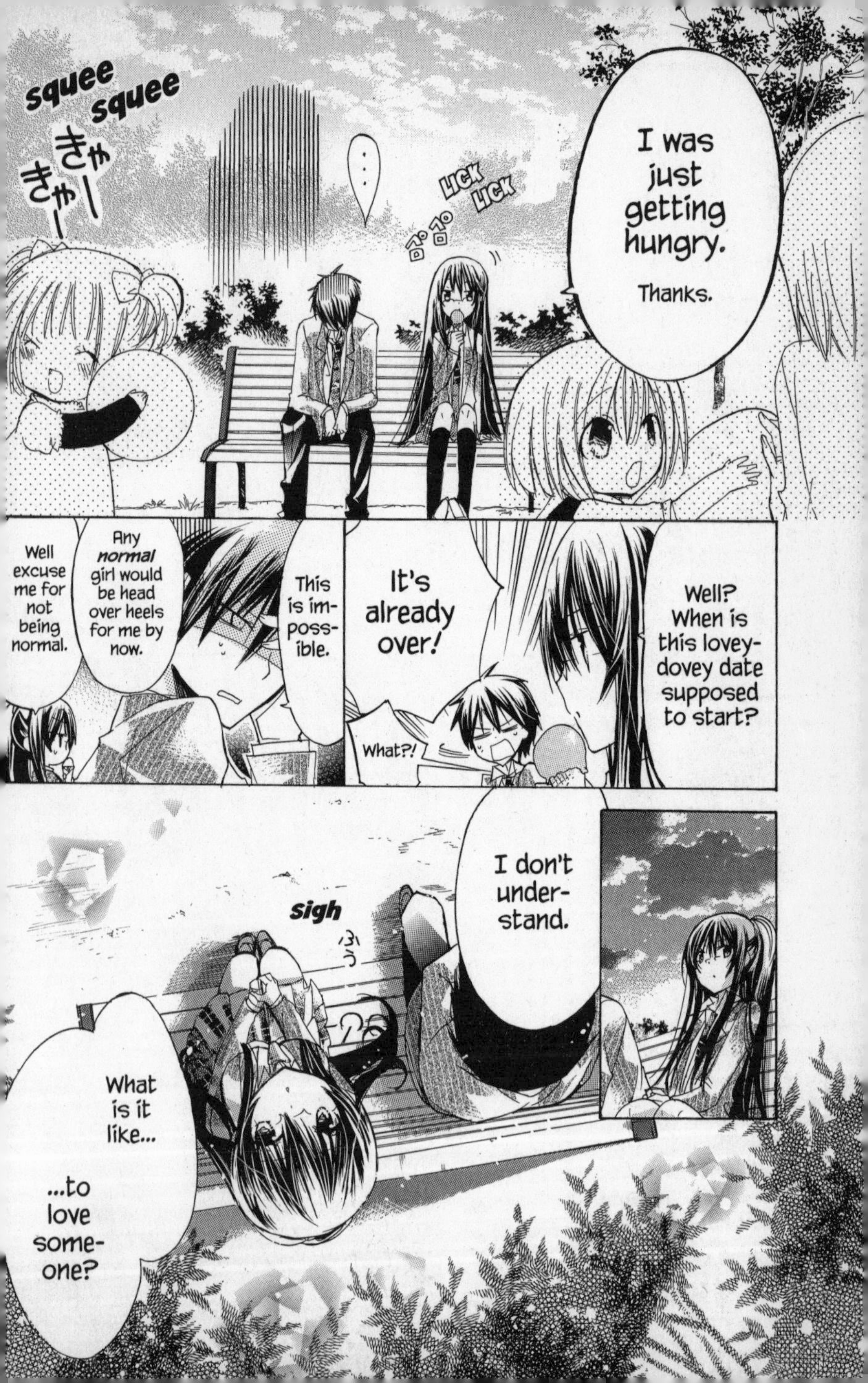

I was just getting hungry.
Thanks.
LICK LICK
...
squee squee
きゃーきゃー
Well? When is this lovey-dovey date supposed to start?
It's already over!
What?!
This is im-poss-ible.
Any *normal* girl would be head over heels for me by now.
Well excuse me for not being normal.
I don't under-stand.
Sigh
ふぅ
What is it like...
...to love some-one?

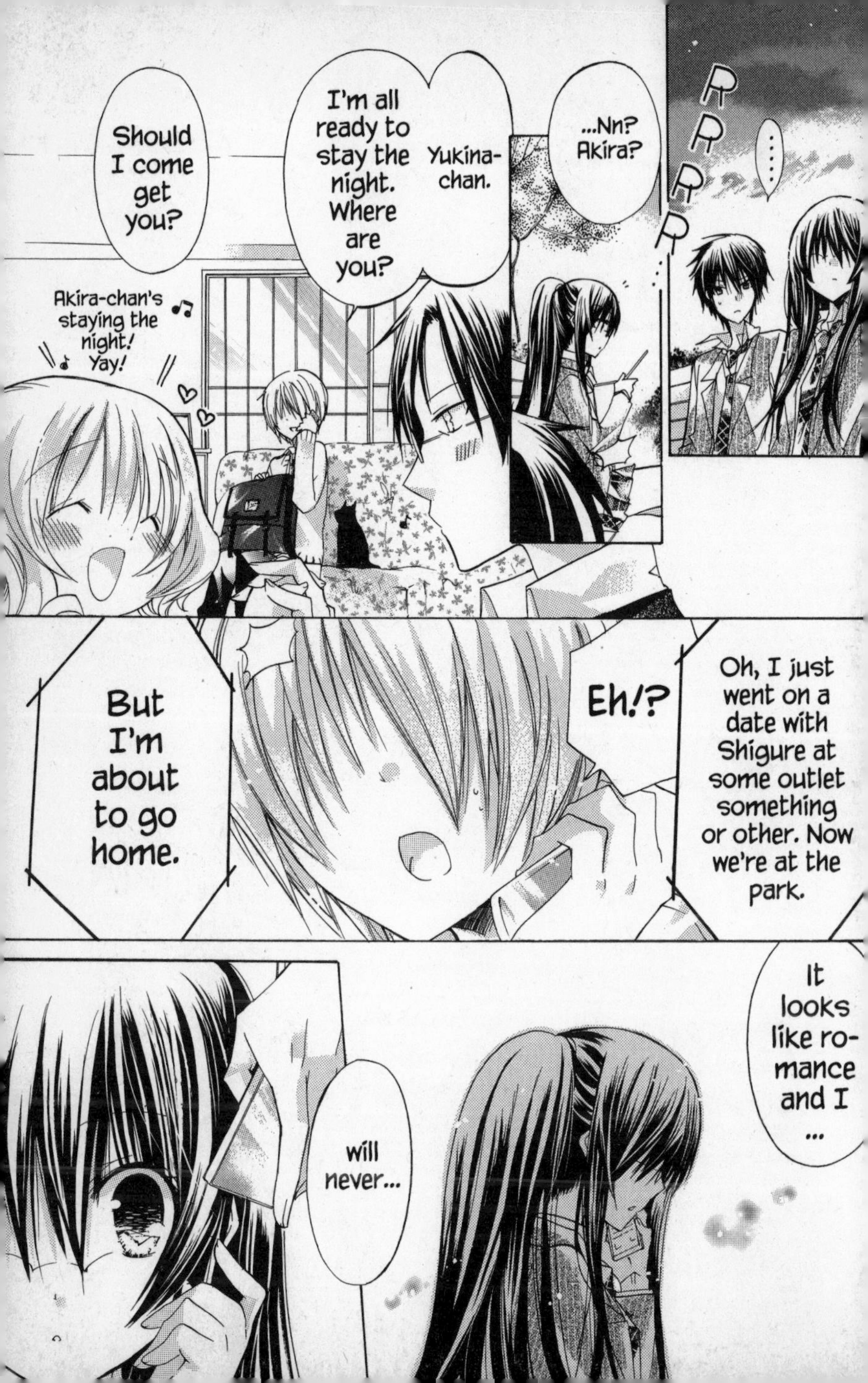
RRRR
......
...Nn? Akira?
Yukina-chan.
I'm all ready to stay the night. Where are you?
Should I come get you?
Akira-chan's staying the night! Yay!
Oh, I just went on a date with Shigure at some outlet something or other. Now we're at the park.
Eh!?
But I'm about to go home.
It looks like ro-mance and I ...
will never...

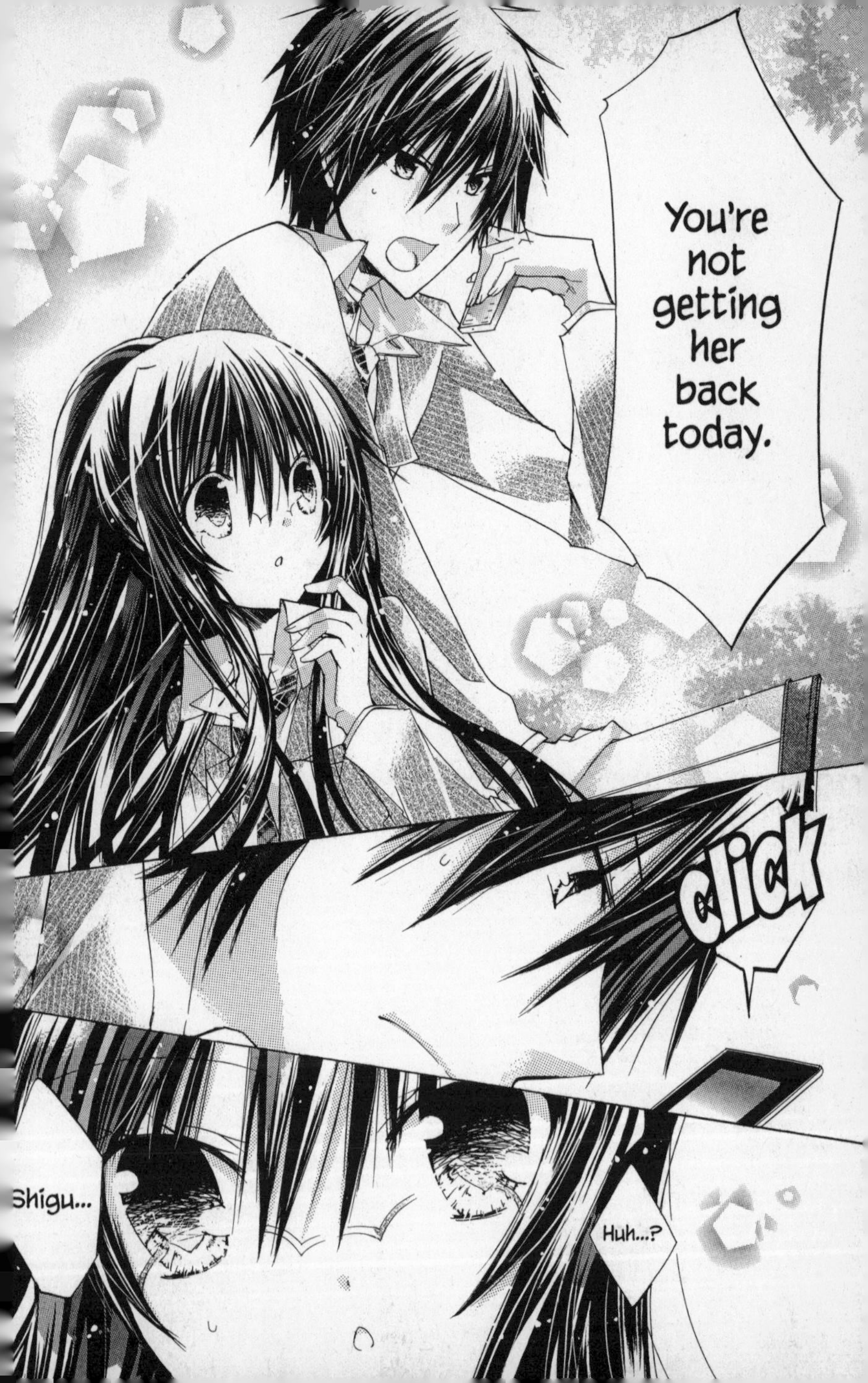
You're not getting her back today.
click
Huh...?
Shigu...

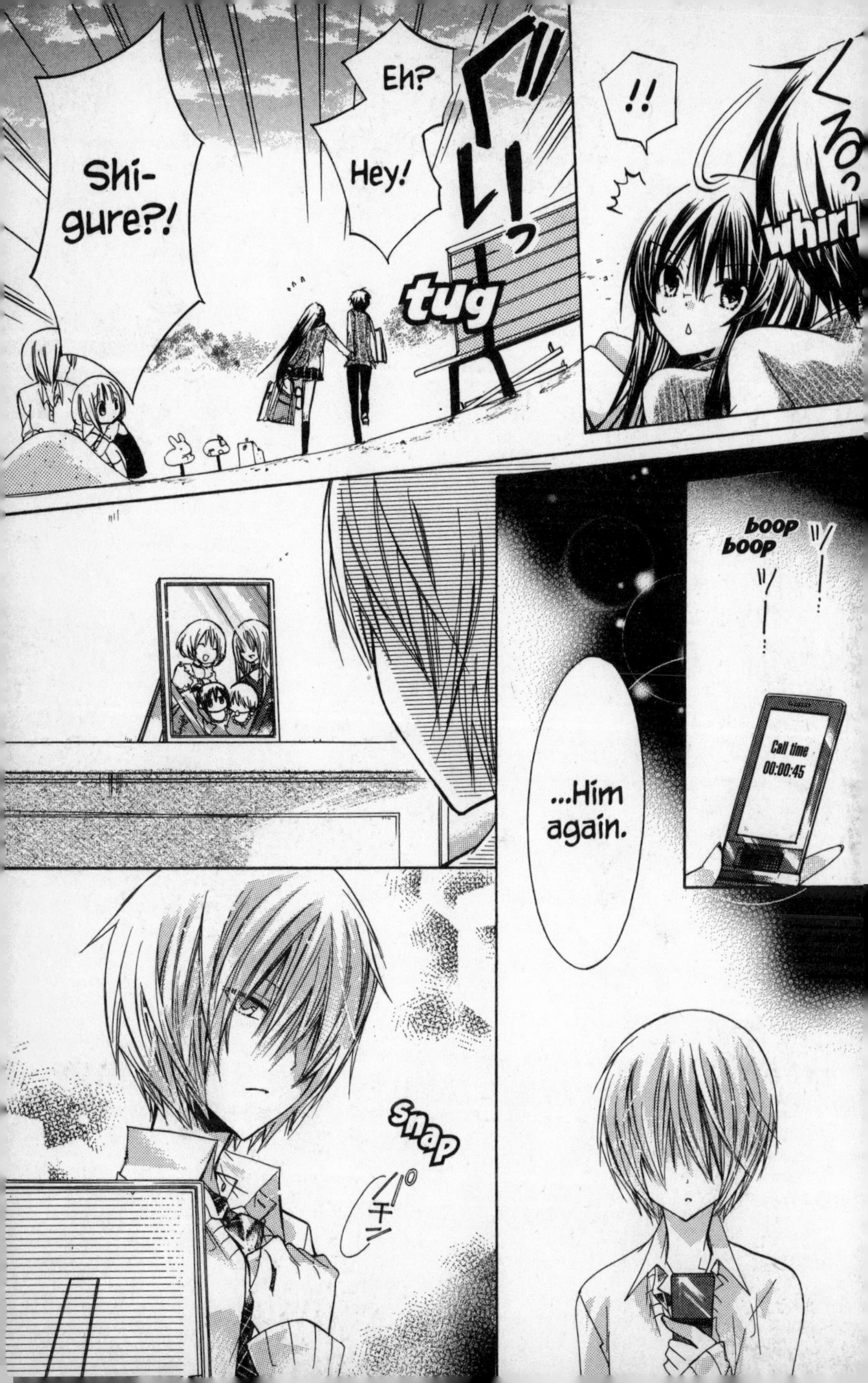
!!
whirl
Eh?
Hey!
tug
Shi-gure?!
boop boop
Call time 00:00:45
...Him again.
snap

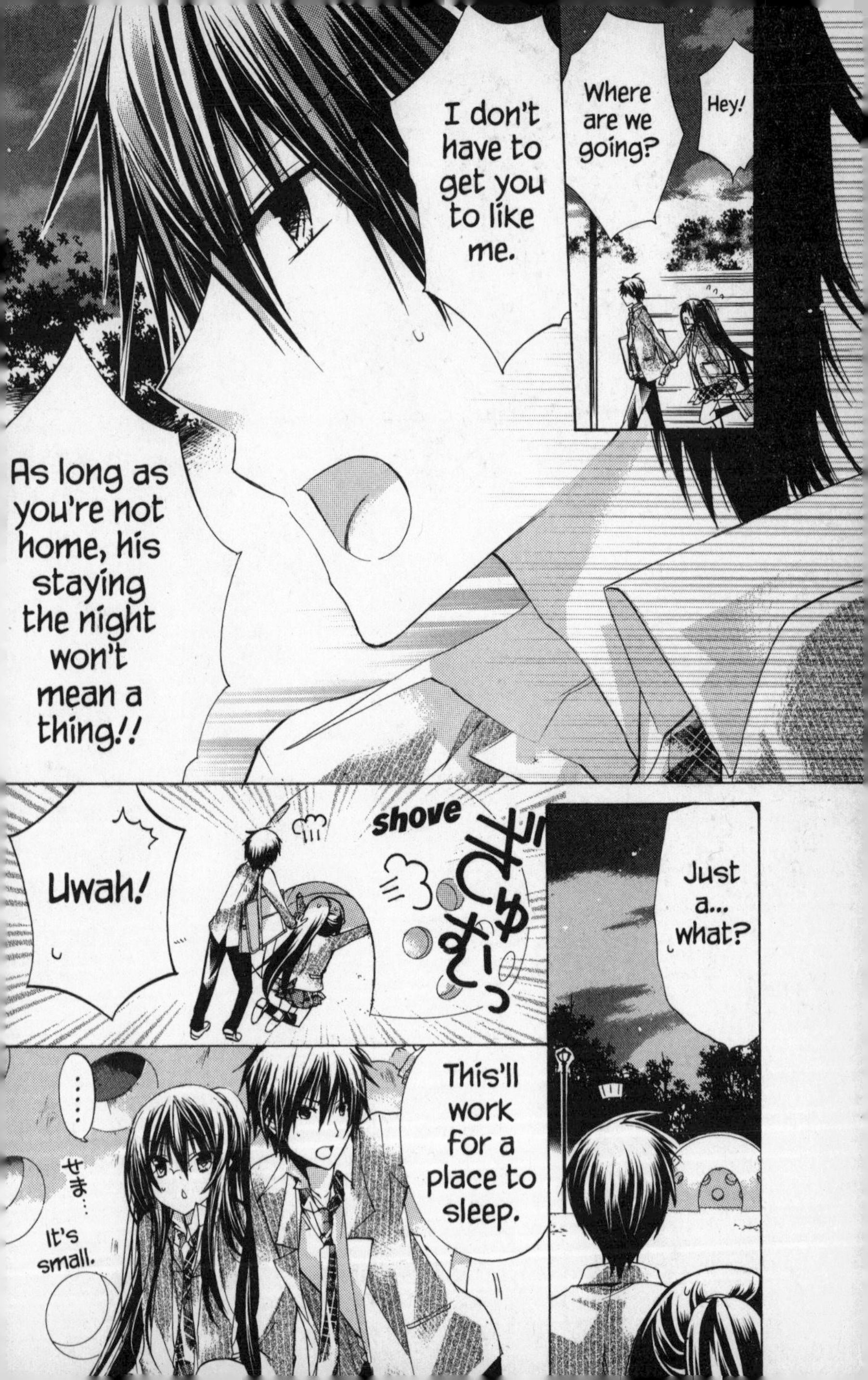
Hey!
Where are we going?
I don't have to get you to like me.
As long as you're not home, his staying the night won't mean a thing!!
Just a... what?
shove
Uwah!
This'll work for a place to sleep.
......
せま…
It's small.

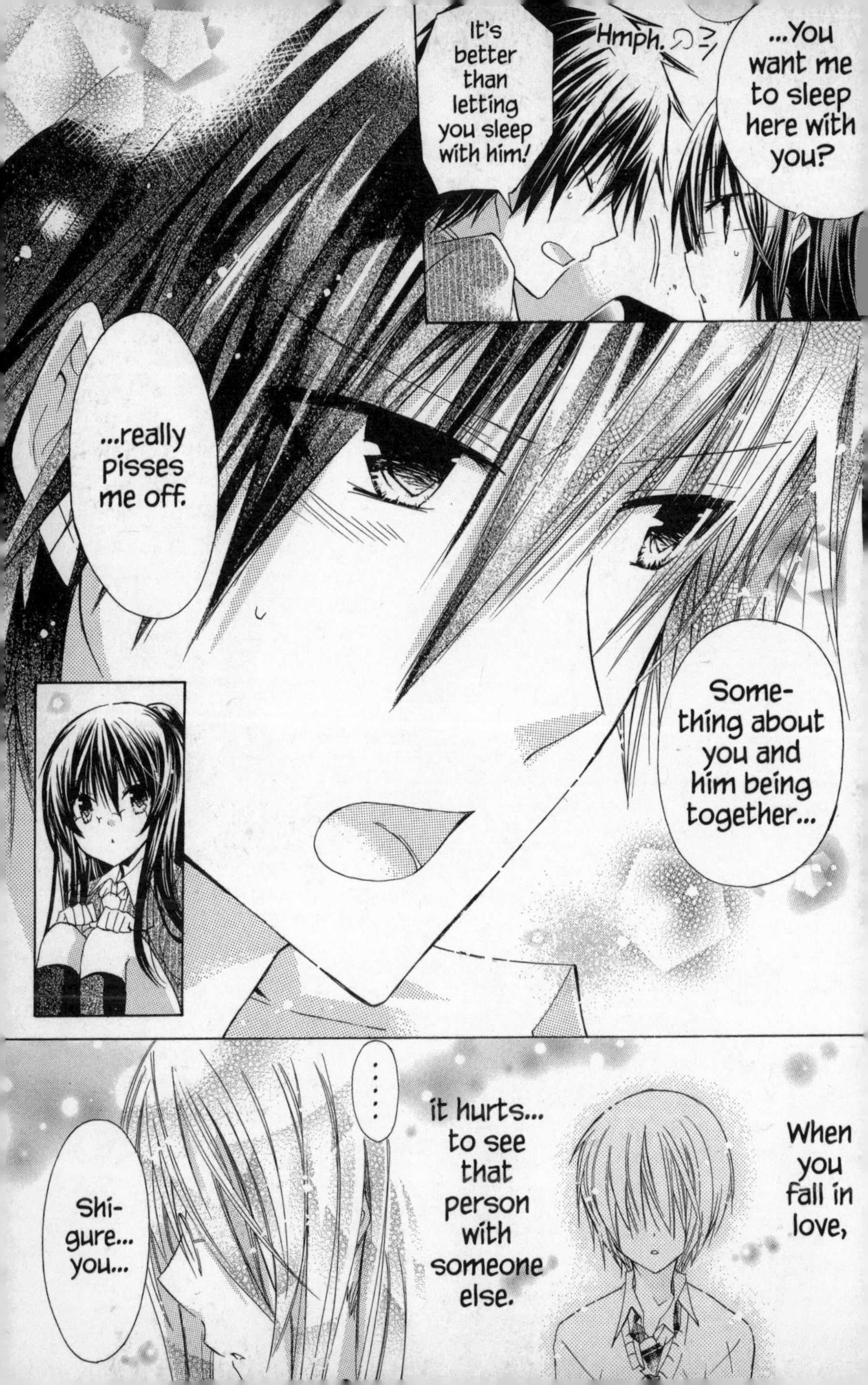
...You want me to sleep here with you?
Hmph.
It's better than letting you sleep with him!
Some-thing about you and him being together...
...really pisses me off.
When you fall in love,
it hurts... to see that person with someone else.
......
Shi-gure... you...

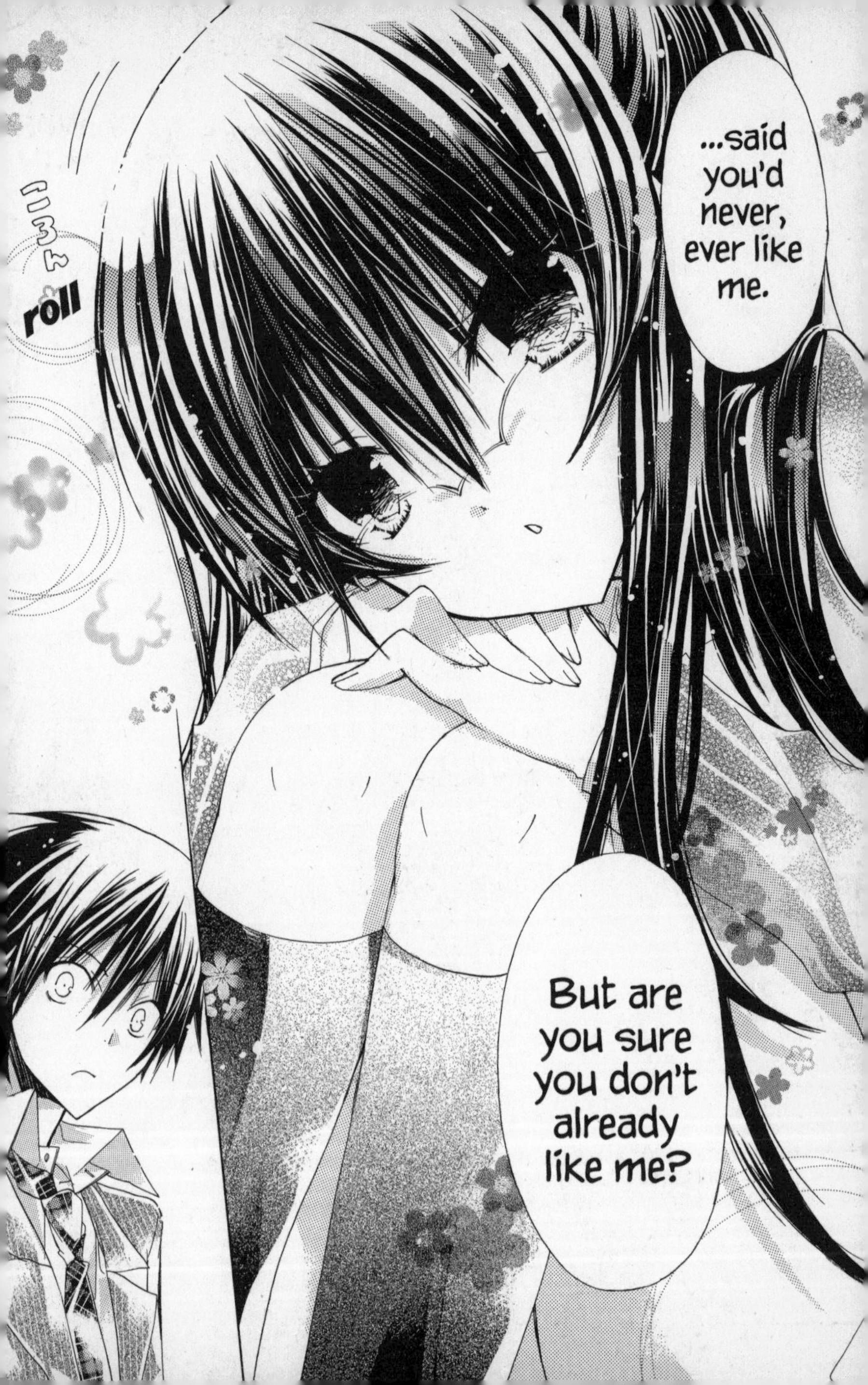

...said you'd never, ever like me.
ころん
roll
But are you sure you don't already like me?

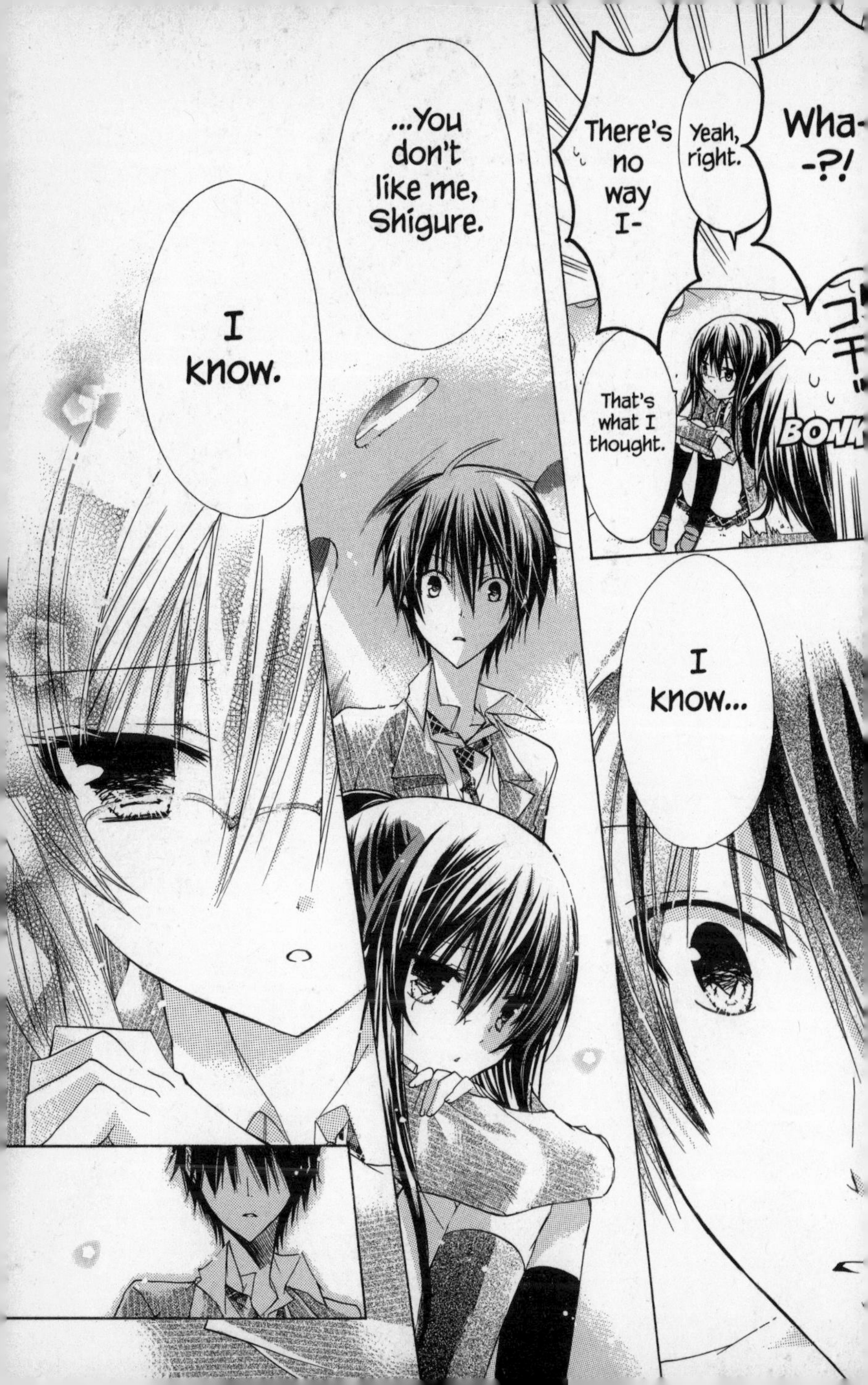
Wha--?!
Yeah, right.
There's no way I-
That's what I thought.
BONK
I know...
...You don't like me, Shigure.
I know.

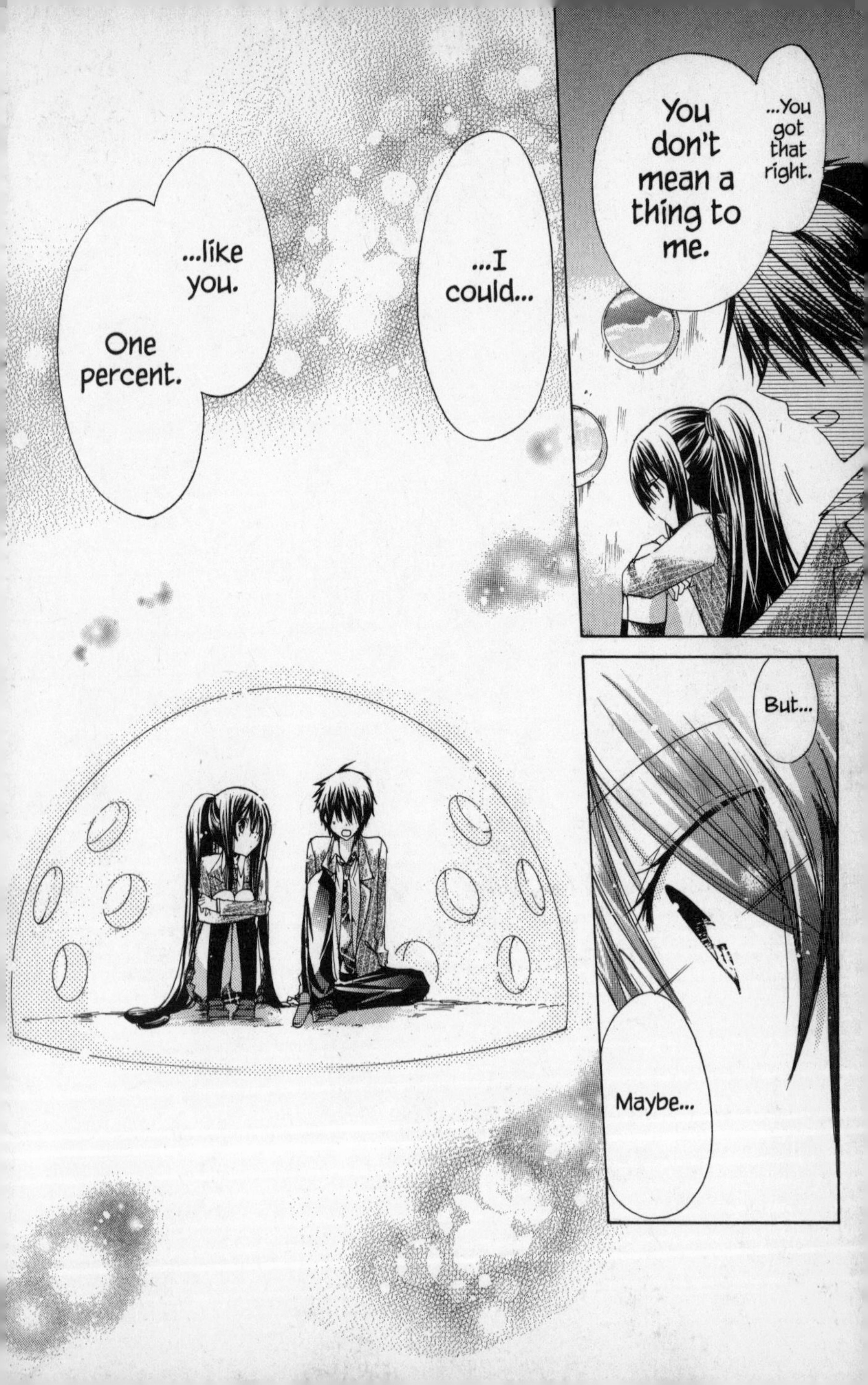

...You got that right.
You don't mean a thing to me.
But...
Maybe...
...I could...
...like you.
One percent.

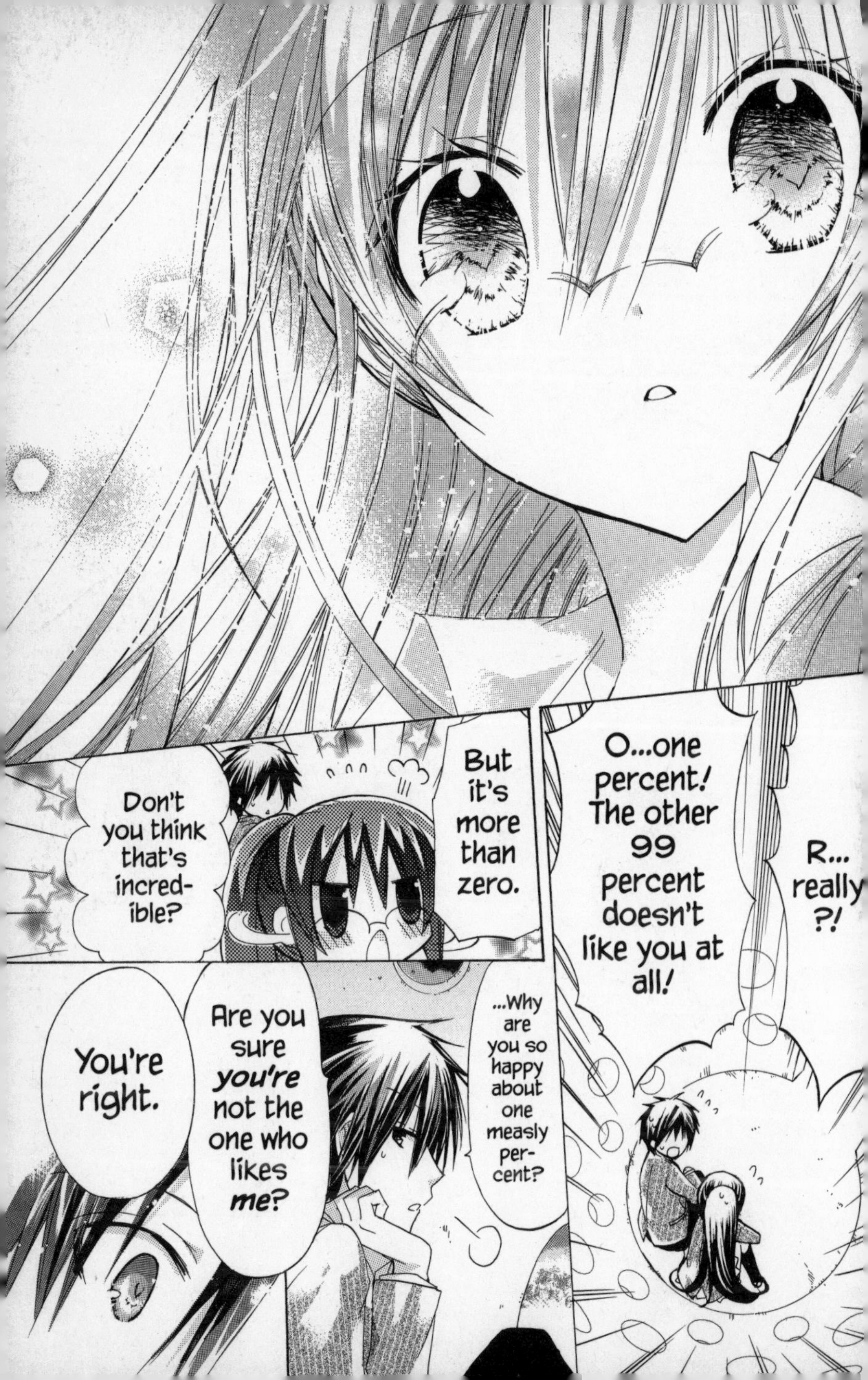
R... really?!
O...one percent! The other 99 percent doesn't like you at all!
But it's more than zero.
Don't you think that's incred-ible?
...Why are you so happy about one measly per-cent?
Are you sure *you're* not the one who likes *me*?
You're right.

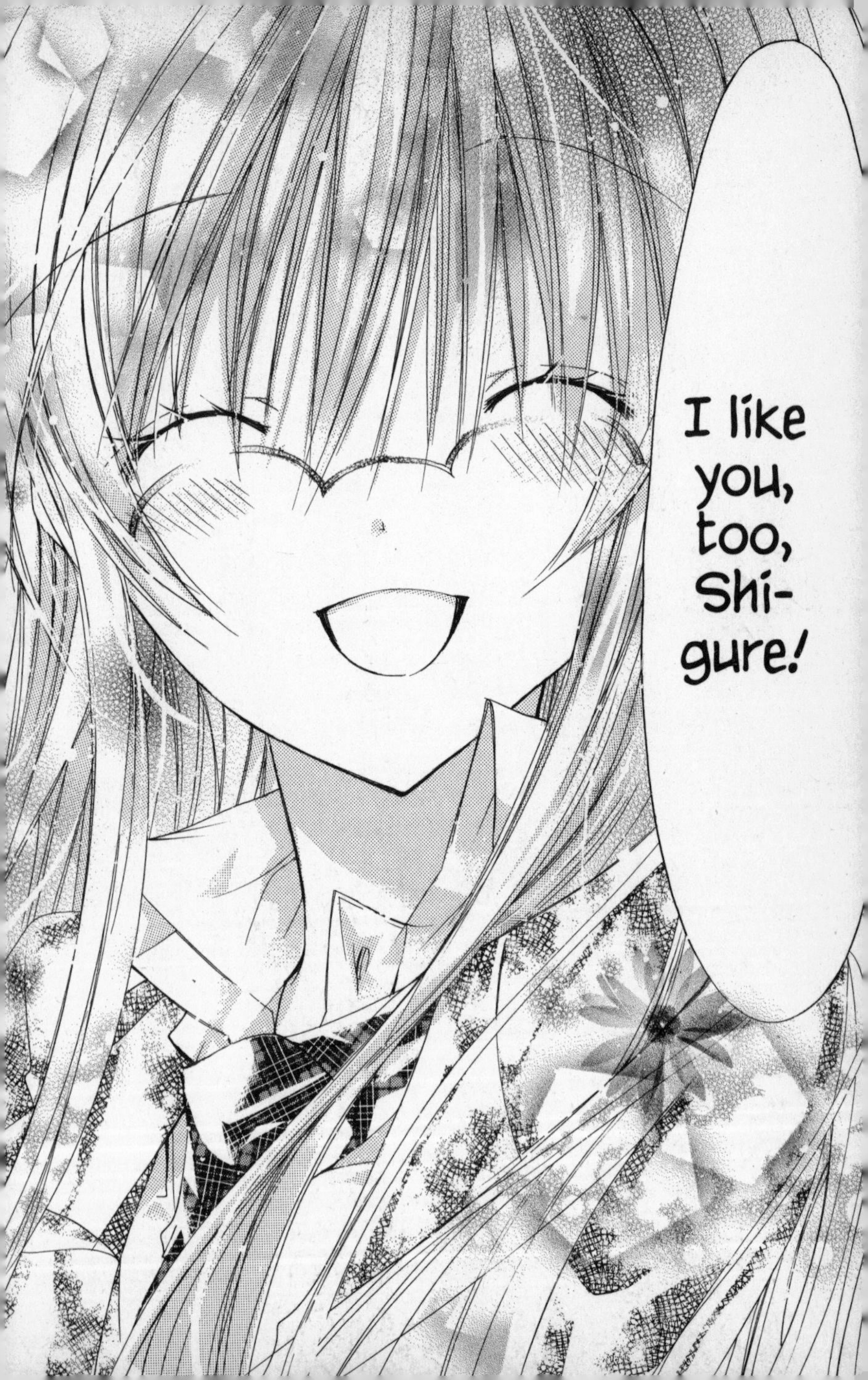
I like you, too, Shi-gure!

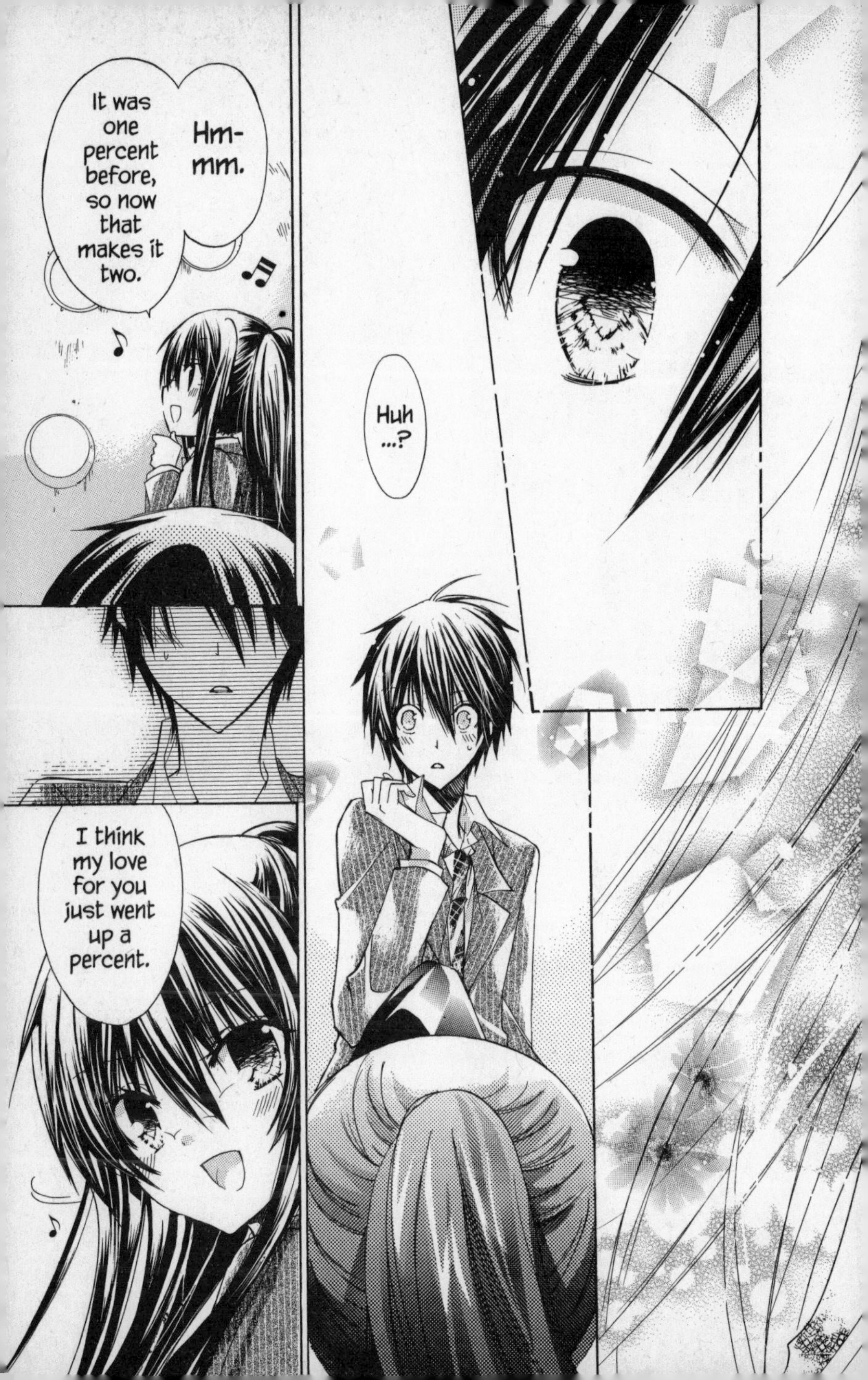
Huh ...?
Hm-mm.
It was one percent before, so now that makes it two.
I think my love for you just went up a percent.

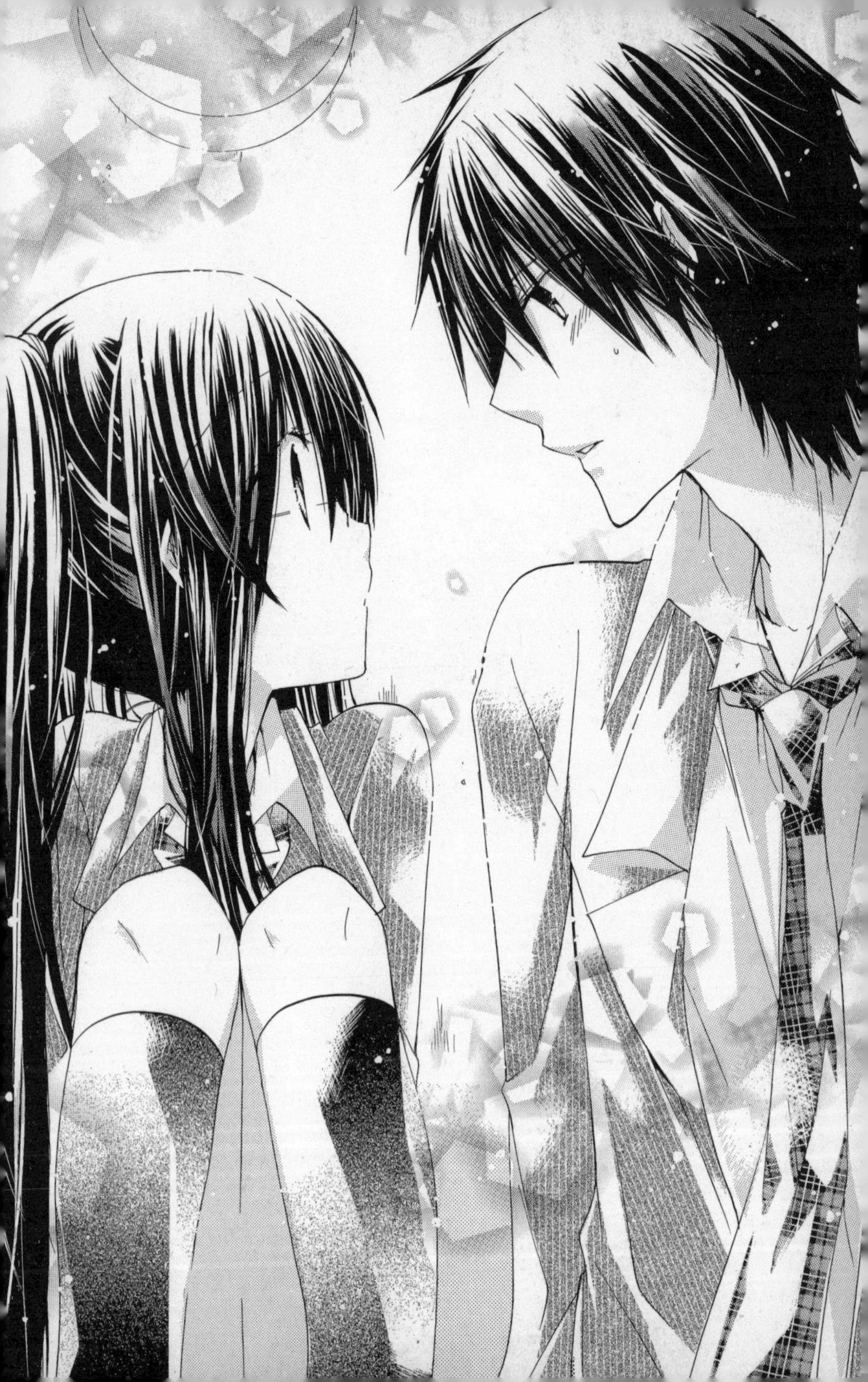

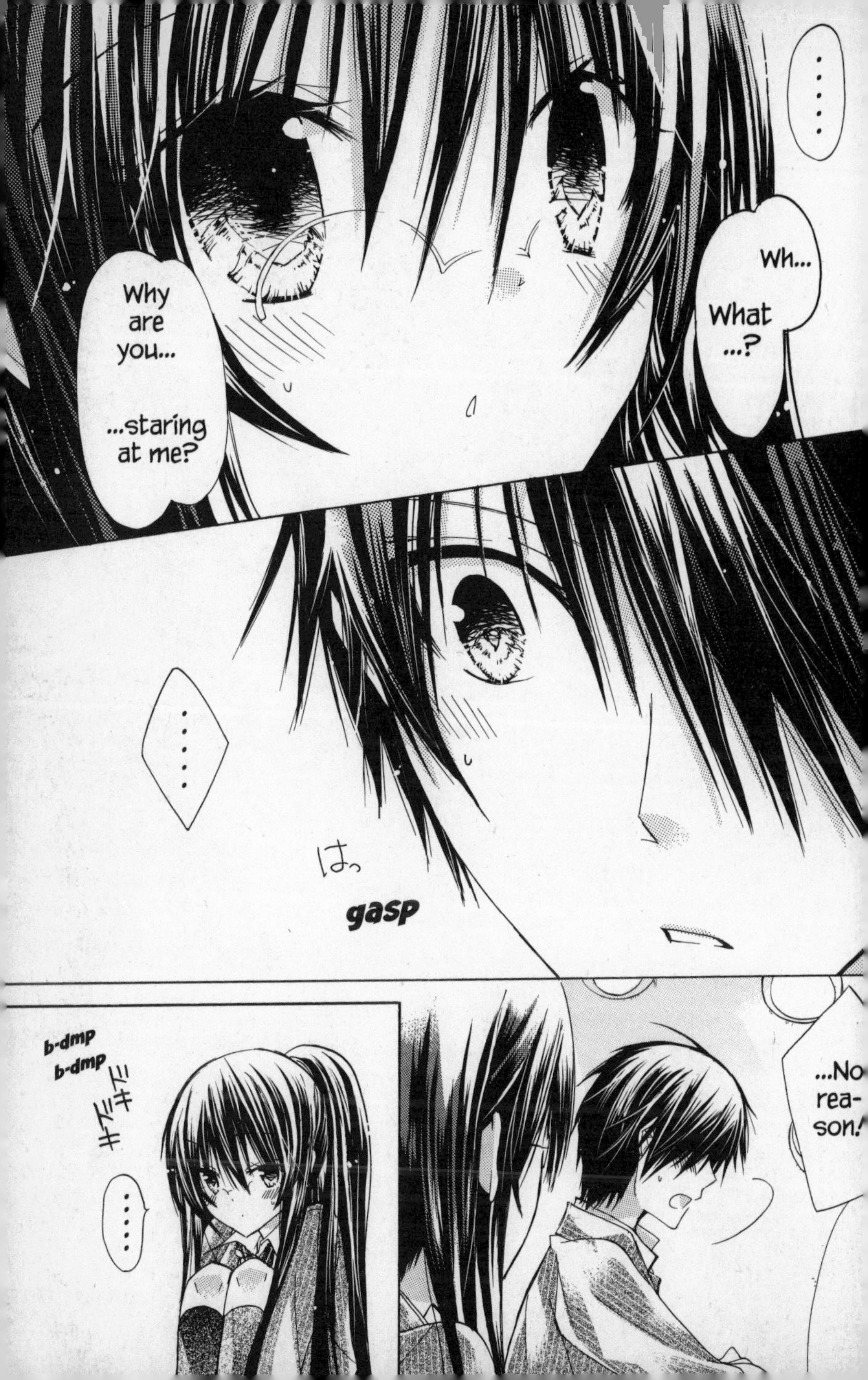

......
Wh... What ...?
Why are you... ...staring at me?
......
はっ
gasp
...No reason!
b-dmp b-dmp
ドキドキ
......

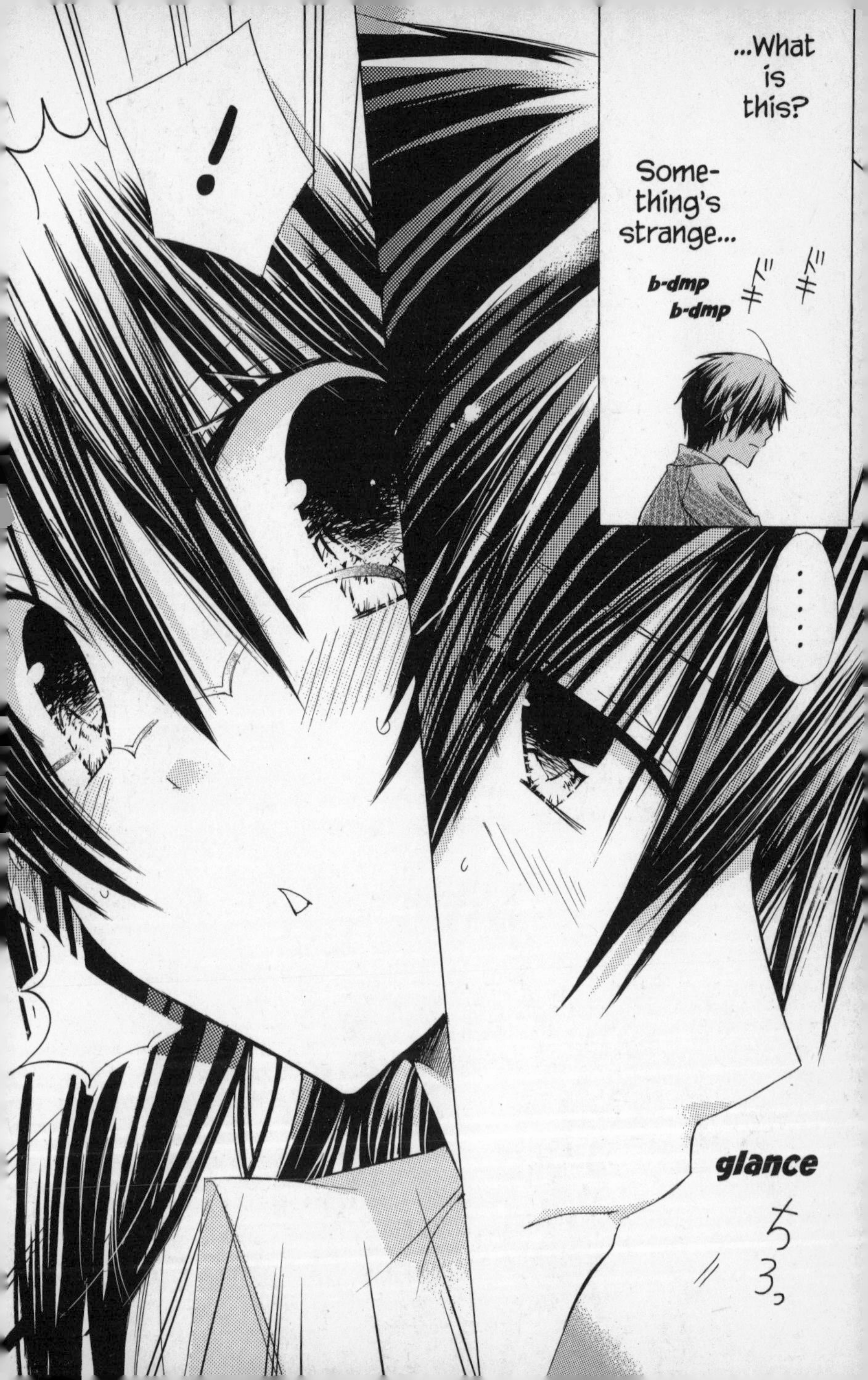
...What is this?
Some-thing's strange...
b-dmp b-dmp
!
......
glance
ちろっ

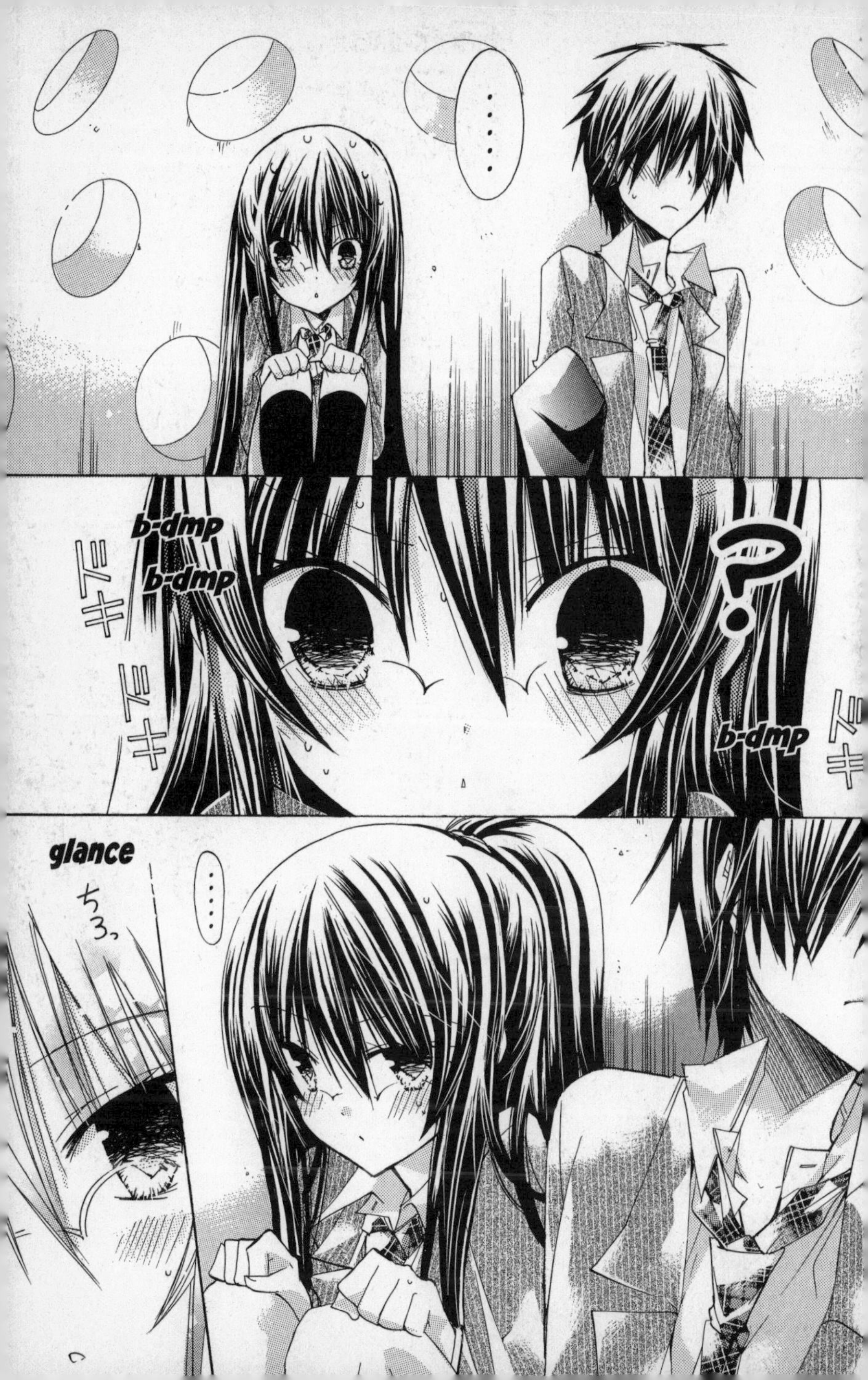
......
?!
b-dmp
ドキ
b-dmp
b-dmp
ドキドキ
ドキドキ
......
glance
ちろっ

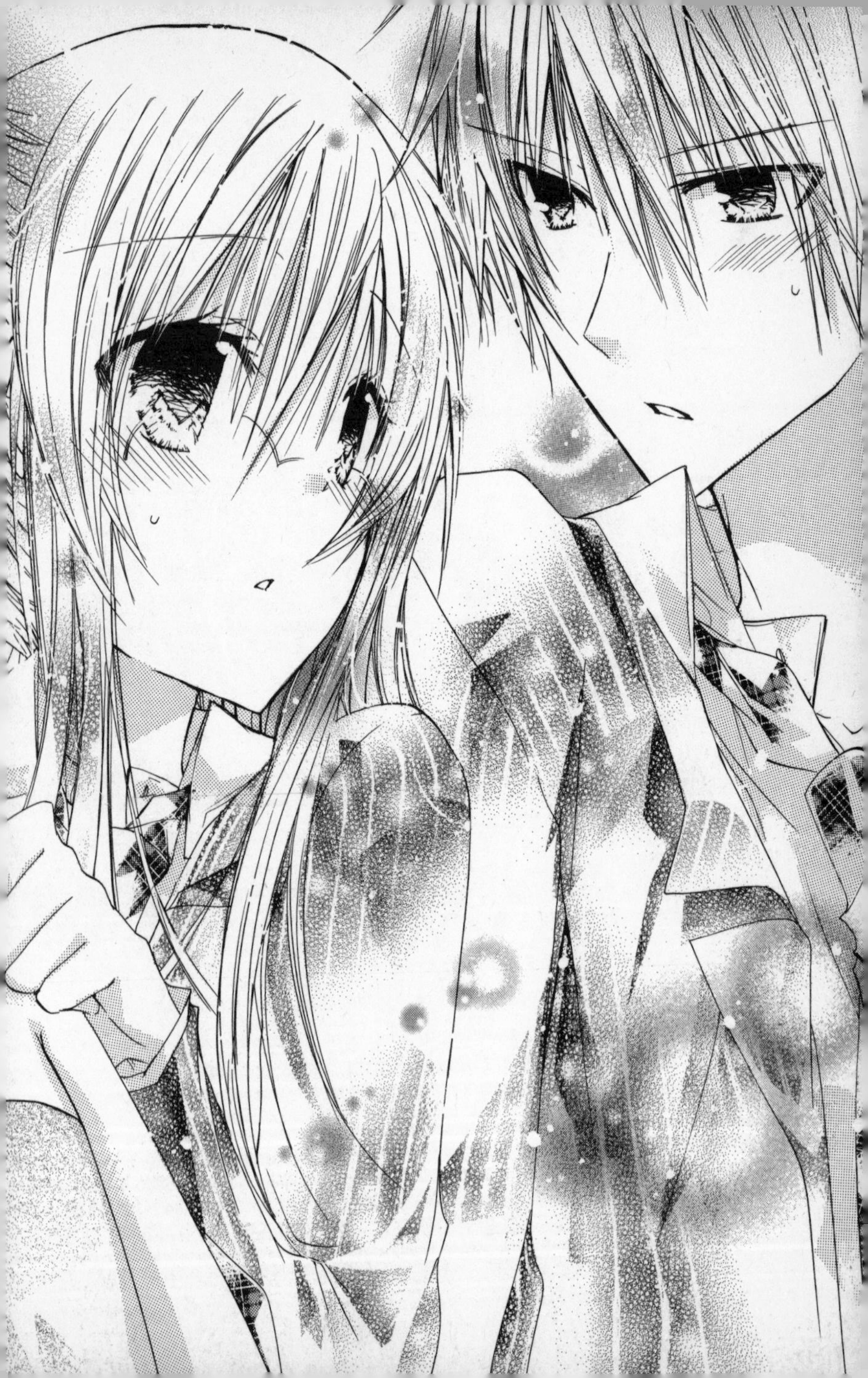

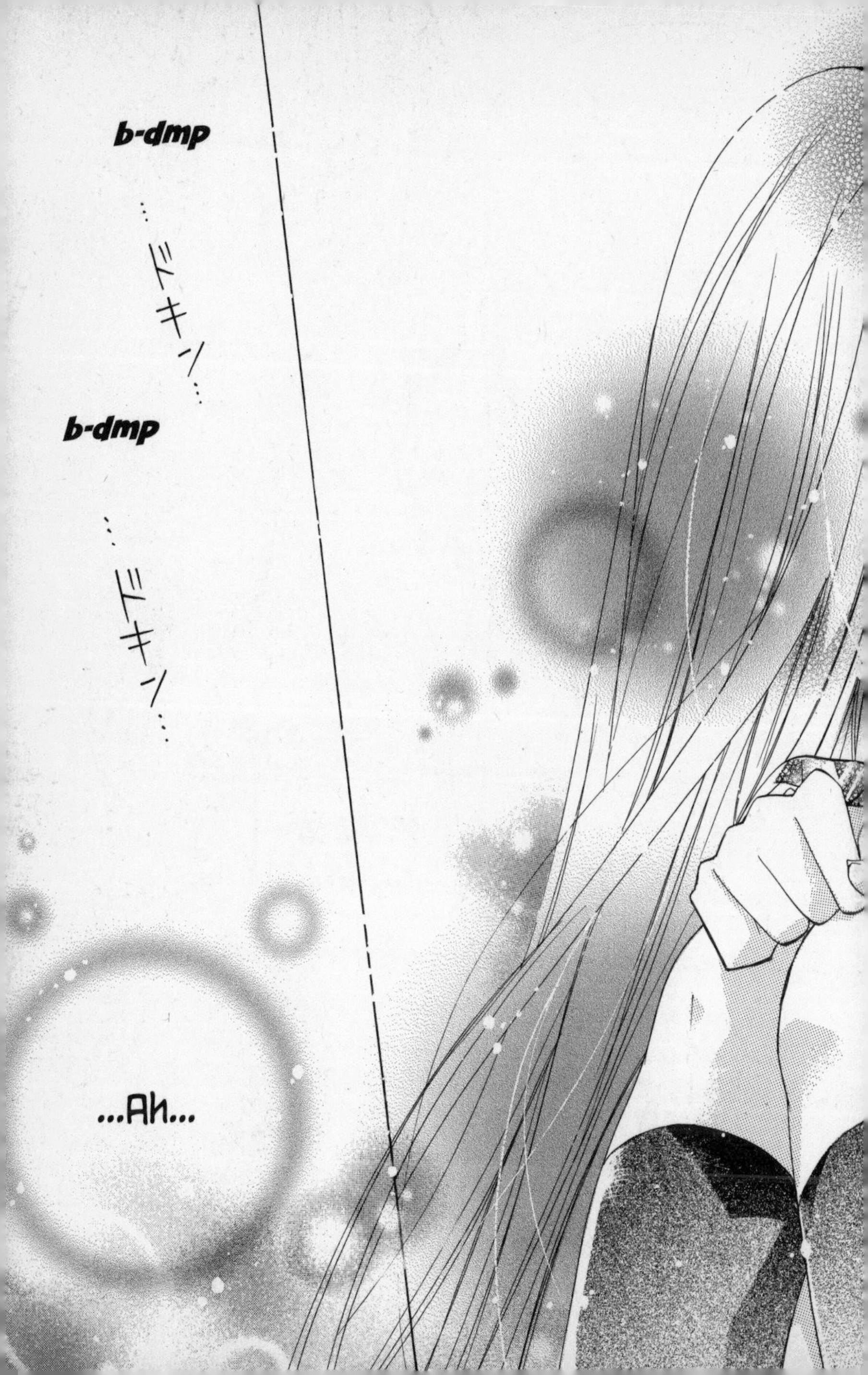
b-dmp
…ドキン…
b-dmp
…ドキン…
...Ah...

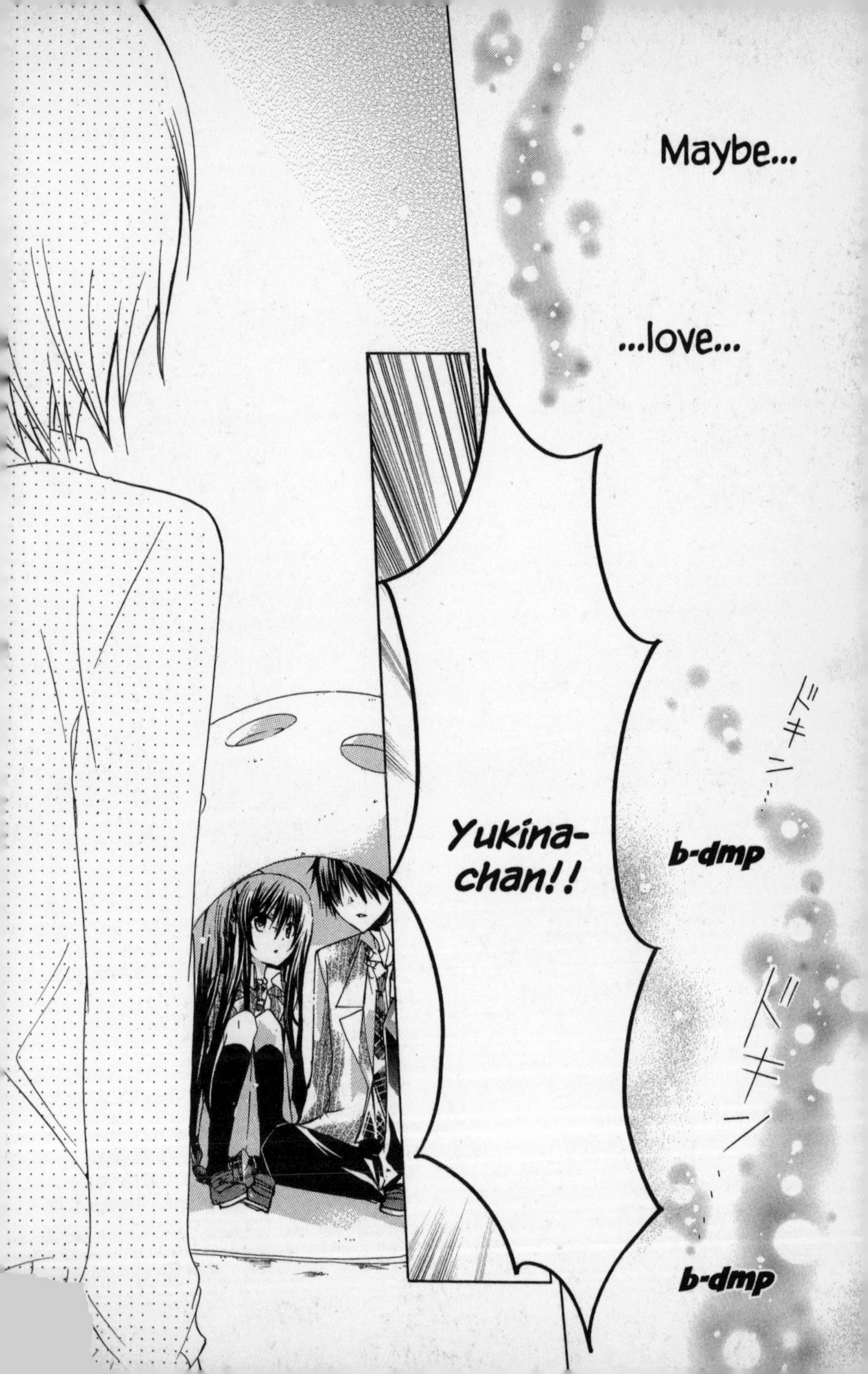
Maybe...
...love...
Yukina-chan!!
ドキン…
b-dmp
ドキン
b-dmp

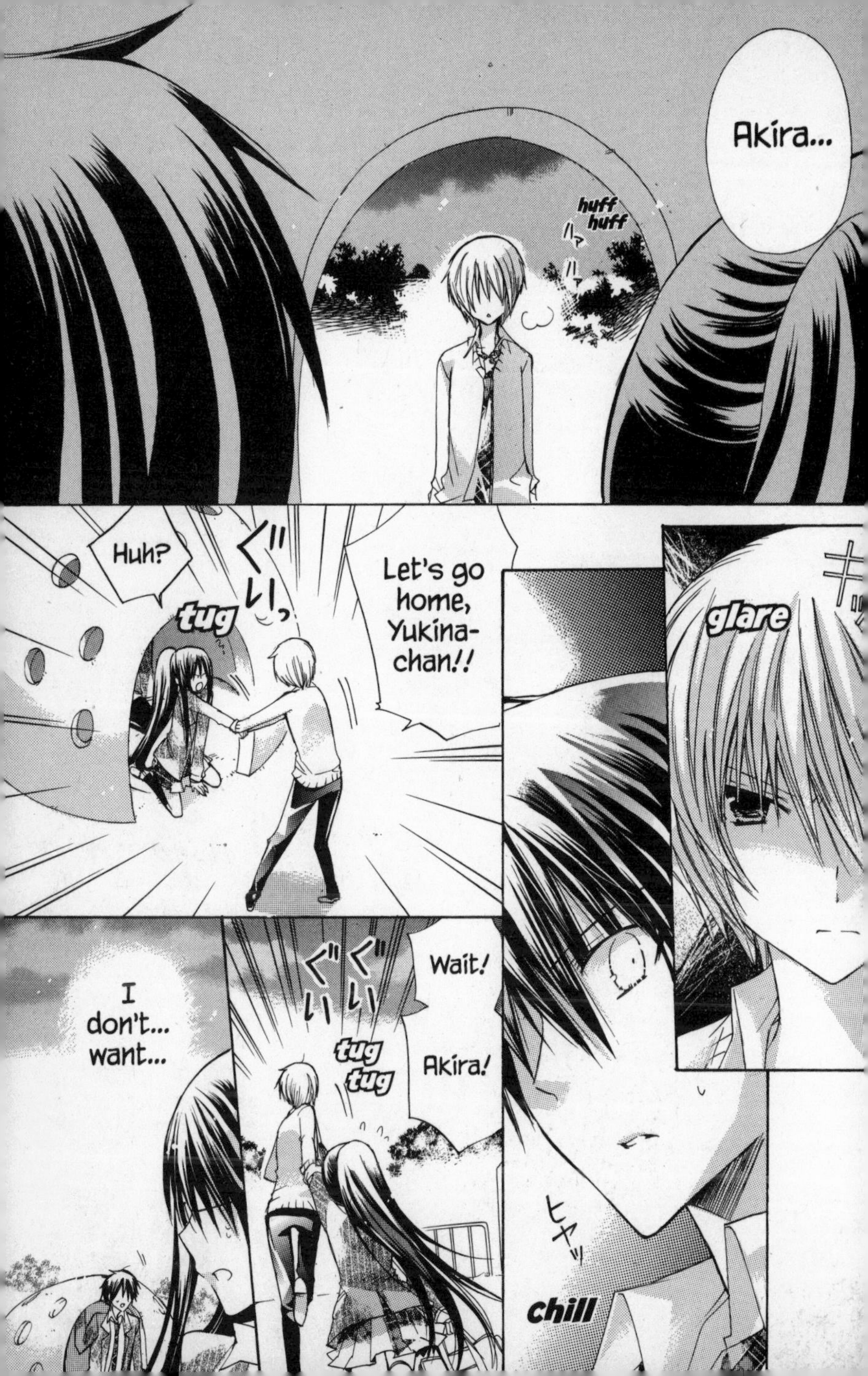
Akira...
huff huff
ハァ ハァ
キッ
glare
ヒヤッ
chill
Let's go home, Yukina-chan!!
Huh?
ぐいっ
tug
Wait!
Akira!
ぐいぐいい
tug tug
I don't... want...

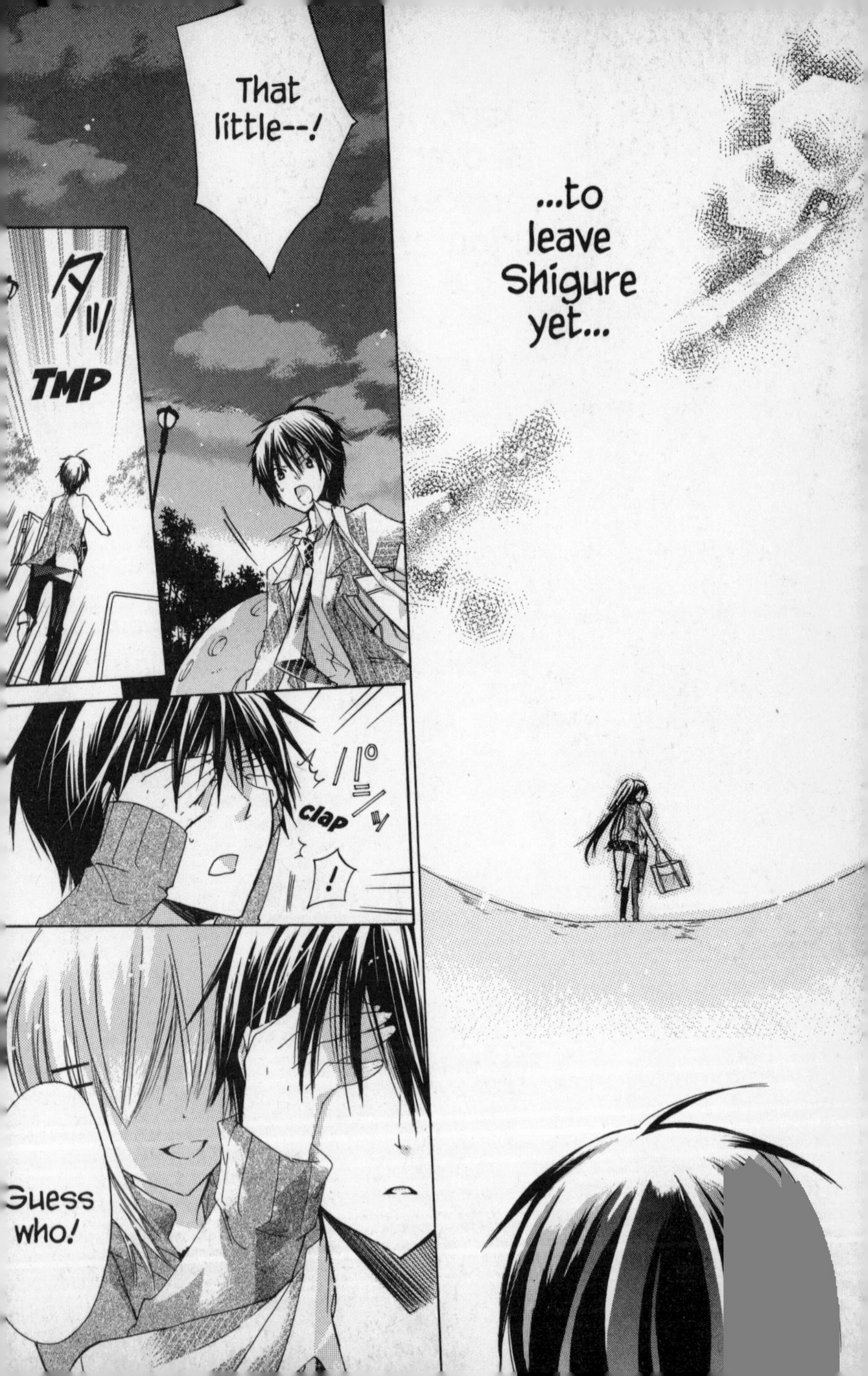
...to leave Shigure yet...
That little--!
TMP
clap
!
Guess who!

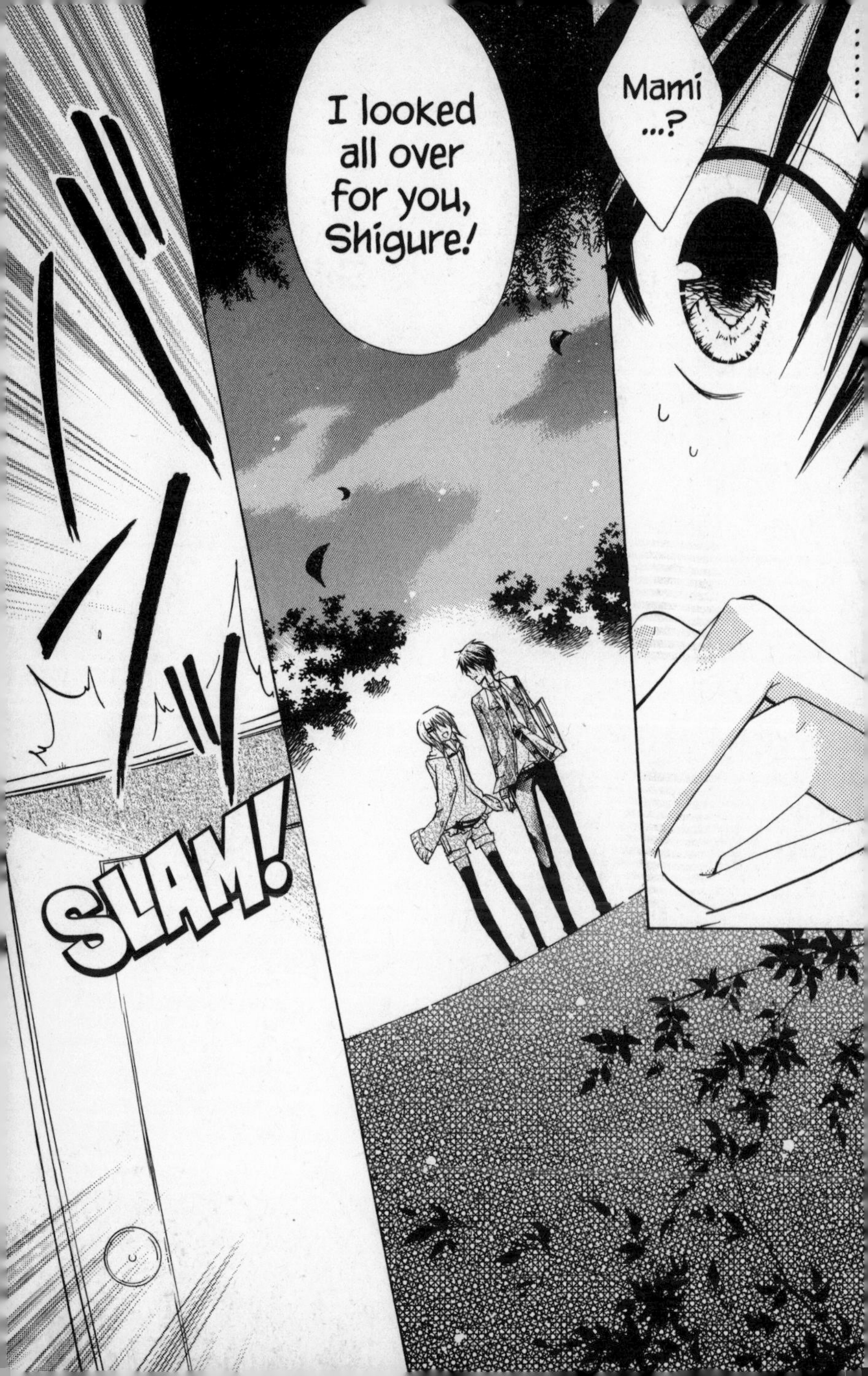
Mami ...?
I looked all over for you, Shigure!
SLAM!

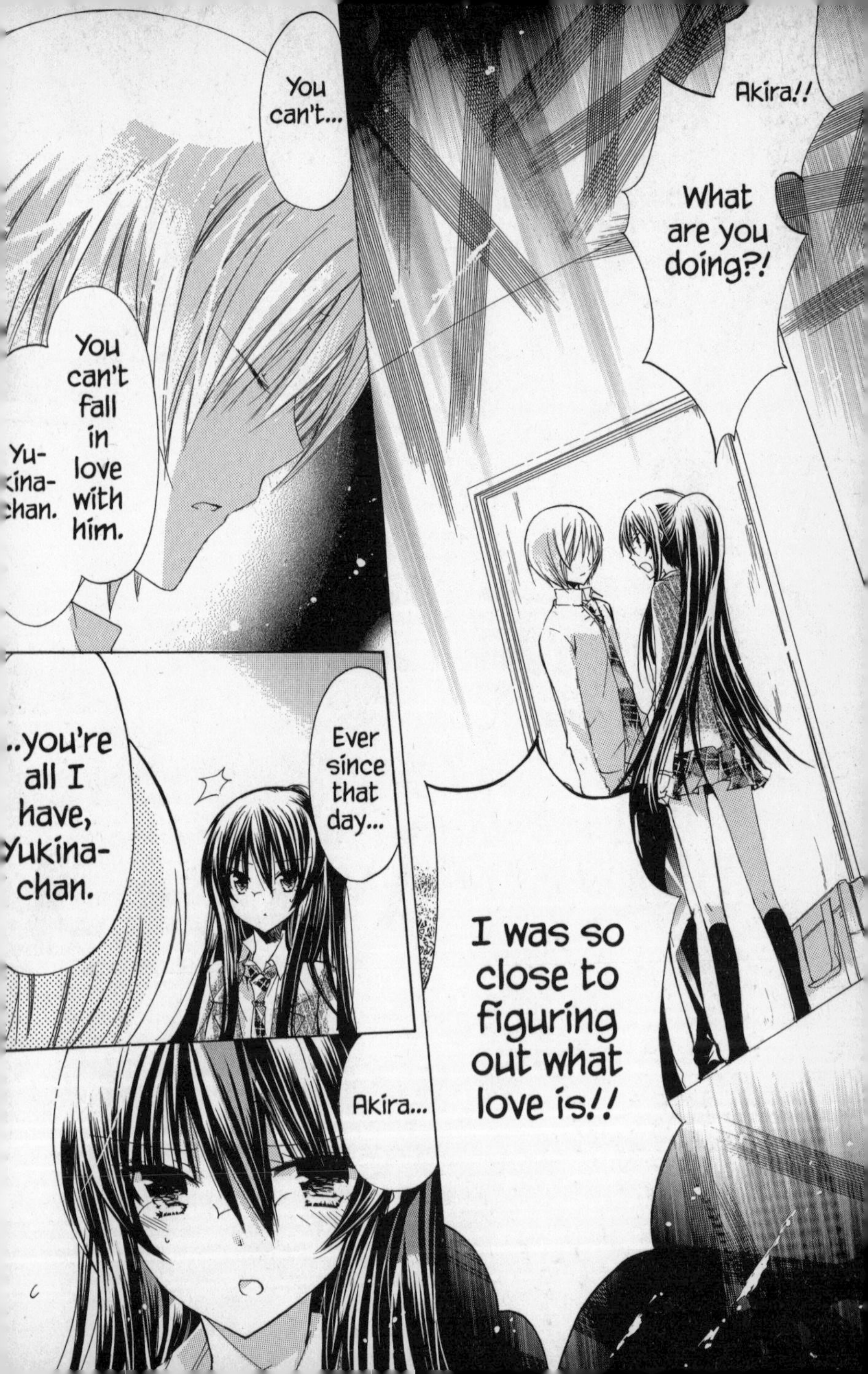

Akira!!
What are you doing?!
I was so close to figuring out what love is!!
You can't...
You can't fall in love with him.
Yu-kina-chan.
Ever since that day...
..you're all I have, Yukina-chan.
Akira...

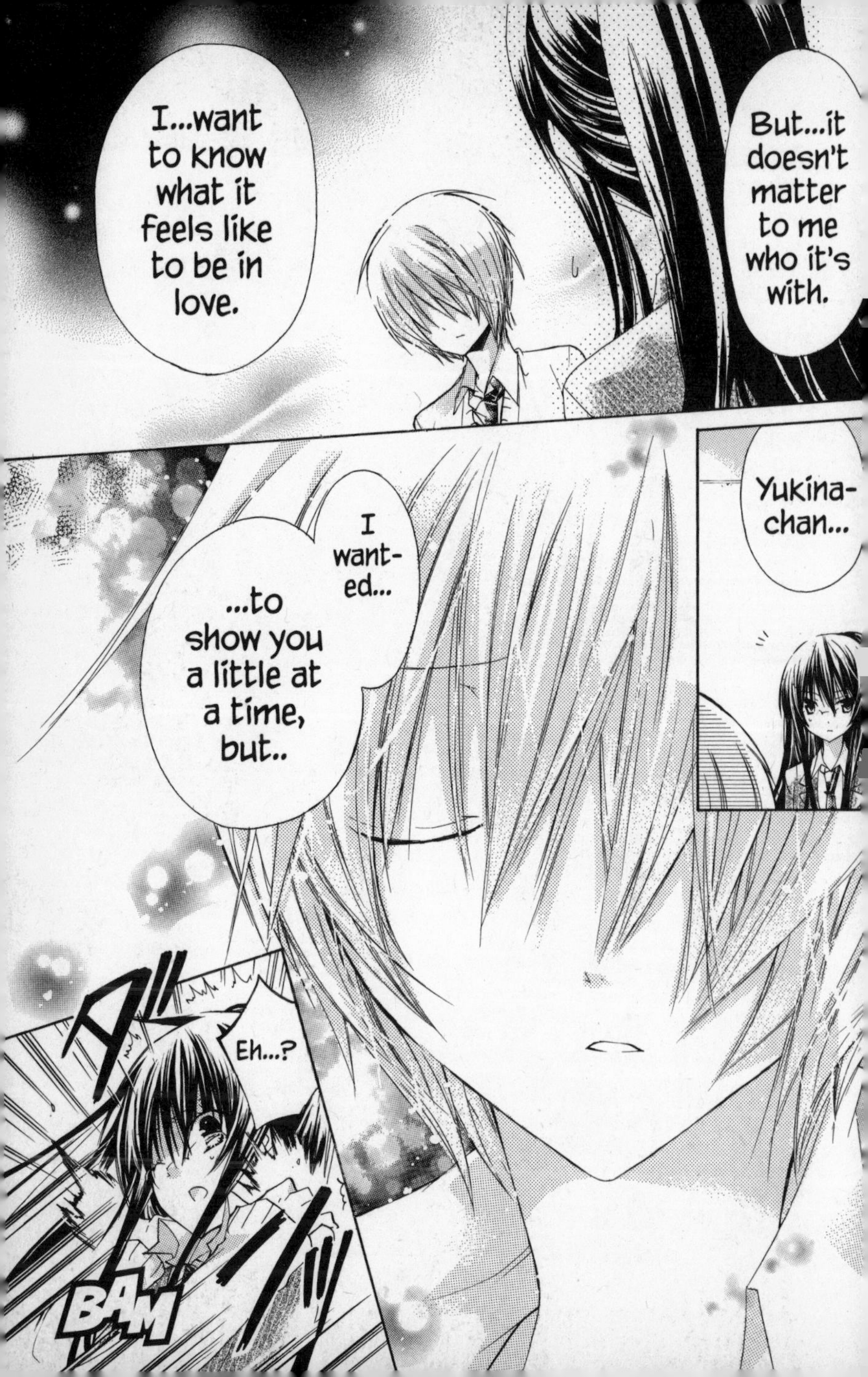
But...it doesn't matter to me who it's with.
I...want to know what it feels like to be in love.
Yukina-chan...
I wanted...
...to show you a little at a time, but..
Eh...?
BAM

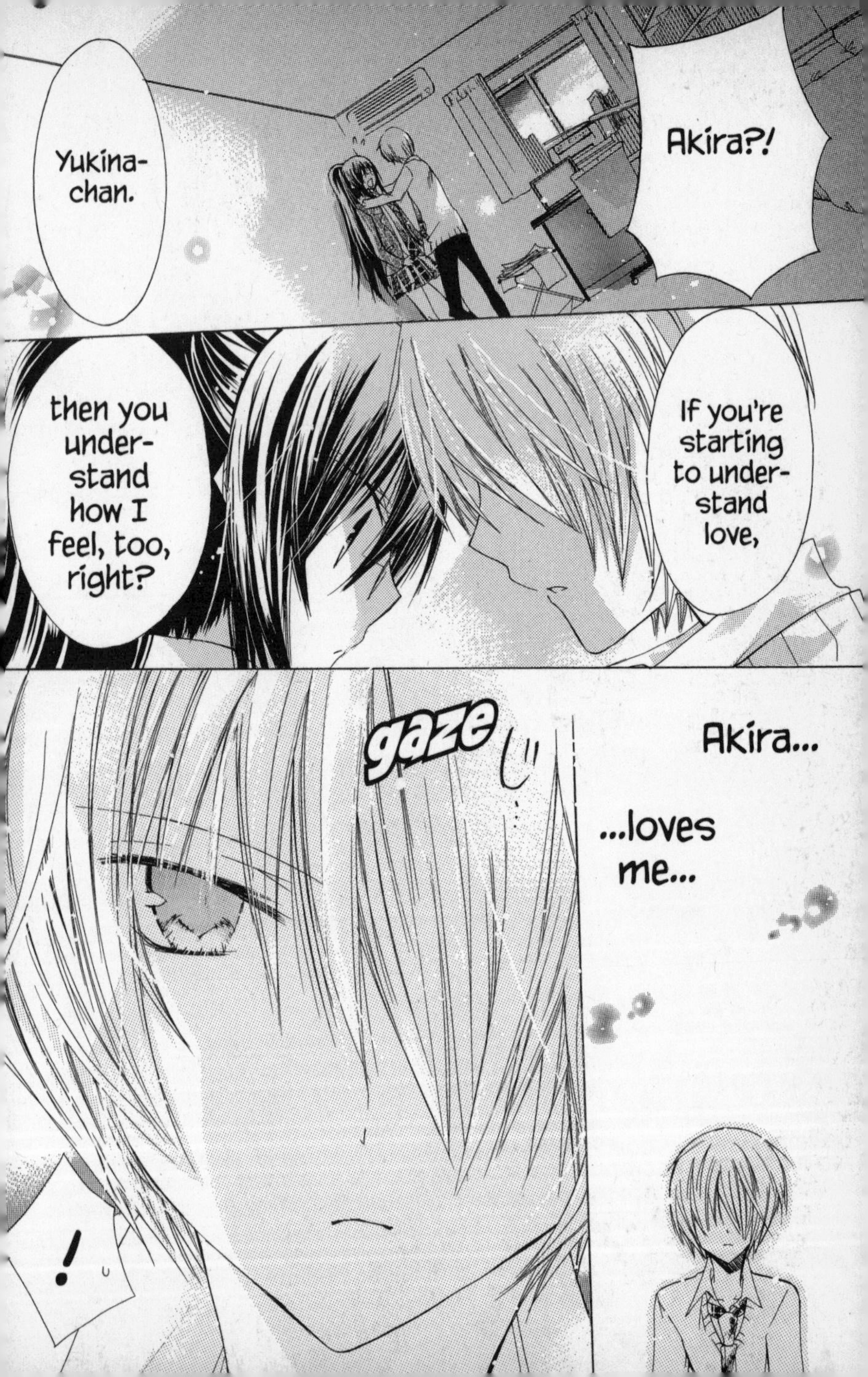
Akira?!
Yukina-chan.
If you're starting to understand love,
then you understand how I feel, too, right?
Akira...
...loves me...
gaze
!

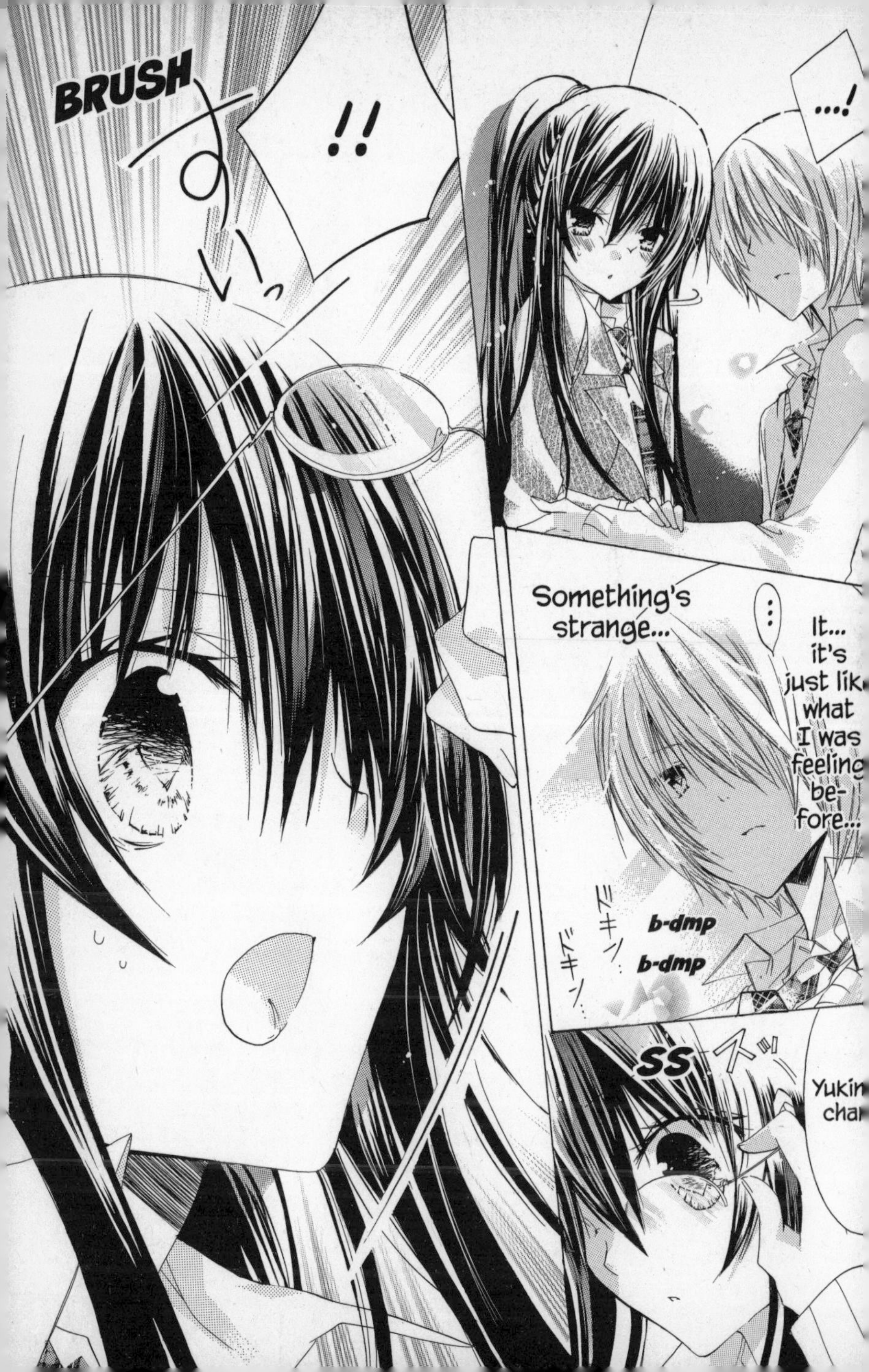

...!
It... it's just lik what I was feeling be-fore...
...
Something's strange...
b-dmp
b-dmp
Yukin cha
SS
!!
BRUSH

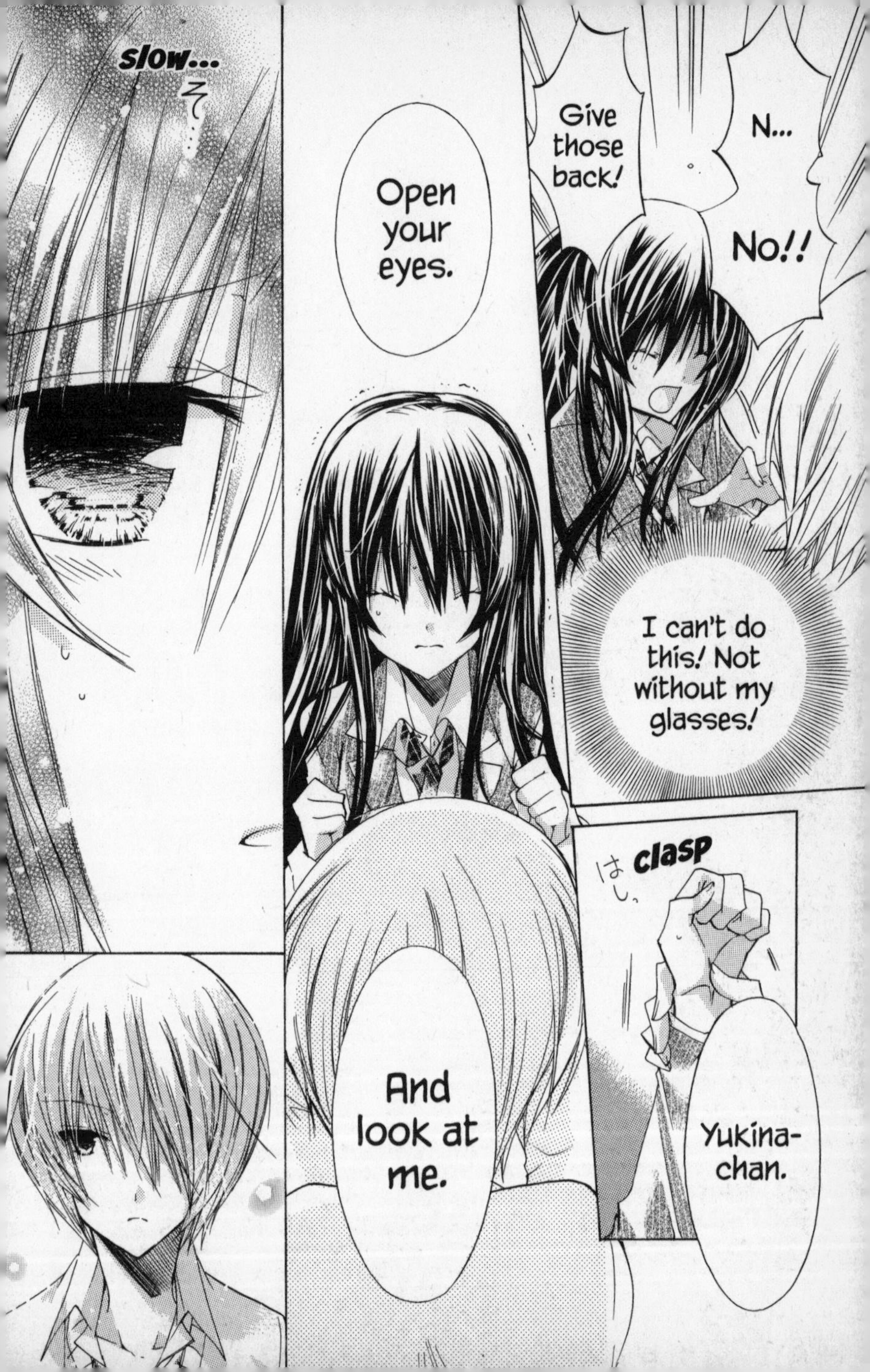

N...
No!!
Give those back!
I can't do this! Not without my glasses!
Open your eyes.
slow...
clasp
Yukina-chan.
And look at me.

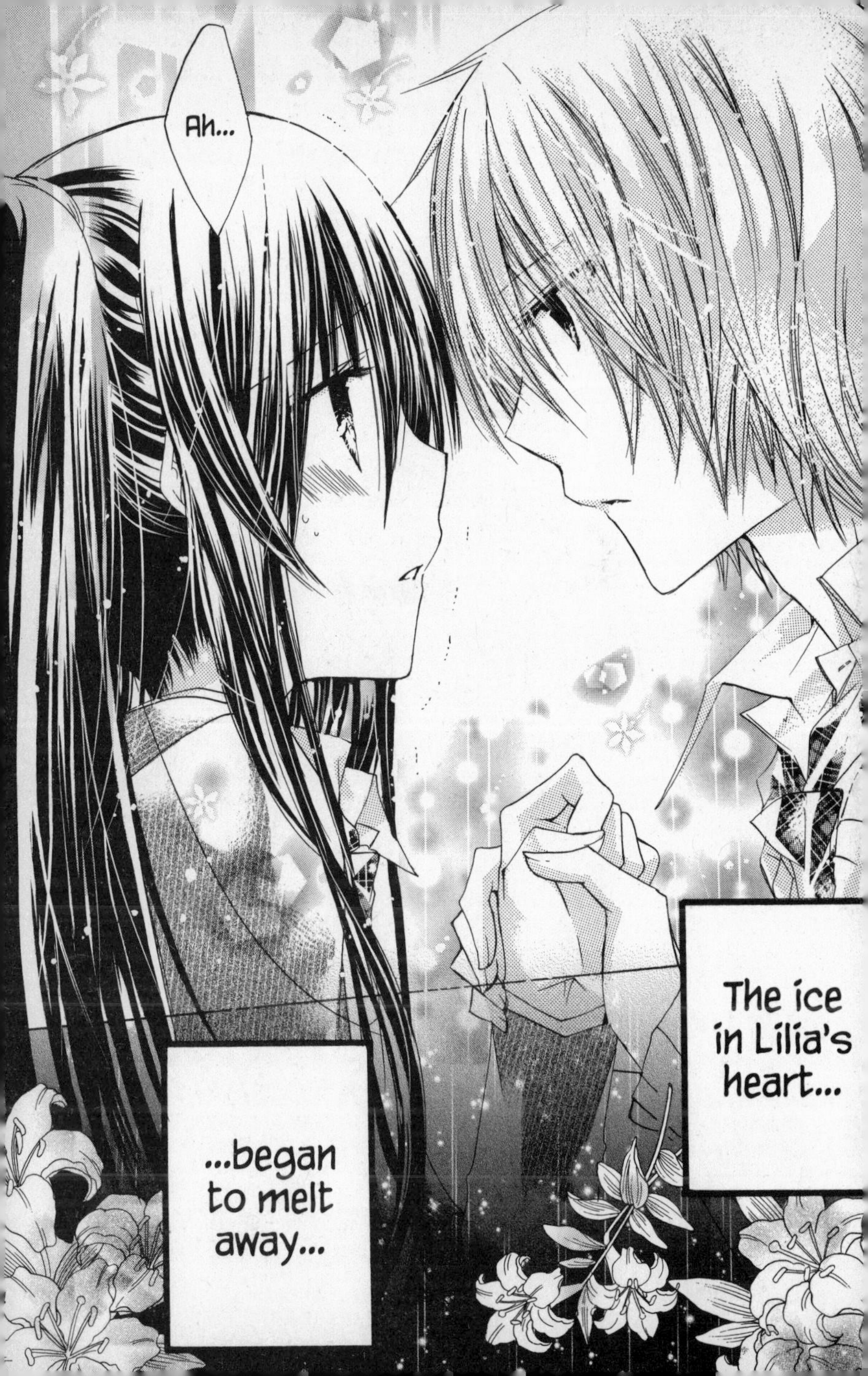
Ah...
The ice in Lilia's heart...
...began to melt away...

# Missions of Love

**It is time for love.
Secret cell phone
novelist vs. the most
popular boy in school.
A mission of love for
absolute servitude.**

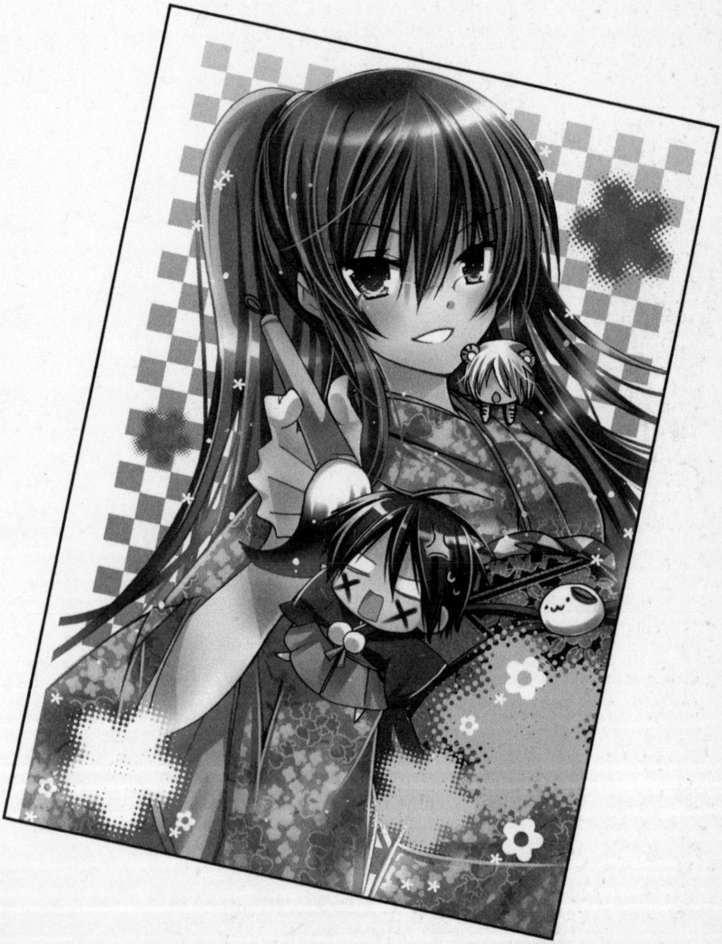

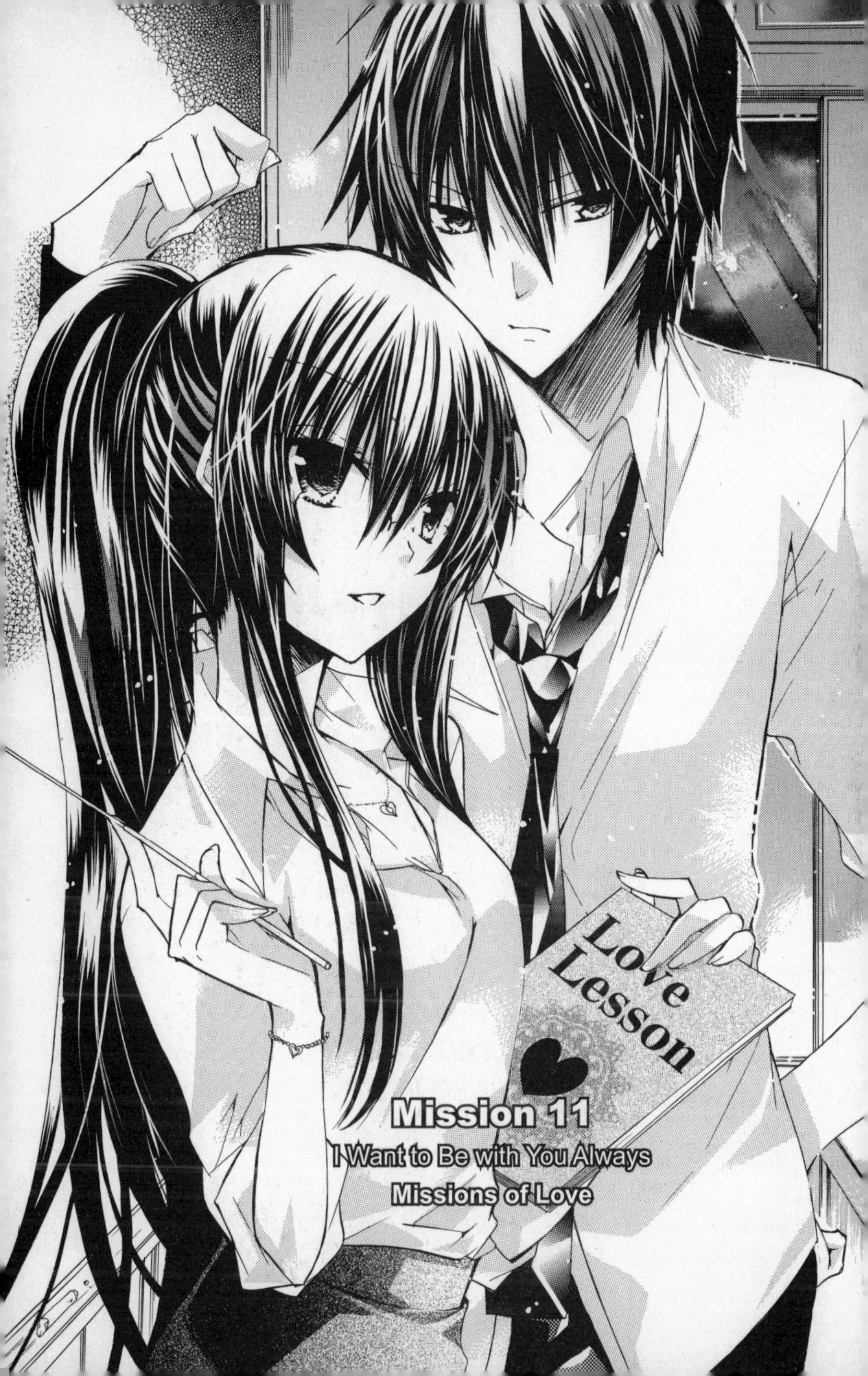
Love Lesson
Mission 11
I Want to Be with You Always
Missions of Love

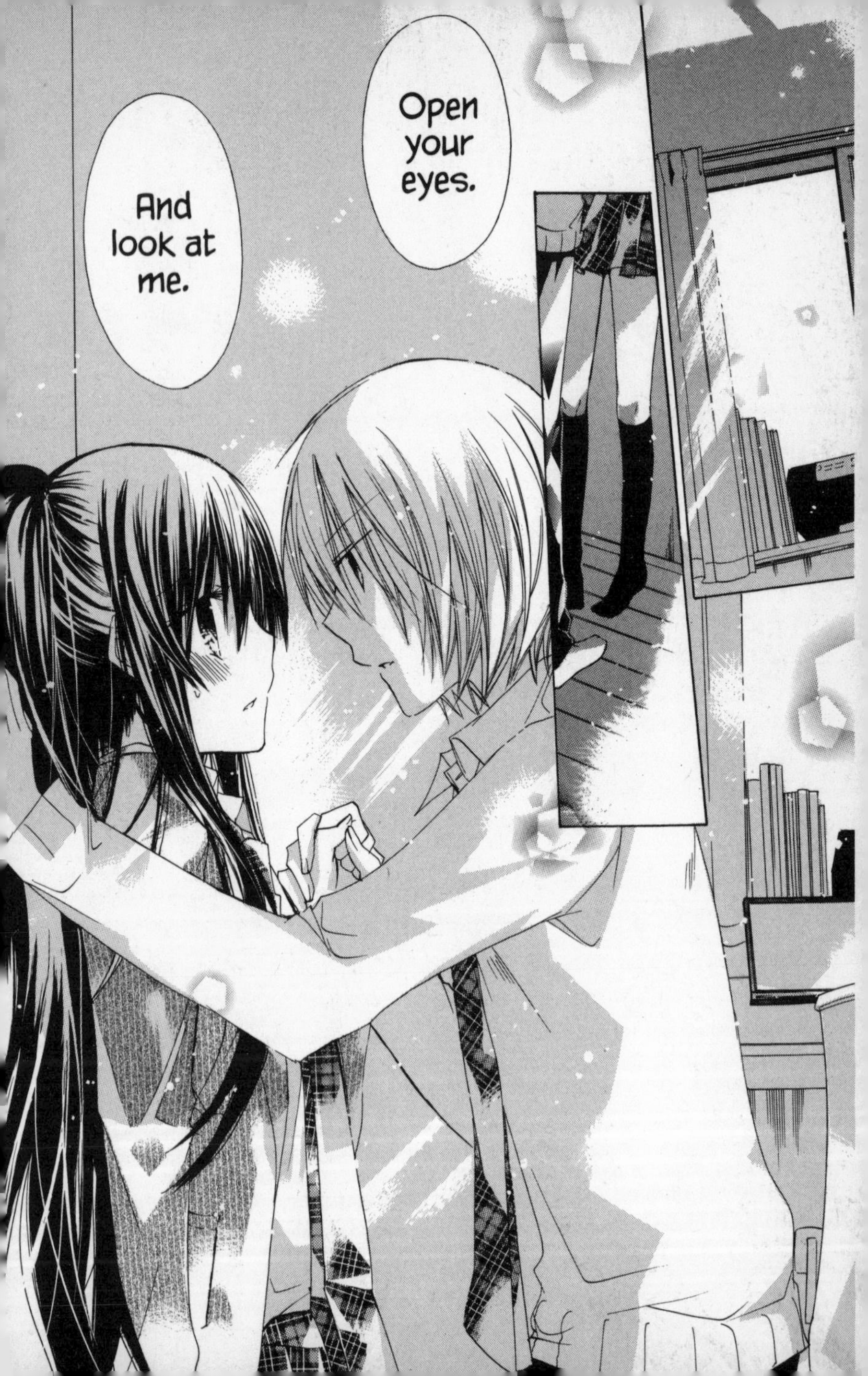
Open your eyes.
And look at me.

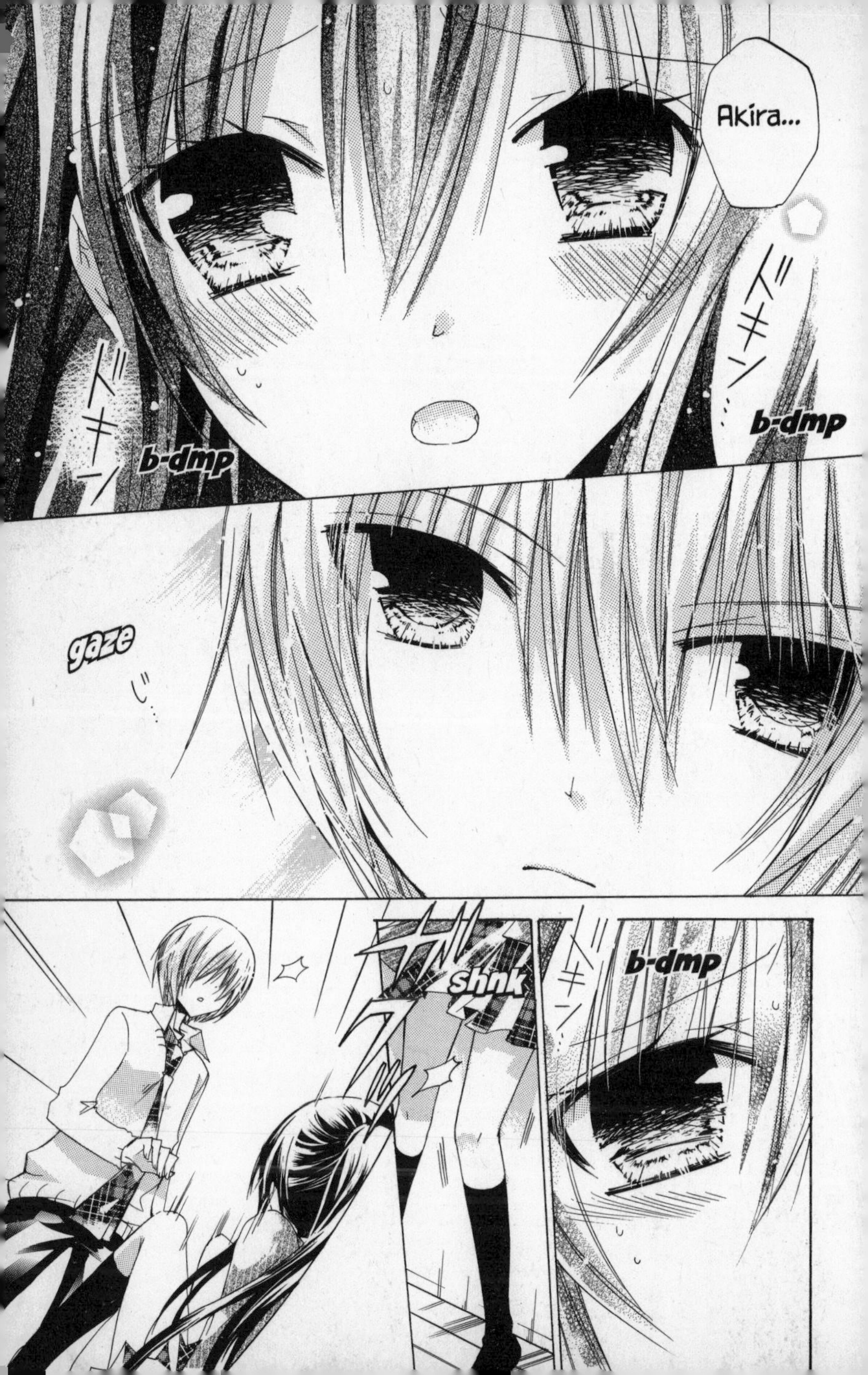
Akira...
ドキン…
b-dmp
b-dmp
gaze
じ…
b-dmp
shnk

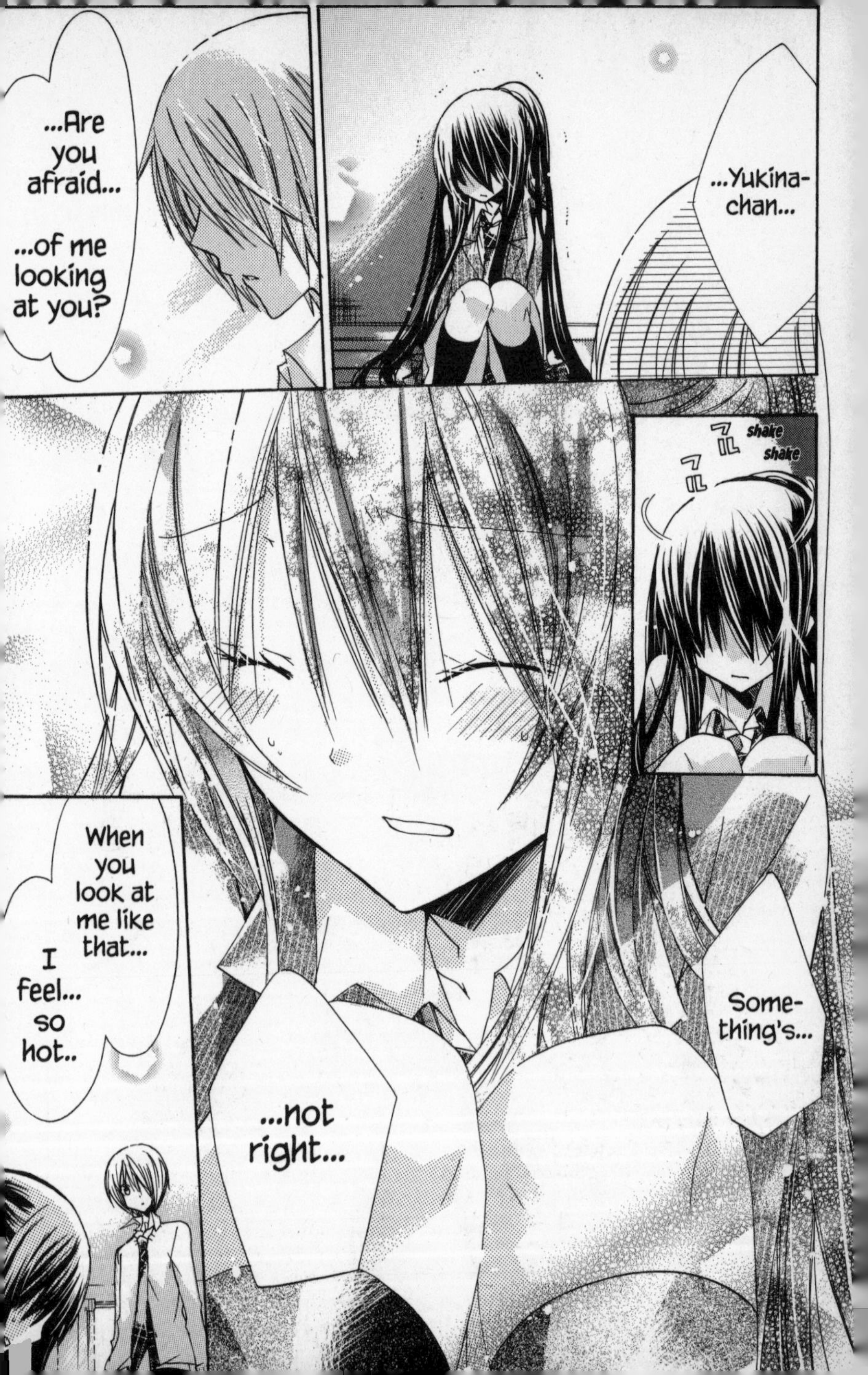
...Yukina-chan...
...Are you afraid...
...of me looking at you?
フル フル
shake shake
Some-thing's...
...not right...
When you look at me like that...
I feel... so hot..

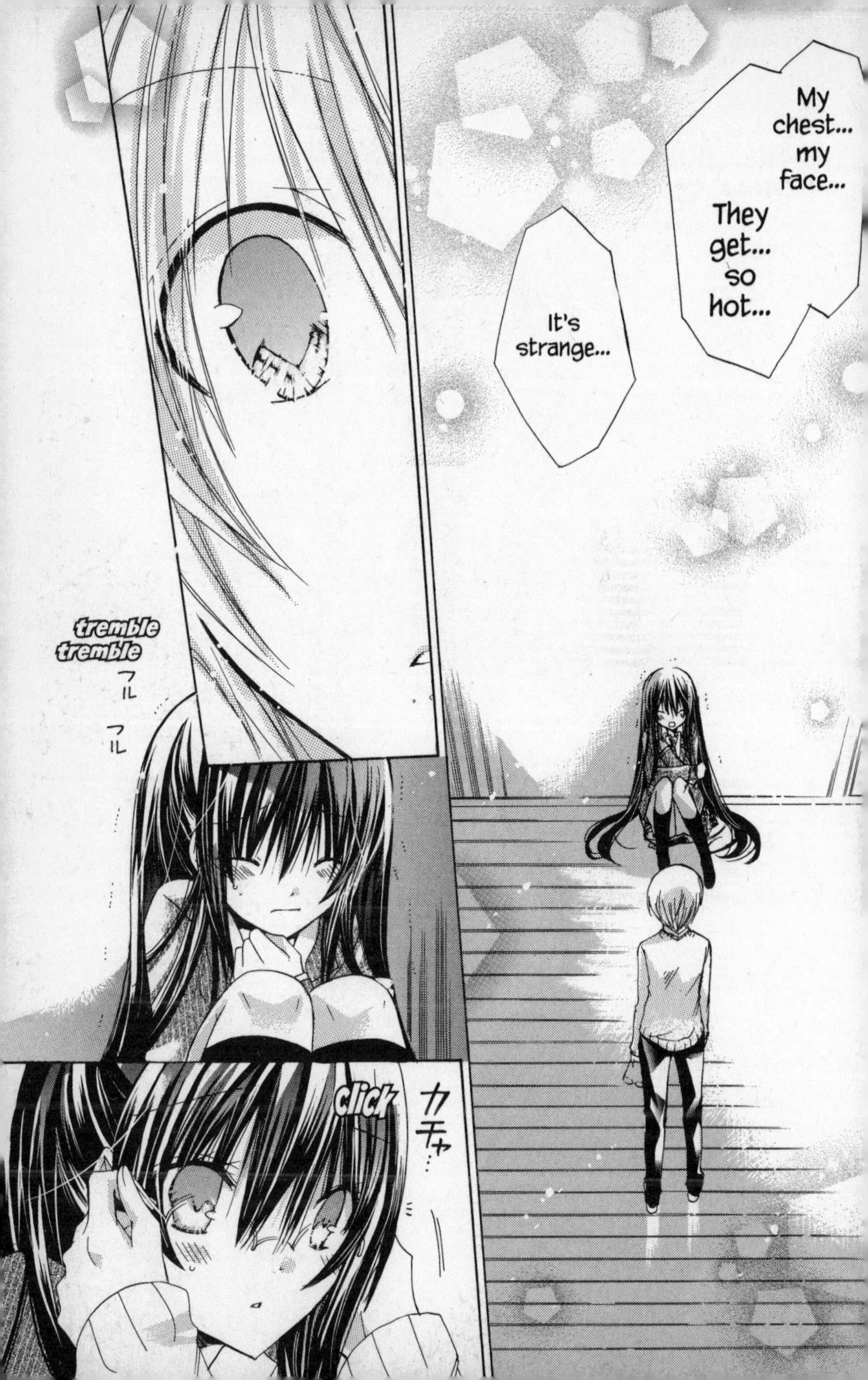
My chest... my face... They get... so hot...
It's strange...
tremble tremble
フル フル
click
カチャ...

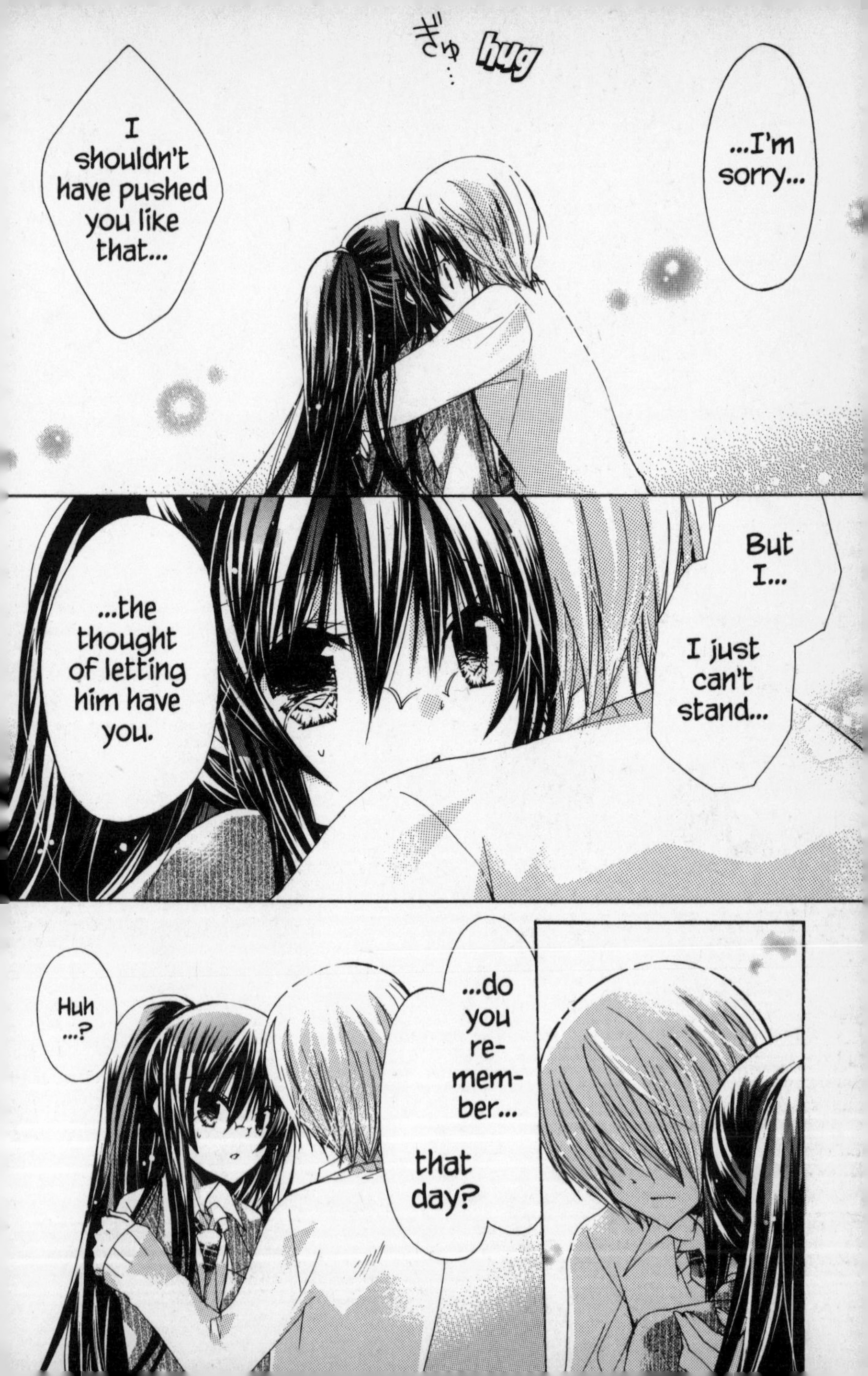
ぎゅ…
hug
...I'm sorry...
I shouldn't have pushed you like that...
But I...
I just can't stand...
...the thought of letting him have you.
...do you re-mem-ber...
that day?
Huh ...?

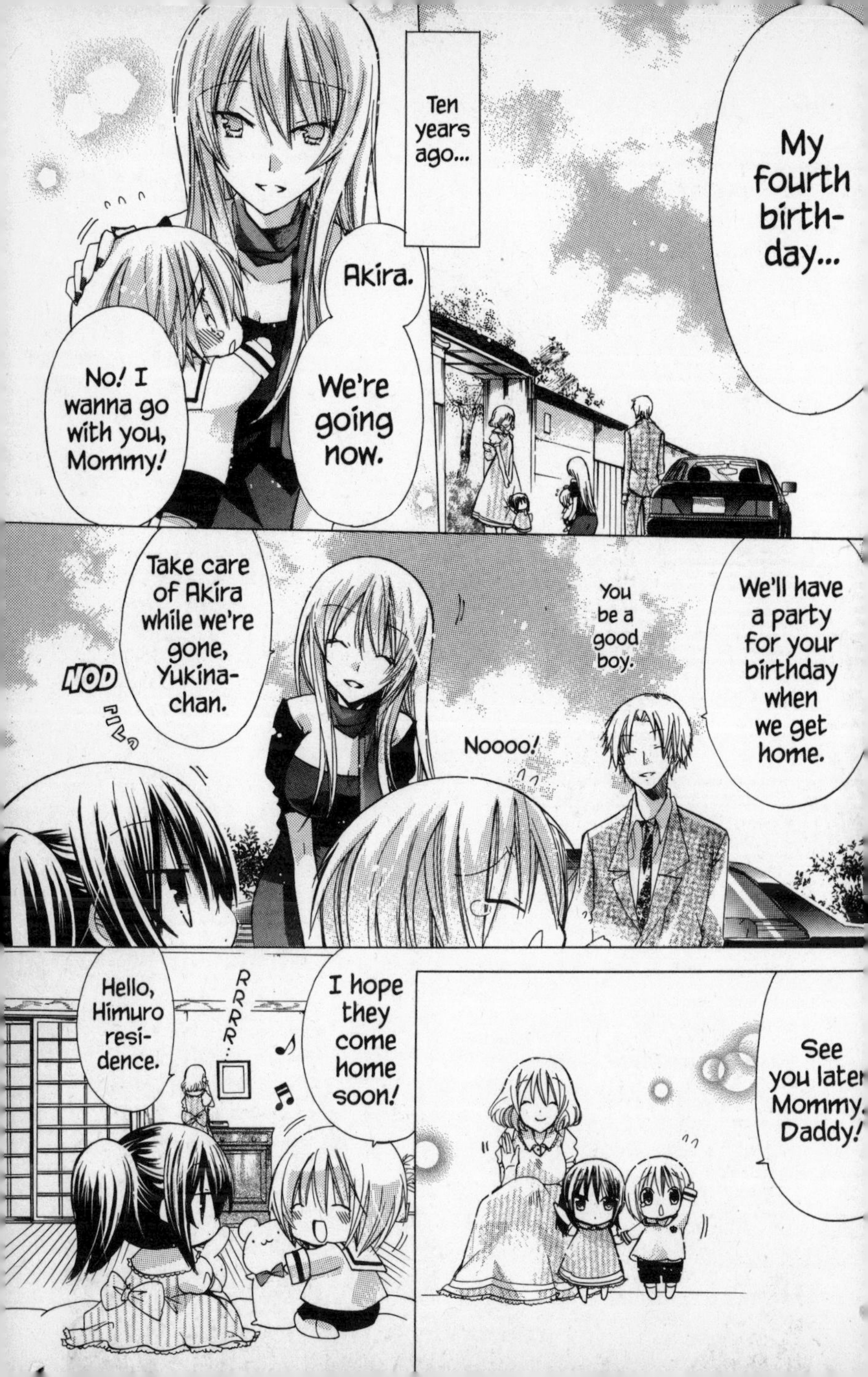
My fourth birth-day...
Ten years ago...
Akira.
We're going now.
No! I wanna go with you, Mommy!
We'll have a party for your birthday when we get home.
You be a good boy.
Noooo!
Take care of Akira while we're gone, Yukina-chan.
NOD
See you later Mommy, Daddy!
I hope they come home soon!
RRRR...
Hello, Himuro resi-dence.

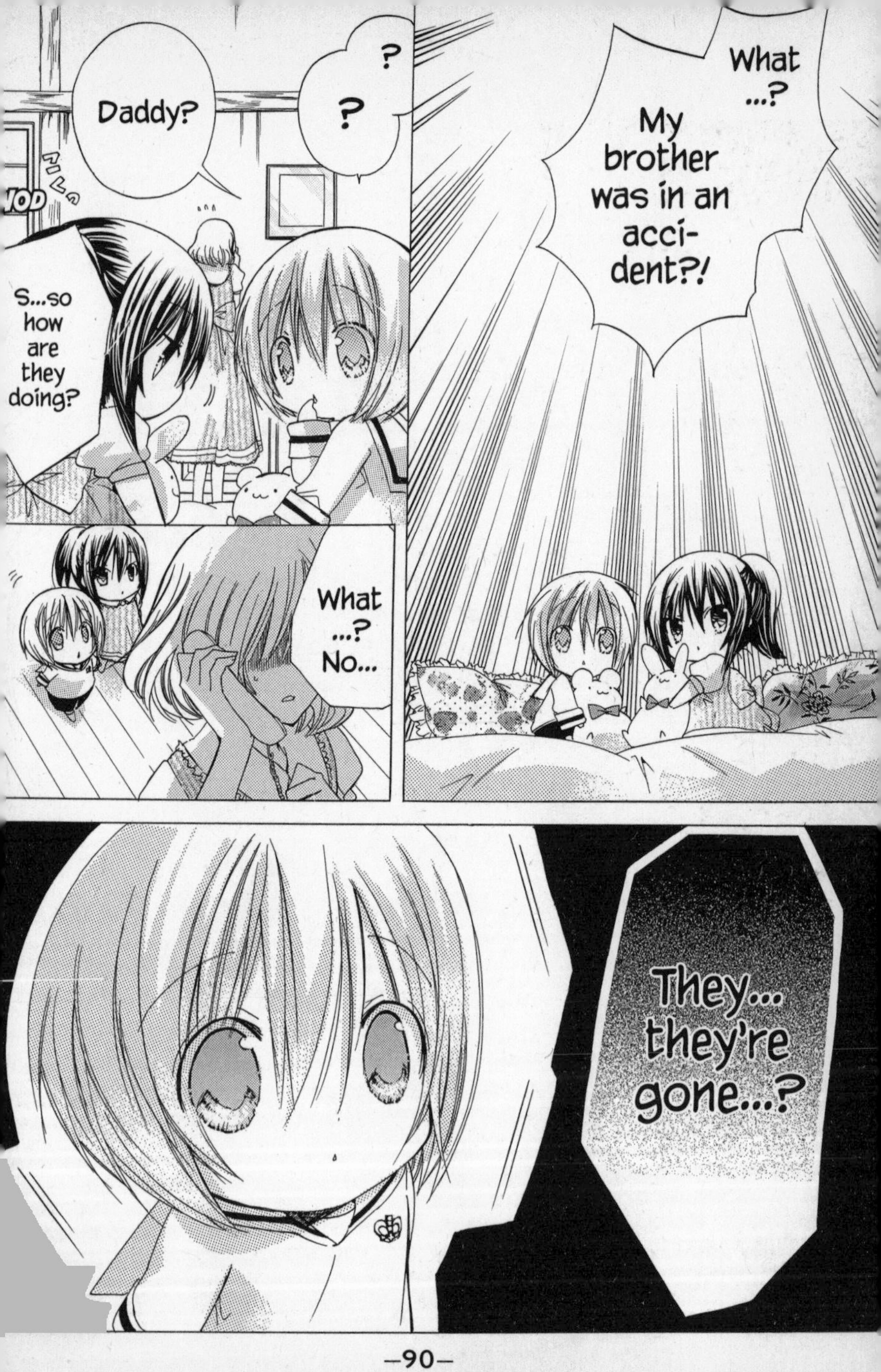
What ...?
My brother was in an acci- dent?!
? ?
Daddy?
NOD
S...so how are they doing?
What ...? No...
They... they're gone...?

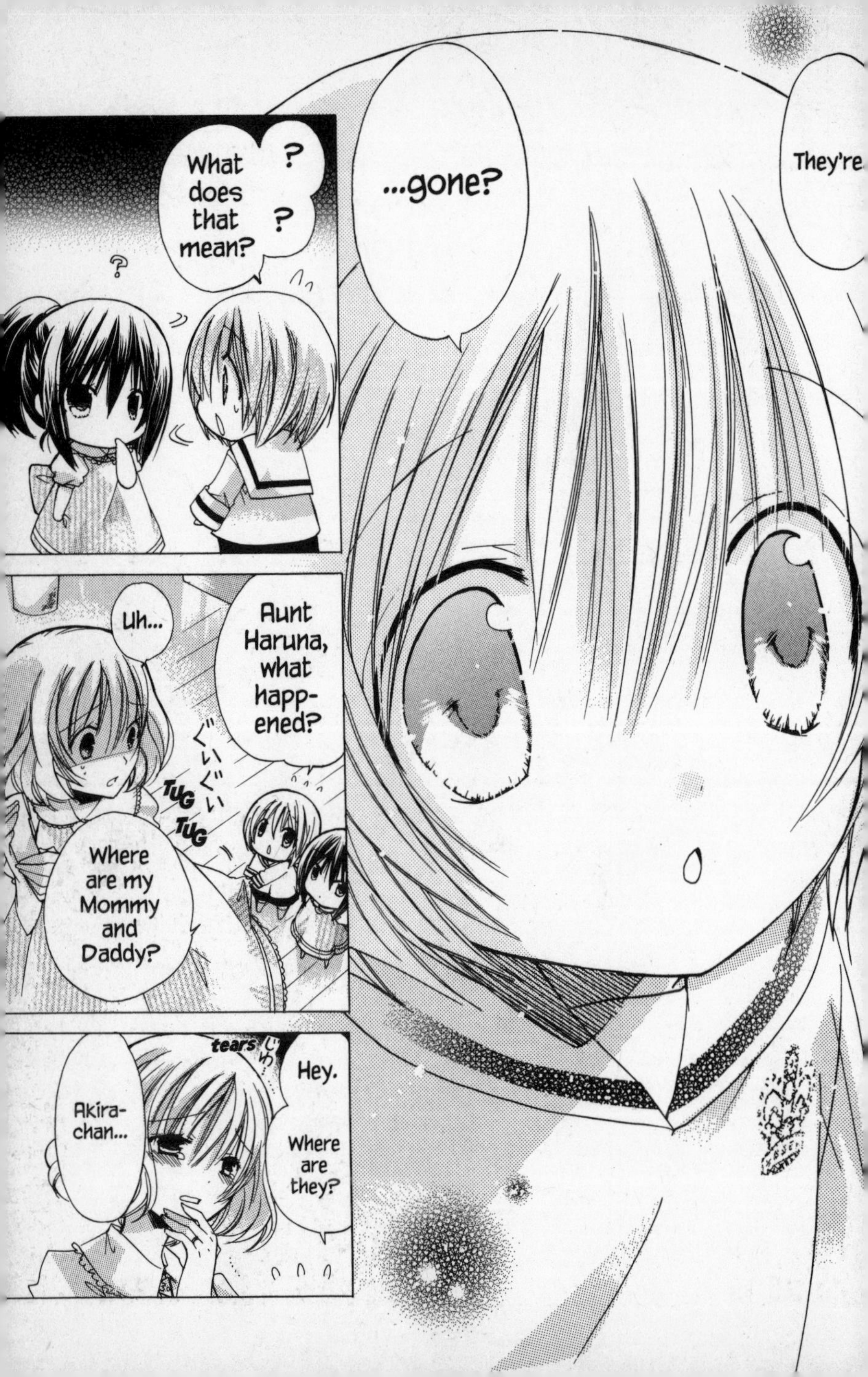
They're
...gone?
What does that mean?
?
?
?
Aunt Haruna, what happened?
Uh...
ぐいぐい
TUG TUG
Where are my Mommy and Daddy?
Hey.
Where are they?
tears
Akira-chan...

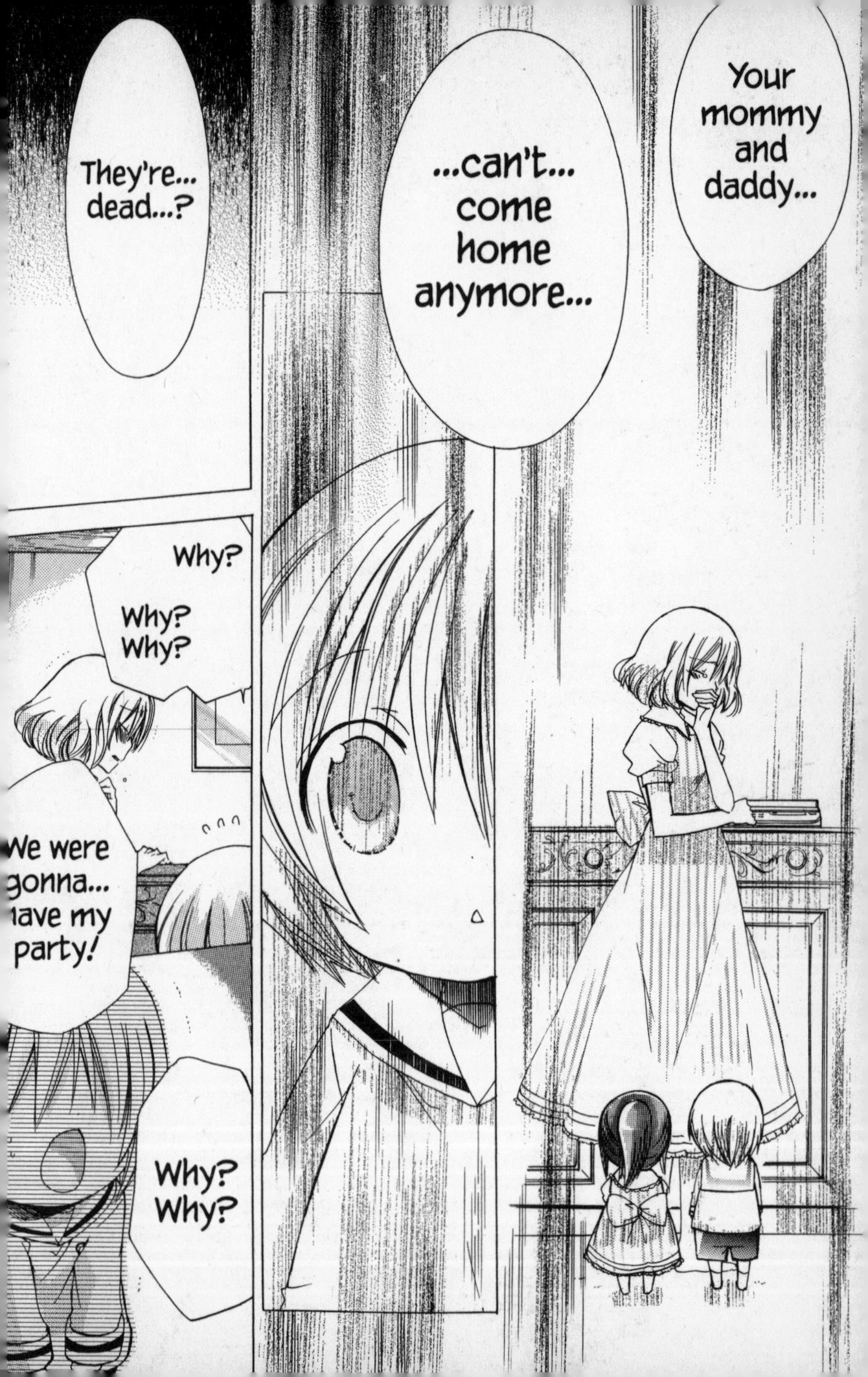
Your mommy and daddy...
...can't... come home anymore...
They're... dead...?
Why?
Why? Why?
We were gonna... have my party!
Why? Why?

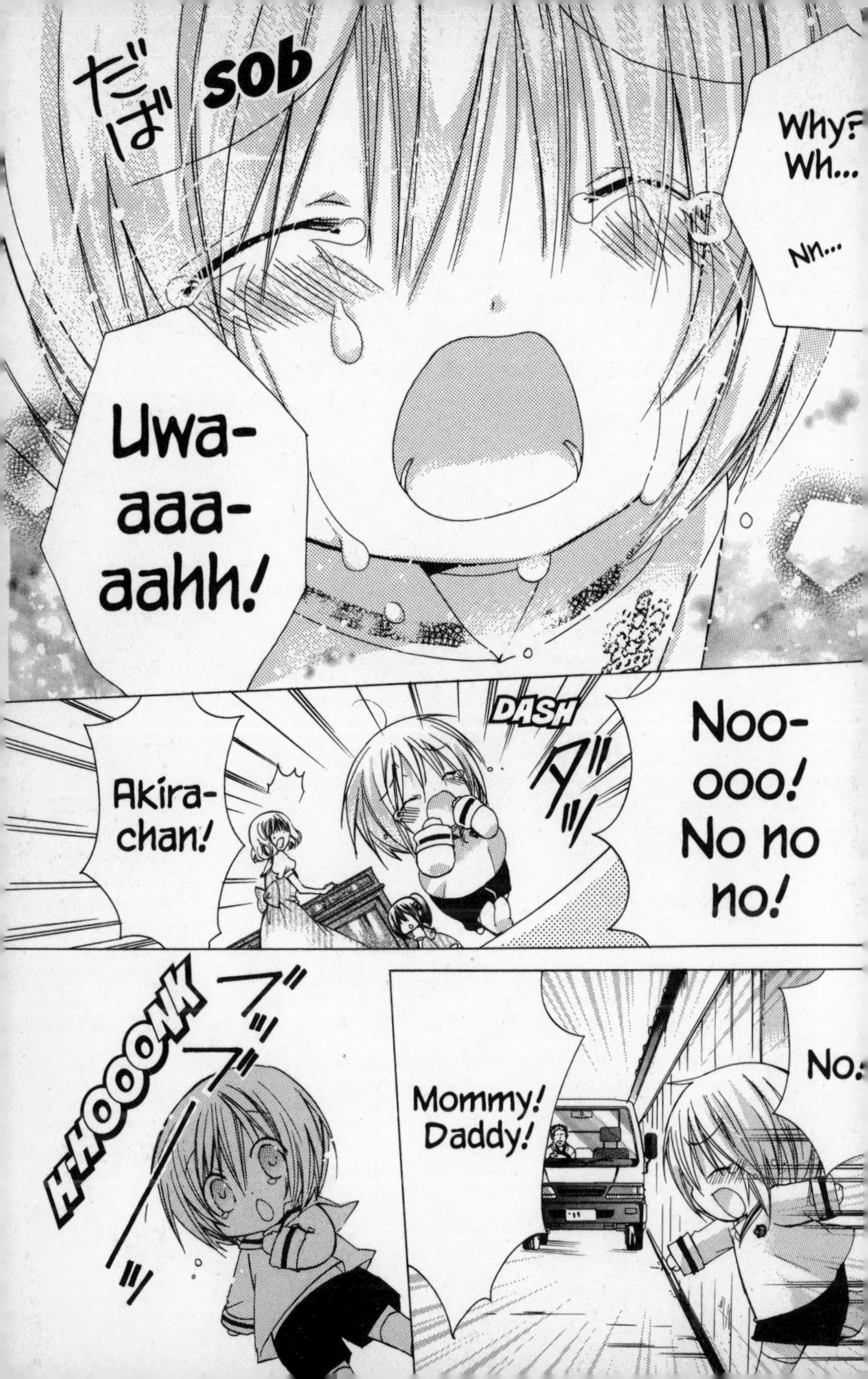
Why? Wh...
Nn...
Uwa-aaa-aahh!
だば
SOB
Noo-ooo! No no no!
DASH
ダッ
Akira-chan!
No
Mommy! Daddy!
H-HOOONK

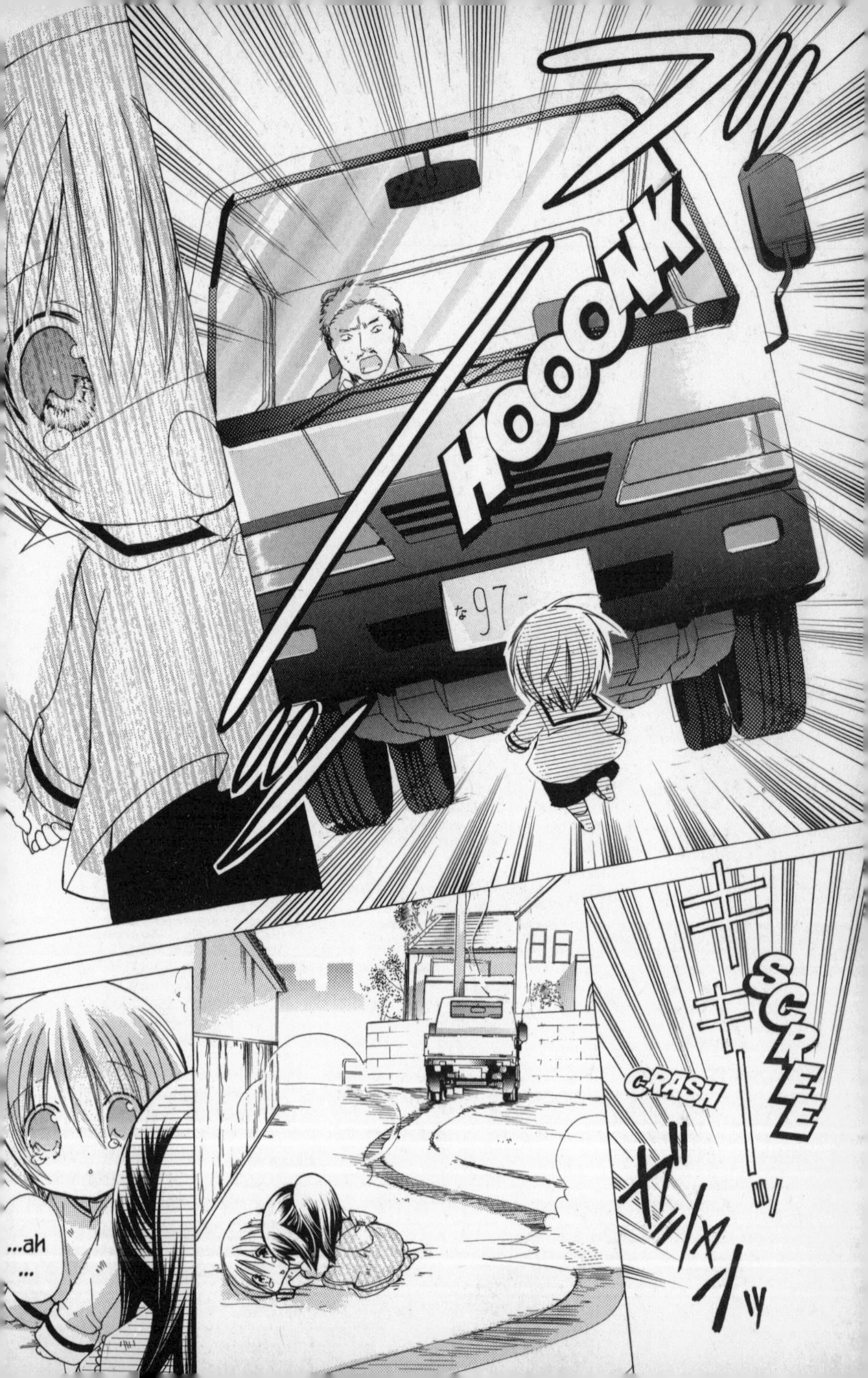
HOOONK
な97-
SCREE
CRASH
...ah ...

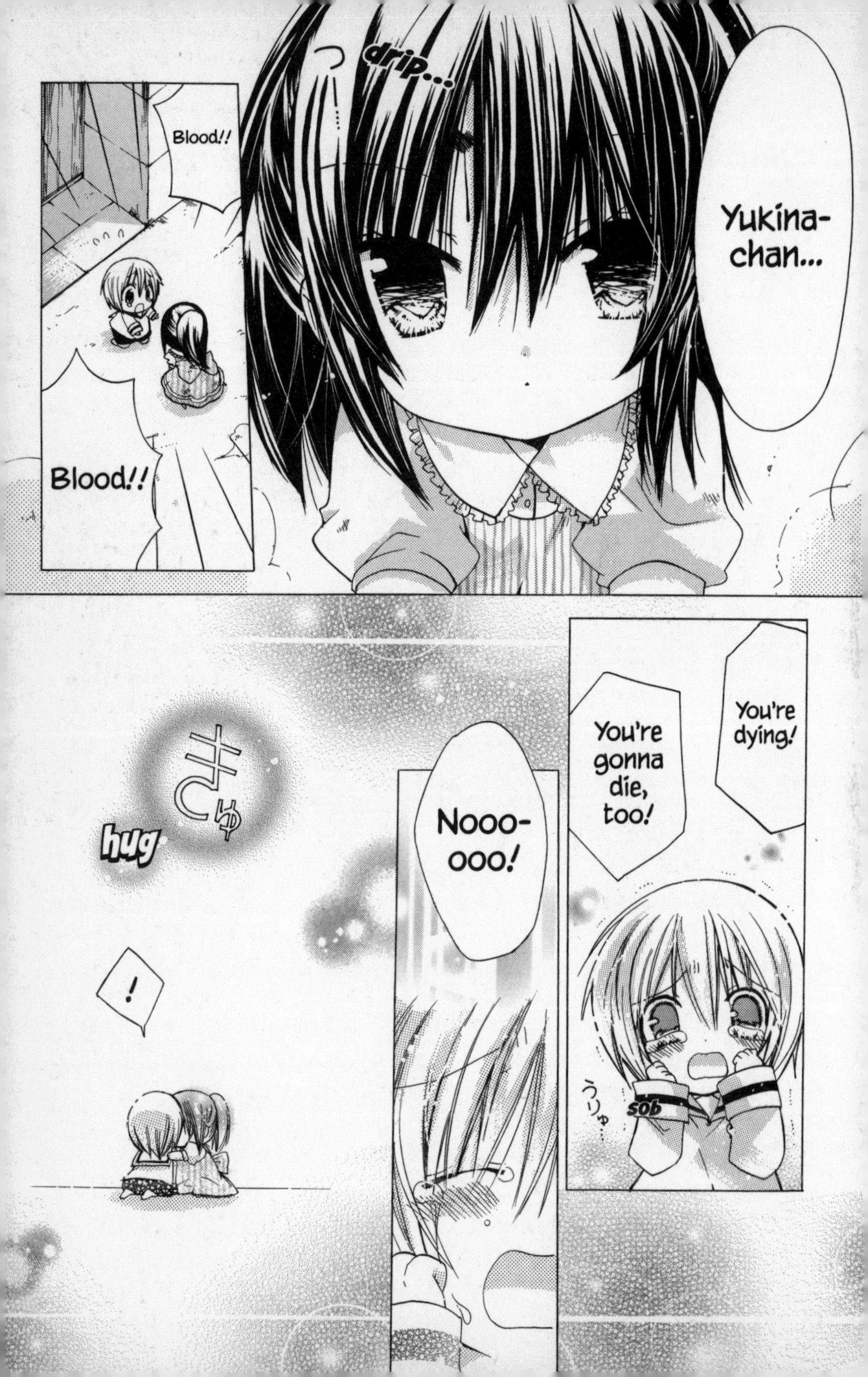
Yukina-chan...
drip...
Blood!!
Blood!!
You're dying!
You're gonna die, too!
Nooo-ooo!
うりゅ...
sob
!
hug

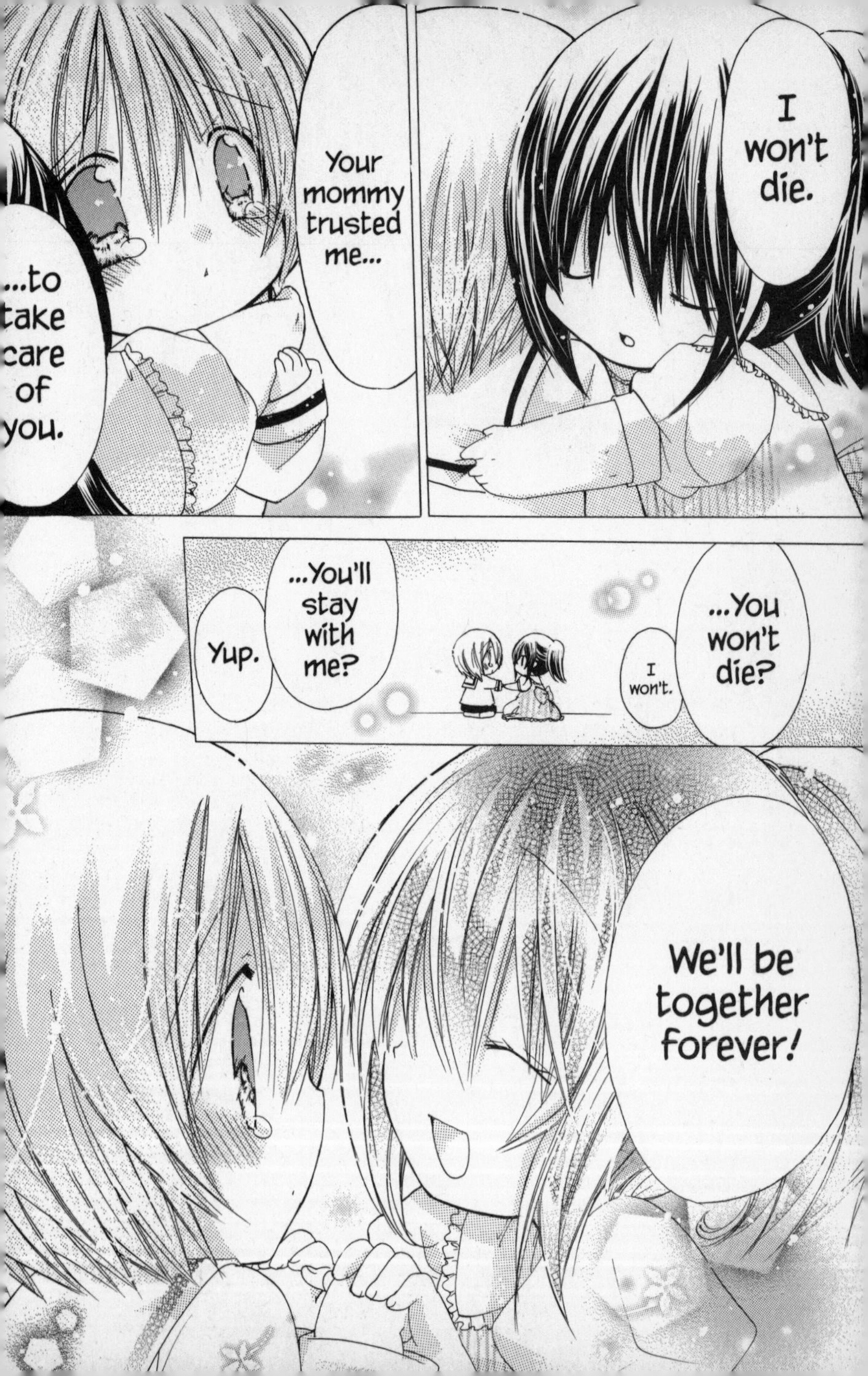
I won't die.
Your mommy trusted me...
...to take care of you.
...You won't die?
I won't.
...You'll stay with me?
Yup.
We'll be together forever!

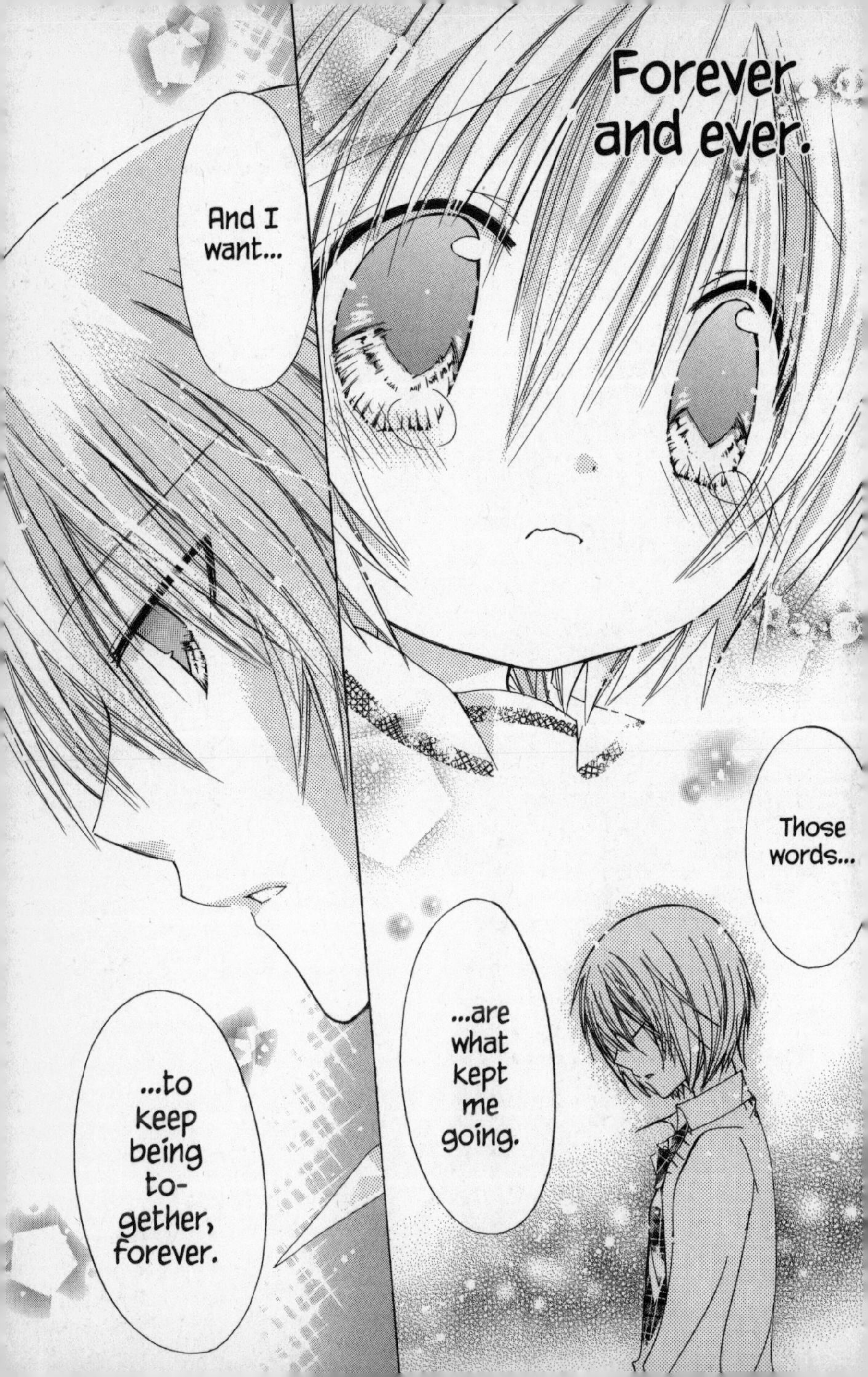
Forever and ever.
Those words...
...are what kept me going.
And I want...
...to keep being together, forever.

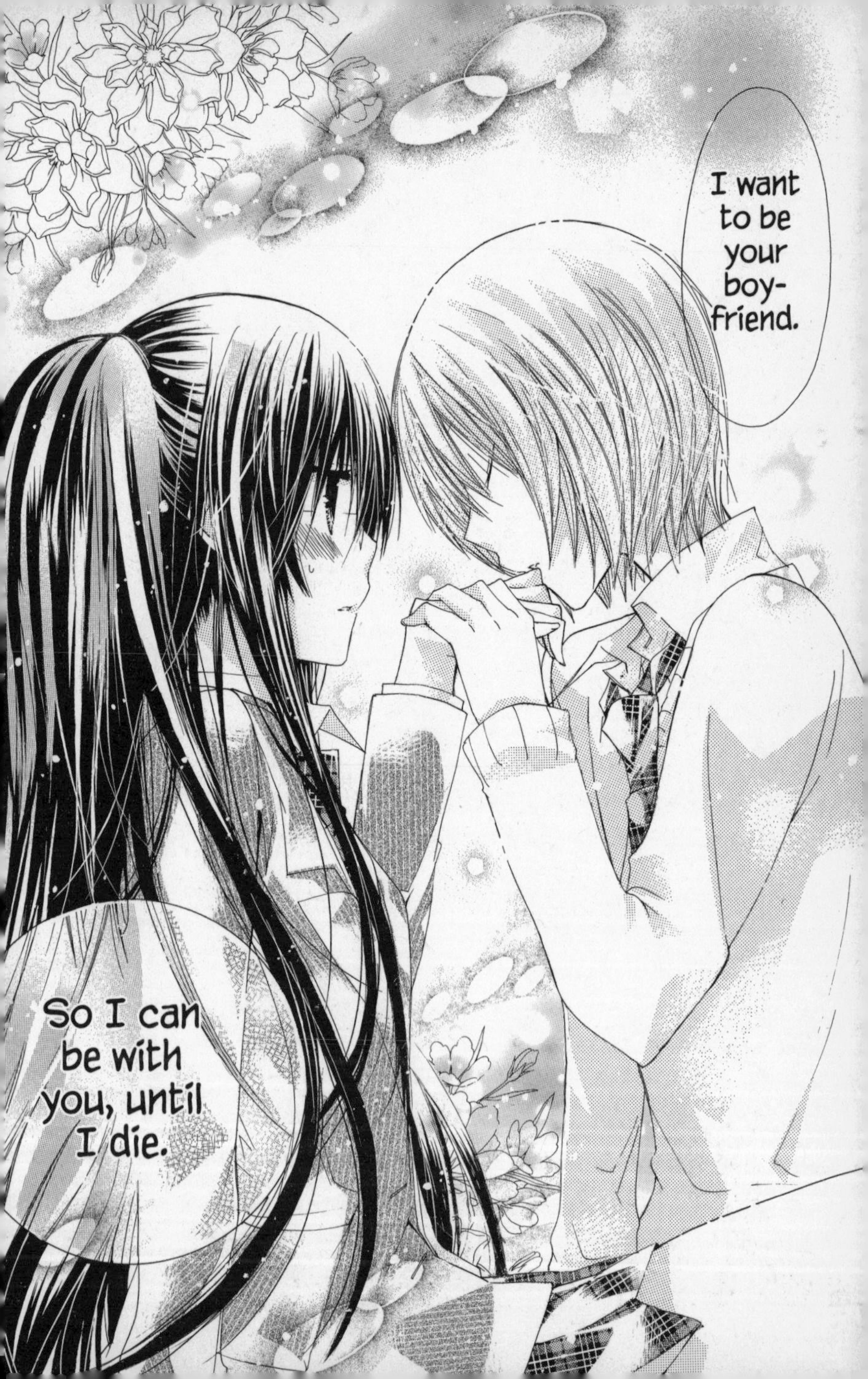
I want to be your boy-friend.
So I can be with you, until I die.

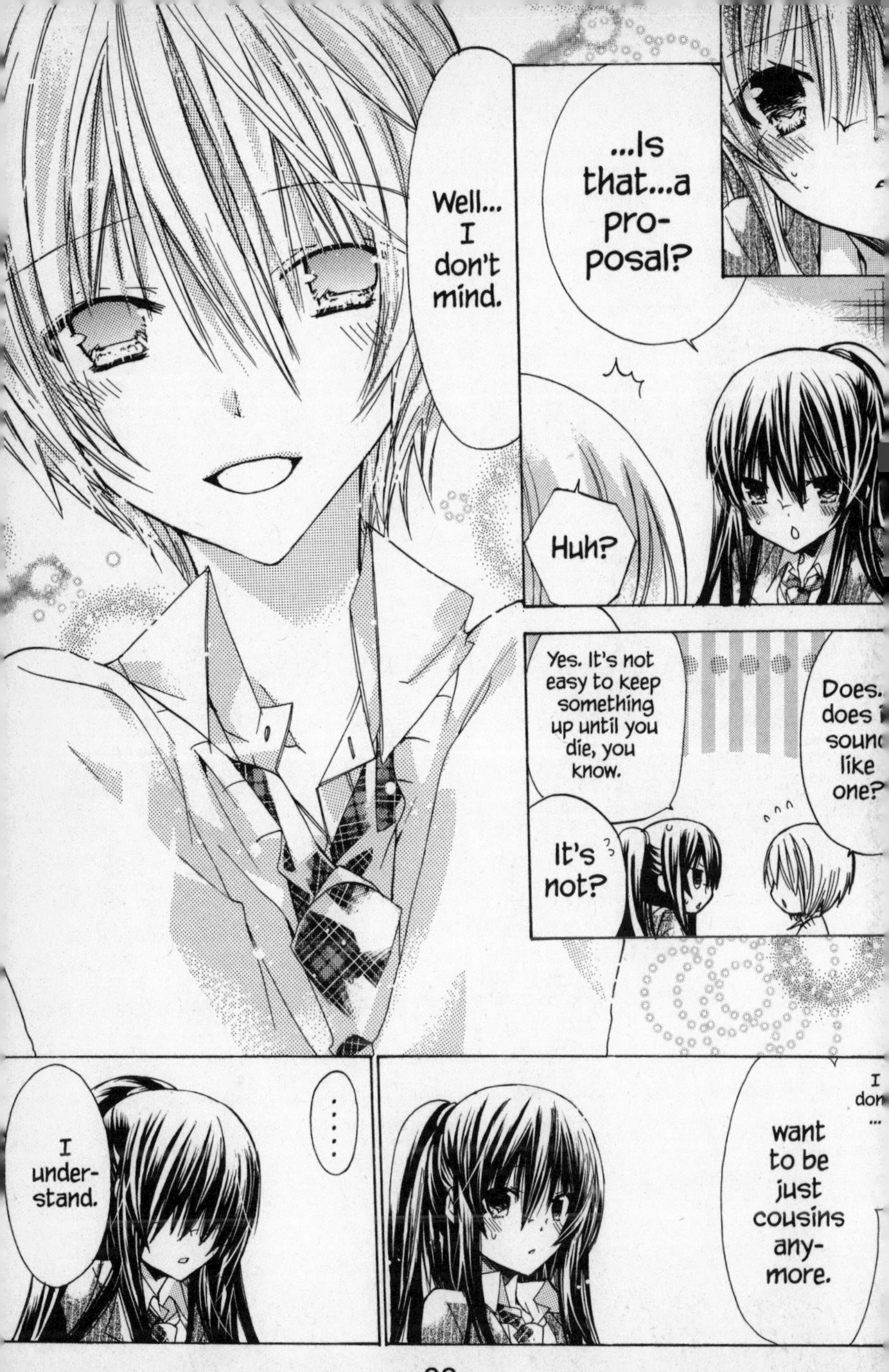
...Is that...a pro-posal?
Huh?
Does.. does i sounc like one?
Yes. It's not easy to keep something up until you die, you know.
It's not?
Well... I don't mind.
I don ...
want to be just cousins any-more.
......
I under-stand.

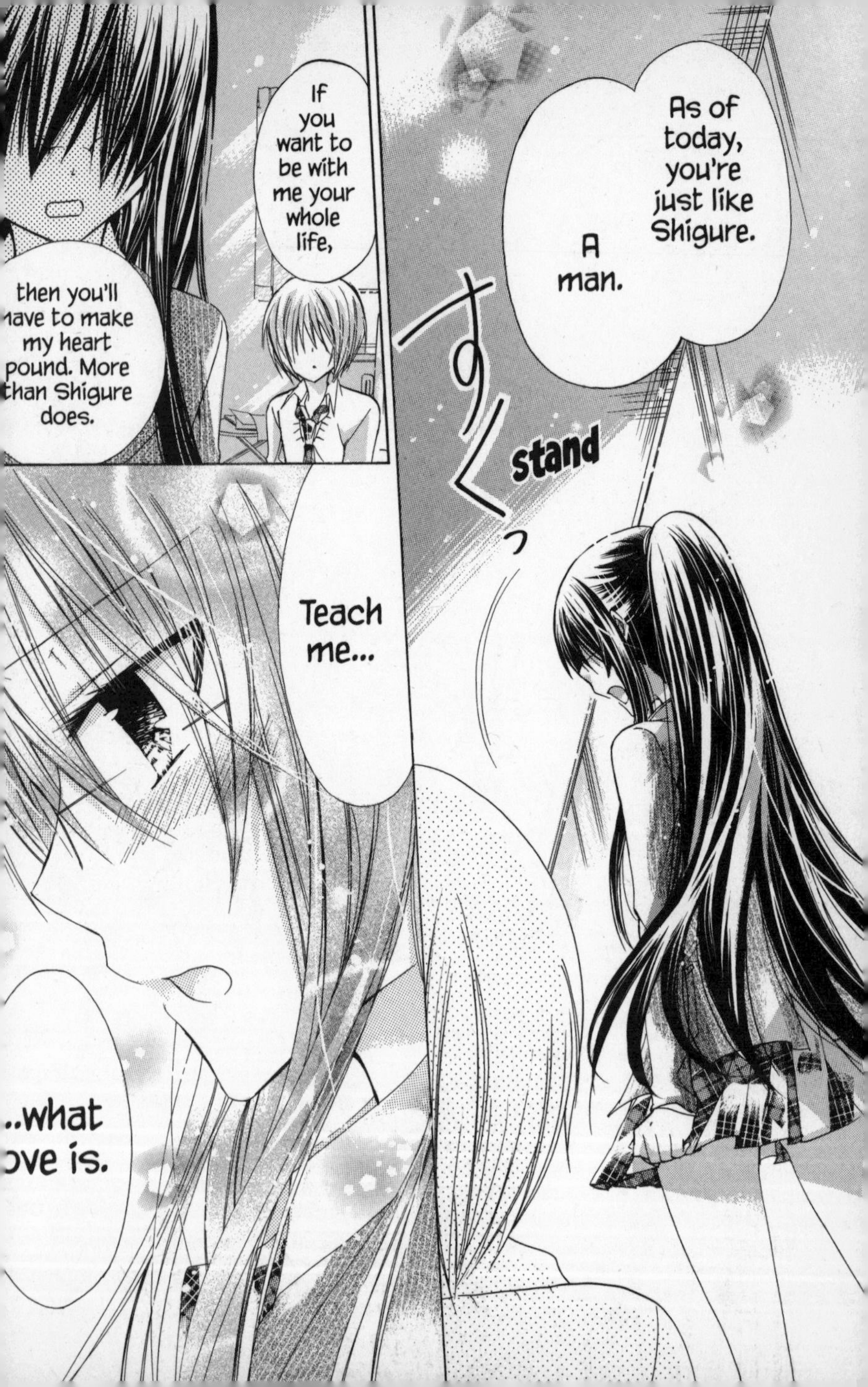
As of today, you're just like Shigure.
A man.
すくっ
stand
If you want to be with me your whole life,
then you'll ave to make my heart pound. More than Shigure does.
Teach me...
..what ove is.

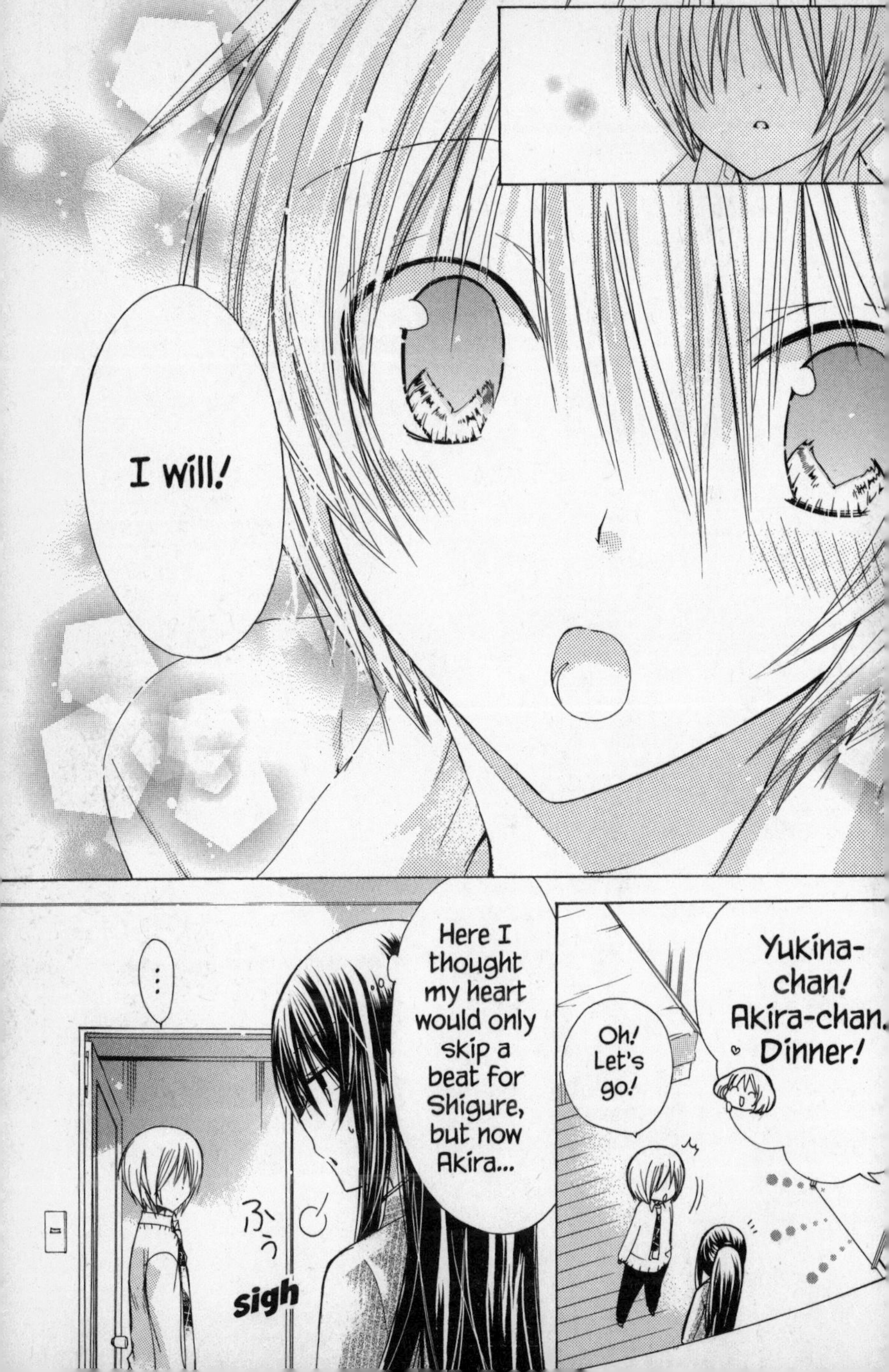
I will!
Yukina-chan! Akira-chan. Dinner!
Oh! Let's go!
Here I thought my heart would only skip a beat for Shigure, but now Akira...
...
ふう
sigh

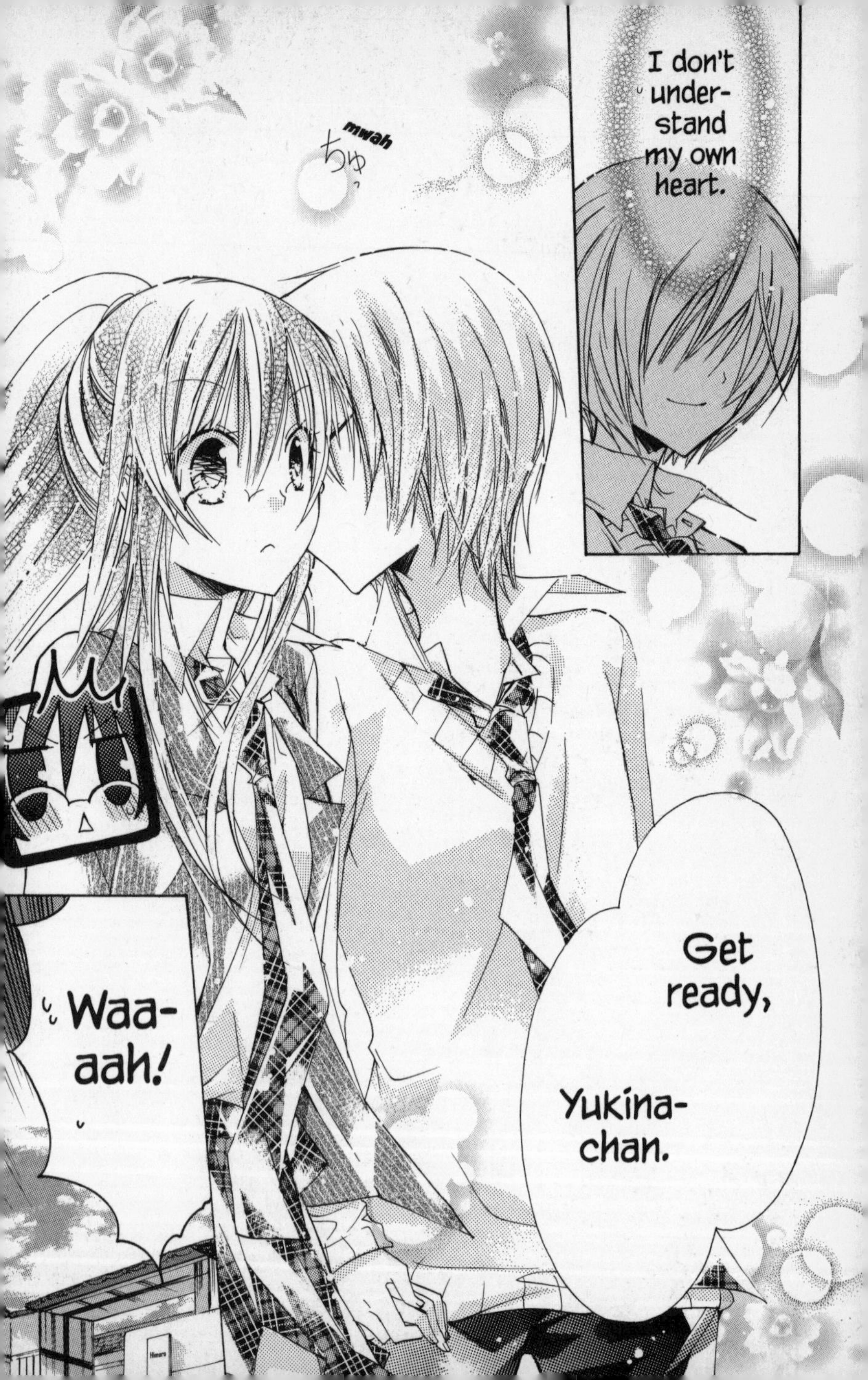
I don't understand my own heart.
ちゅ
mwah
Get ready, Yukina-chan.
Waa-aah!

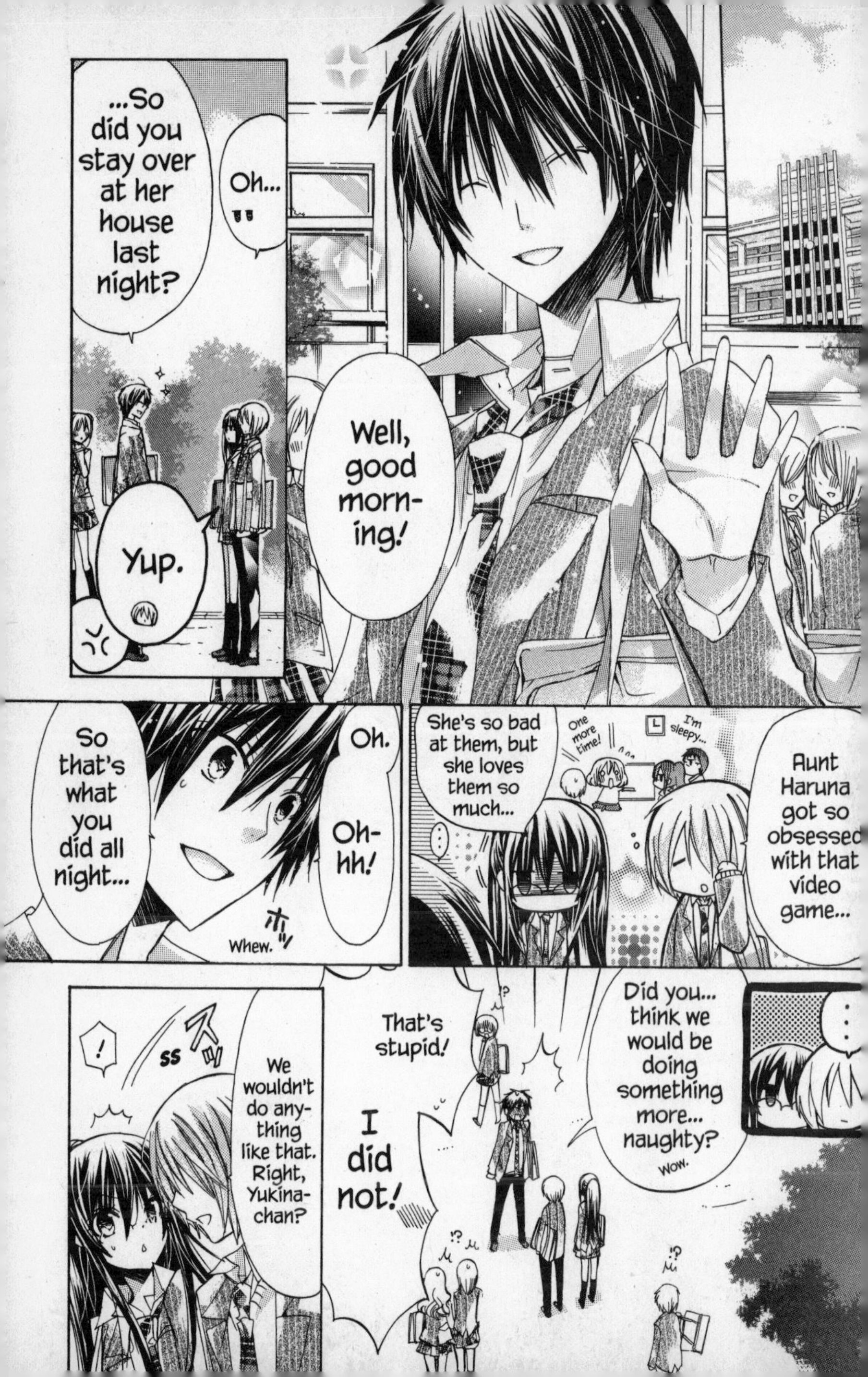
Well, good morning!
...So did you stay over at her house last night?
Oh...
Yup.
Aunt Haruna got so obsessed with that video game...
I'm sleepy...
One more time!
She's so bad at them, but she loves them so much...
Oh.
Oh-hh!
So that's what you did all night...
Whew.
Did you... think we would be doing something more... naughty?
Wow.
That's stupid!
I did not!
We wouldn't do anything like that. Right, Yukina-chan?
SS
!

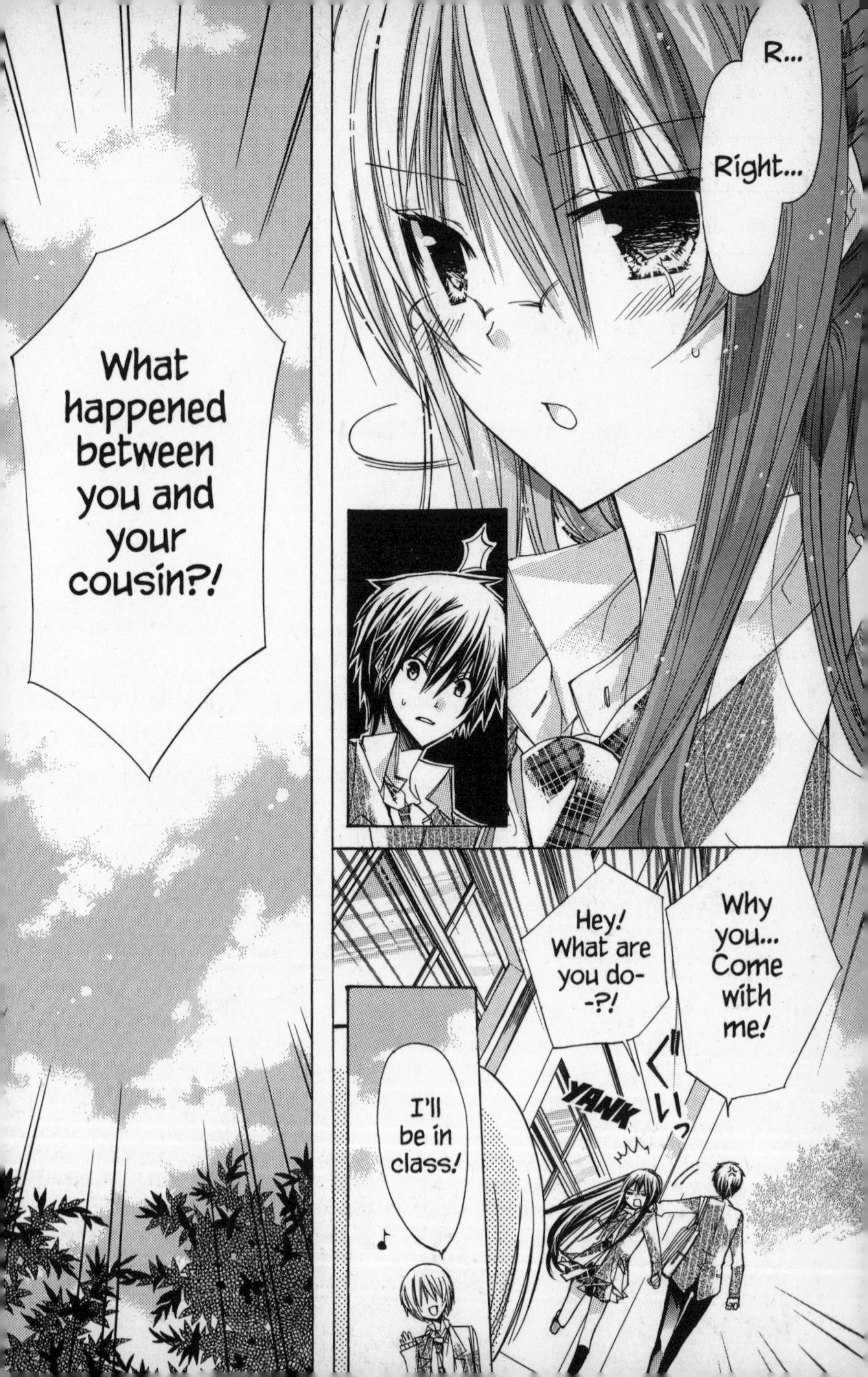
R...
Right...
Why you... Come with me!
Hey! What are you do- -?!
ぐいっ
YANK
I'll be in class!
What happened between you and your cousin?!

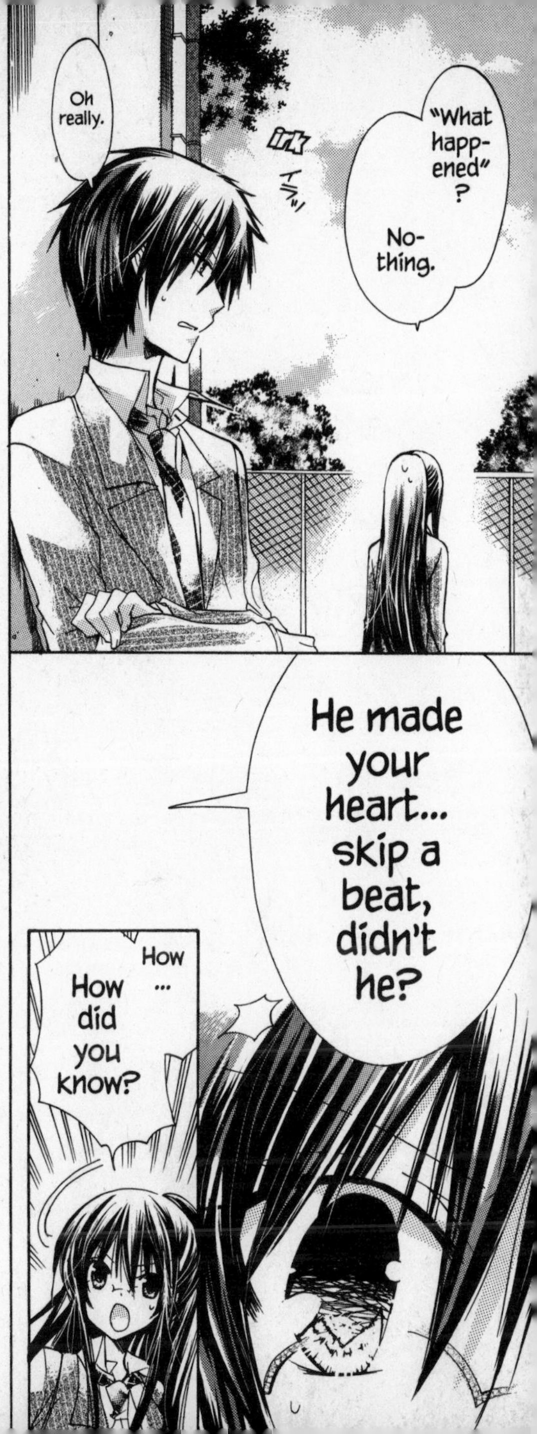
"What happ-ened"? No-thing.
irk
Oh really.
He made your heart... skip a beat, didn't he?
How...
How did you know?

Snow Yukina 3

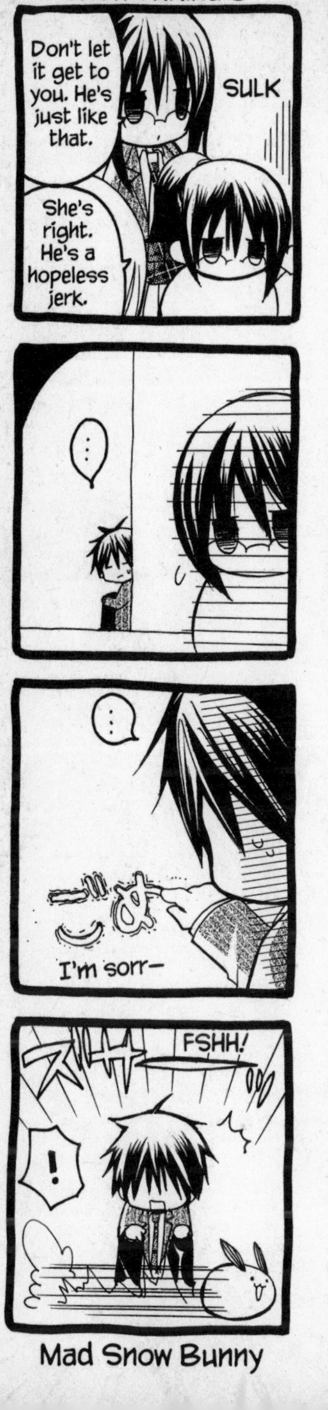
Don't let it get to you. He's just like that.
SULK
She's right. He's a hopeless jerk.
...
...
I'm sorr—
FSHH!
!

Mad Snow Bunny

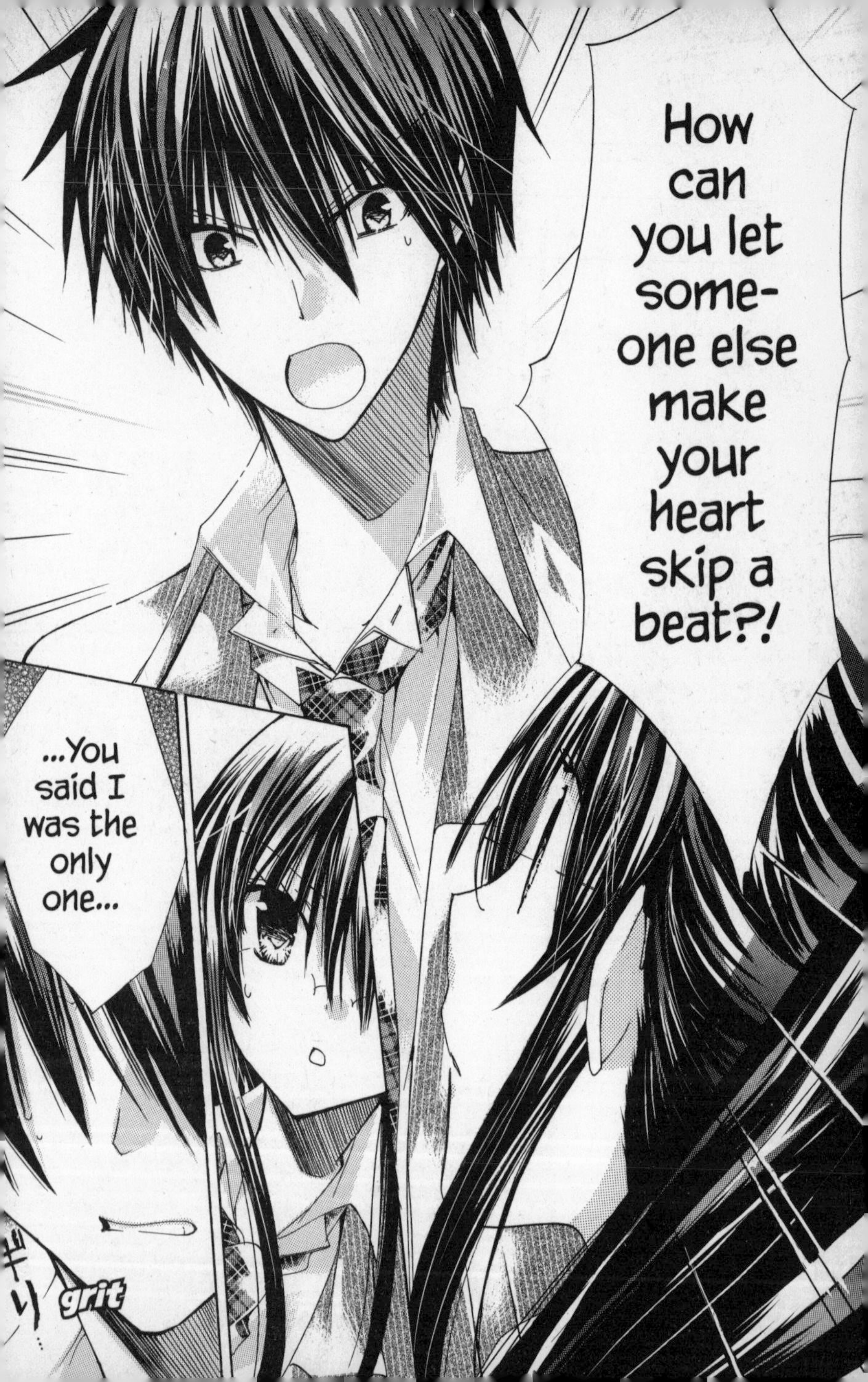
How can you let some-one else make your heart skip a beat?!
...You said I was the only one...
ギリ…
grit

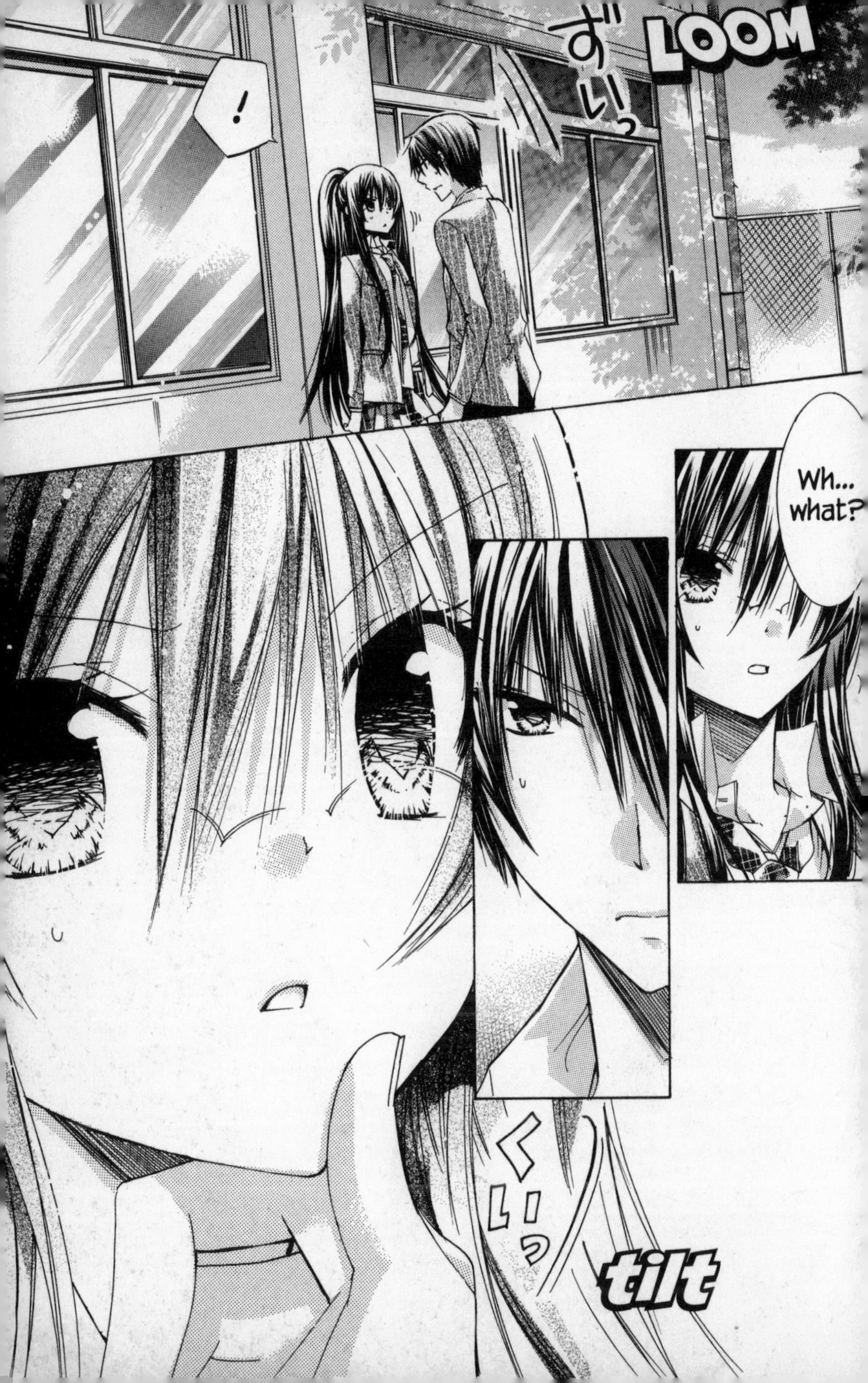
ずいっ
LOOM
!
Wh... what?
くいっ
tilt

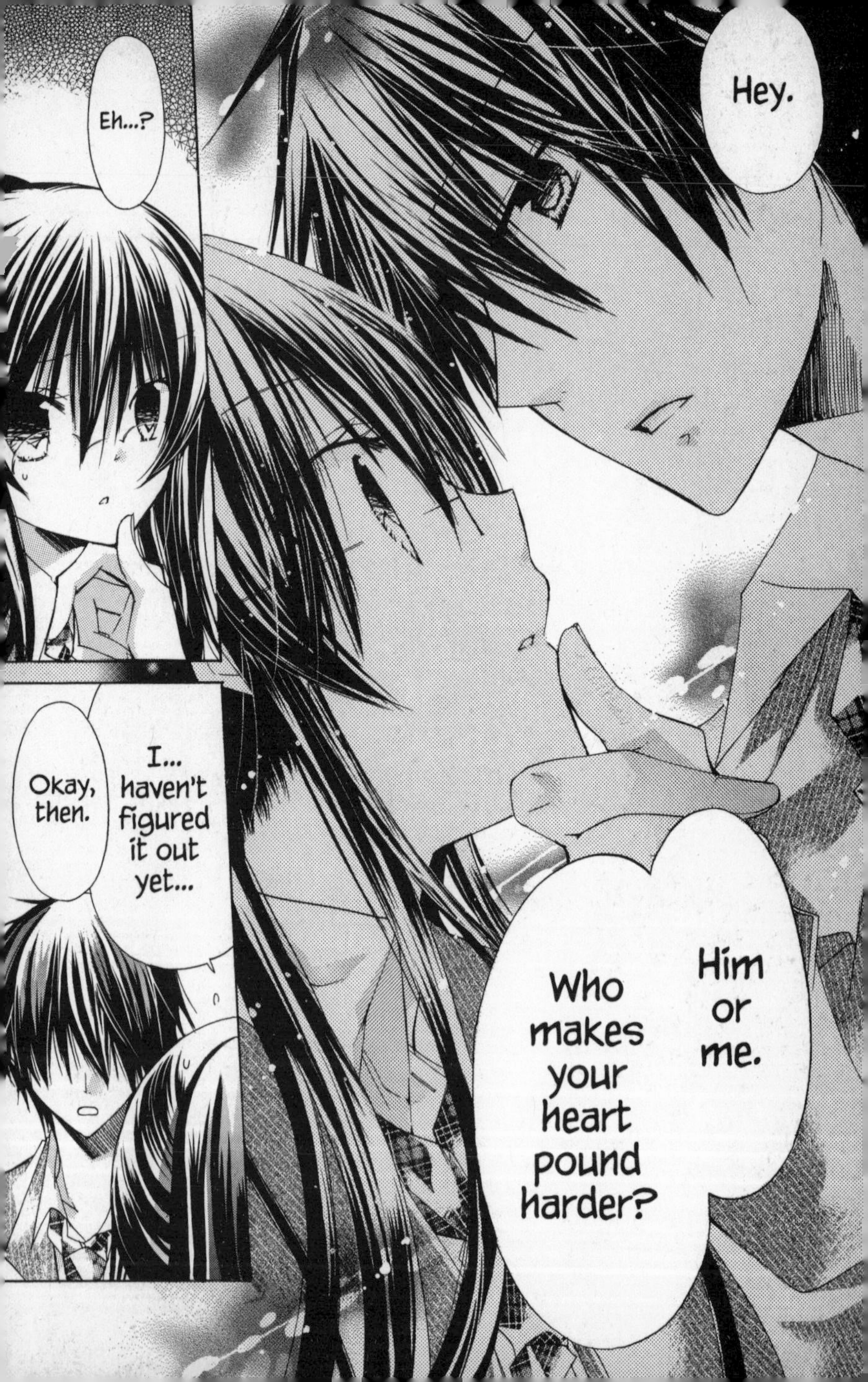
Hey.
Him or me.
Who makes your heart pound harder?
Eh...?
I... haven't figured it out yet...
Okay, then.

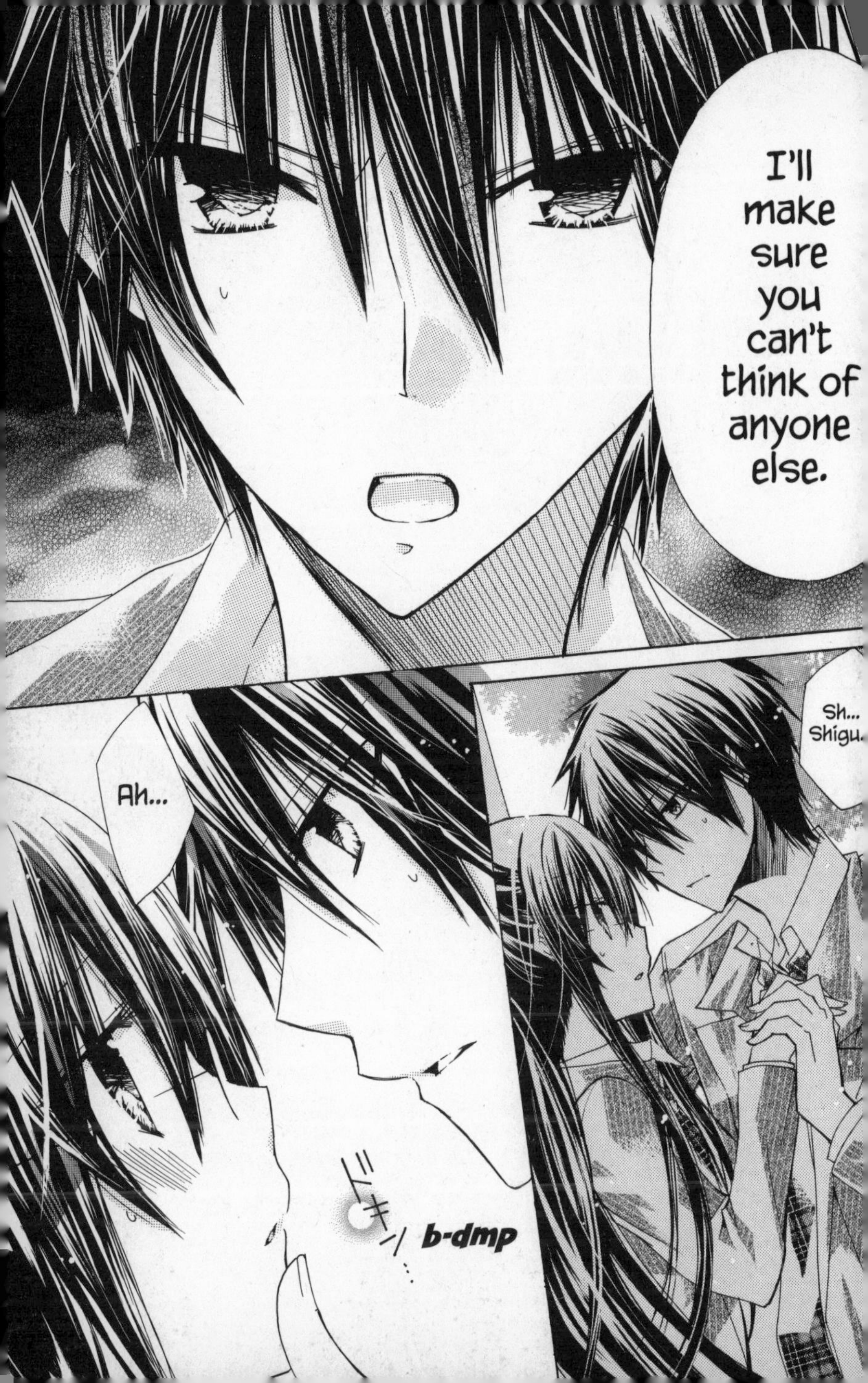
I'll make sure you can't think of anyone else.
Sh... Shigu.
Ah...
b-dmp

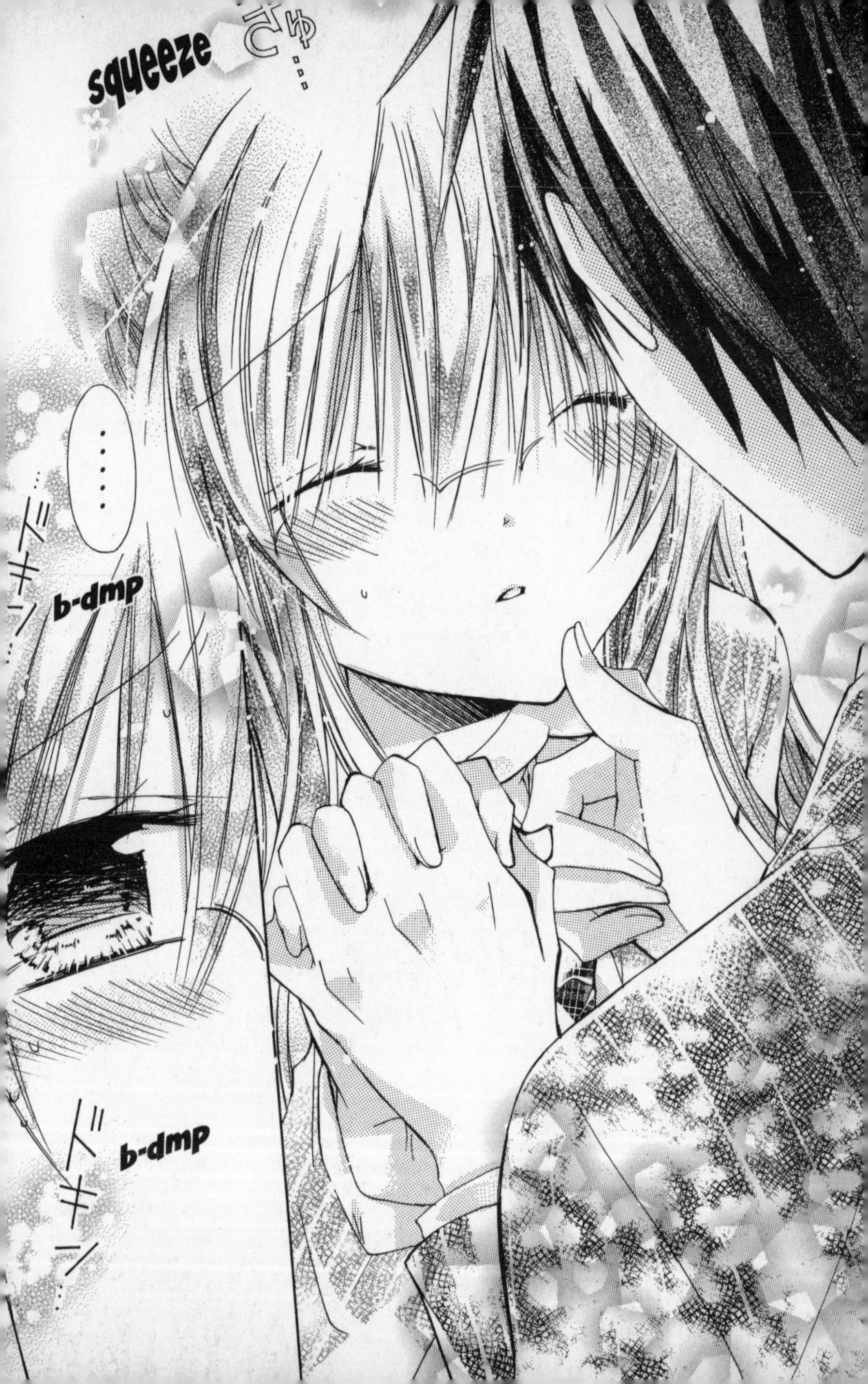
squeeze
ぎゅ…
……
b-dmp
b-dmp
ドキン…

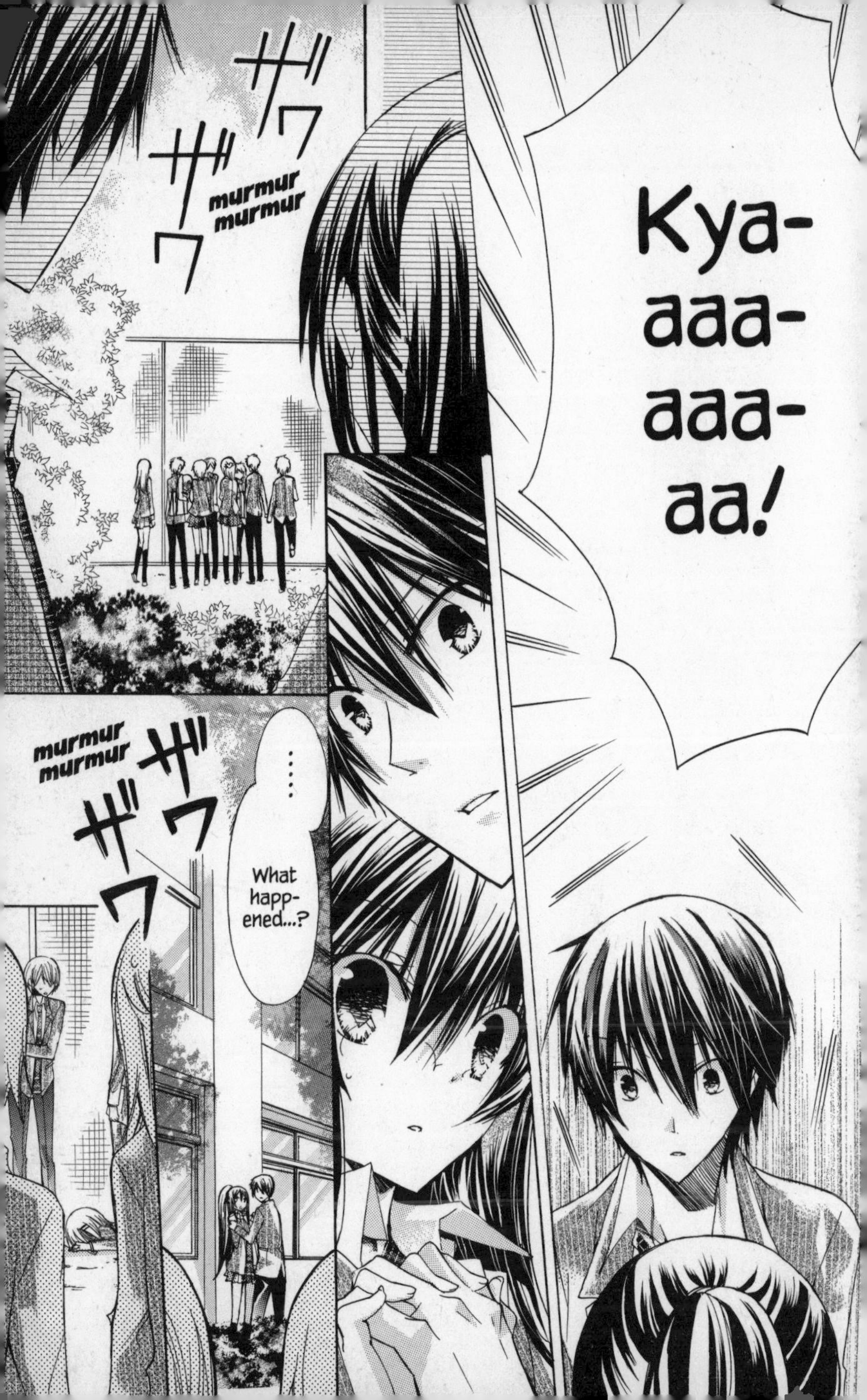
Kya-aaa-aaa-aa!
ザワザワ
murmur murmur
ザワザワ
murmur murmur
.....
What happened...?

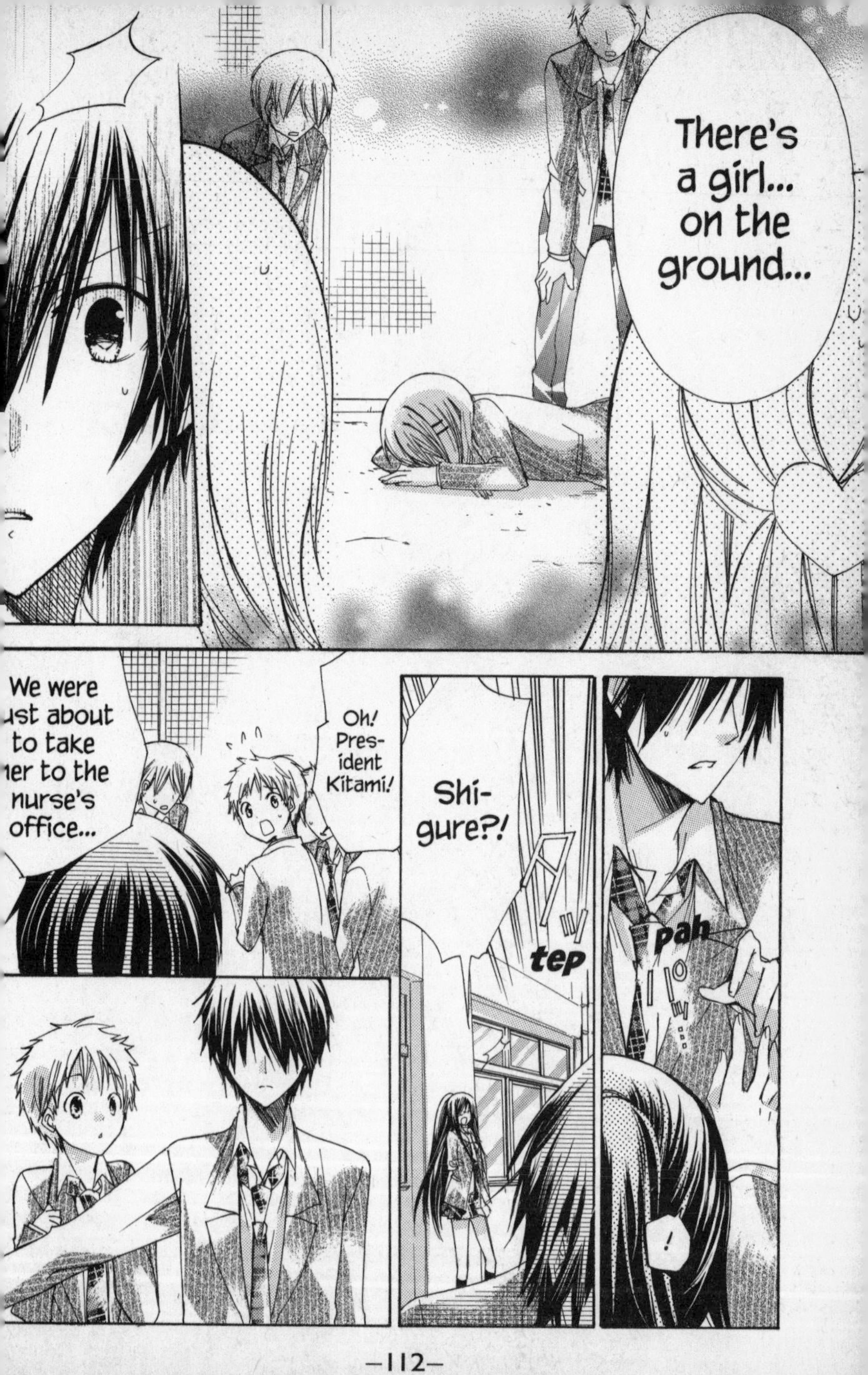
There's a girl... on the ground...
pah
!
tep
Shi-gure?!
Oh! Pres-ident Kitami!
We were ust about to take ner to the nurse's office...

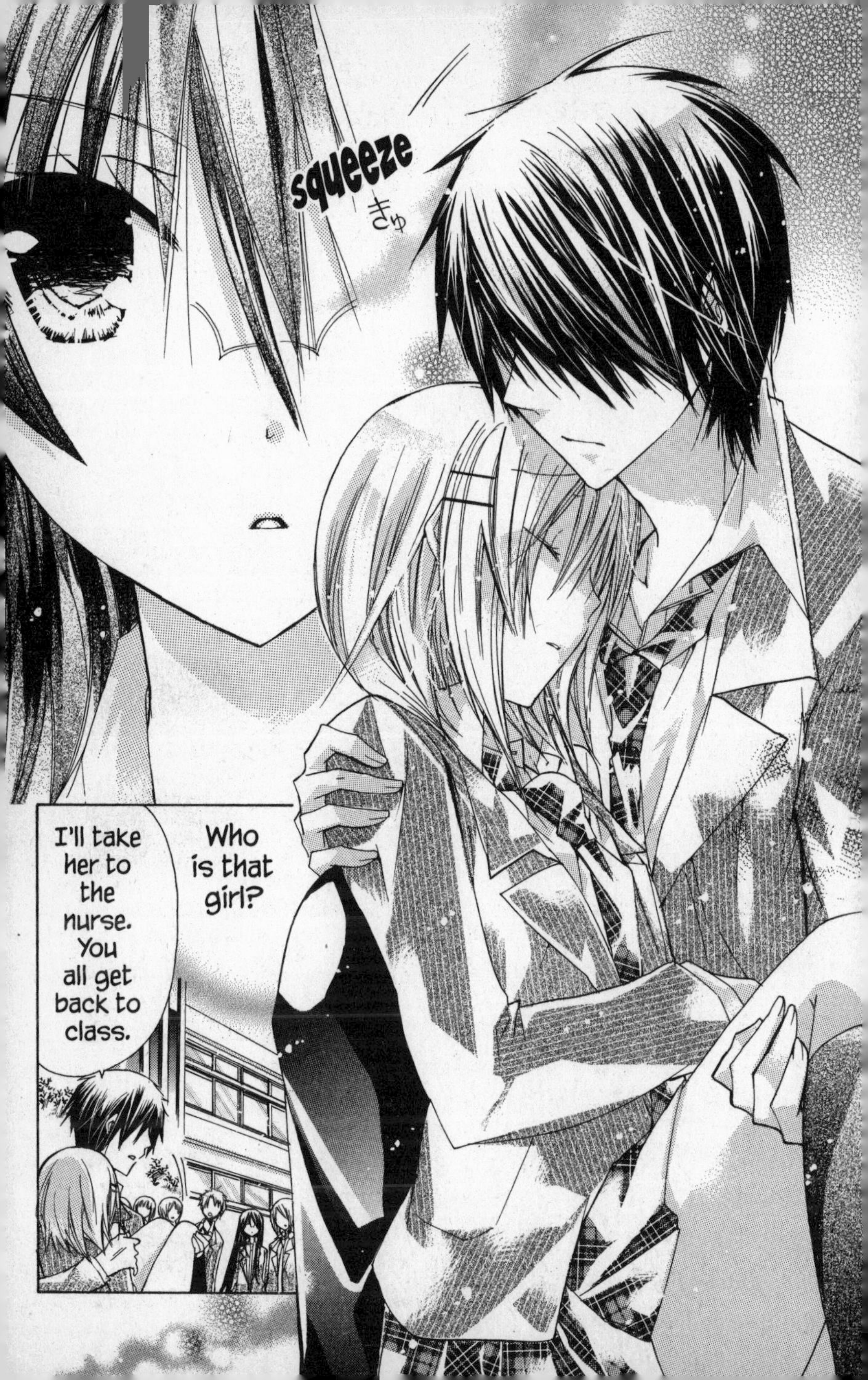
squeeze
きゅ
Who is that girl?
I'll take her to the nurse. You all get back to class.

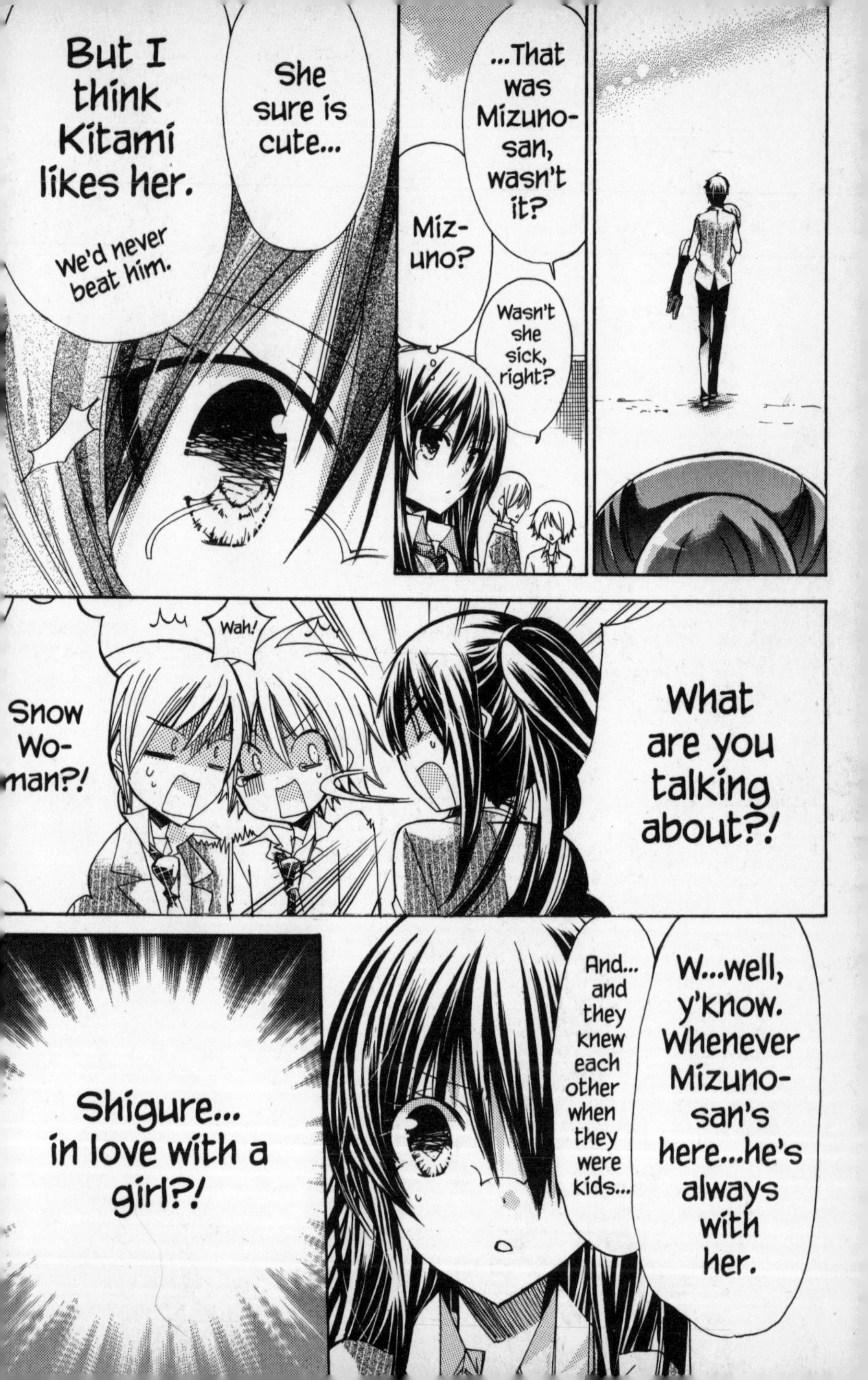
...That was Mizuno-san, wasn't it?
Miz-uno?
Wasn't she sick, right?
She sure is cute...
But I think Kitami likes her.
We'd never beat him.
What are you talking about?!
Wah!
Snow Wo-man?!
W...well, y'know. Whenever Mizuno-san's here...he's always with her.
And... and they knew each other when they were kids...
Shigure... in love with a girl?!

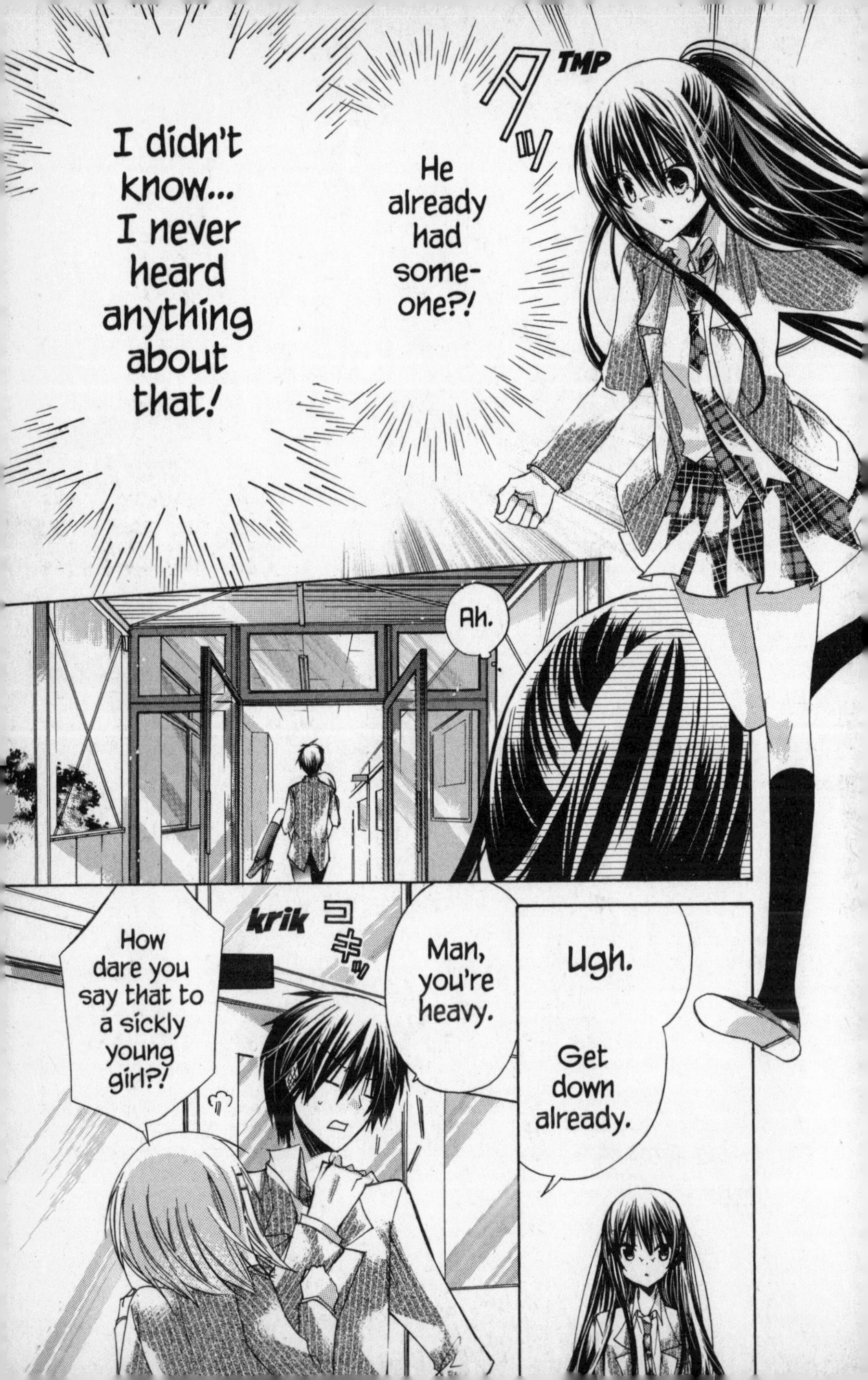
TMP
He already had some-one?!
I didn't know... I never heard anything about that!
Ah.
Ugh.
Get down already.
Man, you're heavy.
krik
How dare you say that to a sickly young girl?!

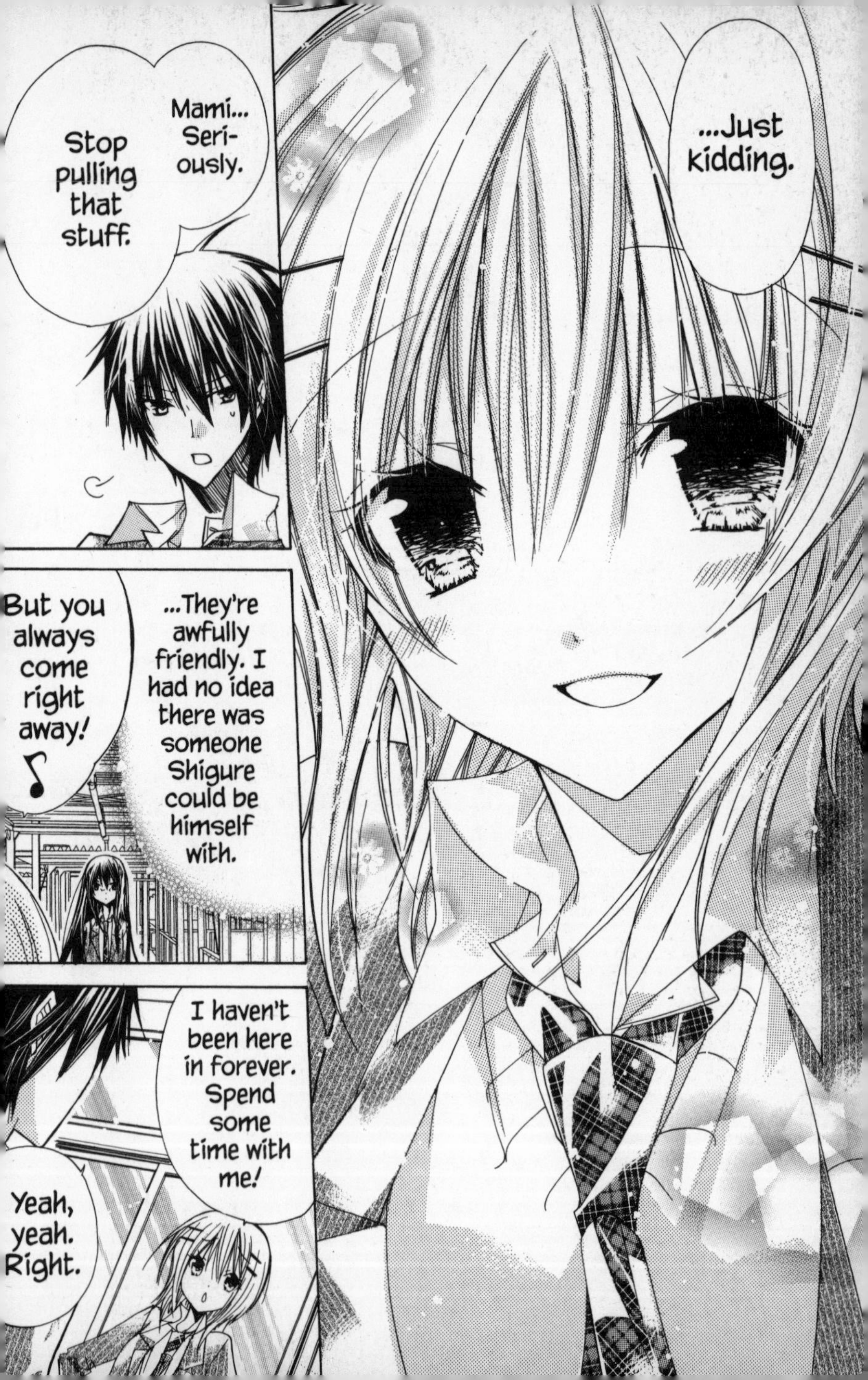
...Just kidding.
Mami... Seriously.
Stop pulling that stuff.
...They're awfully friendly. I had no idea there was someone Shigure could be himself with.
But you always come right away! ♪
I haven't been here in forever. Spend some time with me!
Yeah, yeah. Right.

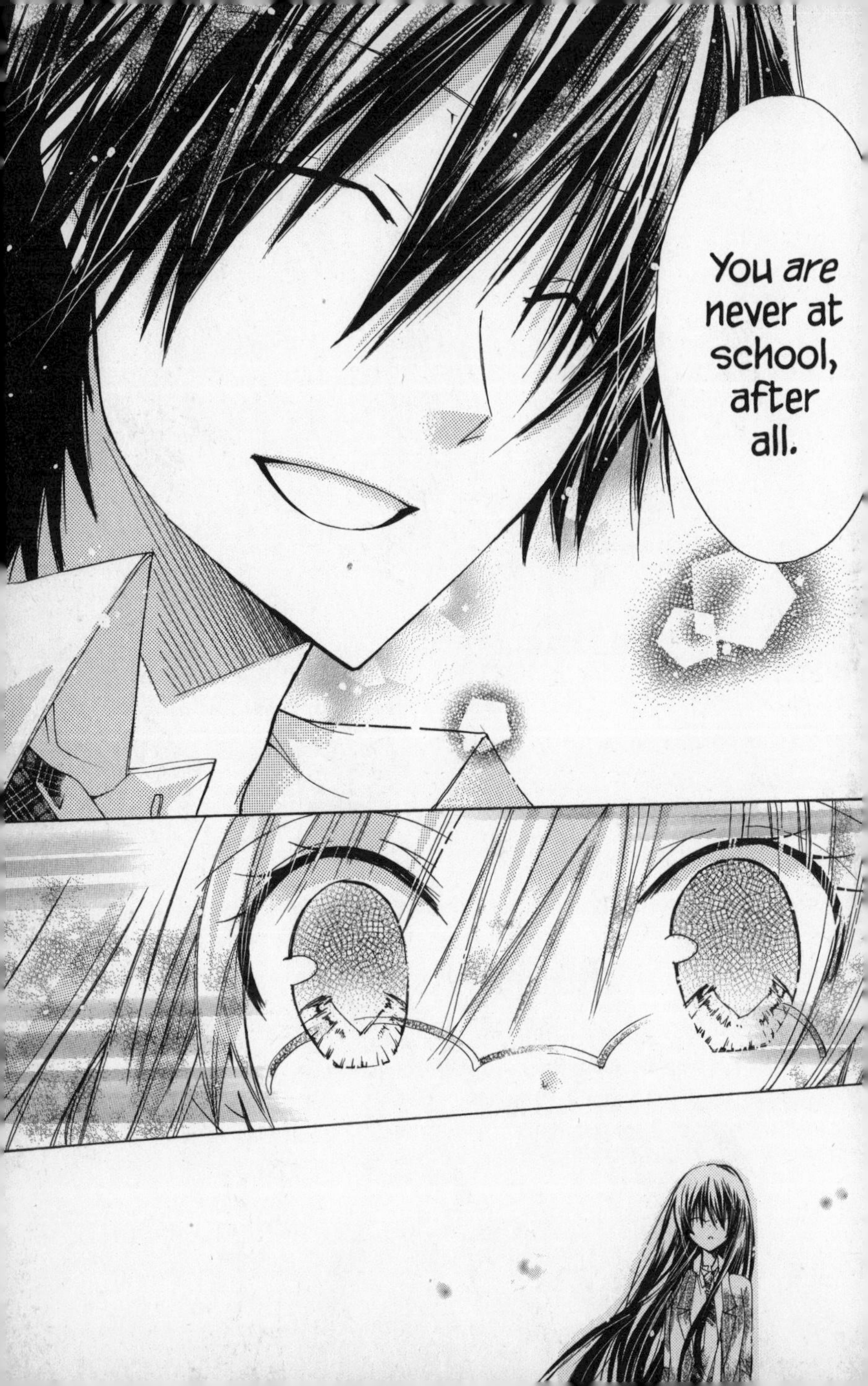
You *are* never at school, after all.

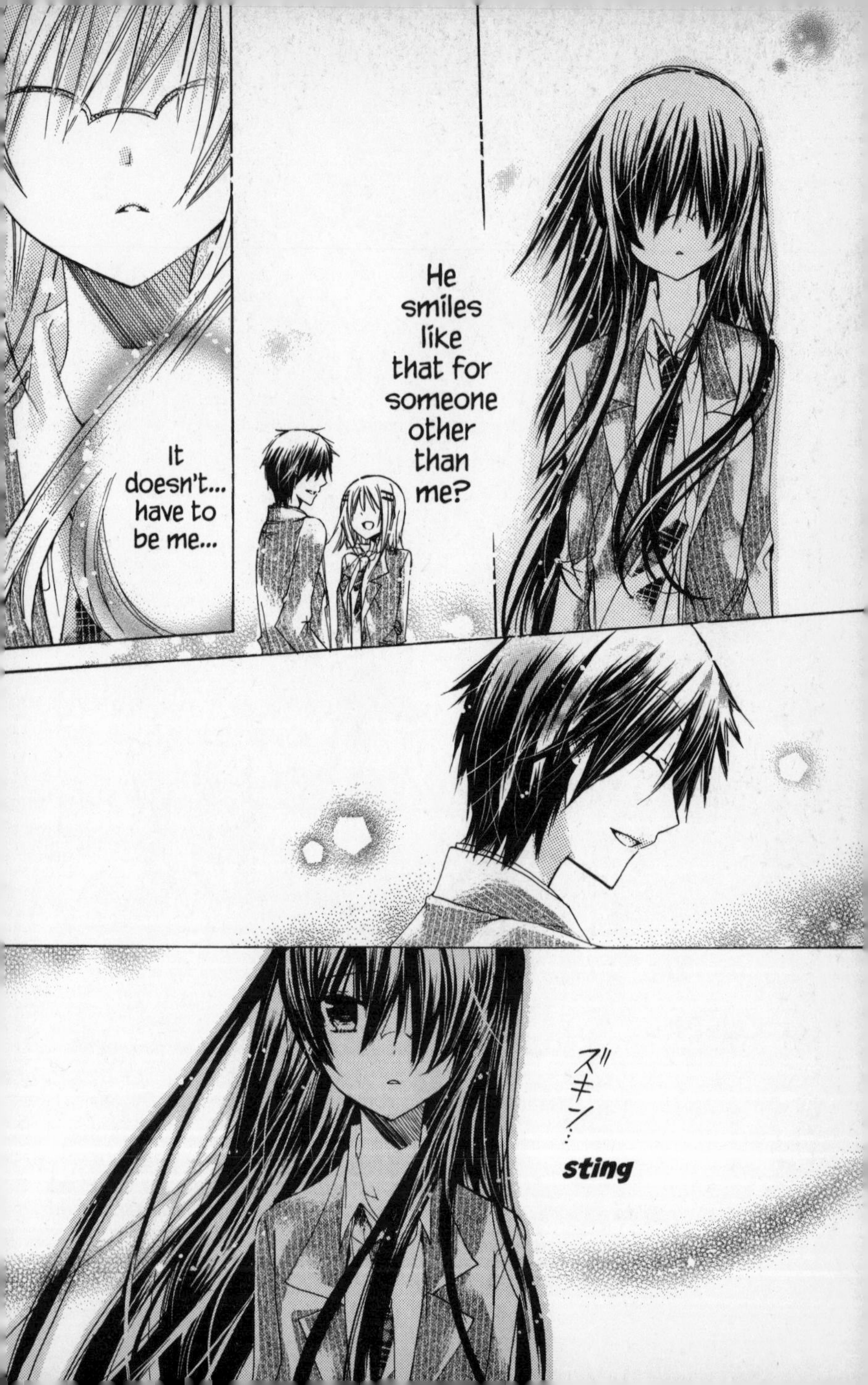
He smiles like that for someone other than me?
It doesn't... have to be me...
ズキン…
sting

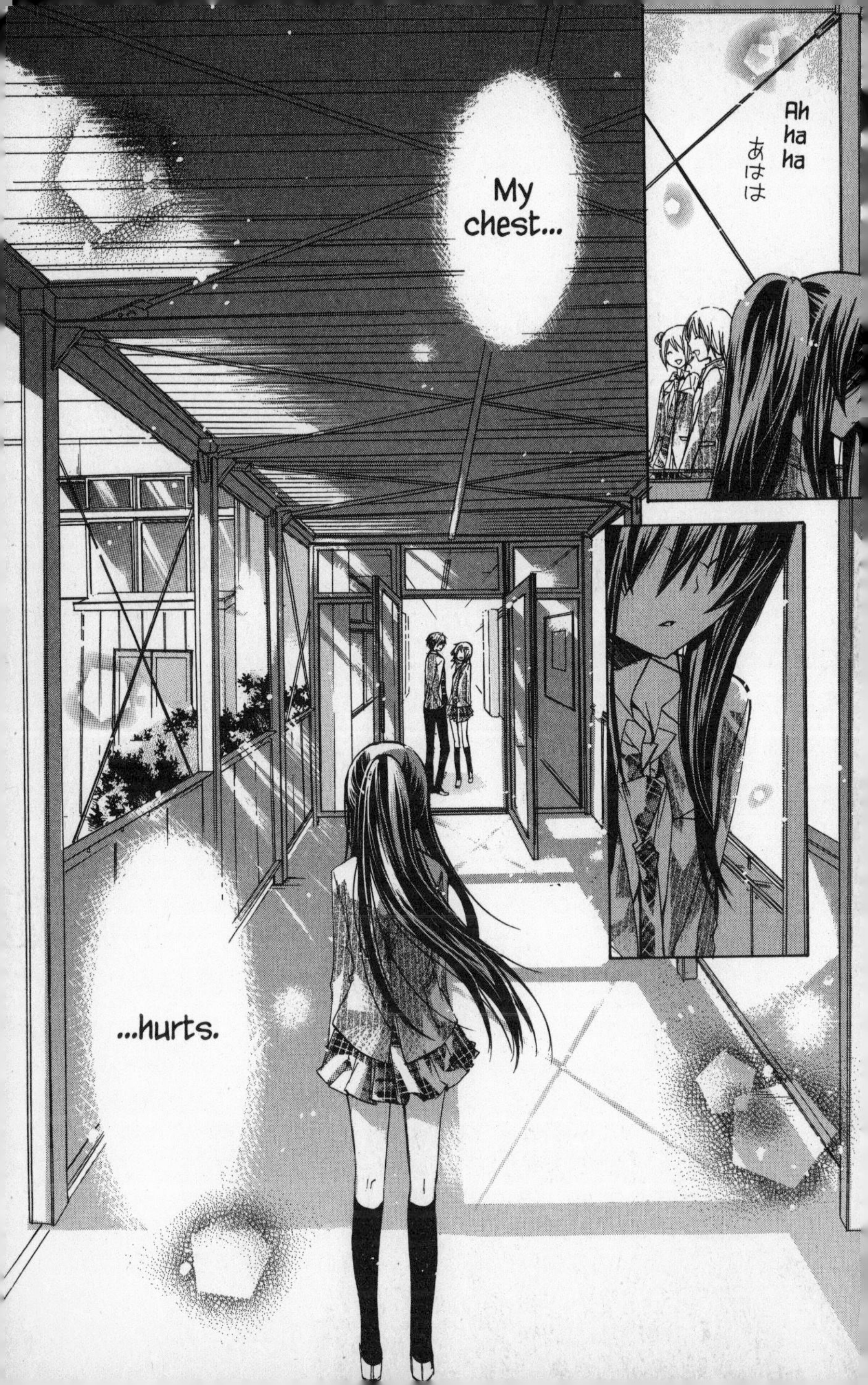
Ah ha ha
あはは
My chest...
...hurts.

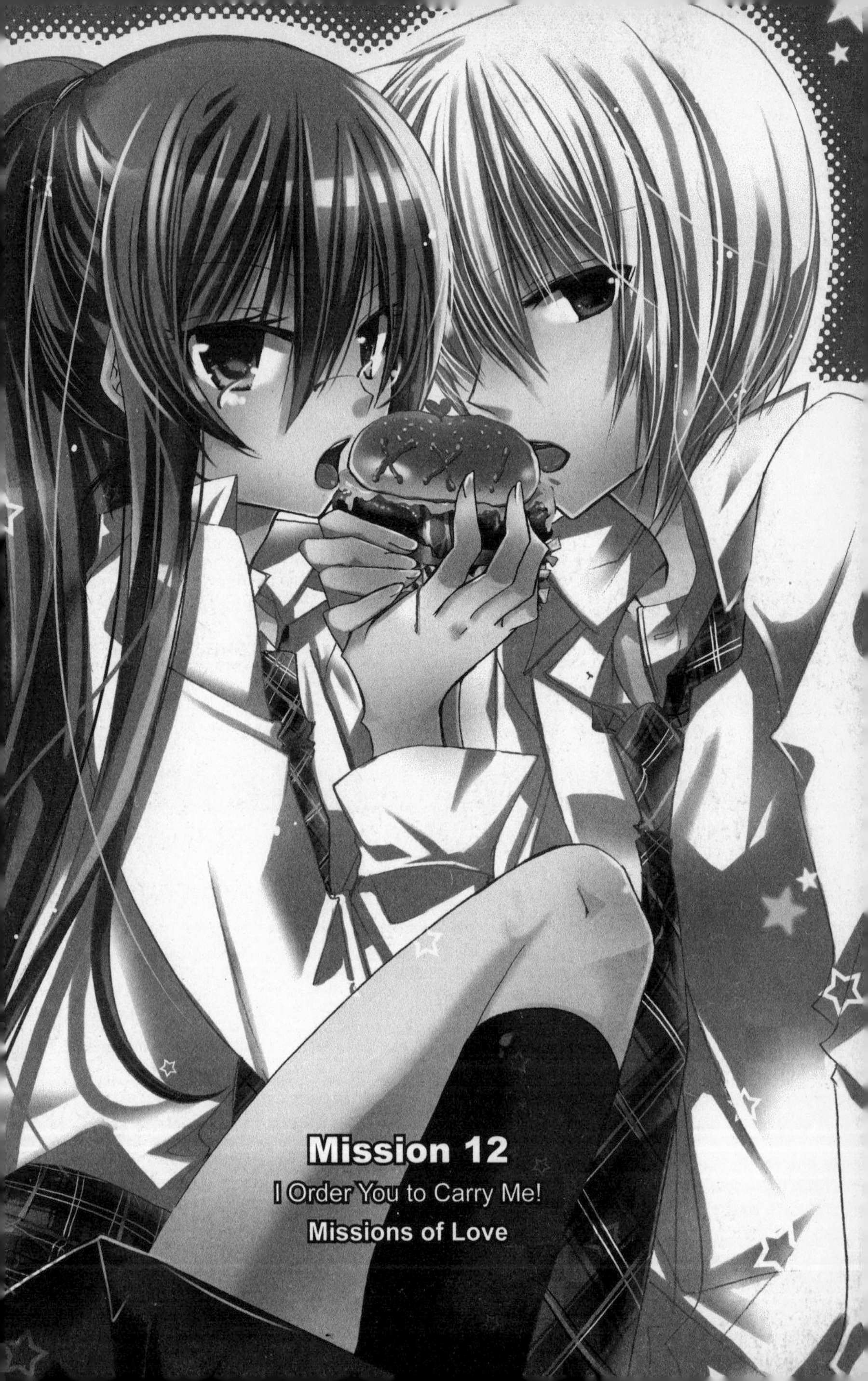
Mission 12
I Order You to Carry Me!
Missions of Love

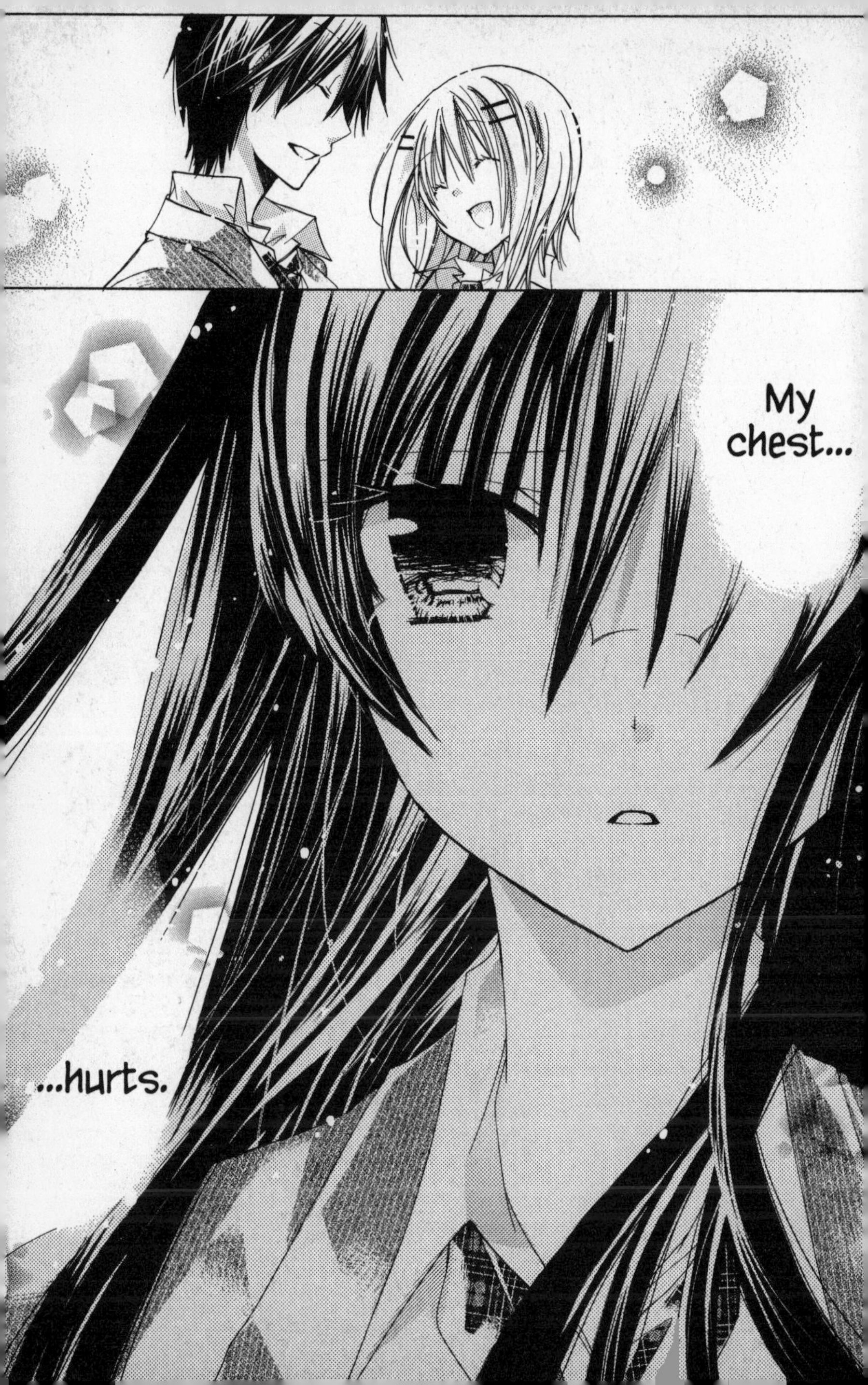
My chest...
...hurts.

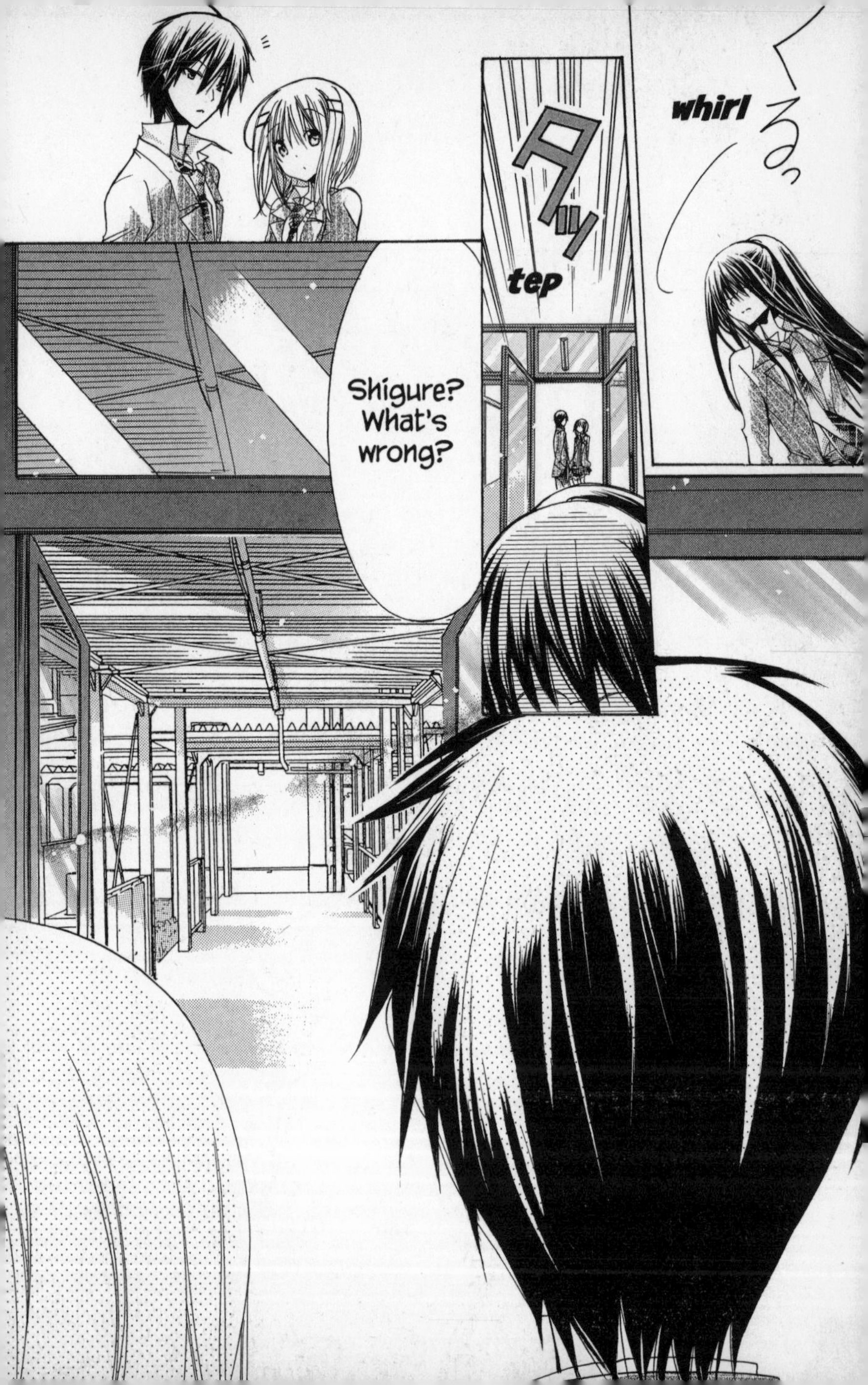
くるっ
whirl
タッ
tep
Shigure? What's wrong?

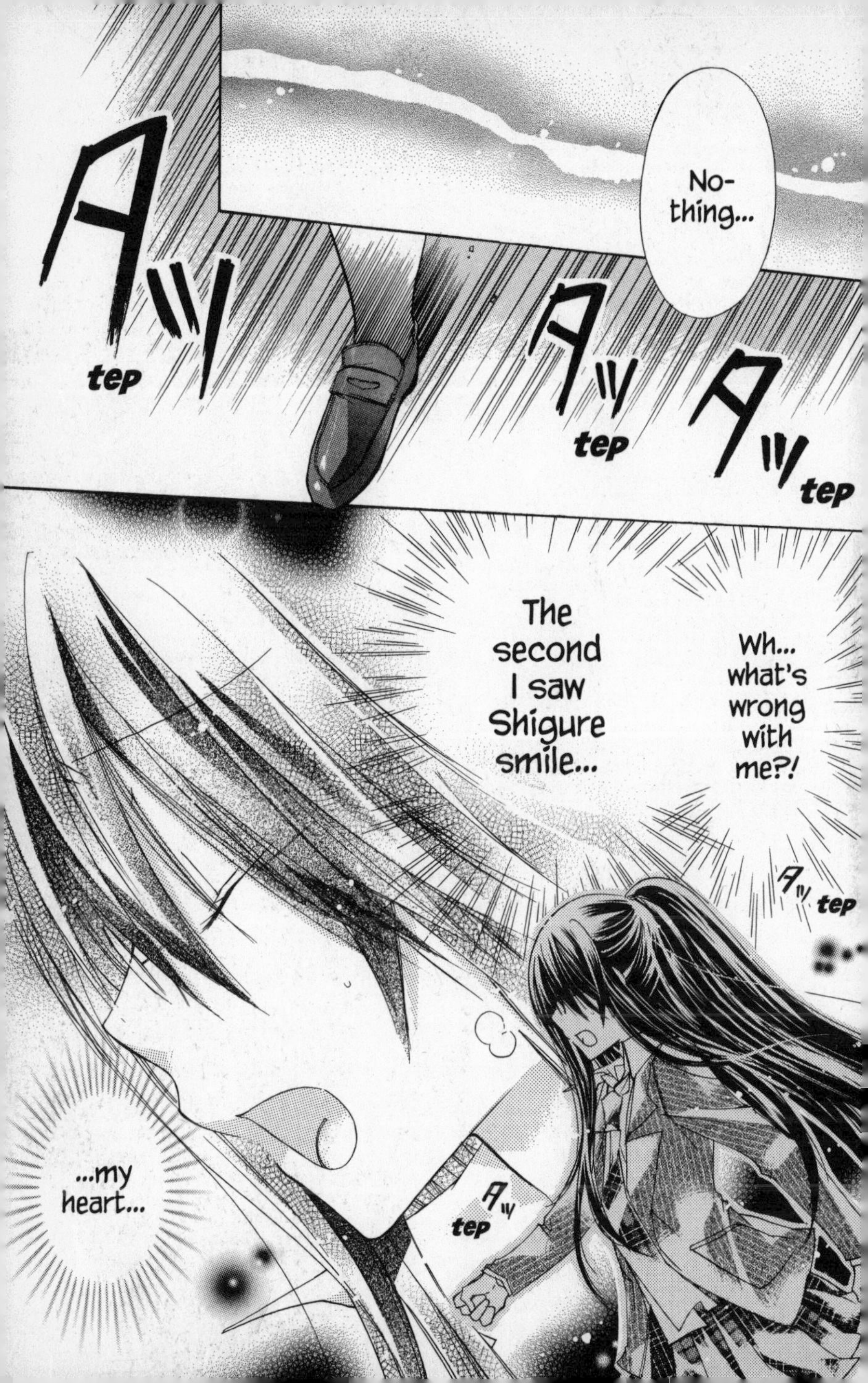
No-thing...
tep
tep
tep
Wh... what's wrong with me?!
The second I saw Shigure smile...
tep
tep
...my heart...

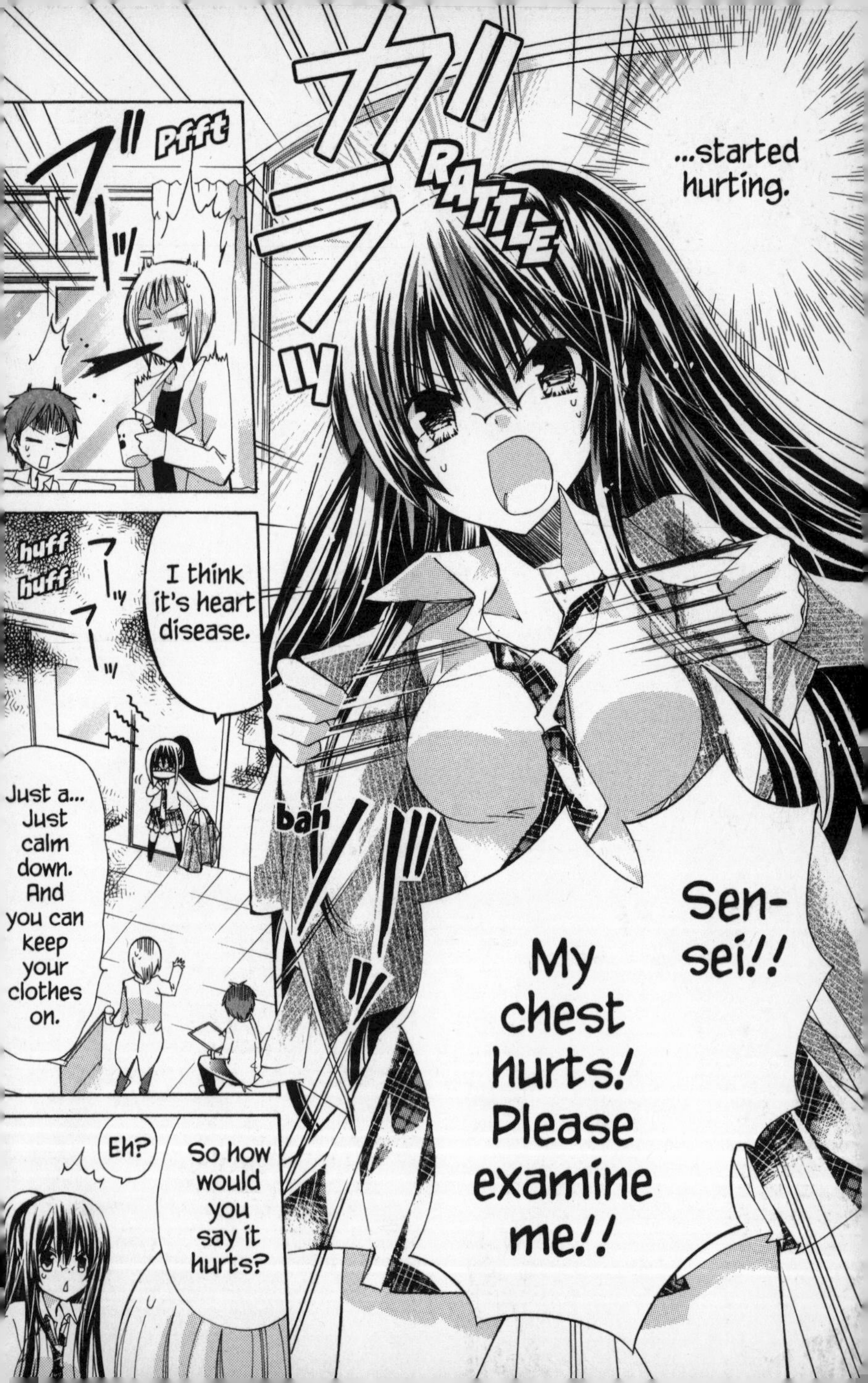
...started hurting.
RATTLE
Sen-sei!!
My chest hurts! Please examine me!!
bah
Pfft
I think it's heart disease.
huff huff
Just a... Just calm down. And you can keep your clothes on.
So how would you say it hurts?
Eh?

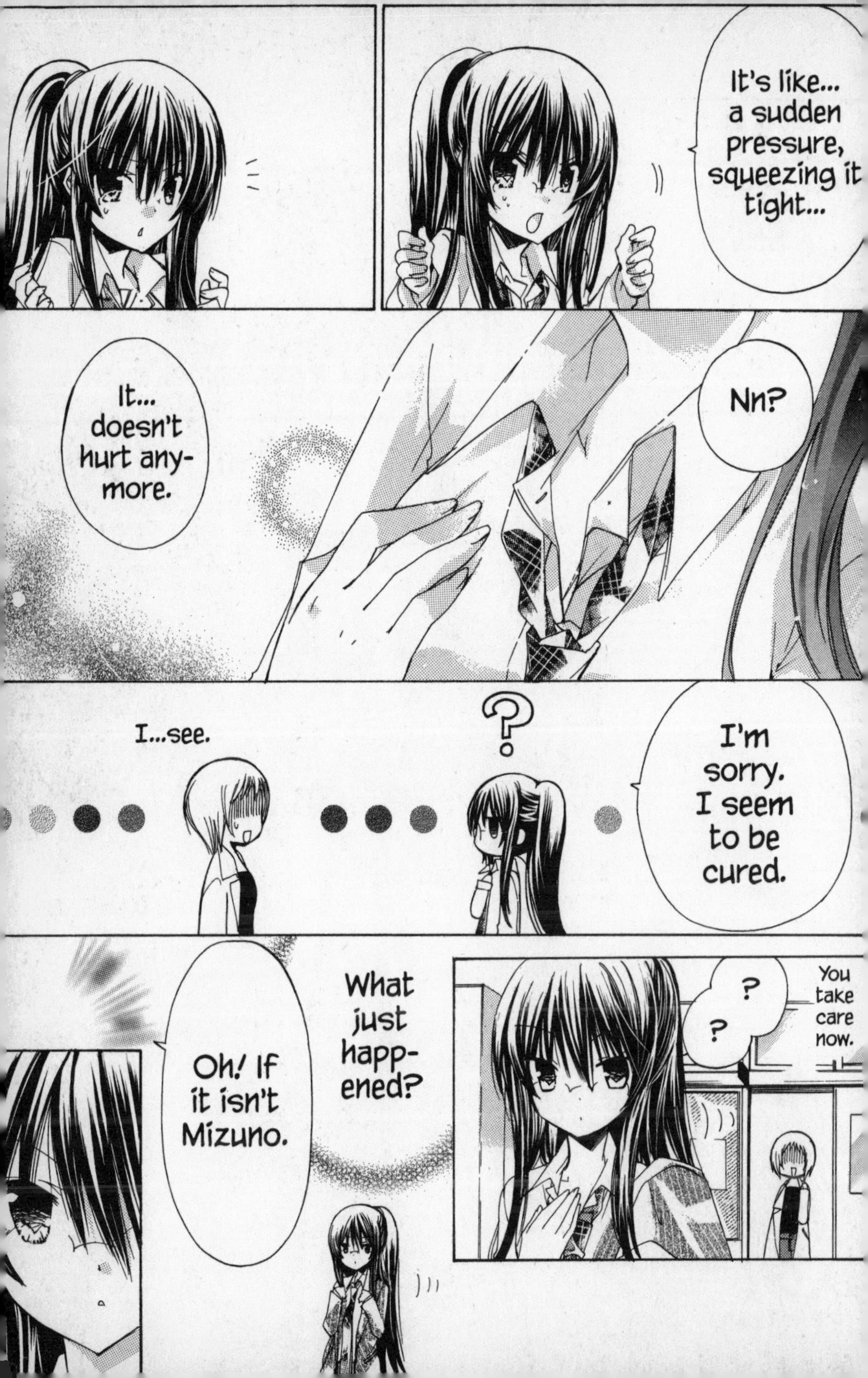

It's like... a sudden pressure, squeezing it tight...
Nn?
It... doesn't hurt anymore.
I'm sorry. I seem to be cured.
I...see.
You take care now.
? ?
What just happened?
Oh! If it isn't Mizuno.

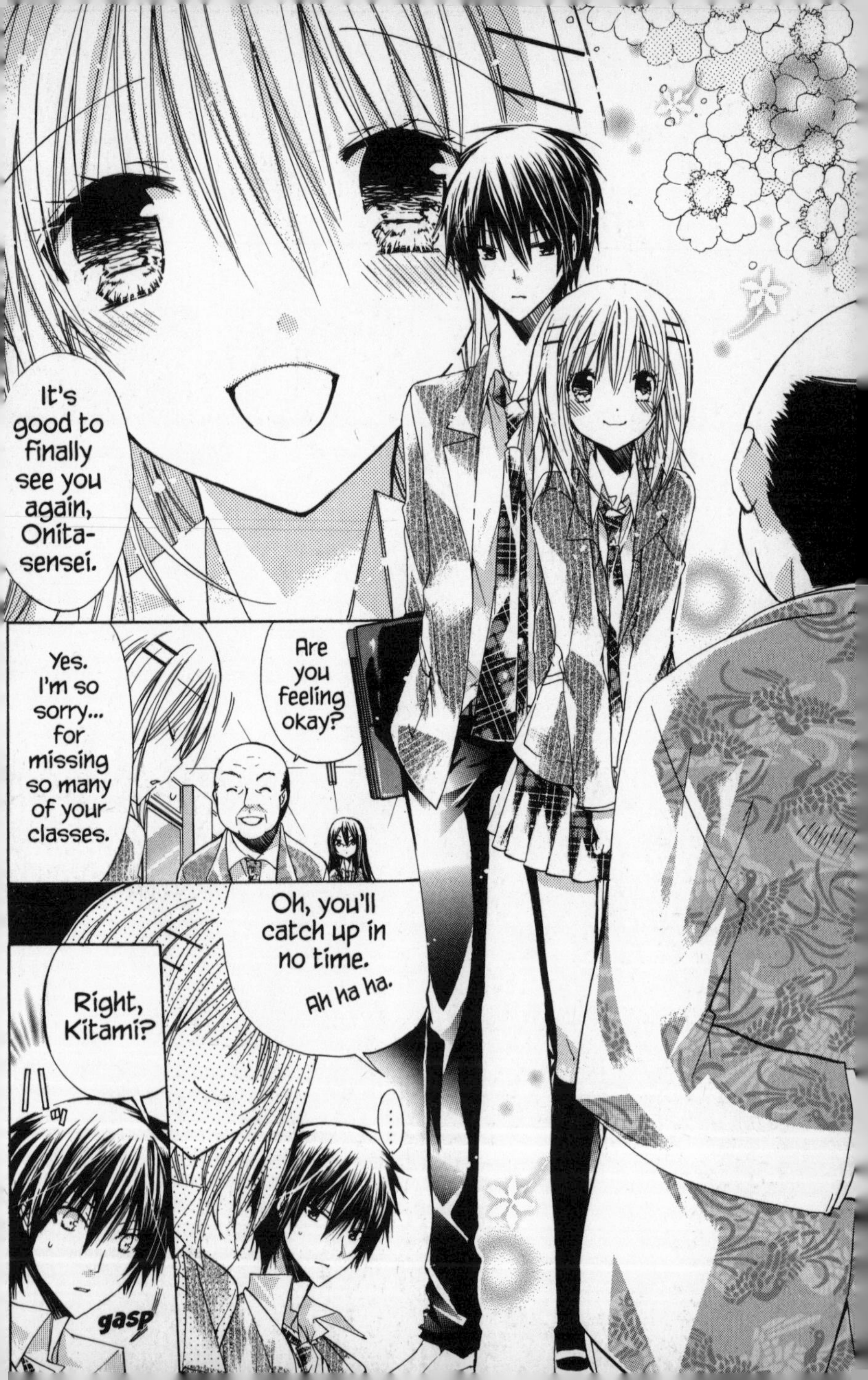
It's good to finally see you again, Onita-sensei.
Are you feeling okay?
Yes. I'm so sorry... for missing so many of your classes.
Oh, you'll catch up in no time.
Ah ha ha.
Right, Kitami?
...
gasp

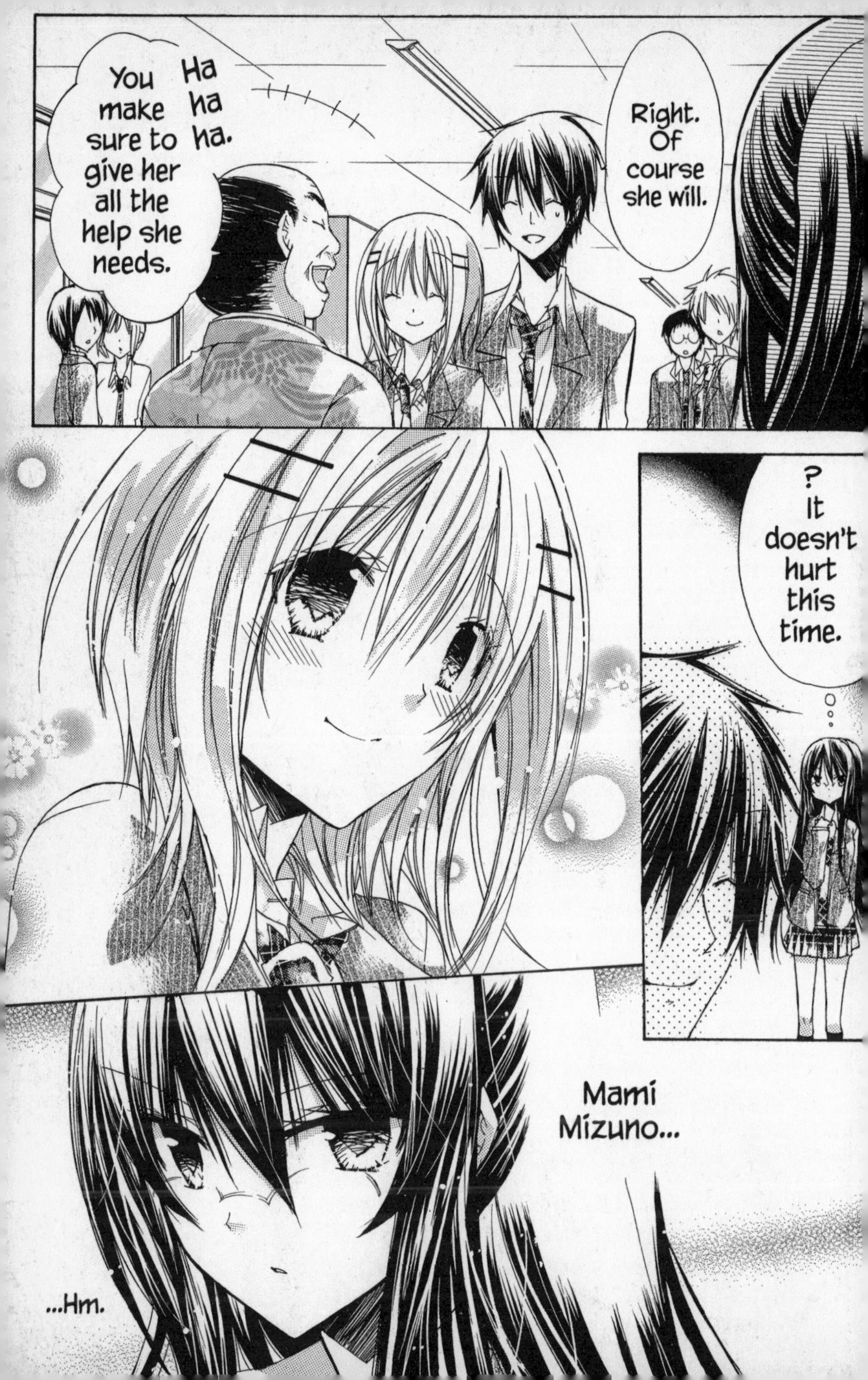
Right. Of course she will.
Ha ha ha.
You make sure to give her all the help she needs.
? It doesn't hurt this time.
Mami Mizuno...
...Hm.

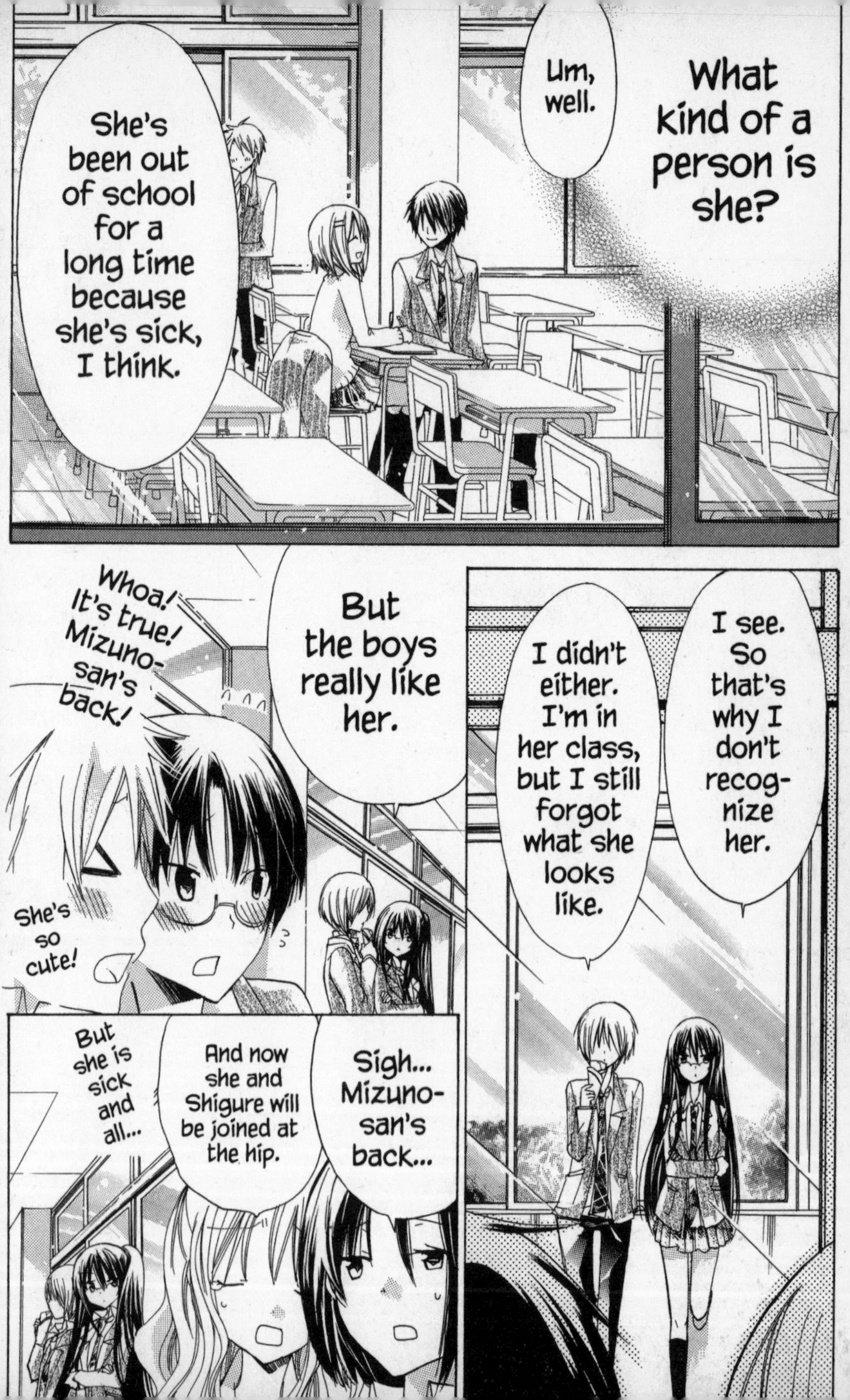
What kind of a person is she?
Um, well.
She's been out of school for a long time because she's sick, I think.
I see. So that's why I don't recognize her.
I didn't either. I'm in her class, but I still forgot what she looks like.
But the boys really like her.
Whoa! It's true! Mizuno-san's back!
She's so cute!
Sigh... Mizuno-san's back...
And now she and Shigure will be joined at the hip.
But she is sick and all...

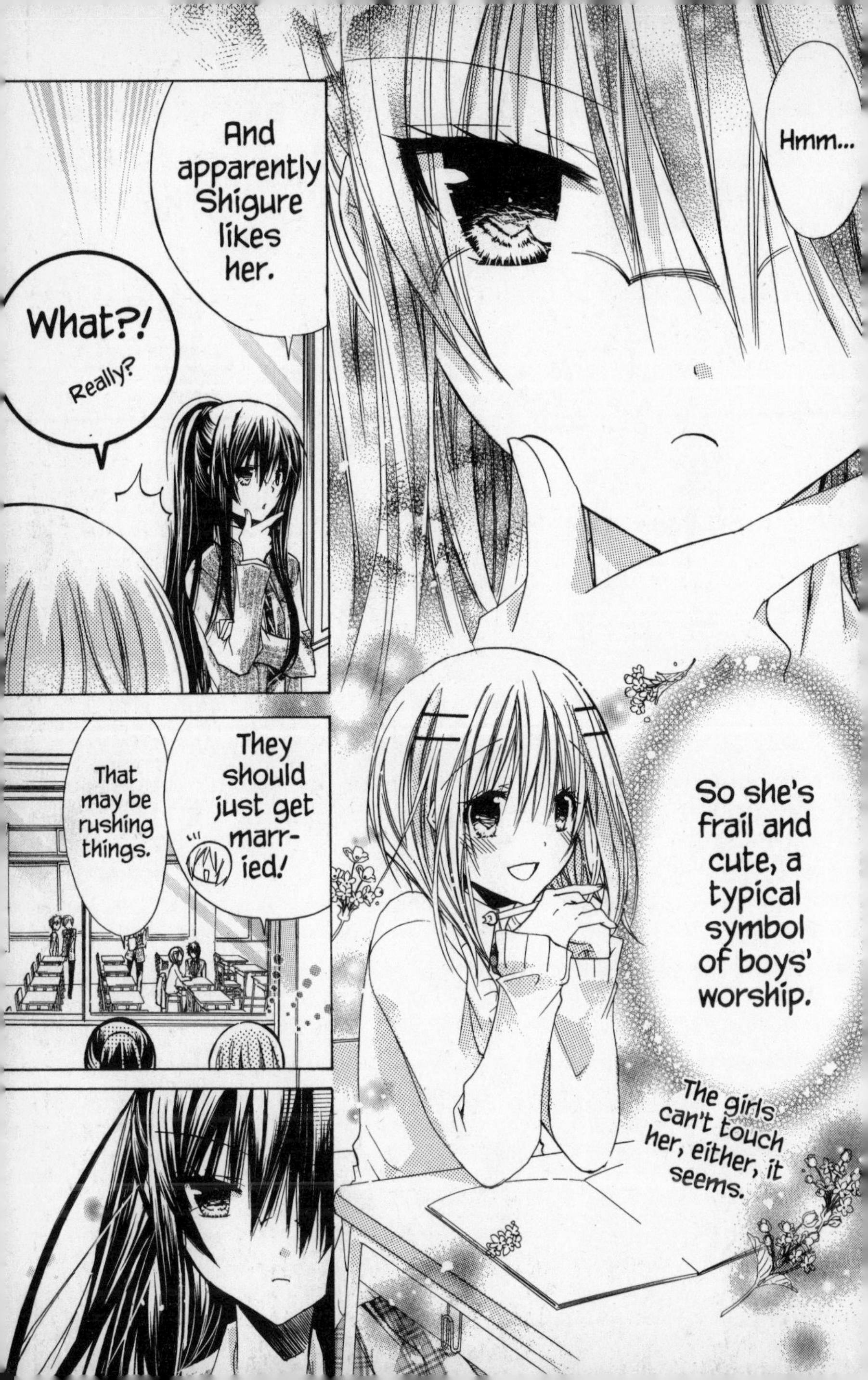
Hmm...
So she's frail and cute, a typical symbol of boys' worship.
The girls can't touch her, either, it seems.
And apparently Shigure likes her.
What?!
Really?
They should just get marr-ied!
That may be rushing things.

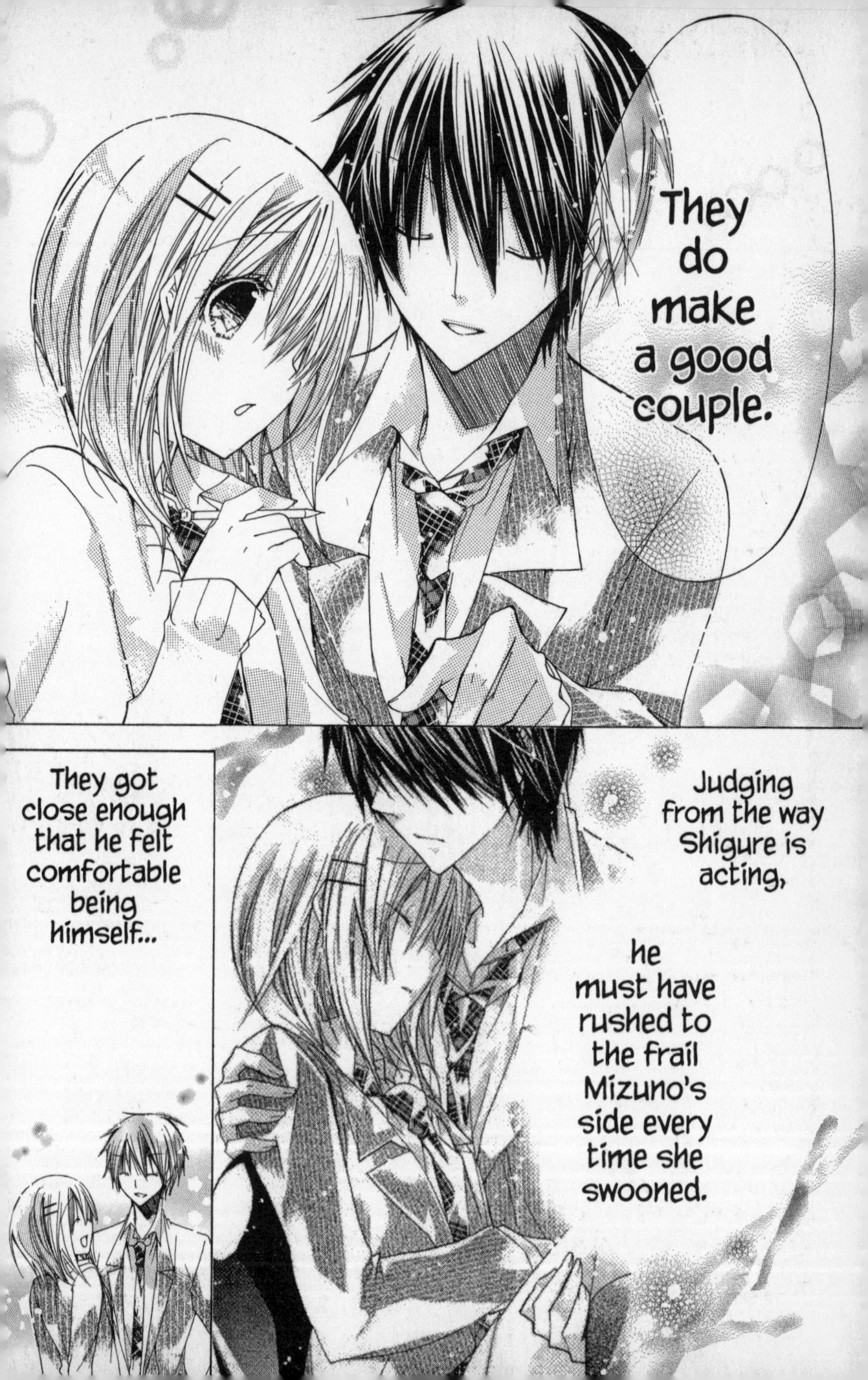
They do make a good couple.
Judging from the way Shigure is acting,
he must have rushed to the frail Mizuno's side every time she swooned.
They got close enough that he felt comfortable being himself...

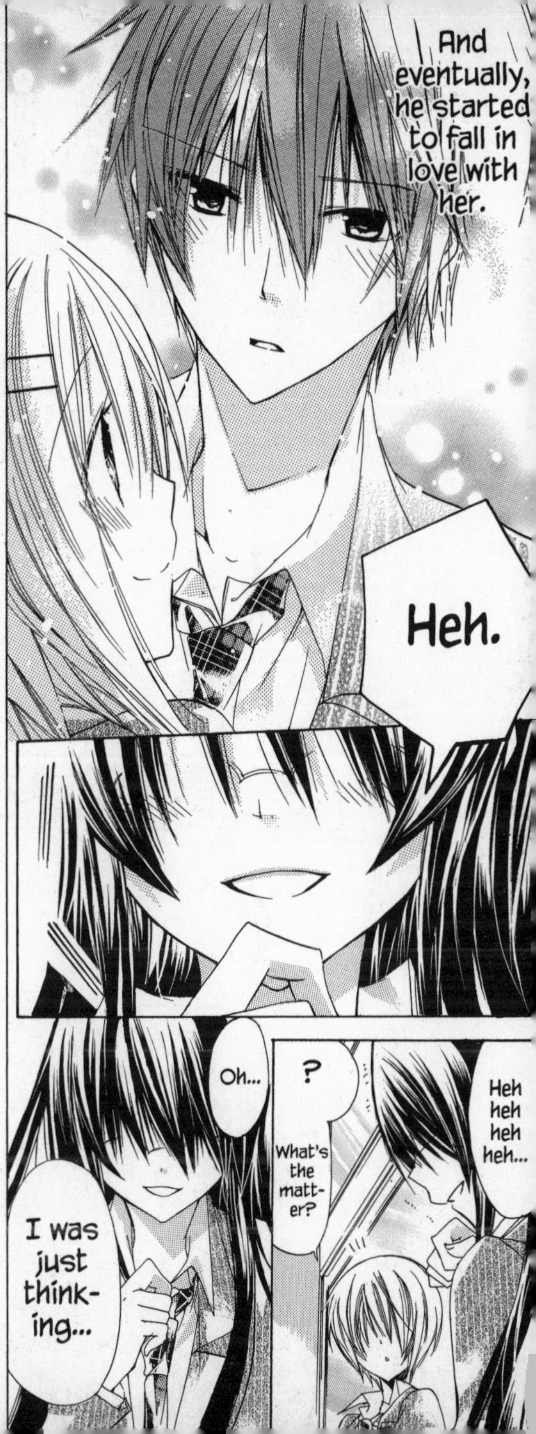
And eventually, he started to fall in love with her.
Heh.
Heh heh heh heh...
?
What's the matter?
Oh...
I was just think-ing...

Snow Yukina 4

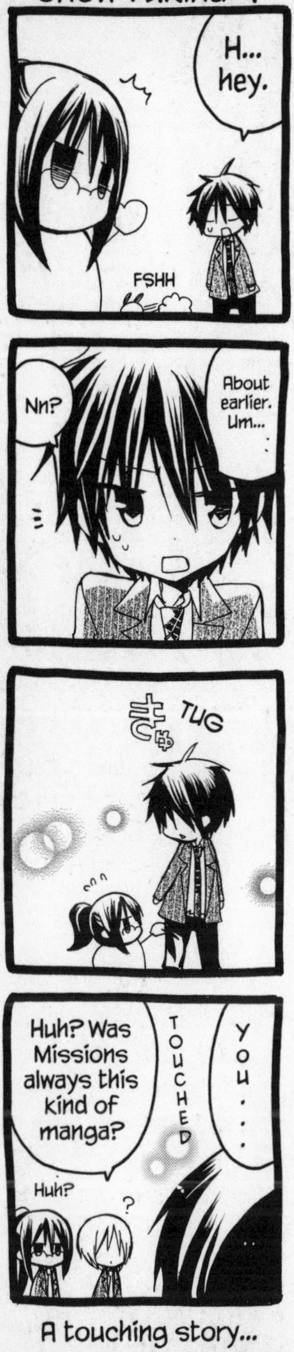
H... hey.
FSHH
About earlier. Um...
Nn?
TUG
You...
TOUCHED
Huh? Was Missions always this kind of manga?
Huh?
?

A touching story...

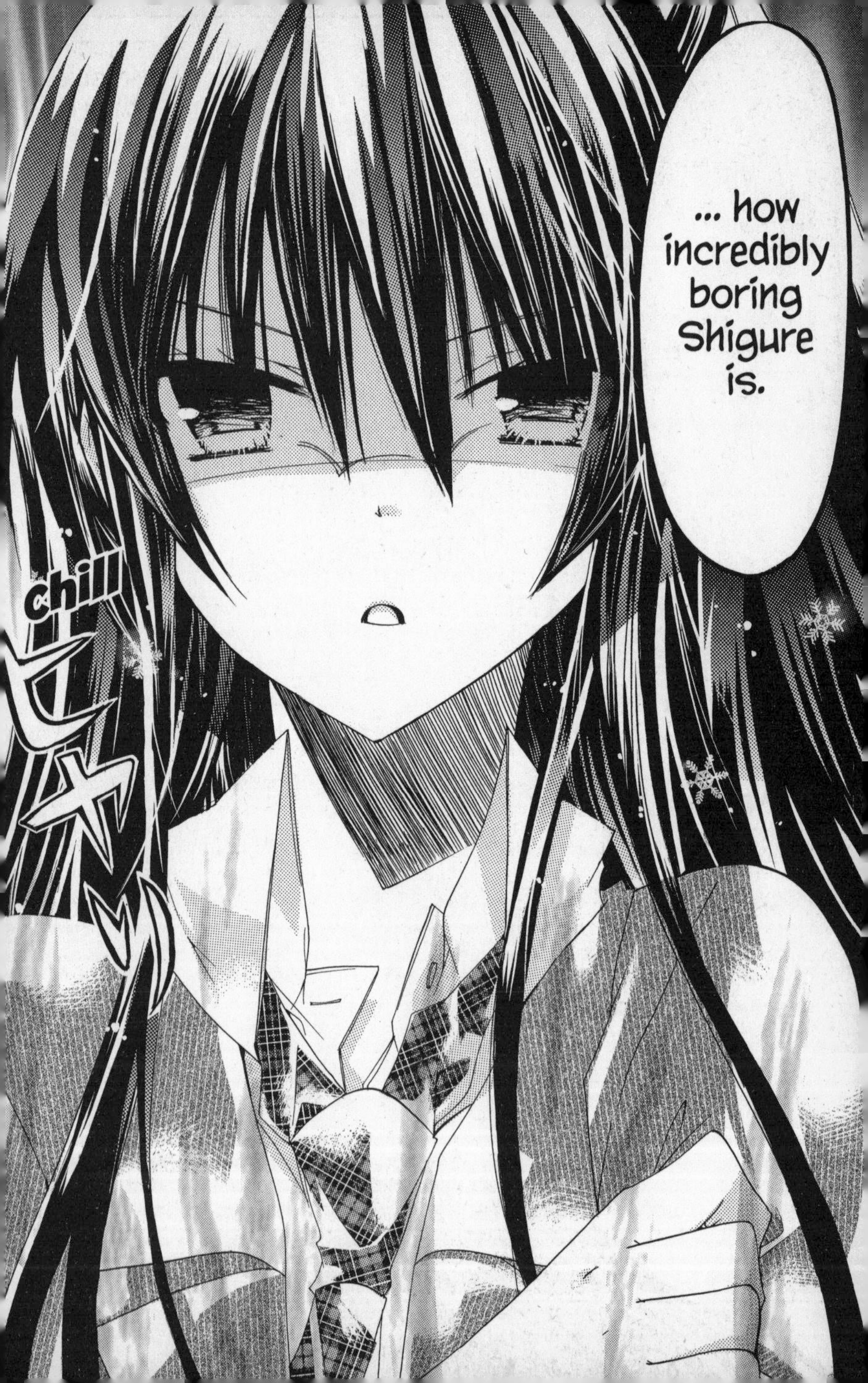
... how incredibly boring Shigure is.
Chill

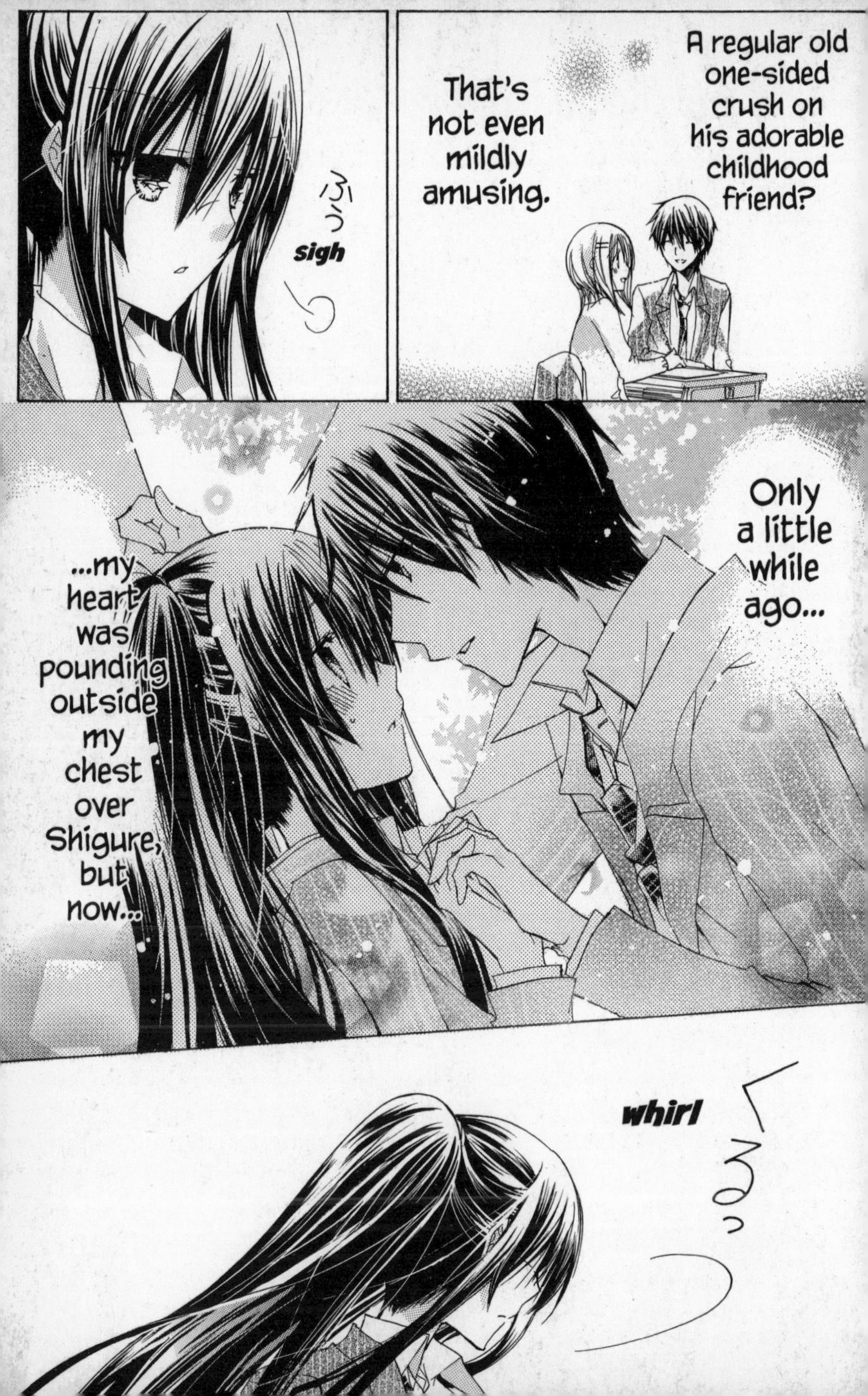
A regular old one-sided crush on his adorable childhood friend?
That's not even mildly amusing.
ふう
sigh
Only a little while ago...
...my heart was pounding outside my chest over Shigure, but now...
くるっ
whirl

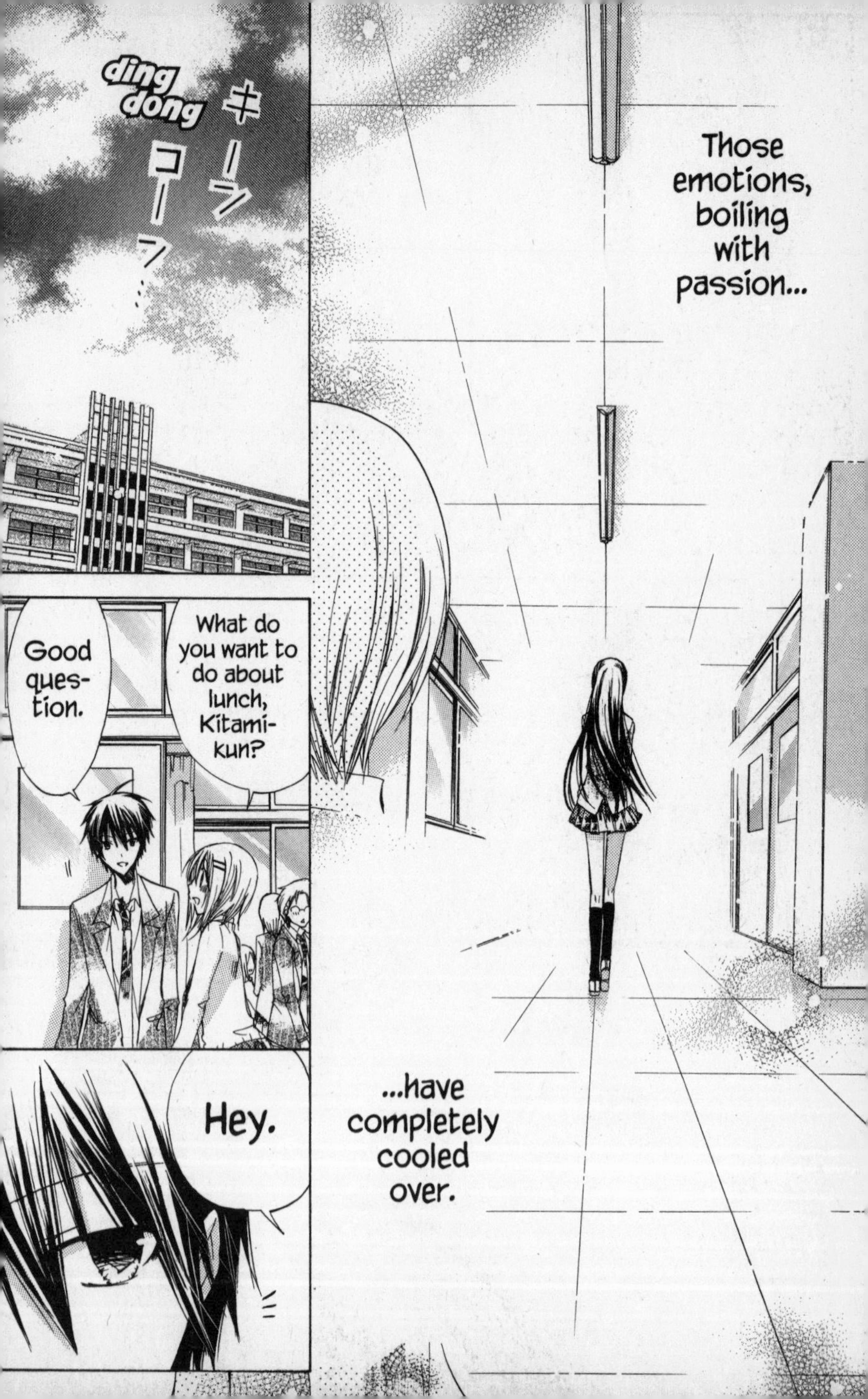
Those emotions, boiling with passion...
...have completely cooled over.
ding dong
キーンコーン…
What do you want to do about lunch, Kitami-kun?
Good question.
Hey.

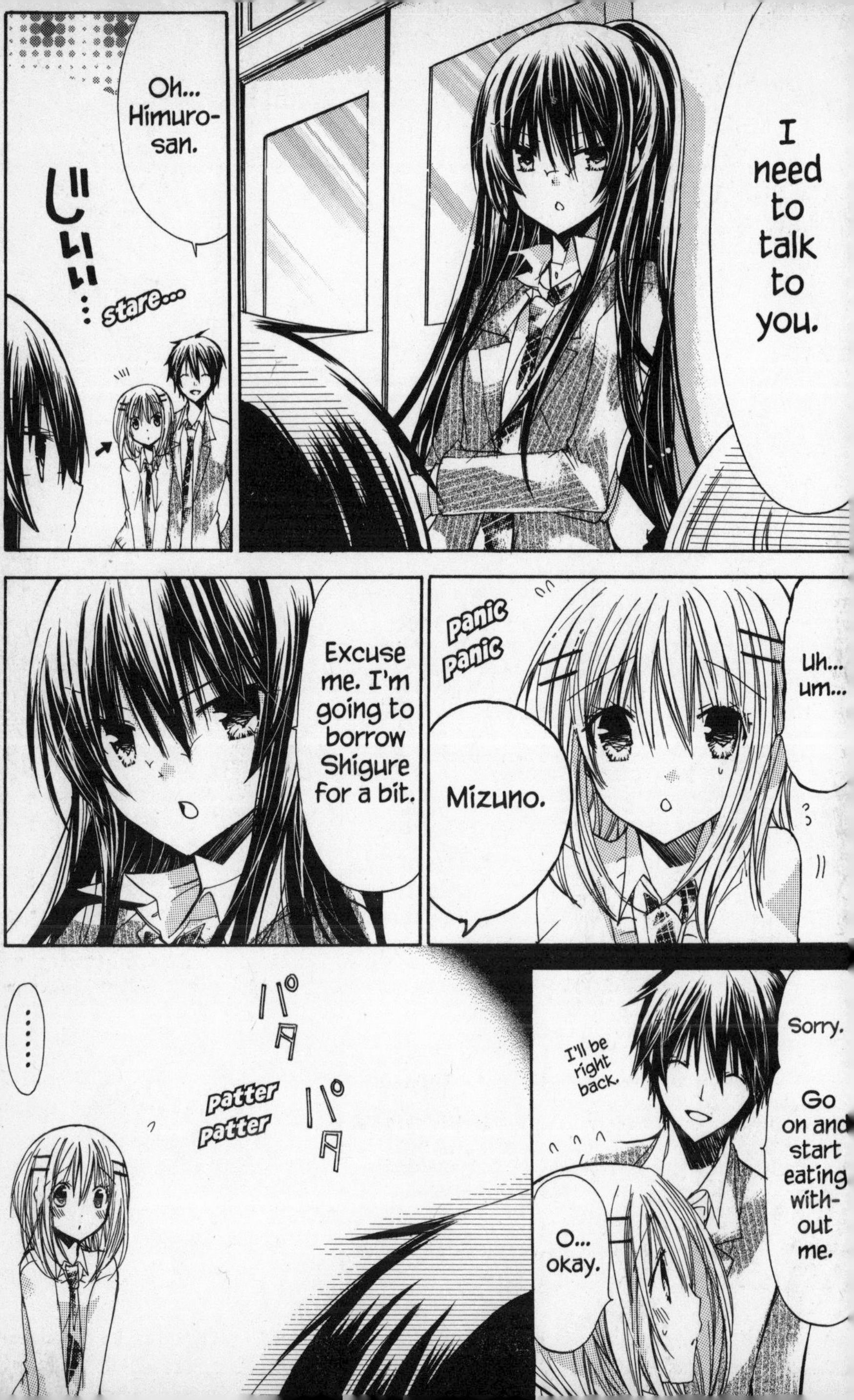
I need to talk to you.
Oh... Himuro-san.
じぃぃ…
stare...
uh... um...
Panic Panic
Mizuno.
Excuse me. I'm going to borrow Shigure for a bit.
Sorry.
Go on and start eating with-out me.
I'll be right back.
O... okay.
......
パタ パタ
patter patter

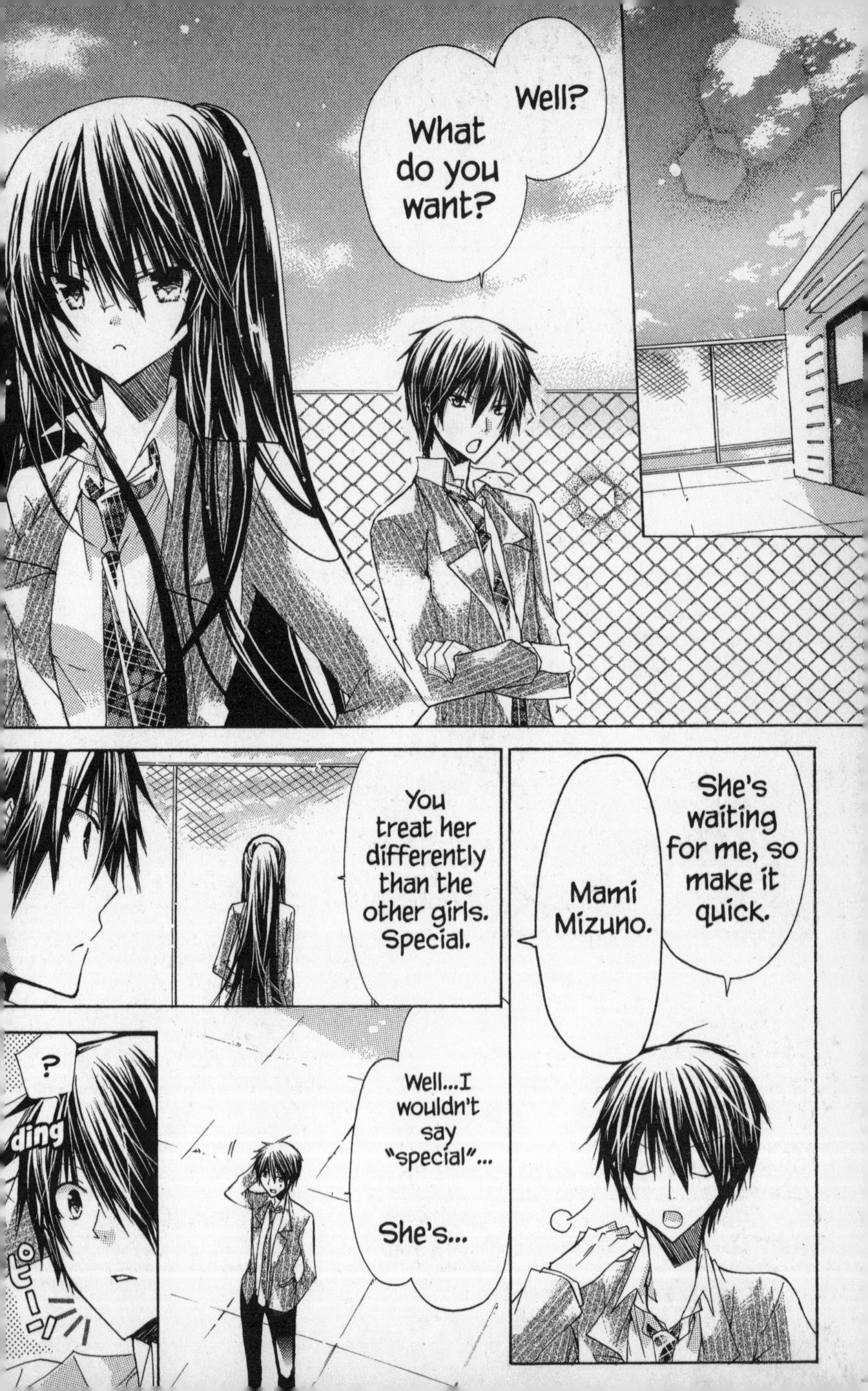

Well? What do you want?
She's waiting for me, so make it quick.
Mami Mizuno.
You treat her differently than the other girls. Special.
Well...I wouldn't say "special"...
She's...
?
ding
ピーー!

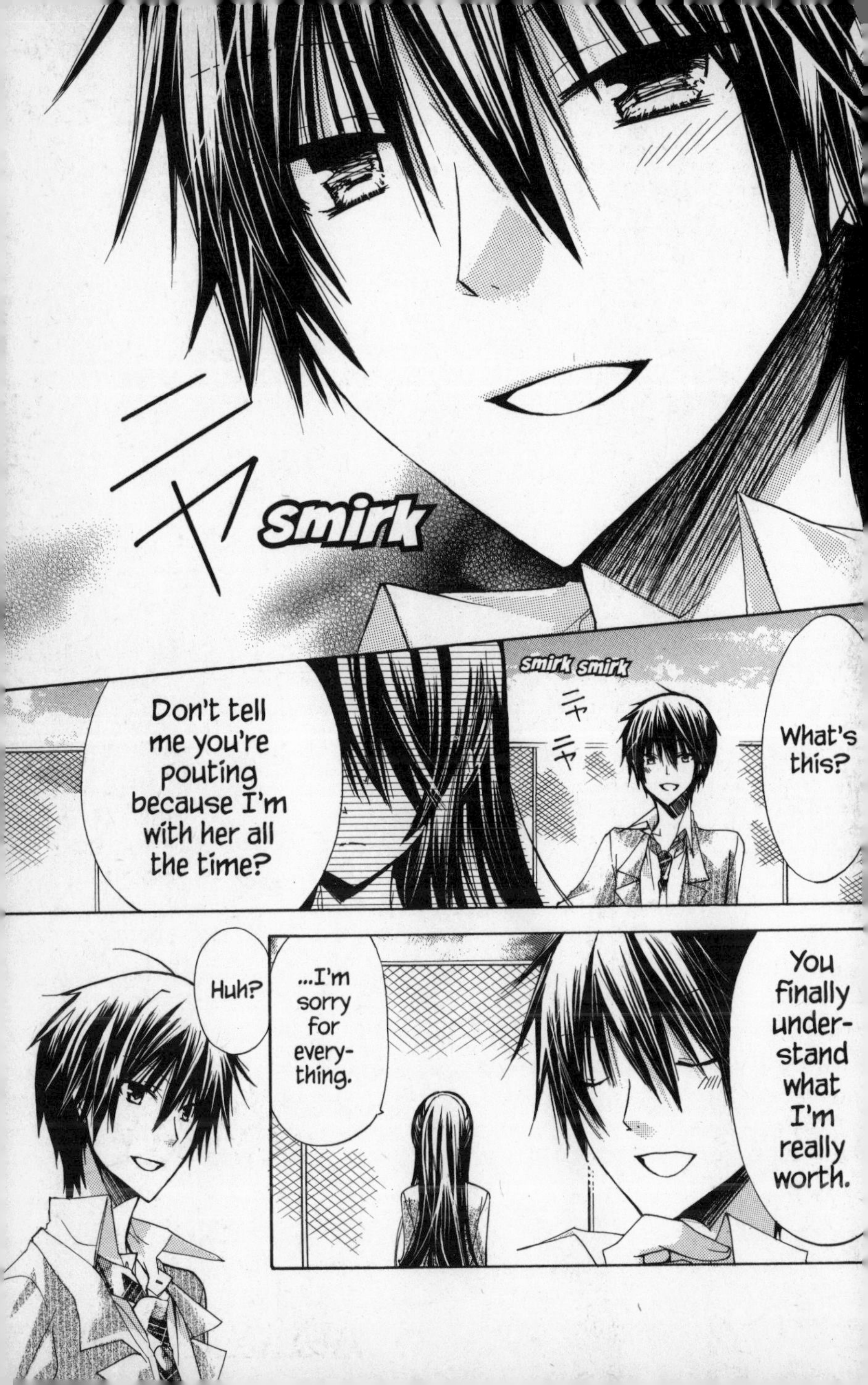
ニヤ
smirk
What's this?
smirk smirk
ニヤニヤ
Don't tell me you're pouting because I'm with her all the time?
You finally under-stand what I'm really worth.
...I'm sorry for everything.
Huh?

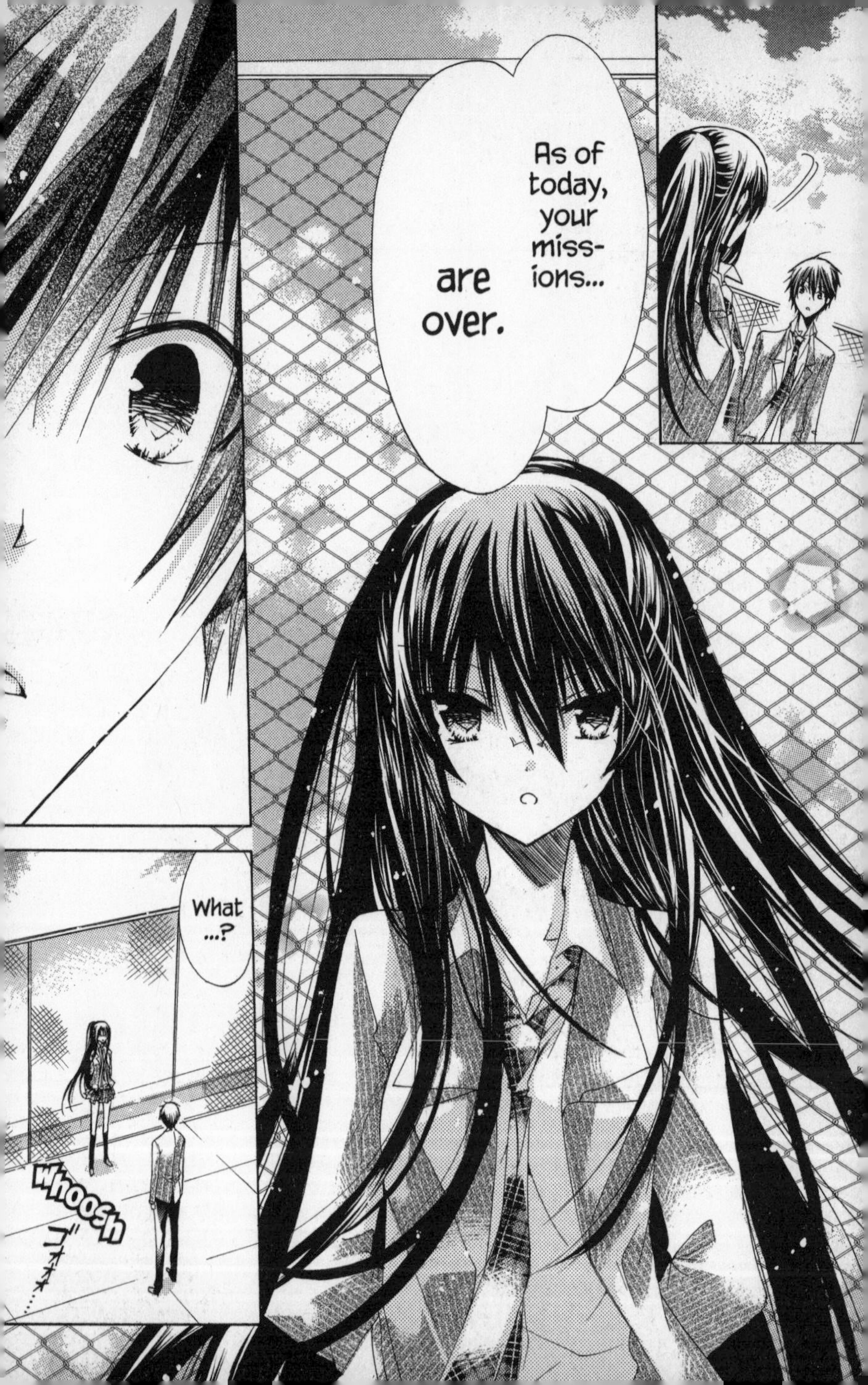
As of today, your missions...
are over.
What ...?
Whoosh
ゴオオオ…

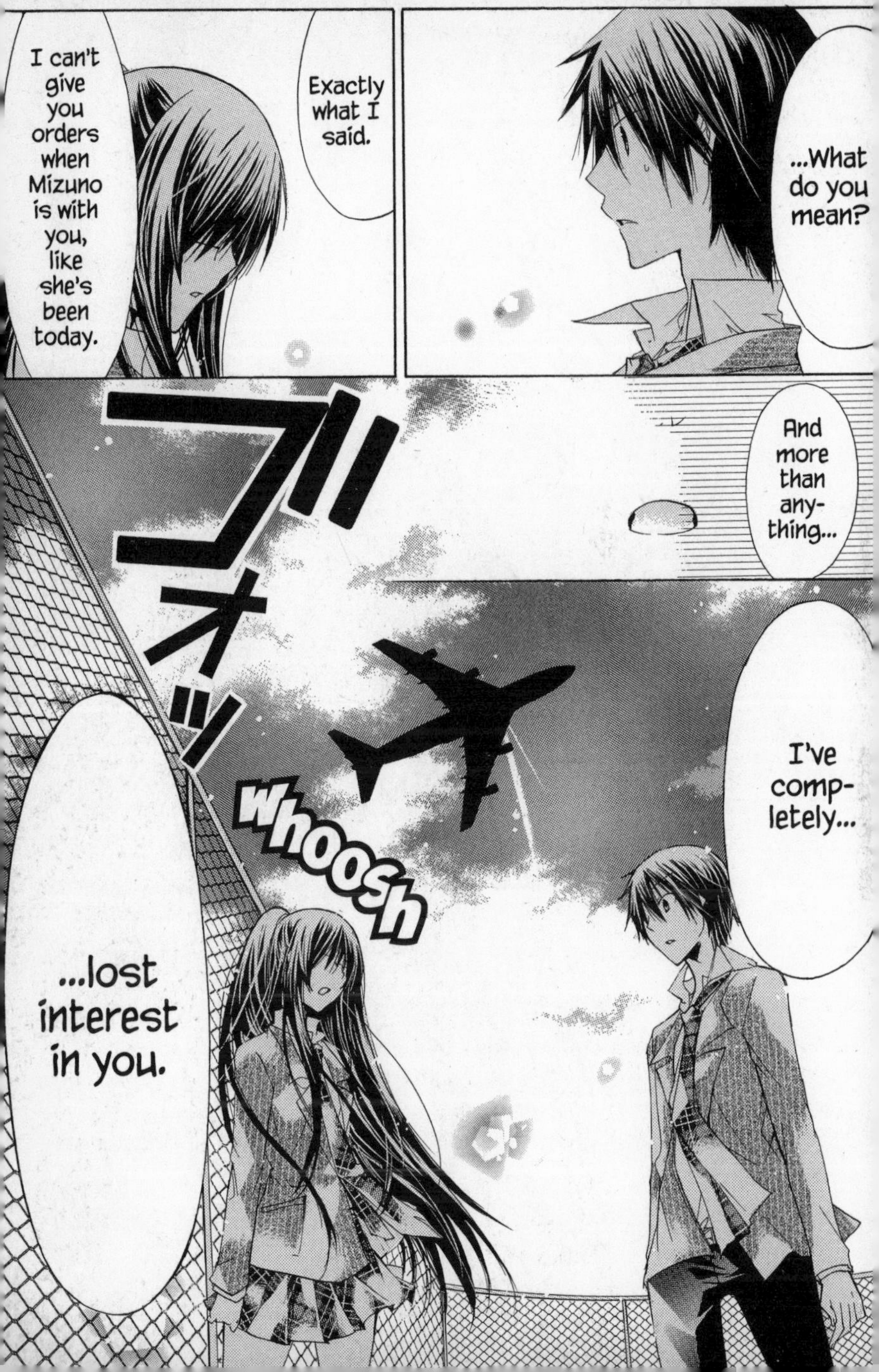
...What do you mean?
Exactly what I said.
I can't give you orders when Mizuno is with you, like she's been today.
And more than anything...
ブオッ
I've completely...
Whoosh
...lost interest in you.

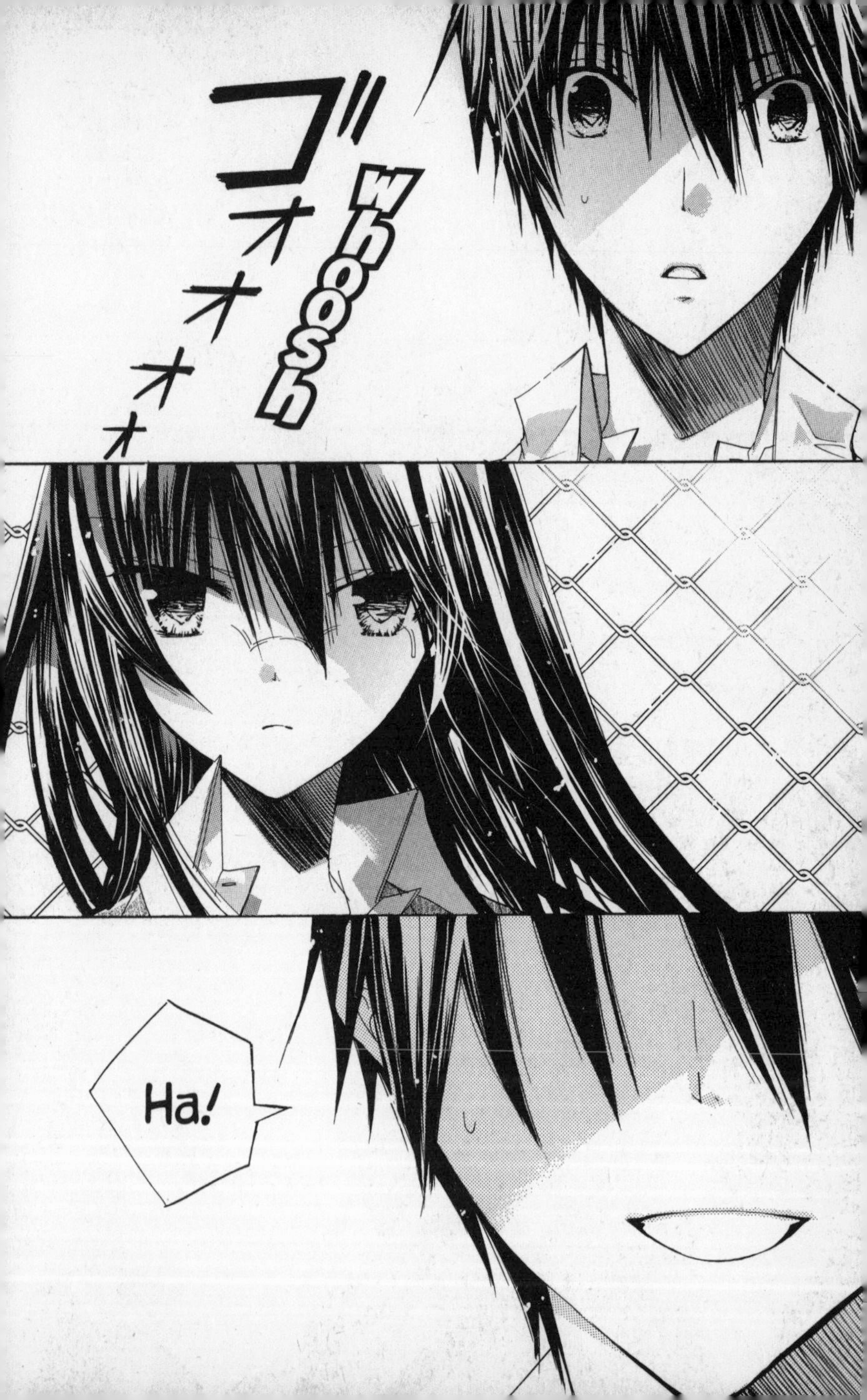
ゴオオオオ
whoosh
Ha!

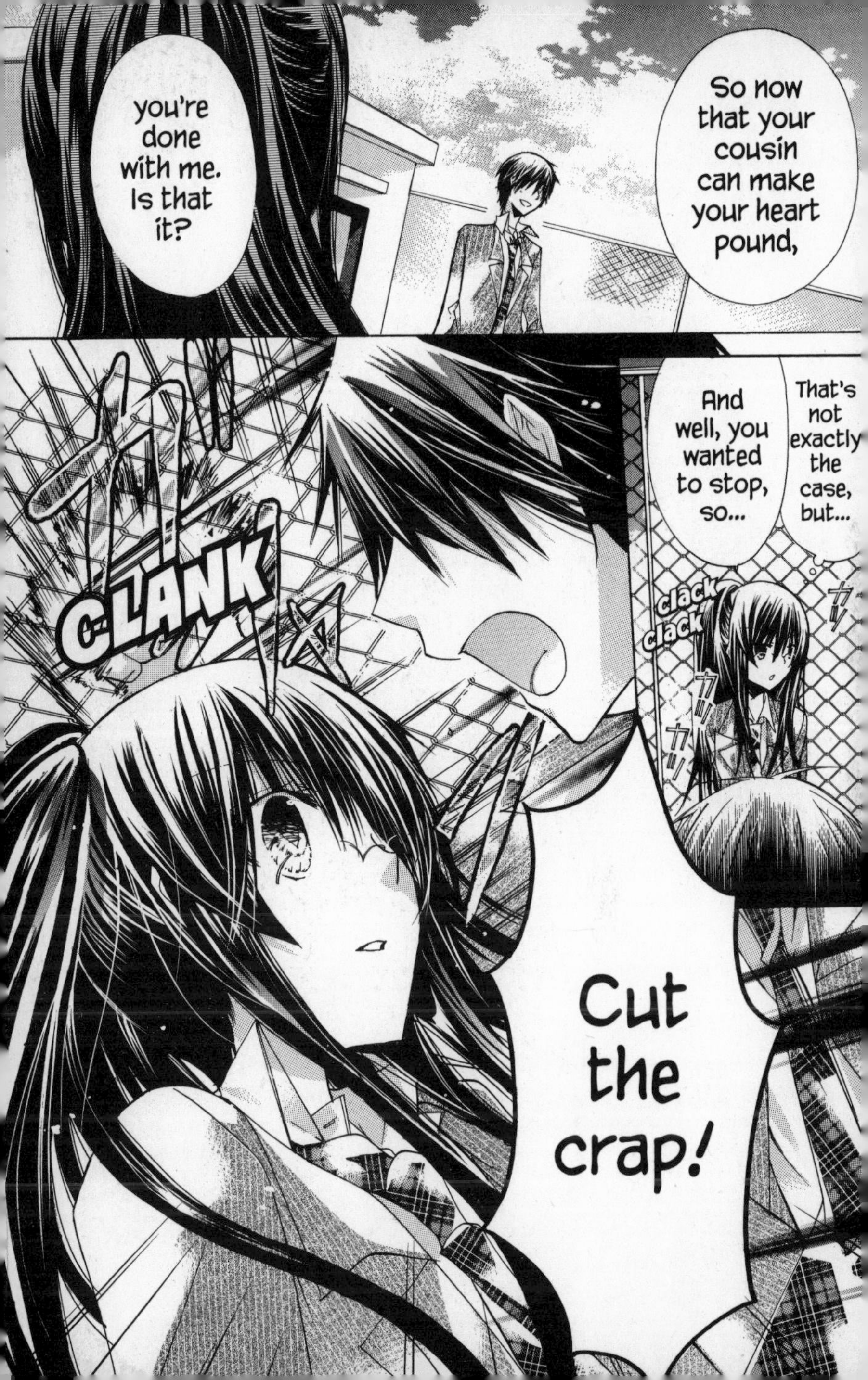
So now that your cousin can make your heart pound,
you're done with me. Is that it?
That's not exactly the case, but...
And well, you wanted to stop, so...
clack clack
CLANK
Cut the crap!

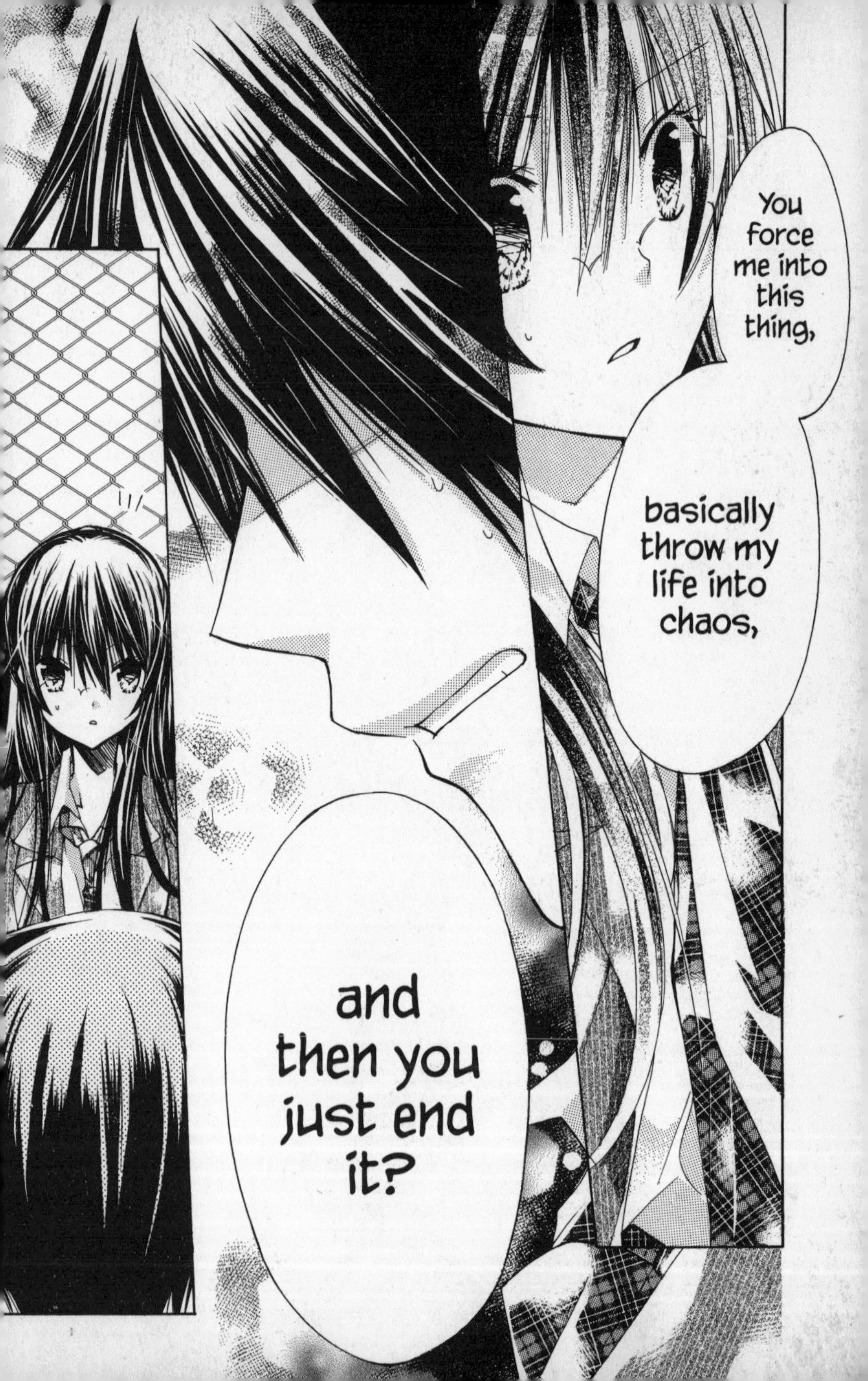
You force me into this thing,
basically throw my life into chaos,
and then you just end it?

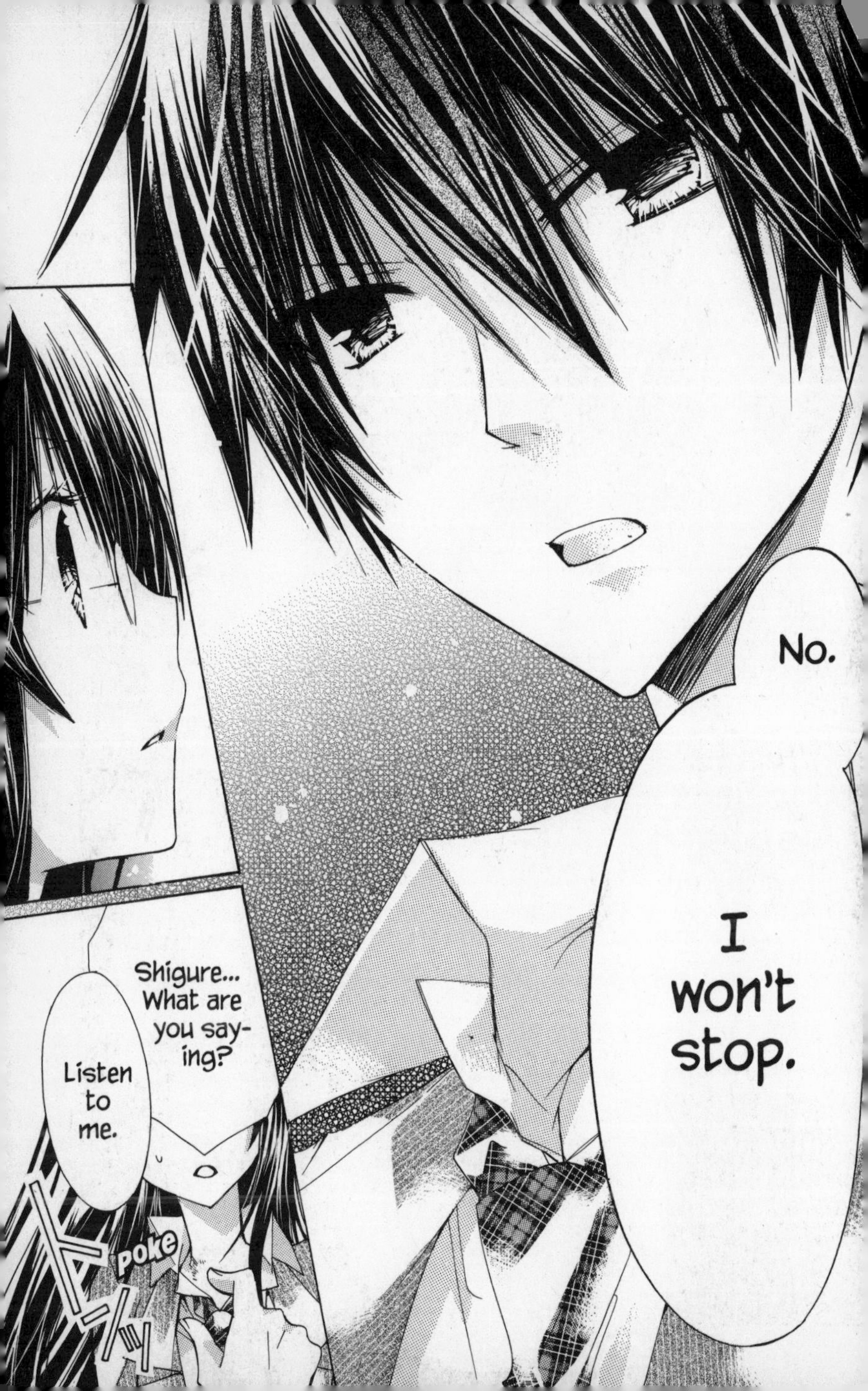
No.
I won't stop.
Shigure... What are you saying?
Listen to me.
poke

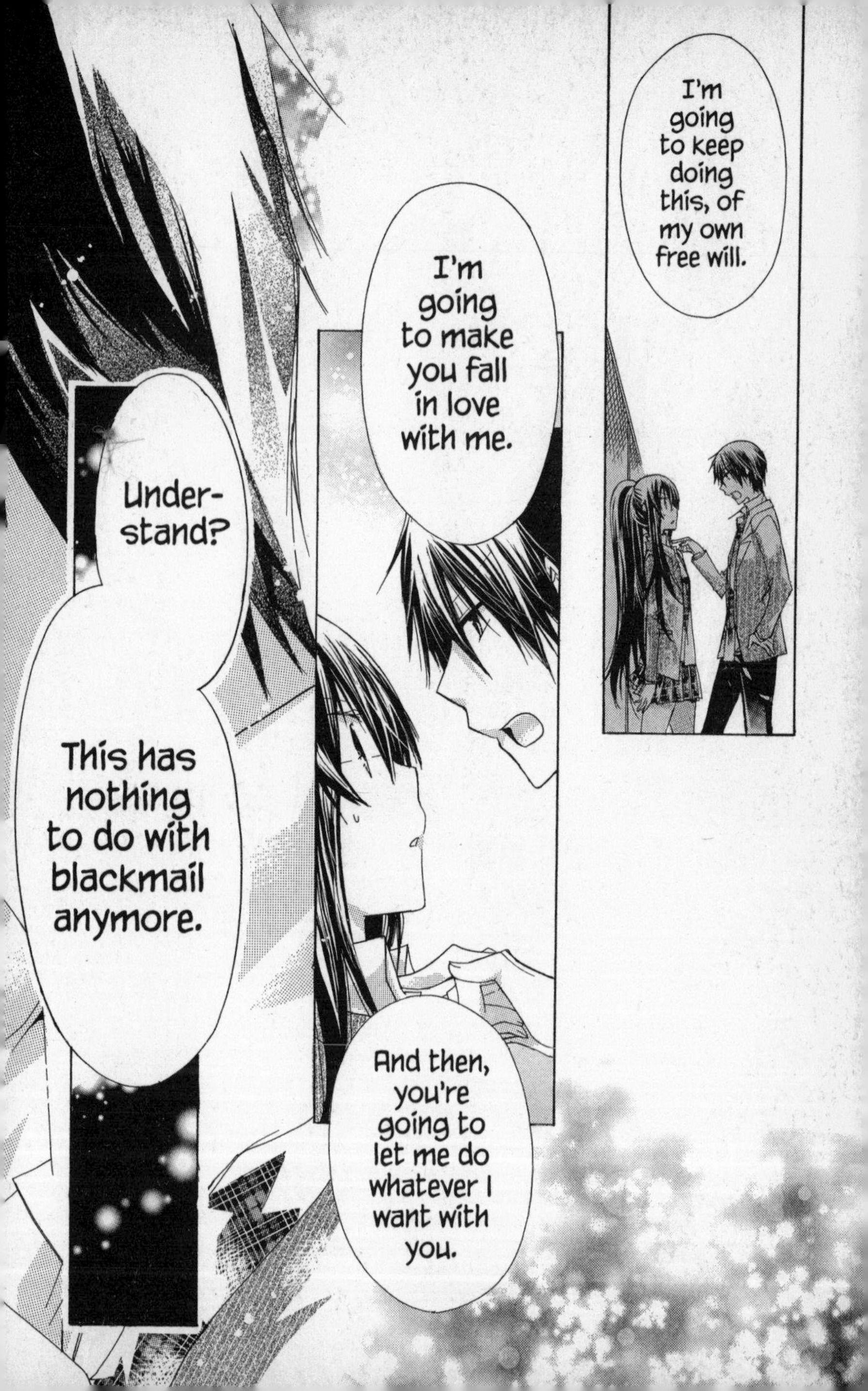
I'm going to keep doing this, of my own free will.
I'm going to make you fall in love with me.
And then, you're going to let me do whatever I want with you.
Understand?
This has nothing to do with blackmail anymore.

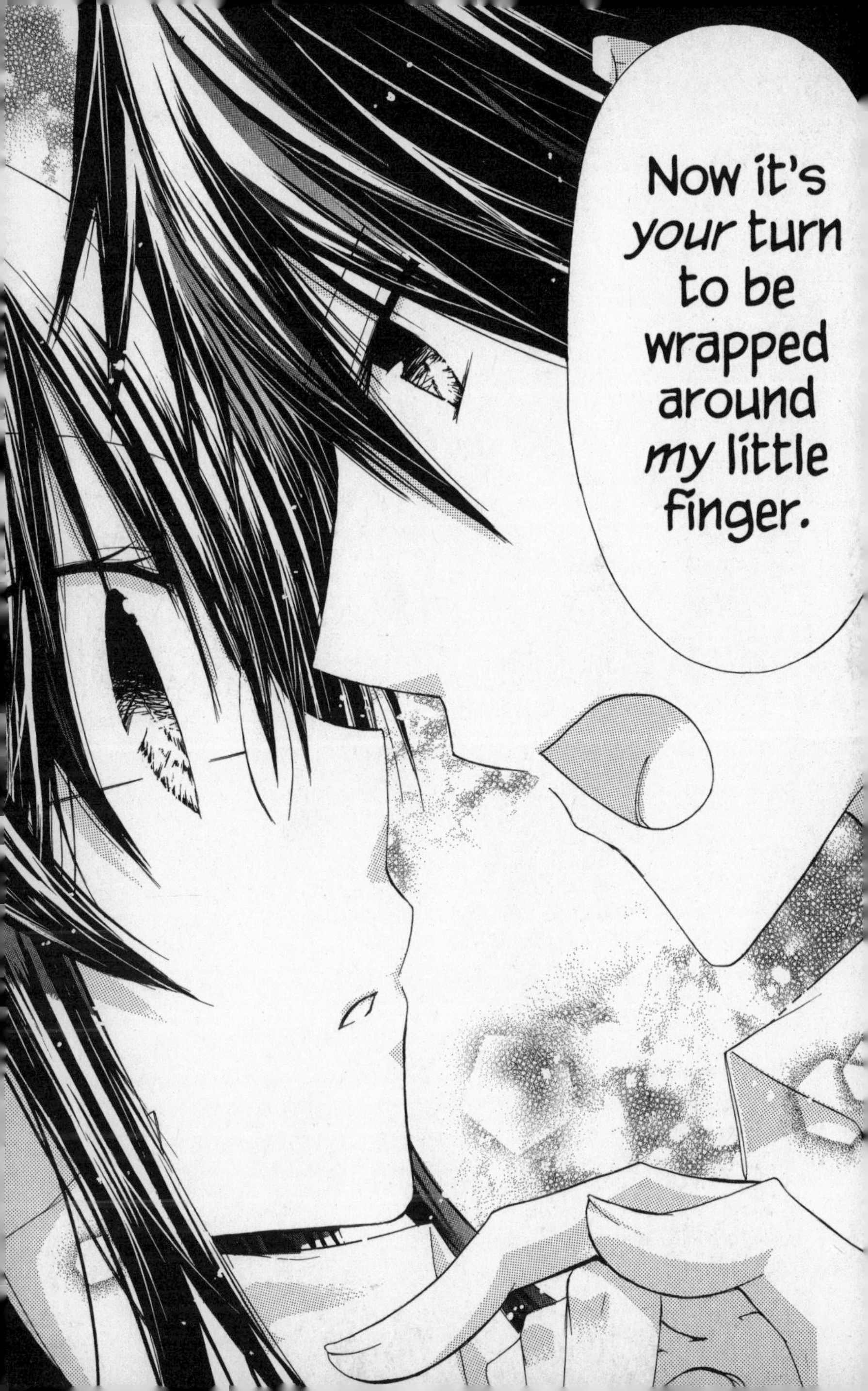
Now it's *your* turn to be wrapped around *my* little finger.

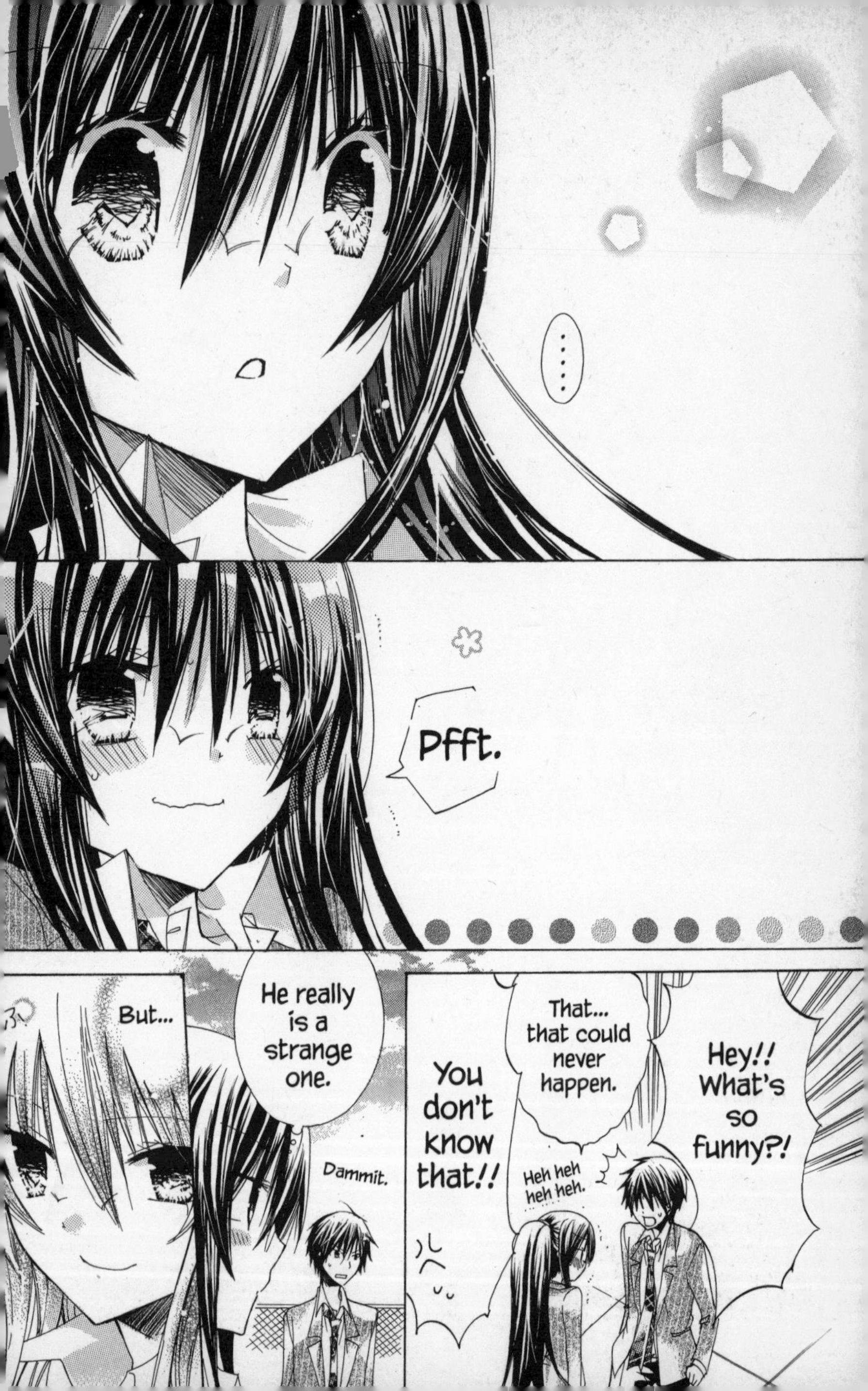
......
Pfft.
Hey!! What's so funny?!
That... that could never happen.
You don't know that!!
Heh heh heh heh.
He really is a strange one.
But...
Dammit.

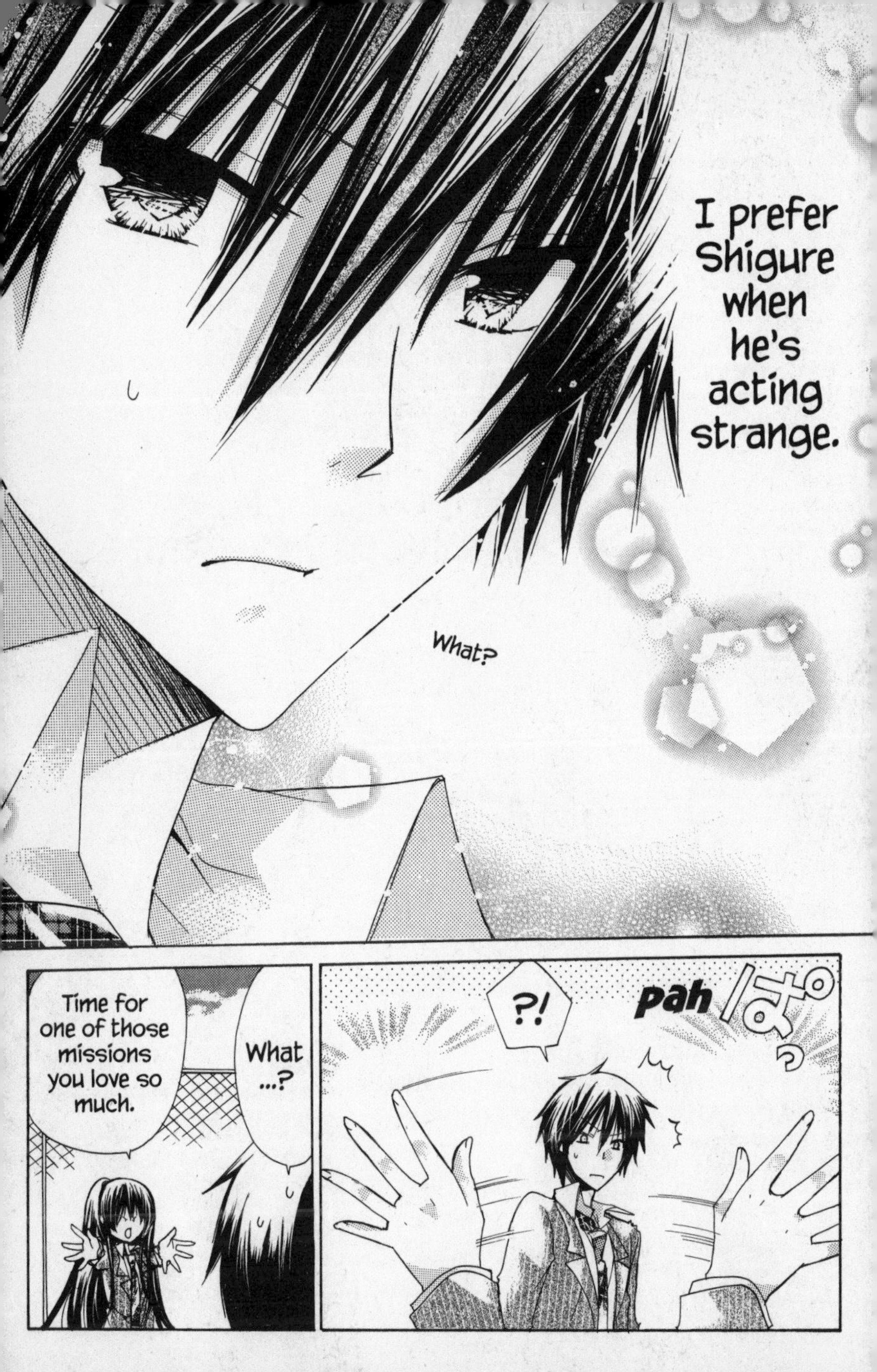
I prefer Shigure when he's acting strange.
What?
pah ぱっ
?!
What ...?
Time for one of those missions you love so much.

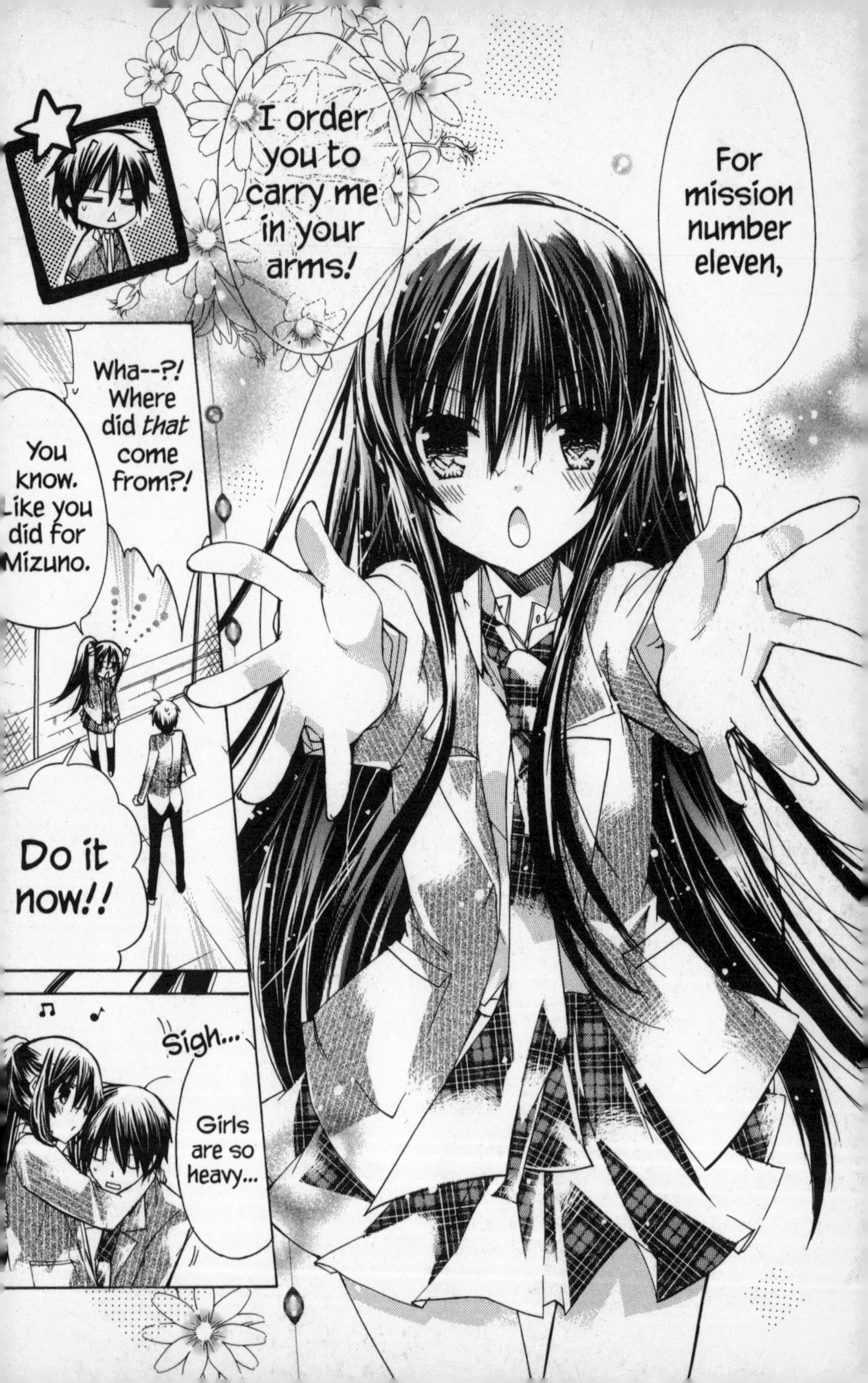
For mission number eleven,
I order you to carry me in your arms!
Wha--?! Where did *that* come from?!
You know. Like you did for Mizuno.
Do it now!!
Sigh...
Girls are so heavy...

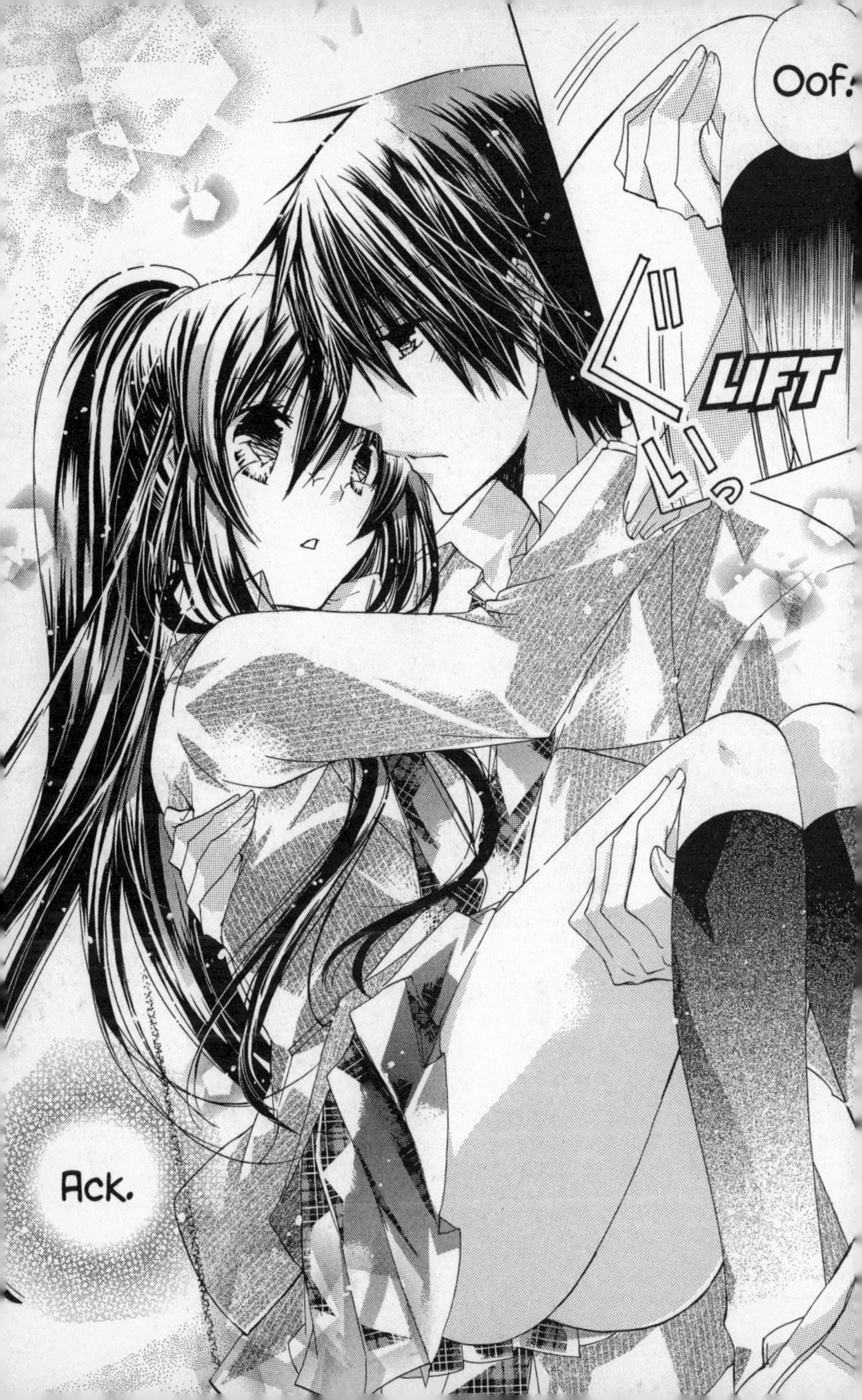
Oof!
LIFT
Ack.

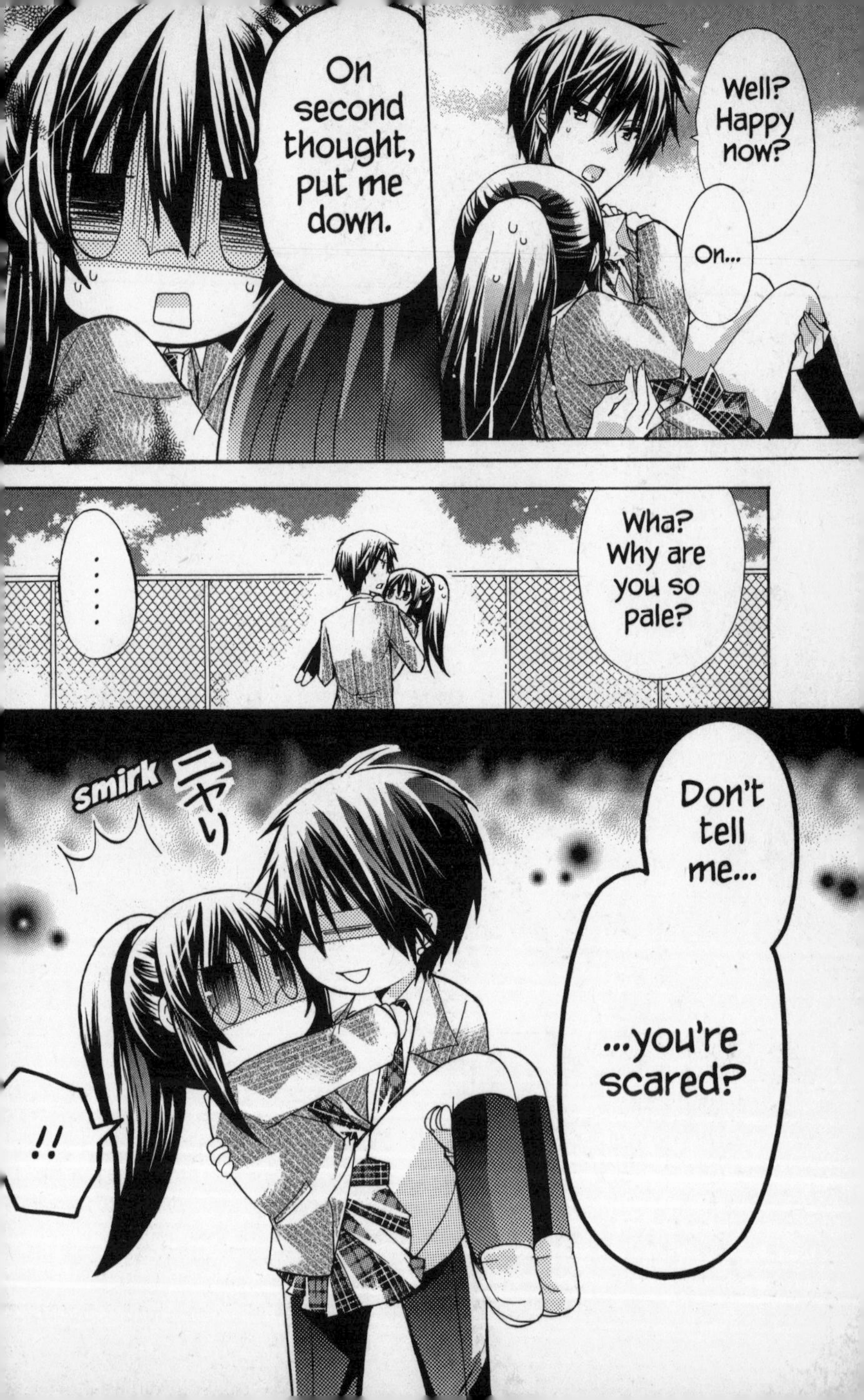

Well? Happy now?
On...
On second thought, put me down.
Wha? Why are you so pale?
.....
Don't tell me...
...you're scared?
smirk
ニヤリ
!!

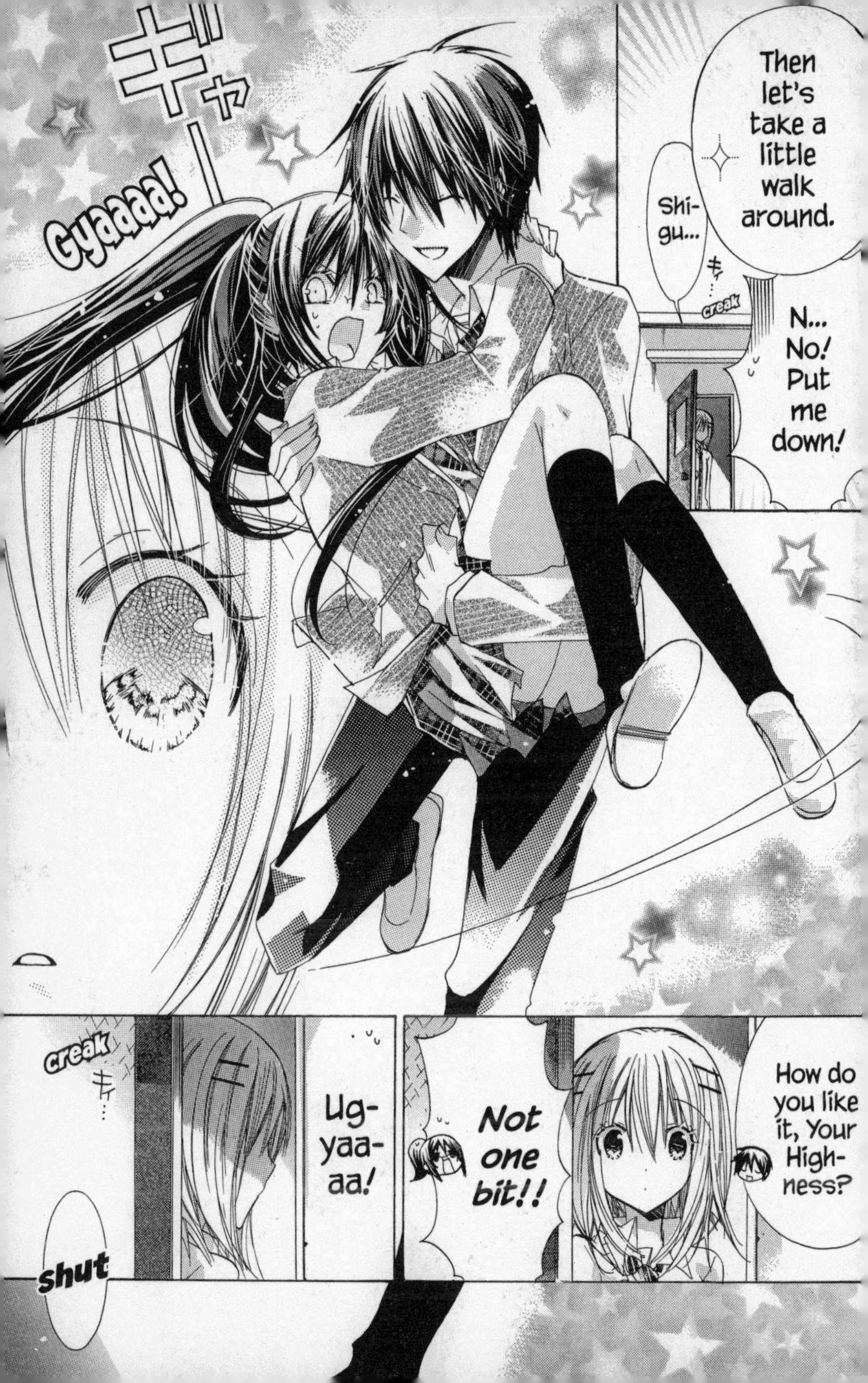
Then let's take a little walk around.
Shi-gu...
キィ…
creak
N... No! Put me down!
ギャー
Gyaaaa!
How do you like it, Your Highness?
Not one bit!!
Ug-yaa-aa!
creak
キィ…
shut

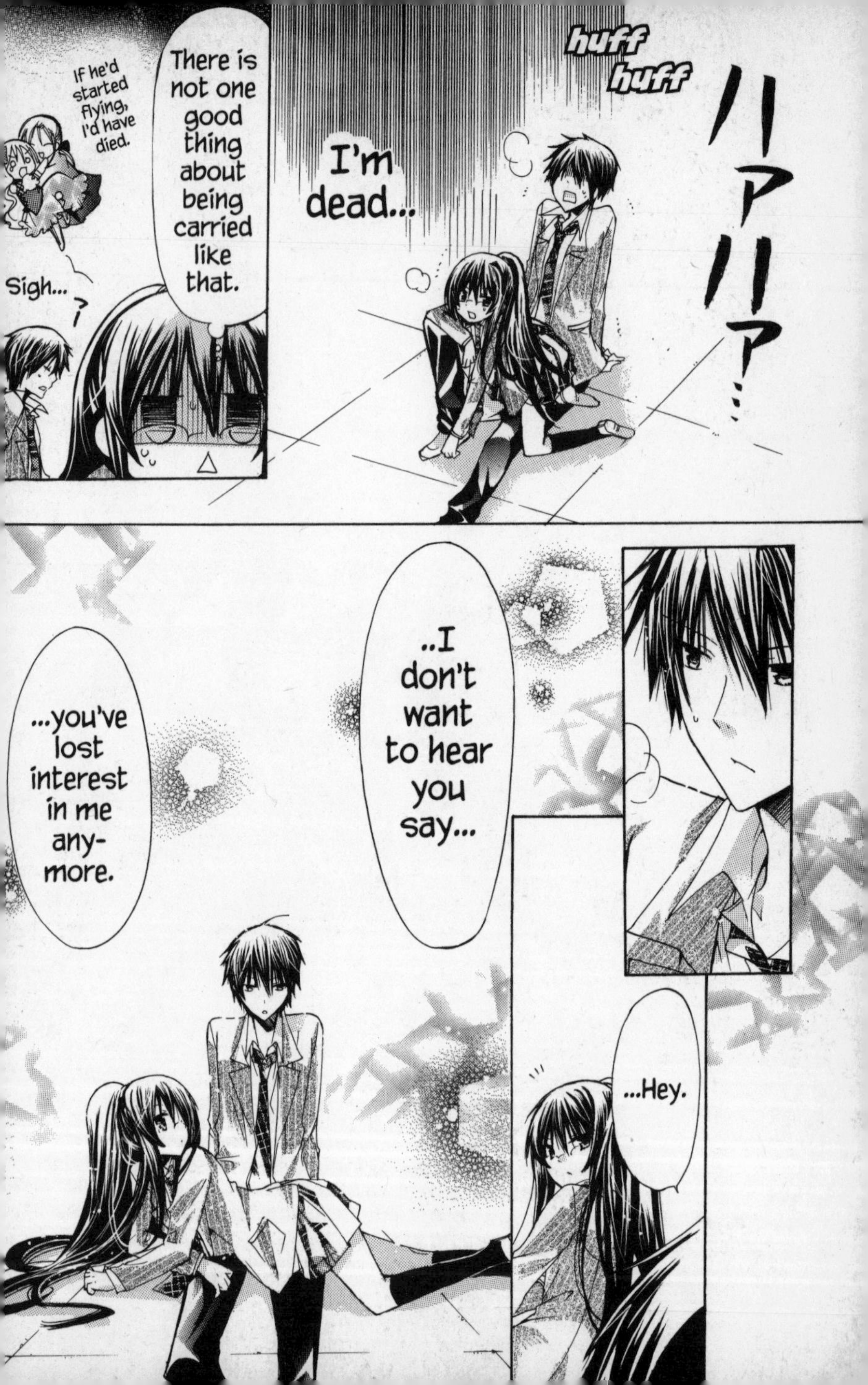
huff huff
ハァハァ…
I'm dead...
There is not one good thing about being carried like that.
If he'd started flying, I'd have died.
Sigh...
?
...Hey.
..I don't want to hear you say...
...you've lost interest in me anymore.

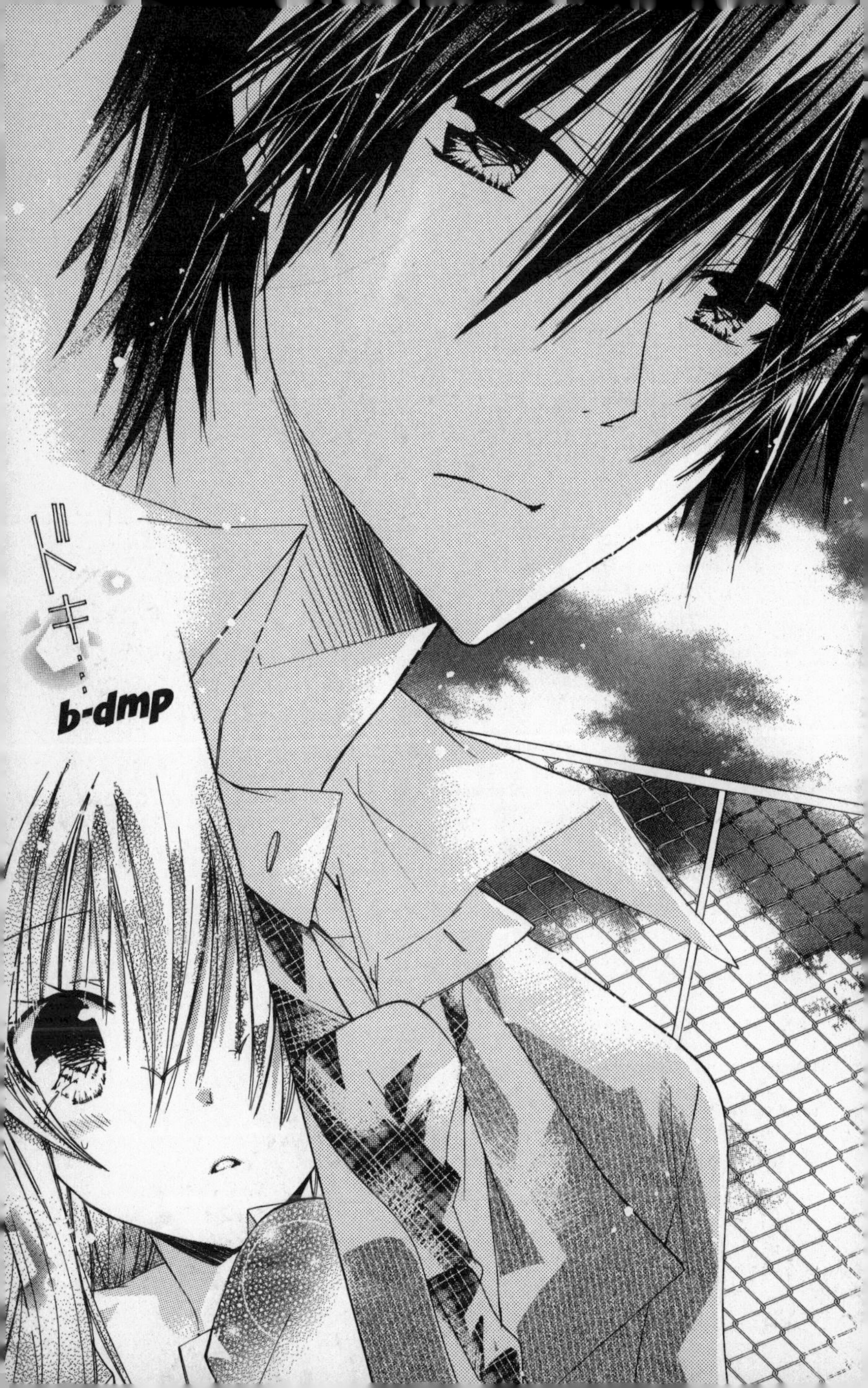
ドキ...
b-dmp

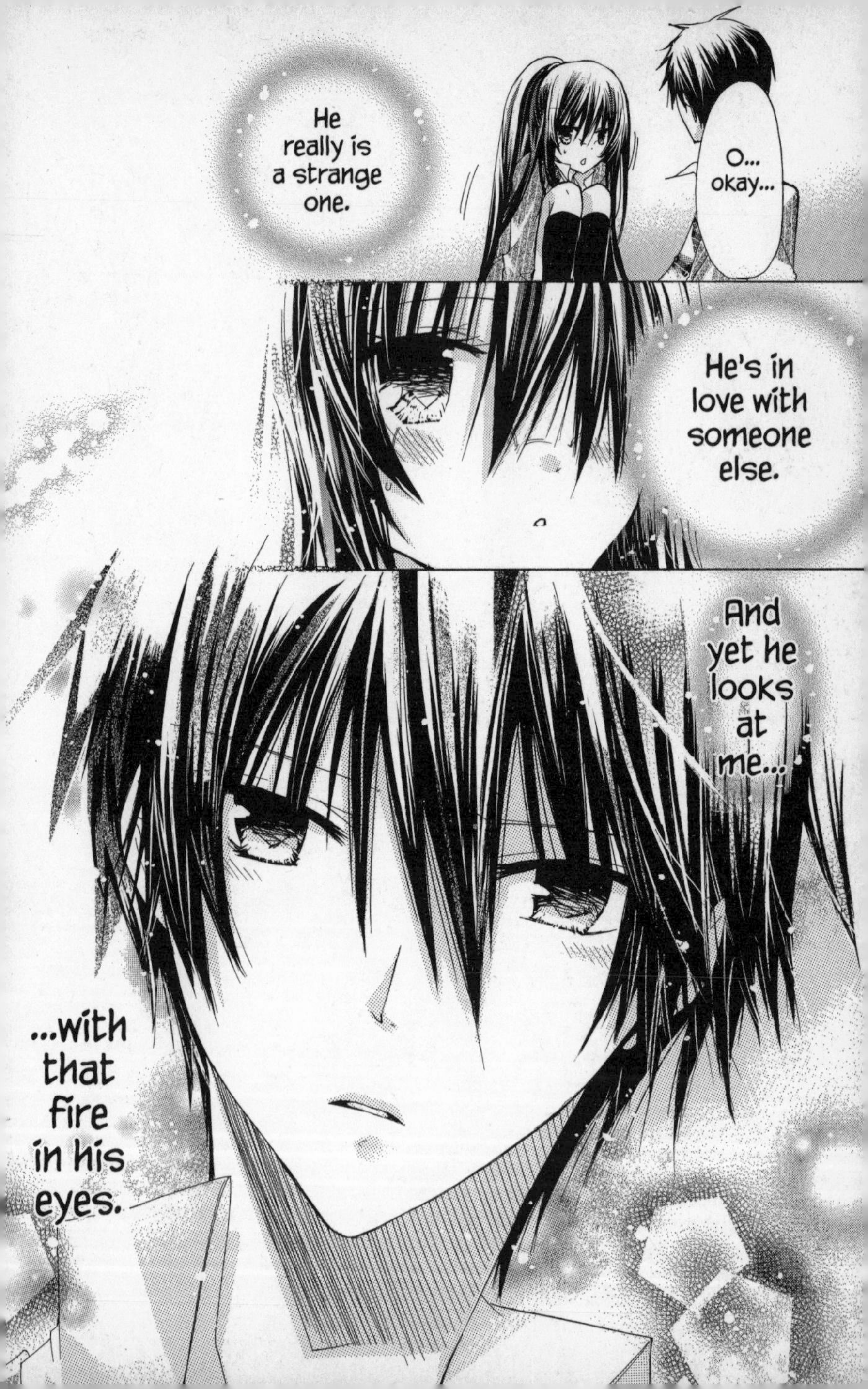
O... okay...
He really is a strange one.
He's in love with someone else.
And yet he looks at me...
...with that fire in his eyes.

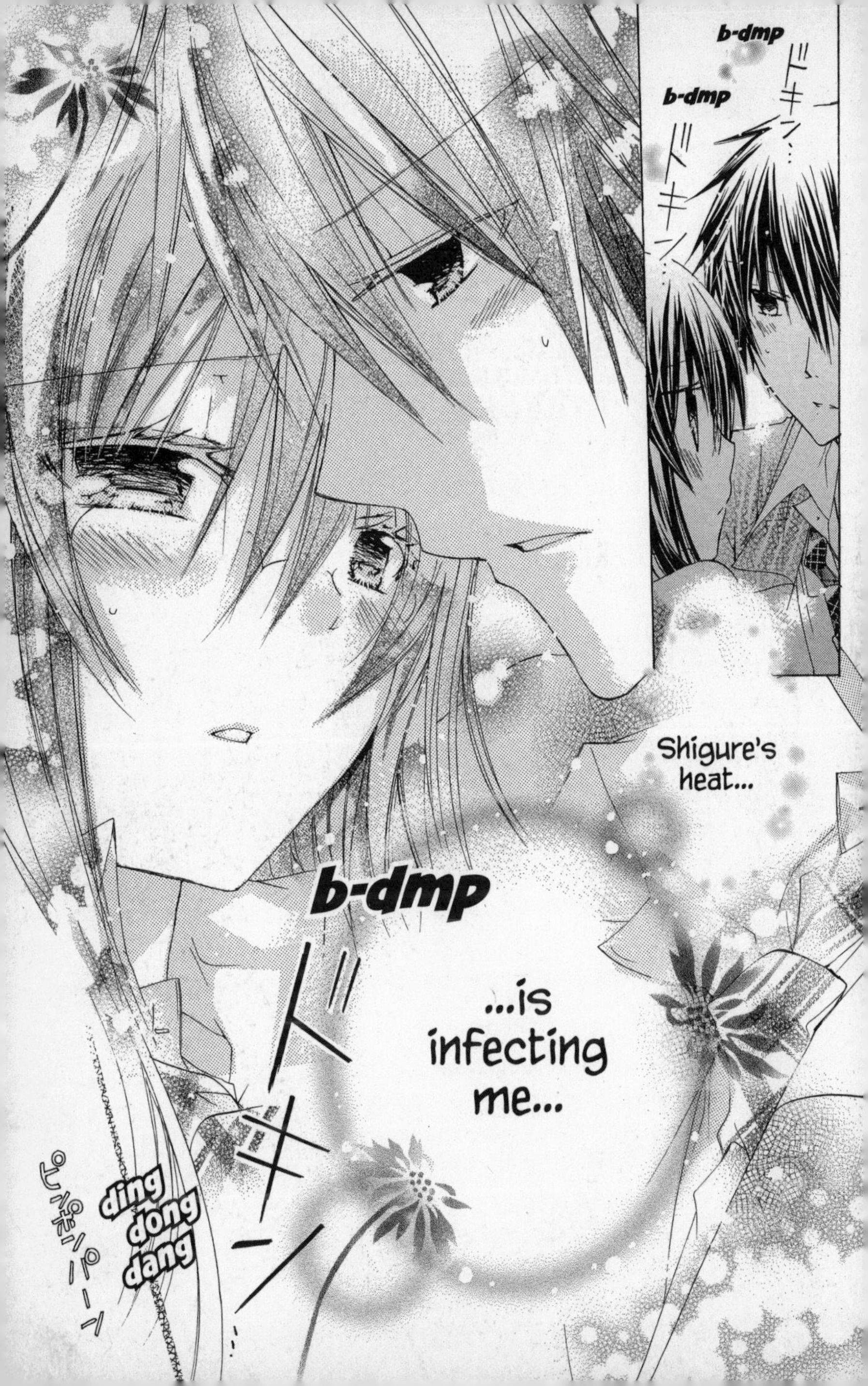

b-dmp
ドキン…
b-dmp
ドキン…
Shigure's heat...
b-dmp
ドキーン
...is infecting me...
ding dong dang

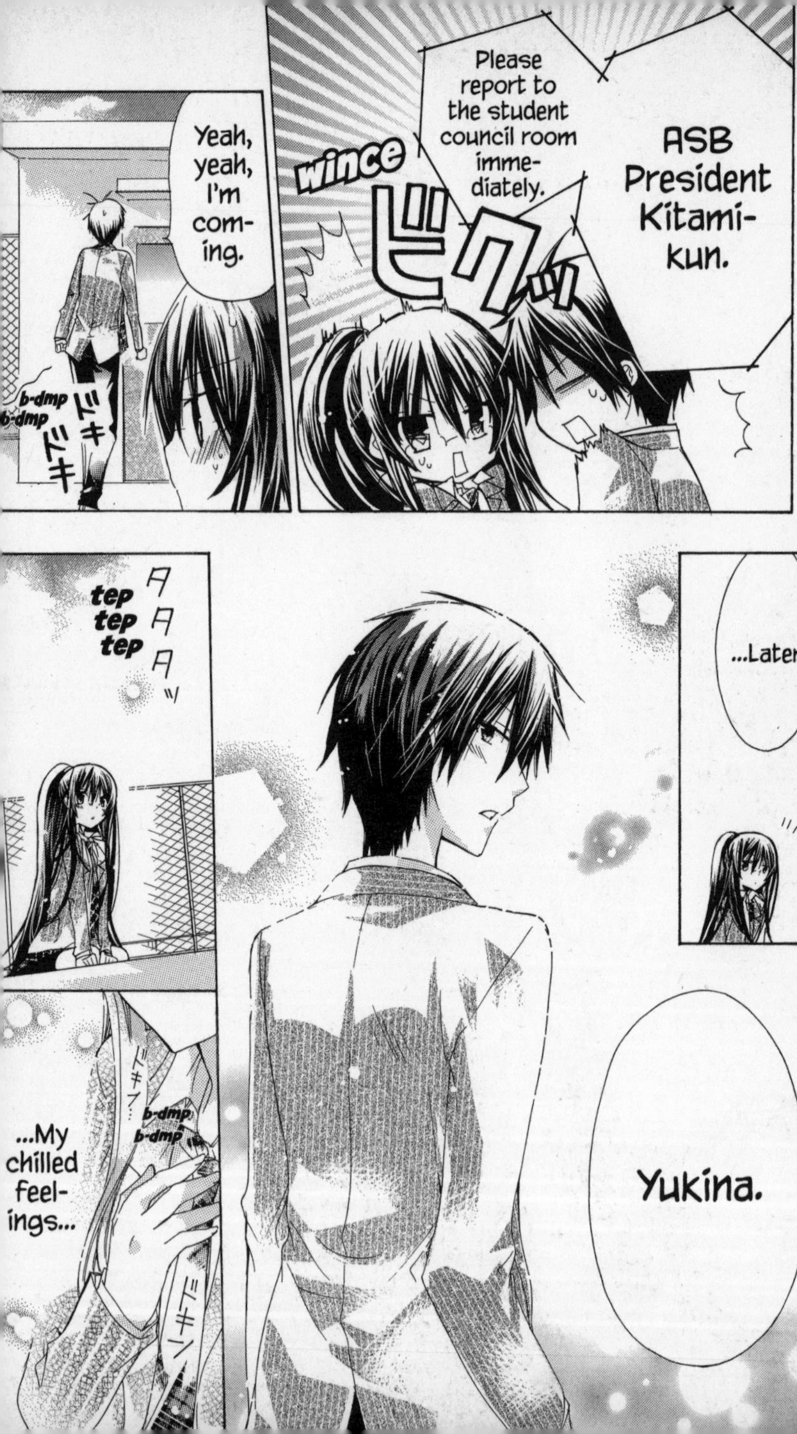
ASB President Kitami-kun.
Please report to the student council room immediately.
wince
ビクッ
Yeah, yeah, I'm coming.
b-dmp b-dmp
ドキドキ
...Later.
Yukina.
tep tep tep
タタタッ
...My chilled feelings...
b-dmp b-dmp
ドキッ…
ドキン

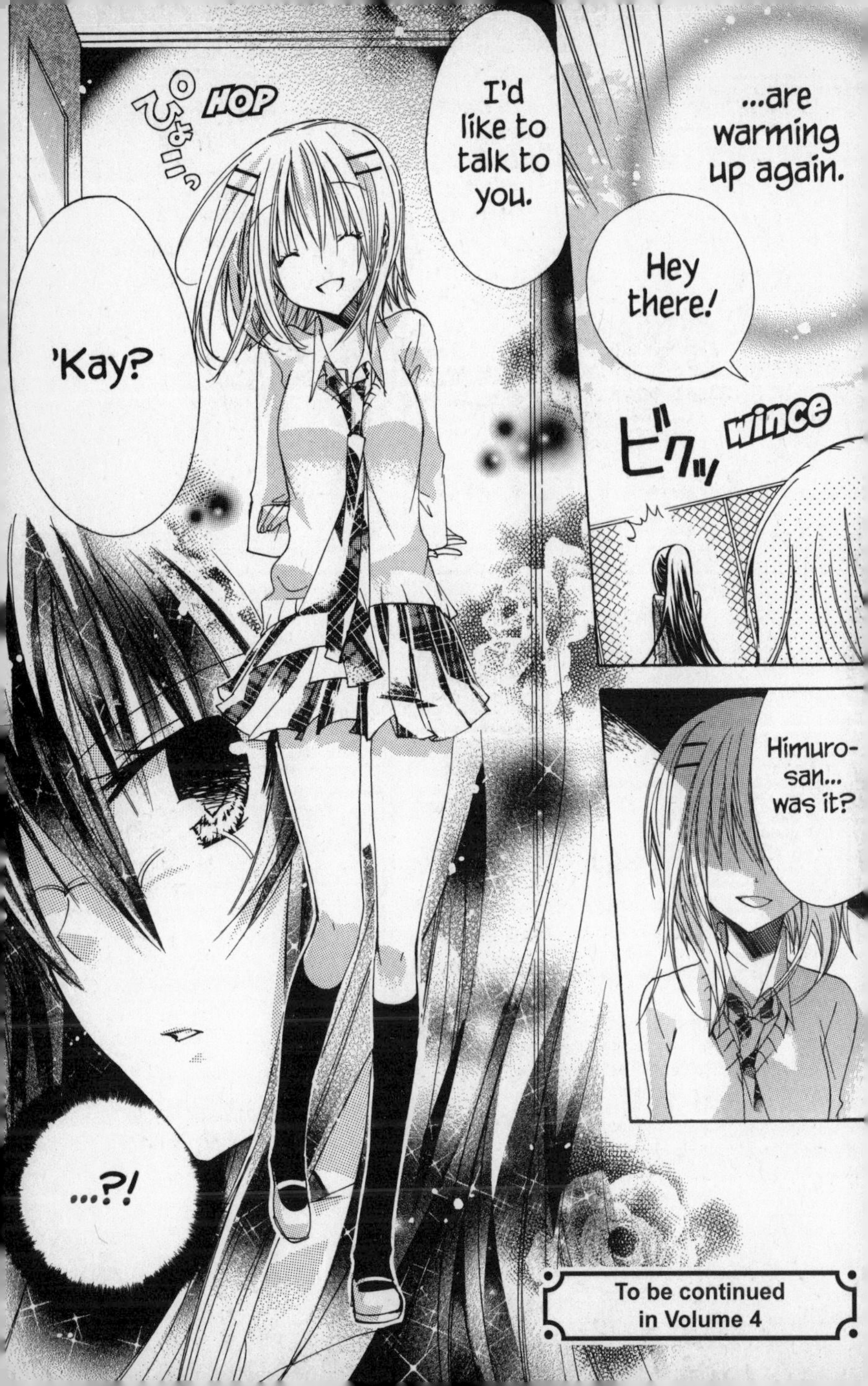
...are warming up again.
Hey there!
ビクッ
wince
Himuro-san... was it?
I'd like to talk to you.
ぴょこっ
HOP
'Kay?
...?!
To be continued in Volume 4

# Afterword

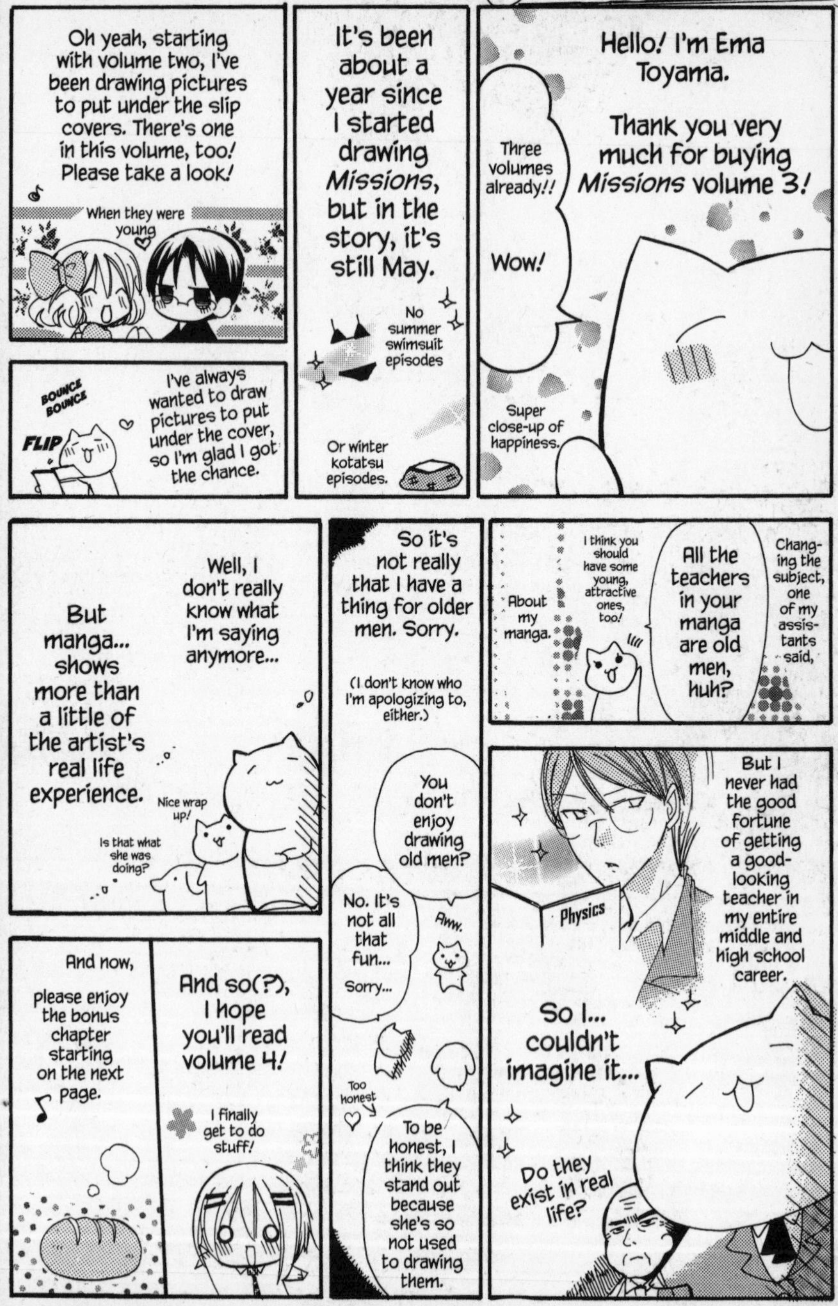

Hello! I'm Ema Toyama.
Thank you very much for buying *Missions* volume 3!
Three volumes already!!
Wow!
Super close-up of happiness.
It's been about a year since I started drawing *Missions*, but in the story, it's still May.
No summer swimsuit episodes
Or winter kotatsu episodes.
Oh yeah, starting with volume two, I've been drawing pictures to put under the slip covers. There's one in this volume, too! Please take a look!
When they were young
BOUNCE BOUNCE
I've always wanted to draw pictures to put under the cover, so I'm glad I got the chance.
FLIP
Changing the subject, one of my assistants said,
All the teachers in your manga are old men, huh?
I think you should have some young, attractive ones, too!
About my manga.
But I never had the good fortune of getting a good-looking teacher in my entire middle and high school career.
Physics
So I... couldn't imagine it...
Do they exist in real life?
So it's not really that I have a thing for older men. Sorry.
(I don't know who I'm apologizing to, either.)
You don't enjoy drawing old men?
No. It's not all that fun...
Aww.
Sorry...
Too honest
To be honest, I think they stand out because she's so not used to drawing them.
Well, I don't really know what I'm saying anymore...
But manga... shows more than a little of the artist's real life experience.
Nice wrap up!
Is that what she was doing?
And so(?), I hope you'll read volume 4!
I finally get to do stuff!
And now, please enjoy the bonus chapter starting on the next page.


Special Thanks ✿ My assistants Ryo-sama and Zo-sama, my editor N-jima-sama.

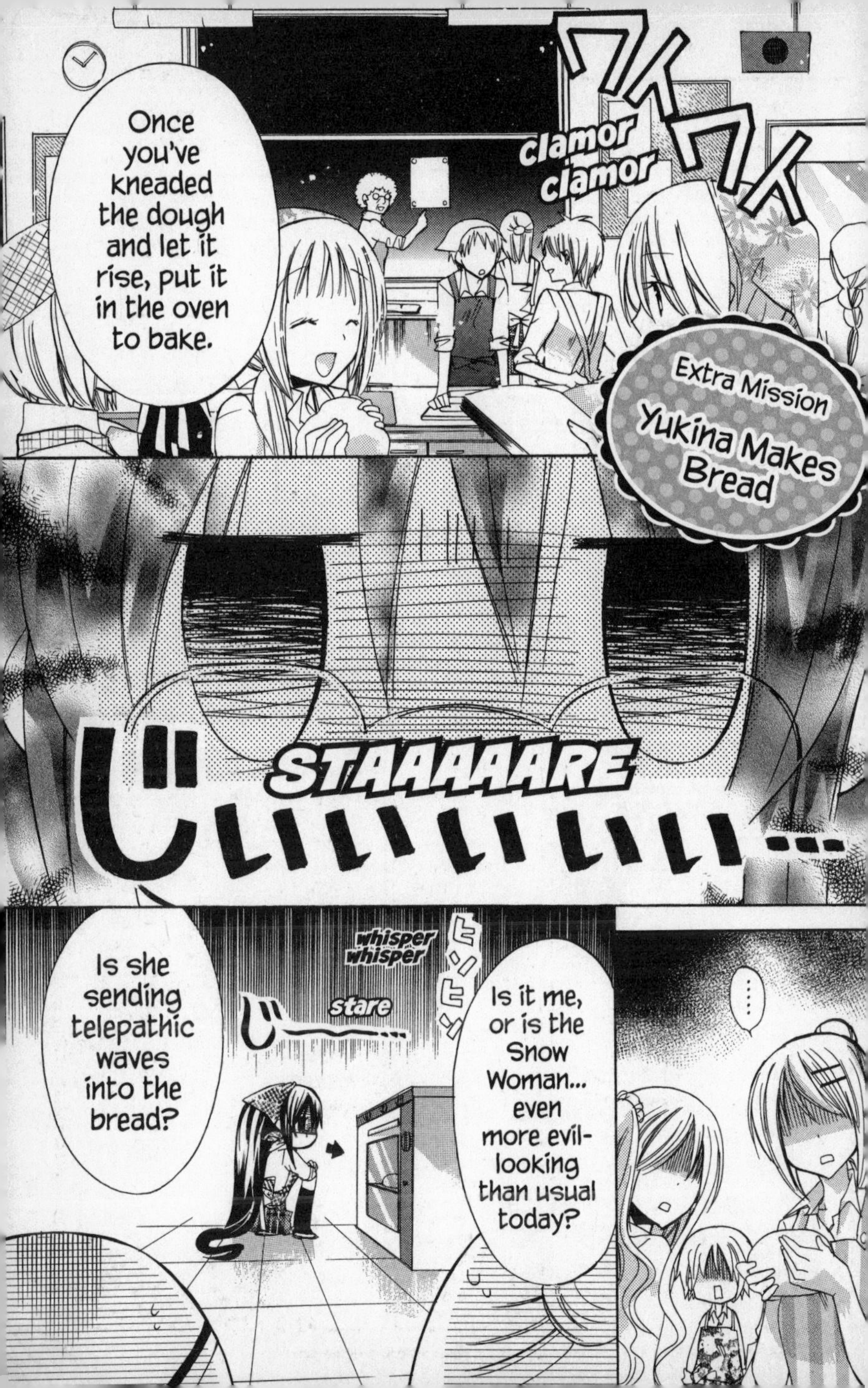
clamor clamor
Extra Mission
Yukina Makes Bread
Once you've kneaded the dough and let it rise, put it in the oven to bake.
STAAAAARE
.....
Is it me, or is the Snow Woman... even more evil-looking than usual today?
whisper whisper
stare
Is she sending telepathic waves into the bread?

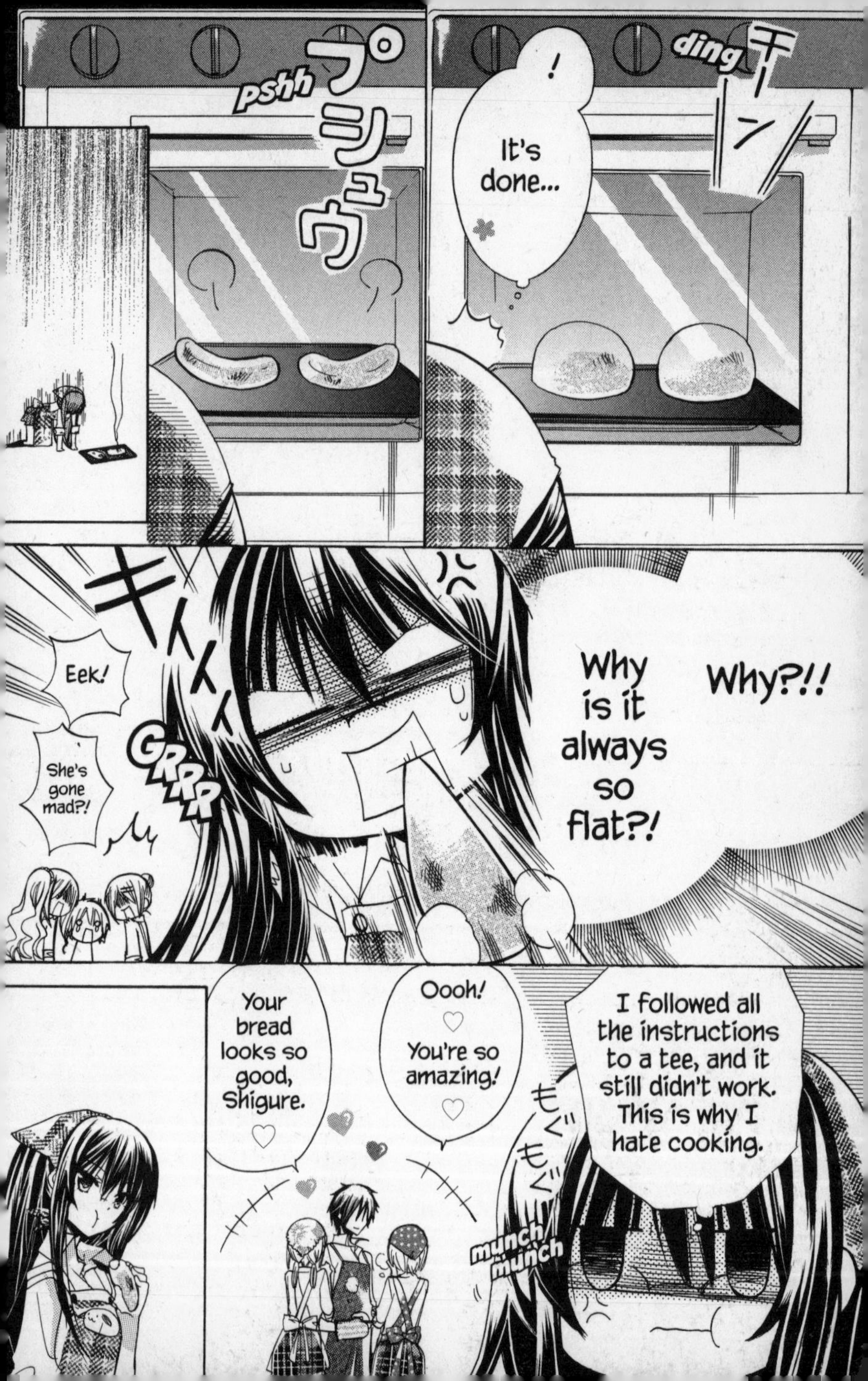

ding
チーン
!
It's done...
pshh
プシュウ
Why?!!
Why is it always so flat?!
キイイイ
GRRR
Eek!
She's gone mad?!
I followed all the instructions to a tee, and it still didn't work. This is why I hate cooking.
もぐもぐ
munch munch
Oooh! You're so amazing!
Your bread looks so good, Shigure.

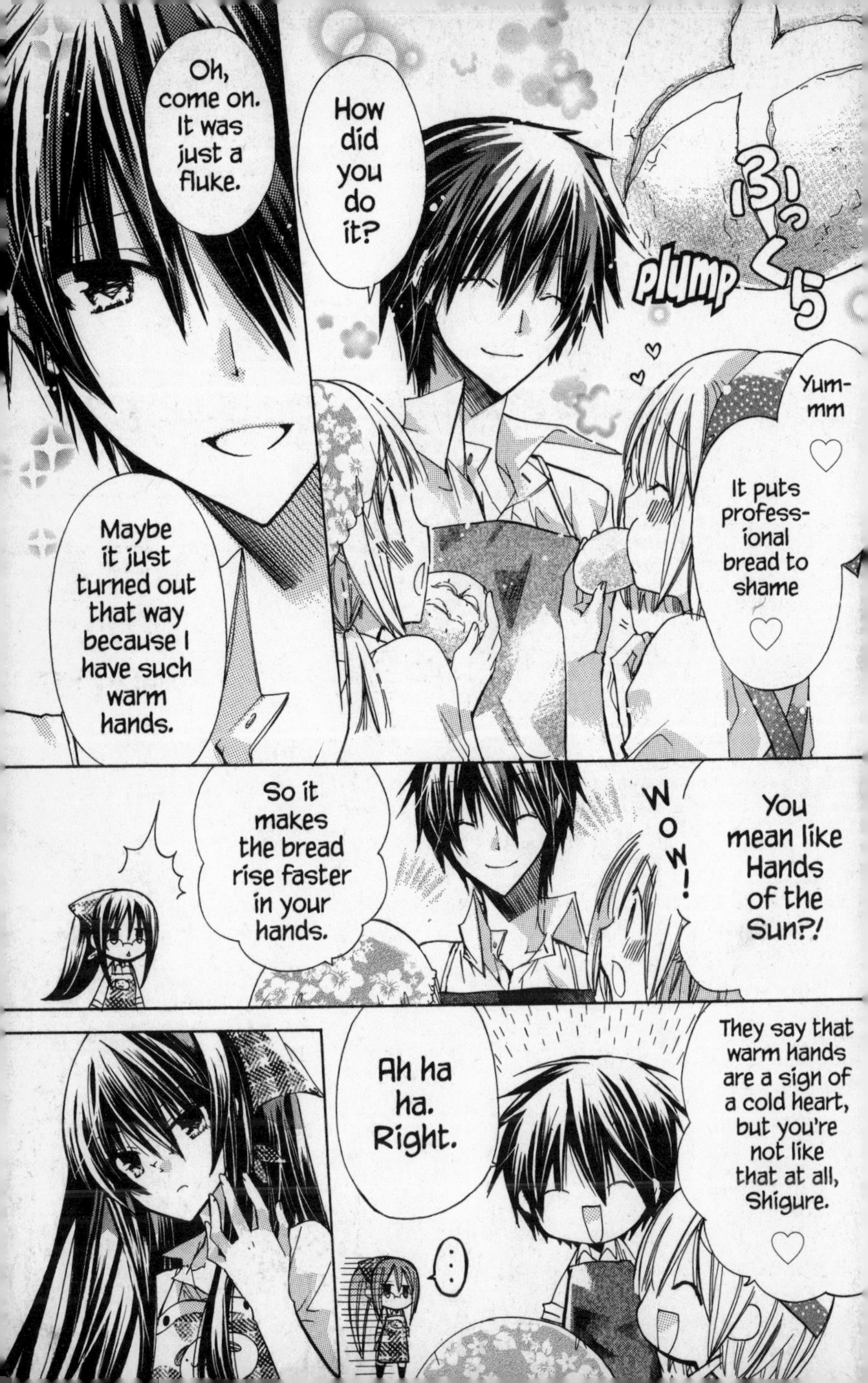
ふっくら
plump
Yumm-mm ♡
It puts professional bread to shame ♡
How did you do it?
Oh, come on. It was just a fluke.
Maybe it just turned out that way because I have such warm hands.
You mean like Hands of the Sun?!
WOW!
So it makes the bread rise faster in your hands.
They say that warm hands are a sign of a cold heart, but you're not like that at all, Shigure. ♡
Ah ha ha. Right.
...

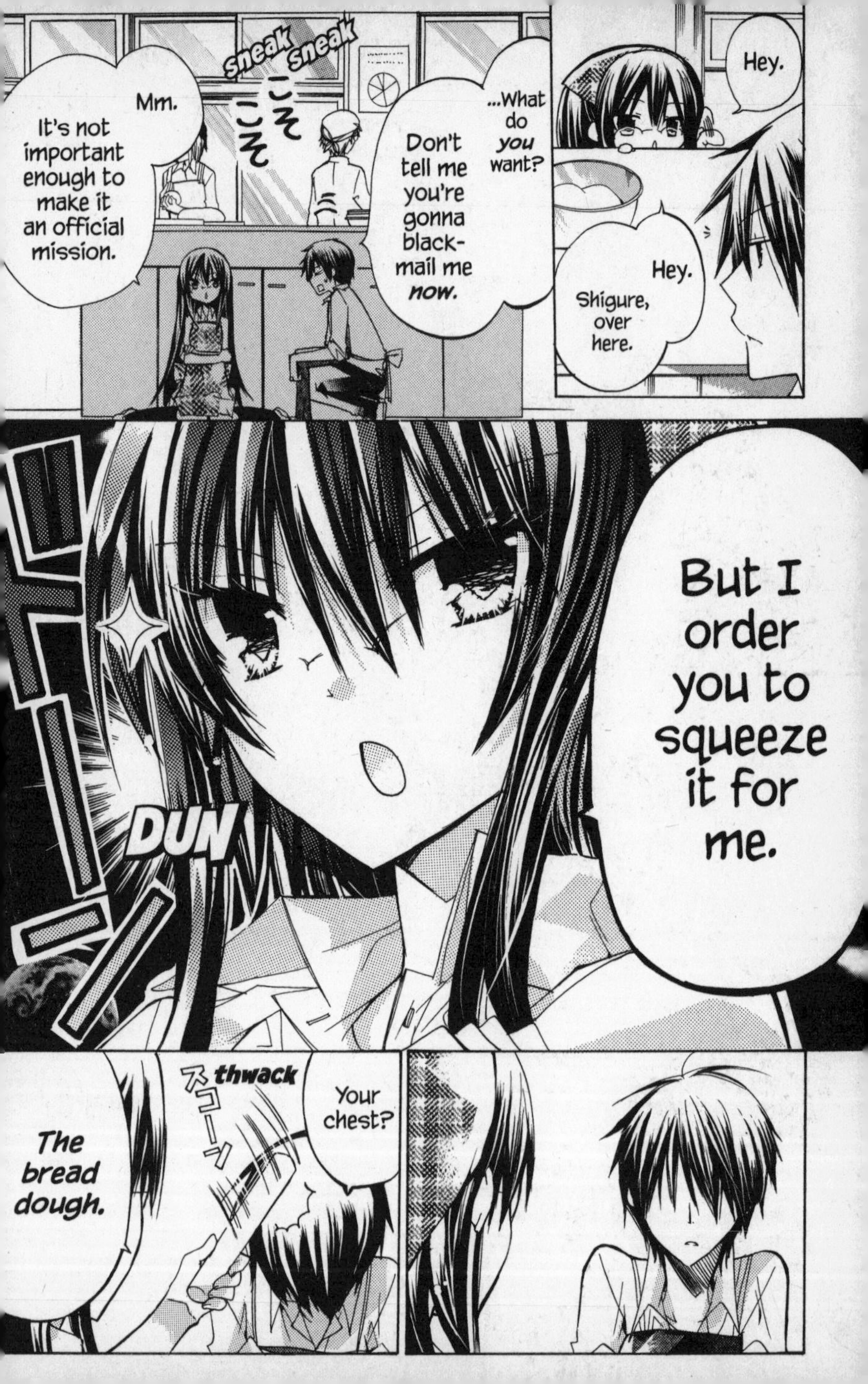
Hey.
Hey. Shigure, over here.
Sneak Sneak
こそこそ
...What do you want?
Don't tell me you're gonna black-mail me now.
Mm.
It's not important enough to make it an official mission.
But I order you to squeeze it for me.
DUN
Your chest?
thwack
スコーン
The bread dough.

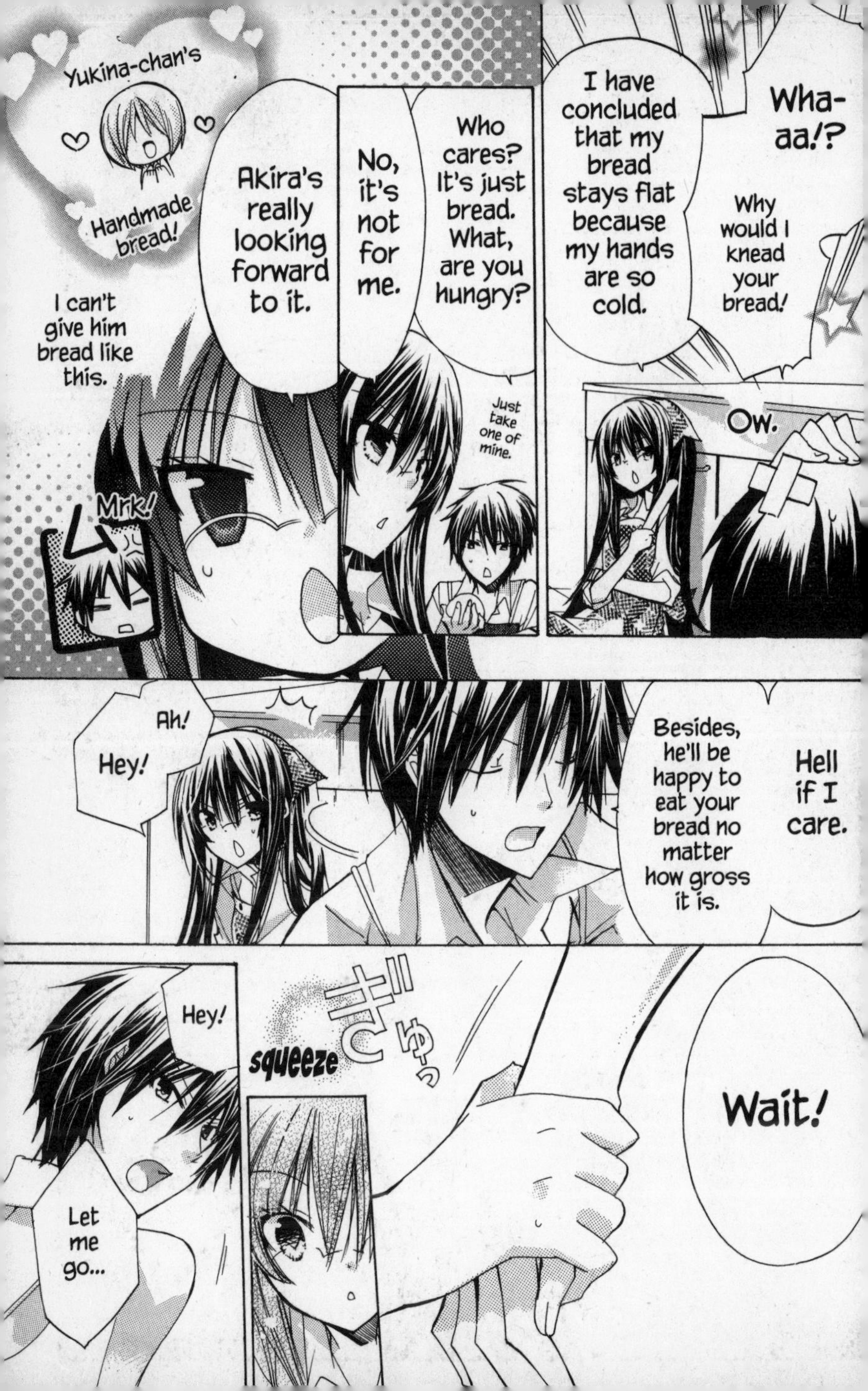
Wha-aa!?
Why would I knead your bread!
I have concluded that my bread stays flat because my hands are so cold.
Ow.
Who cares? It's just bread. What, are you hungry?
No, it's not for me.
Just take one of mine.
Akira's really looking forward to it.
Yukina-chan's Handmade bread!
I can't give him bread like this.
Mrk!
Hell if I care.
Besides, he'll be happy to eat your bread no matter how gross it is.
Ah!
Hey!
Wait!
ぎゅっ
squeeze
Hey!
Let me go...

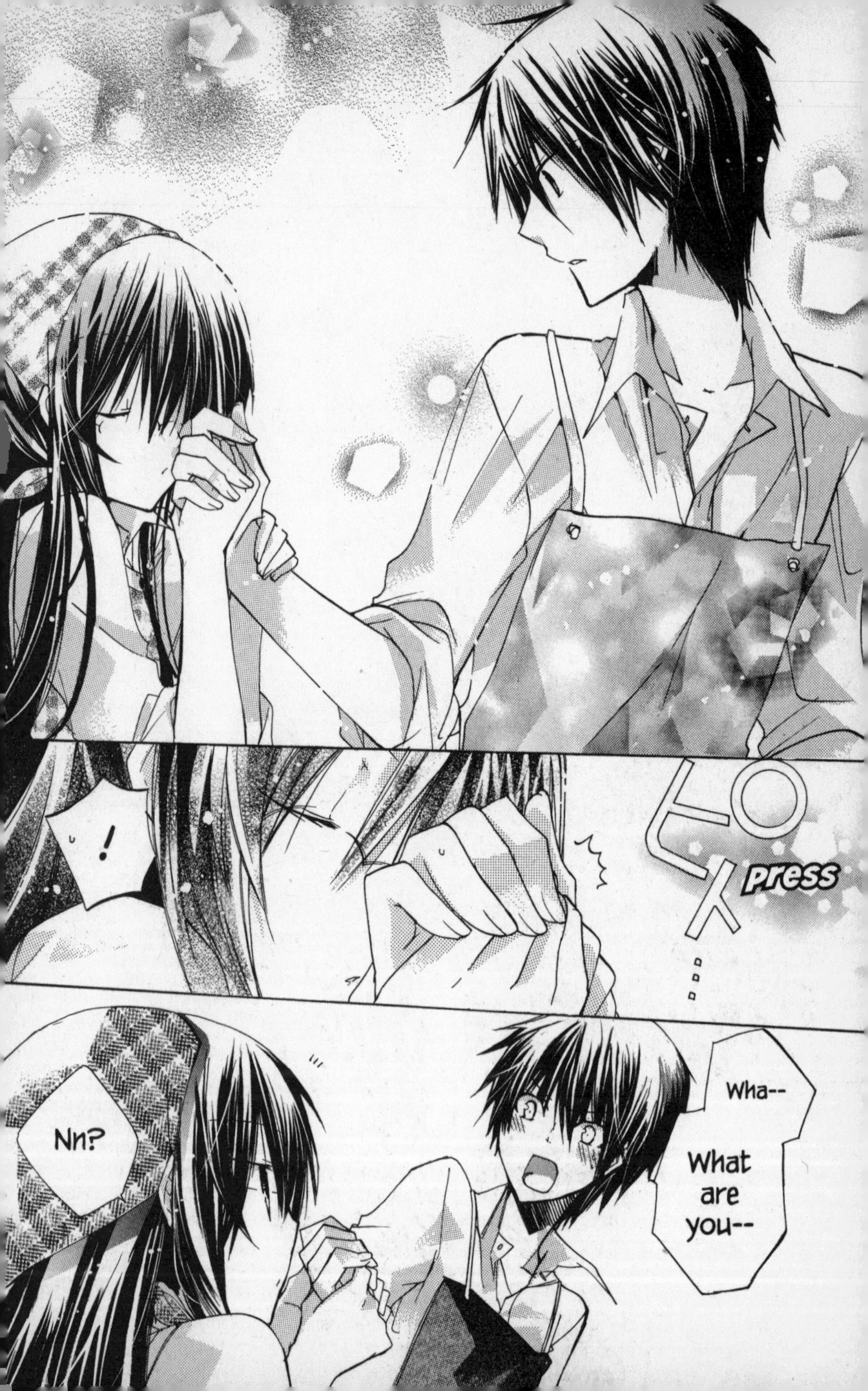
press
!
Wha--
What are you--
Nn?

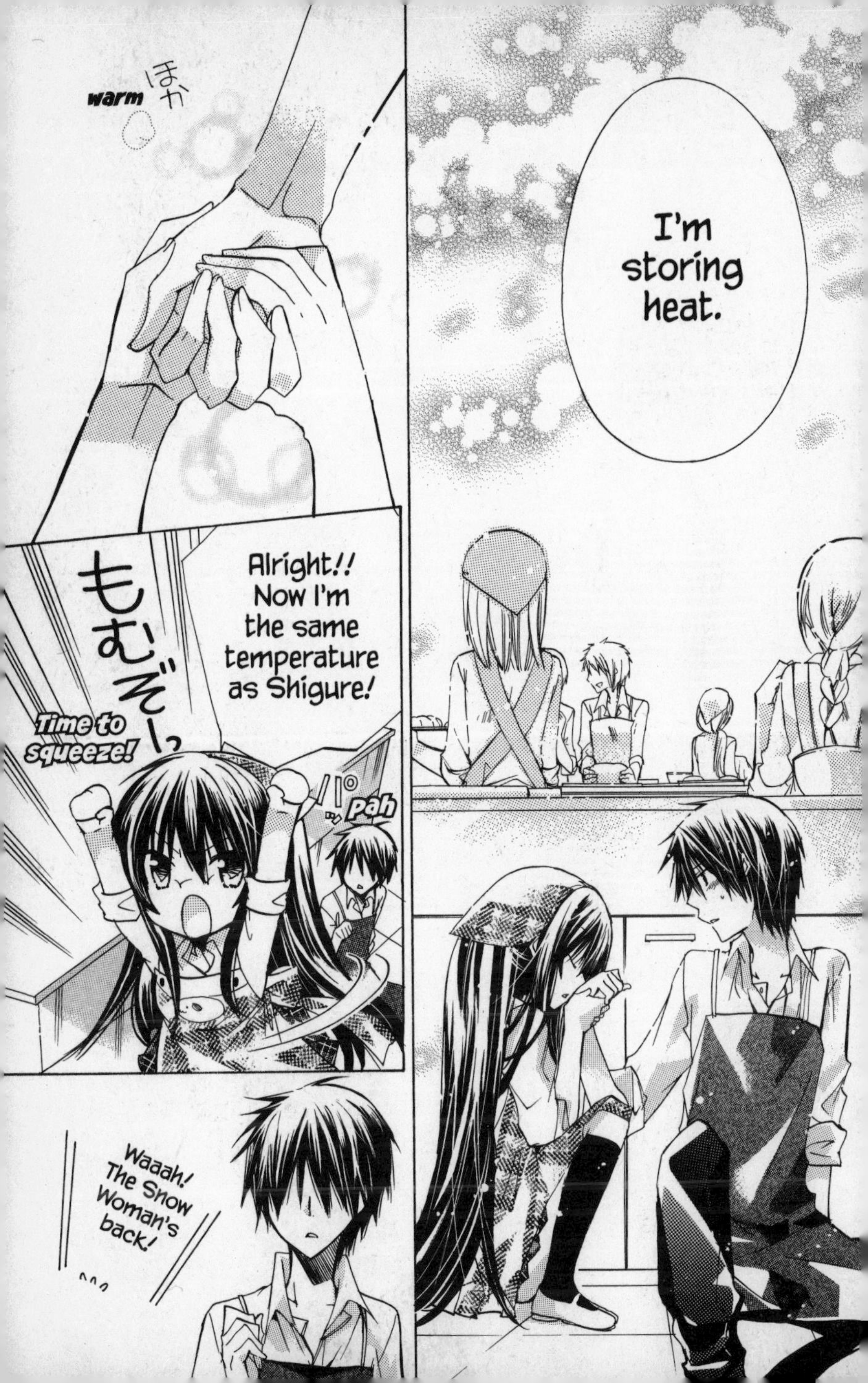

I'm storing heat.
ほか
warm
Alright!! Now I'm the same temperature as Shigure!
もむぞーっ
Time to squeeze!
パッ
Pah
Waaah! The Snow Woman's back!

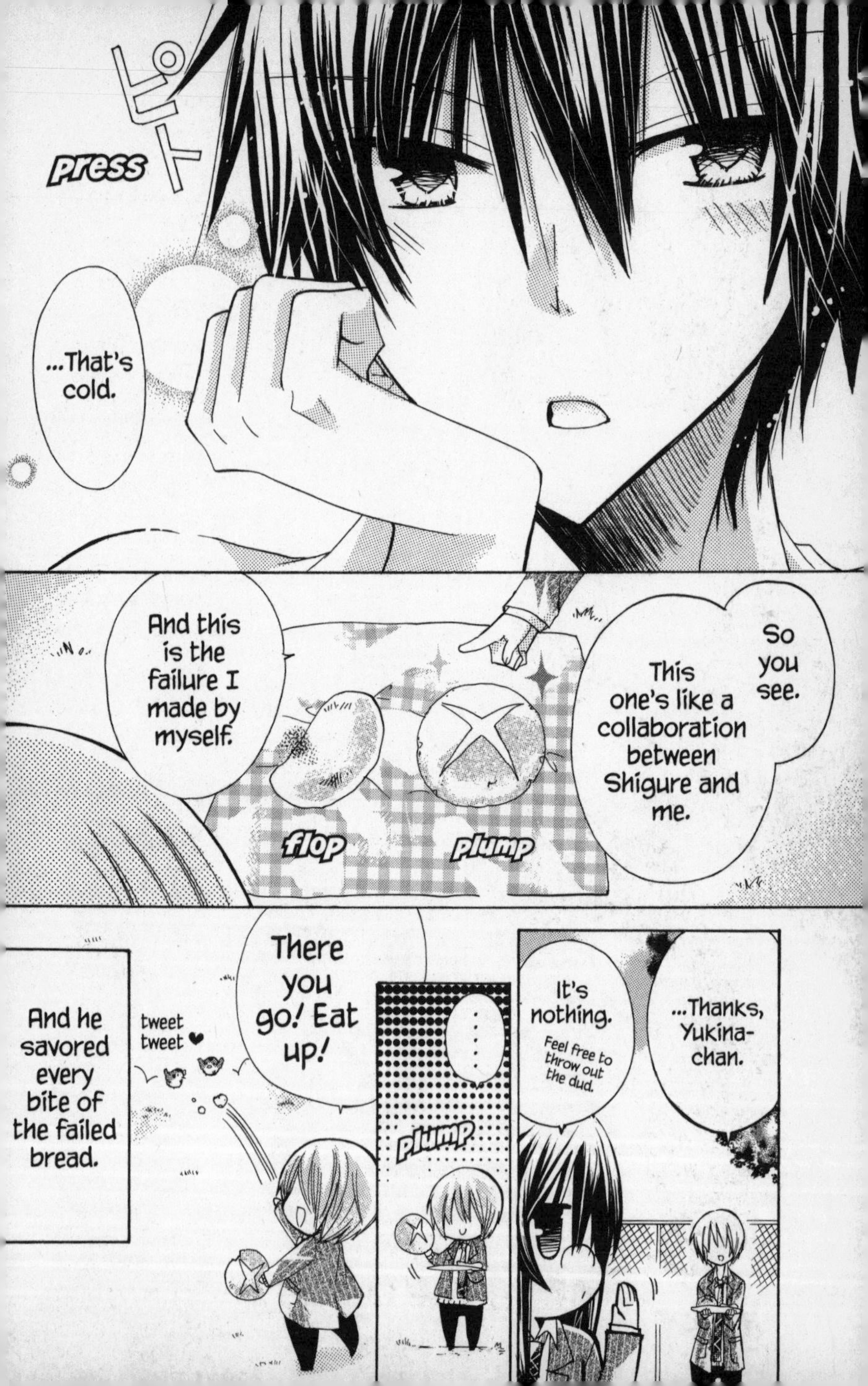
ピト
press
...That's cold.
So you see.
This one's like a collaboration between Shigure and me.
And this is the failure I made by myself.
plump
flop
...Thanks, Yukina-chan.
It's nothing.
Feel free to throw out the dud.
......
plump
There you go! Eat up!
tweet tweet
And he savored every bite of the failed bread.

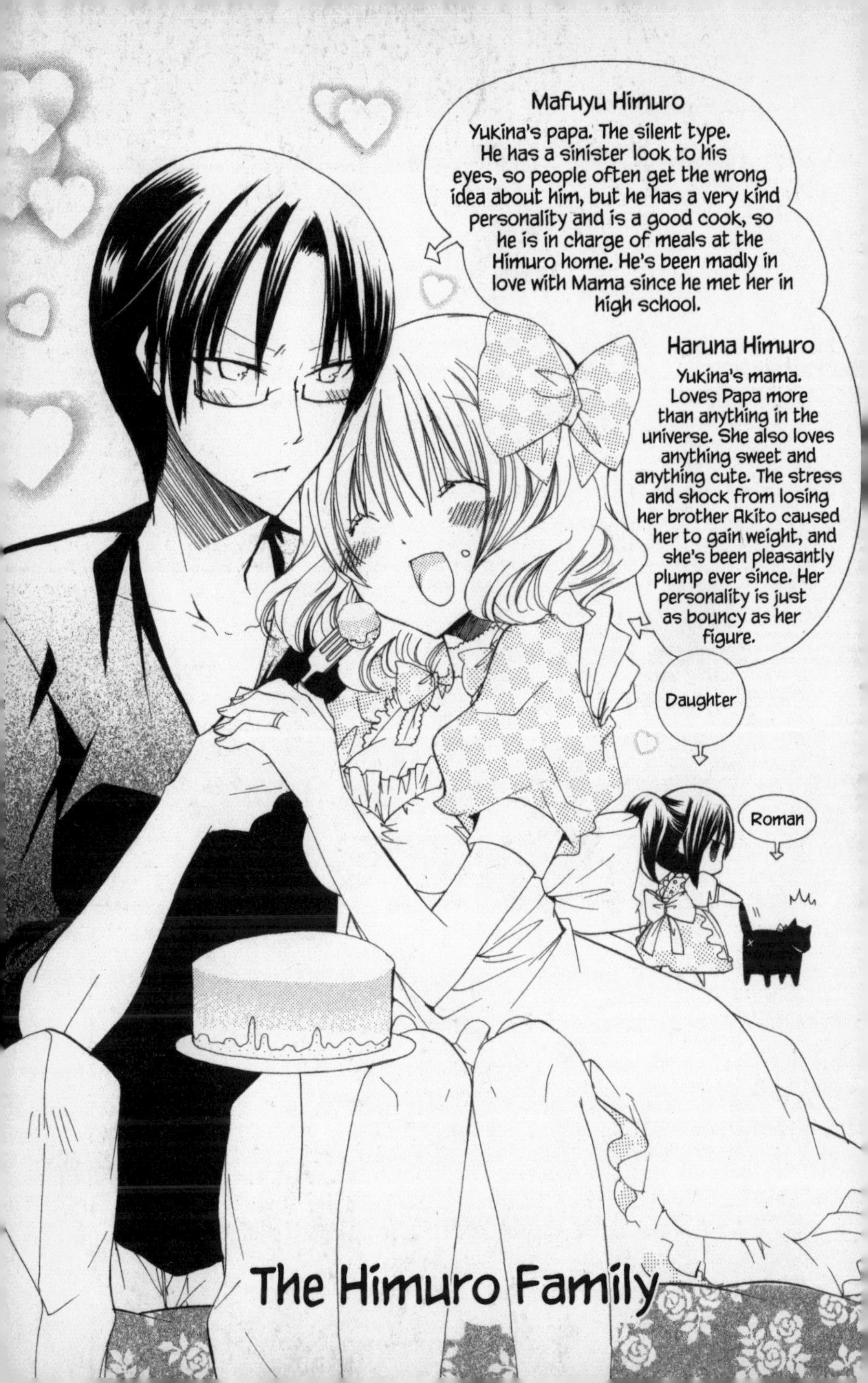
Mafuyu Himuro
Yukina's papa. The silent type. He has a sinister look to his eyes, so people often get the wrong idea about him, but he has a very kind personality and is a good cook, so he is in charge of meals at the Himuro home. He's been madly in love with Mama since he met her in high school.
Haruna Himuro
Yukina's mama. Loves Papa more than anything in the universe. She also loves anything sweet and anything cute. The stress and shock from losing her brother Akito caused her to gain weight, and she's been pleasantly plump ever since. Her personality is just as bouncy as her figure.
Daughter
Roman
The Himuro Family

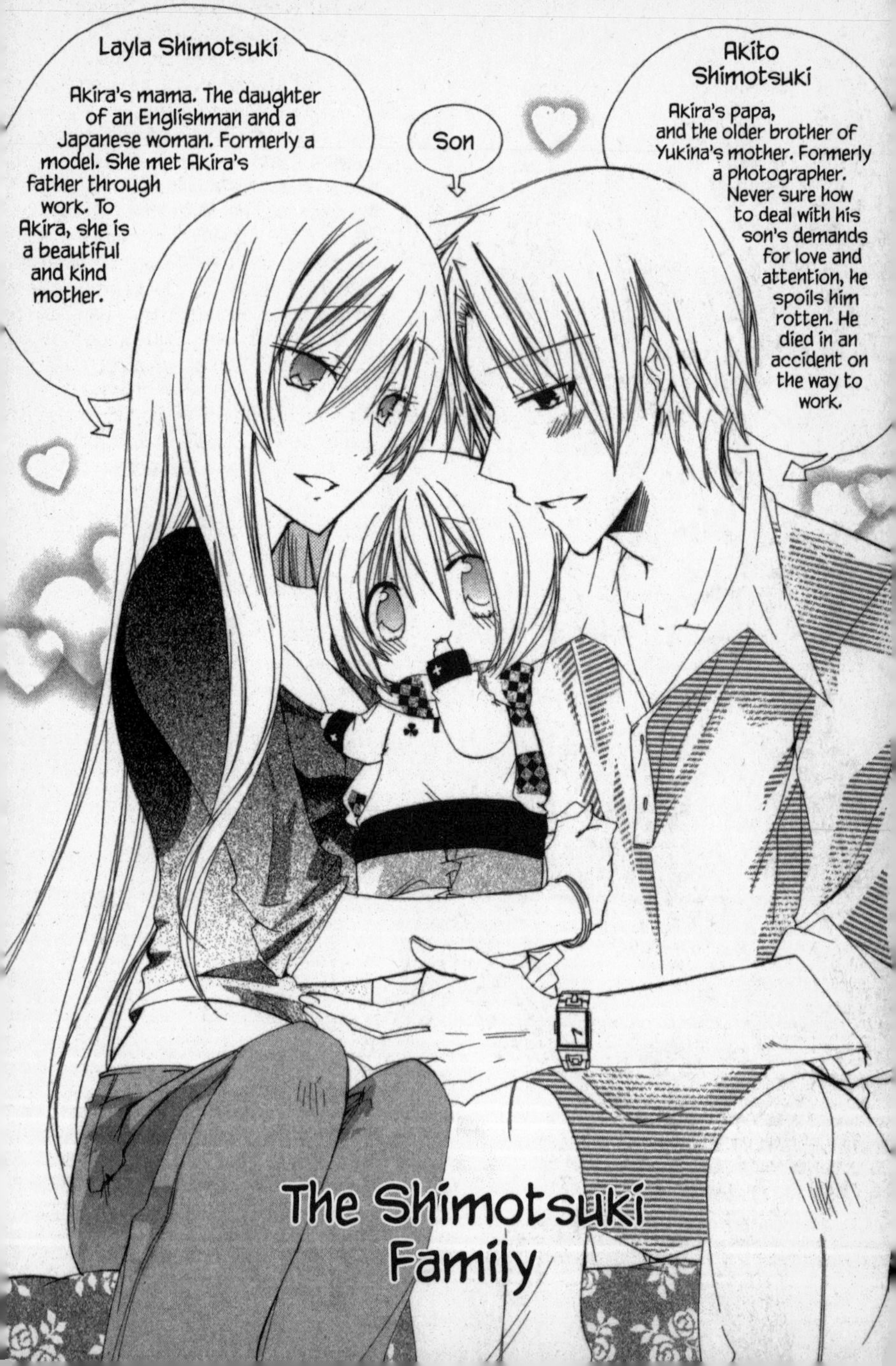
Akito Shimotsuki
Akira's papa, and the older brother of Yukina's mother. Formerly a photographer. Never sure how to deal with his son's demands for love and attention, he spoils him rotten. He died in an accident on the way to work.
Son
Layla Shimotsuki
Akira's mama. The daughter of an Englishman and a Japanese woman. Formerly a model. She met Akira's father through work. To Akira, she is a beautiful and kind mother.
The Shimotsuki Family

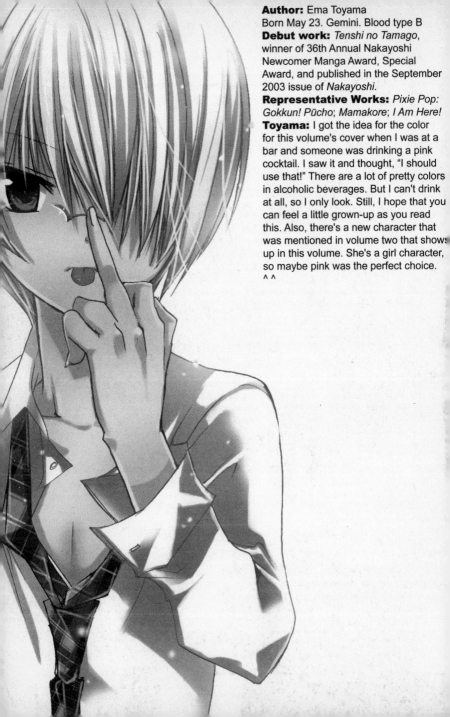

**Author:** Ema Toyama
Born May 23. Gemini. Blood type B
**Debut work:** *Tenshi no Tamago*,
winner of 36th Annual Nakayoshi
Newcomer Manga Award, Special
Award, and published in the September
2003 issue of *Nakayoshi*.
**Representative Works:** *Pixie Pop:
Gokkun! Pūcho*; *Mamakore*; *I Am Here!*
**Toyama:** I got the idea for the color
for this volume's cover when I was at a
bar and someone was drinking a pink
cocktail. I saw it and thought, "I should
use that!" There are a lot of pretty colors
in alcoholic beverages. But I can't drink
at all, so I only look. Still, I hope that you
can feel a little grown-up as you read
this. Also, there's a new character that
was mentioned in volume two that shows
up in this volume. She's a girl character,
so maybe pink was the perfect choice.
^ ^

# Translation Notes

Japanese is a tricky language for most Westerners, and translation is often more art than science. For your edification and reading pleasure, here are notes on some of the places where we could have gone in a different direction with our translation of the work, or where a Japanese cultural reference is used.

## My class is in a different room next period, page 31

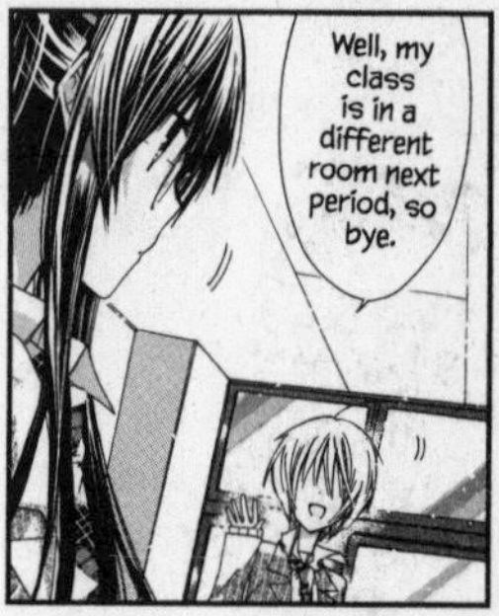
Well, my class is in a different room next period, so bye.

Unlike schools in America, where each teacher has a room and the students all move from room to room throughout the day, in Japan, each set of students has a room, and the teachers will move from class to class to teach their various subjects. However, the class will move for some lessons, such as cooking classes, science labs that require special equipment, etc. This is called idō kyōshitsu (moving classroom), or just idō for short. A more literal translation of Akira's line would be, "My class is on the move next period."

## Your Highness, page 151

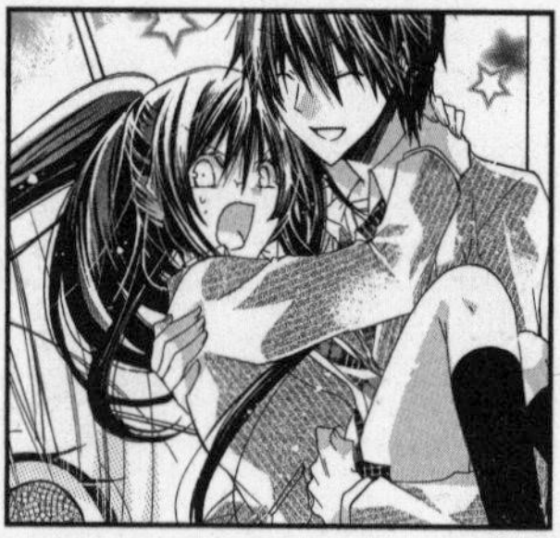

There's a reason that Shigure starts addressing Yukina as he would royalty, other than just to mess with her head (though of course that's probably part of it). In Japanese, the way he's carrying her is called ohimesama dakko. Ohimesama means "honorable princess," and dakko means "to carry in the arms," so together, the terms roughly translate to, "to carry in the arms as you would a princess." In this scenario, Yukina becomes the princess, and Shigure addresses her accordingly.

## Hands of the Sun, page 161

This may be a reference to *Yakitate!! Japan*, a manga series about a boy with exceptionally warm hands, called Hands of the Sun, that aid him in his quest to make the best bread in the world.

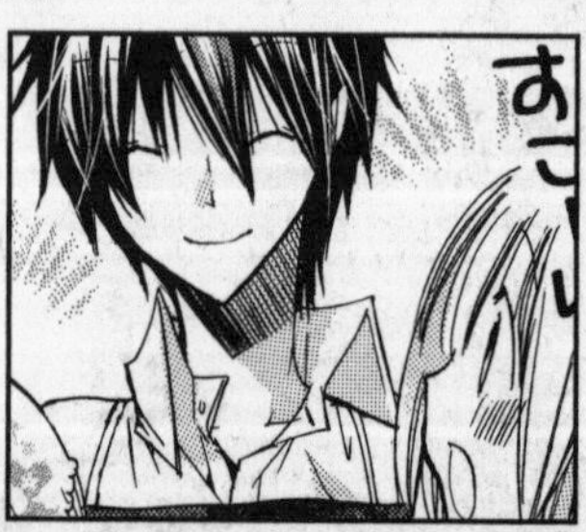

# Mami vs. Yukina

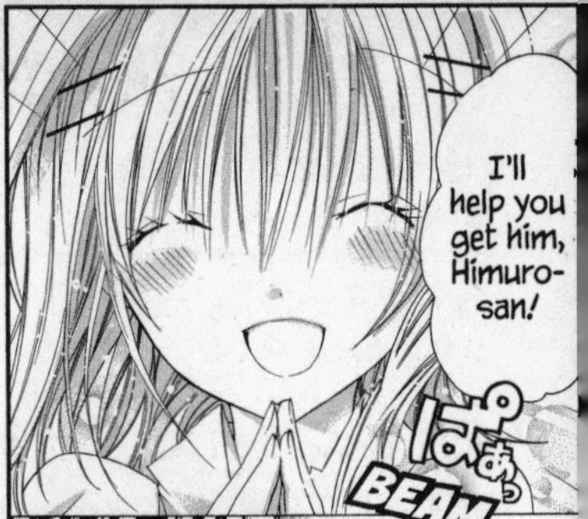
I'll help you get him, Himuro-san!
ぱあっ
BEAM

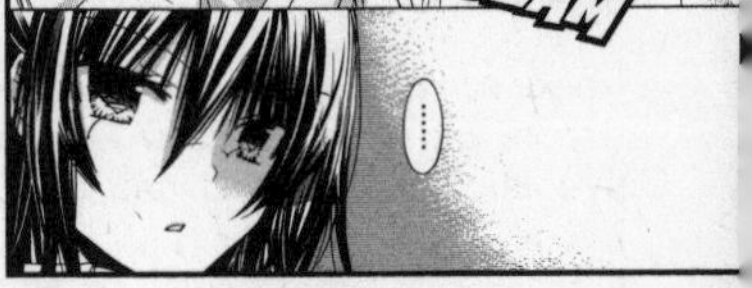
......

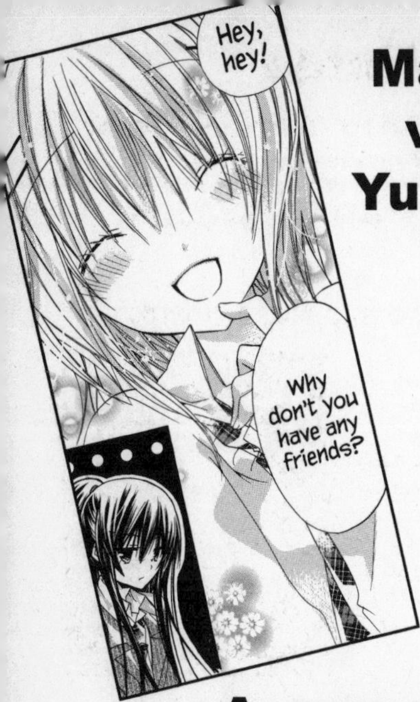
Hey, hey!
Why don't you have any friends?

## A woman's battle!? Or...

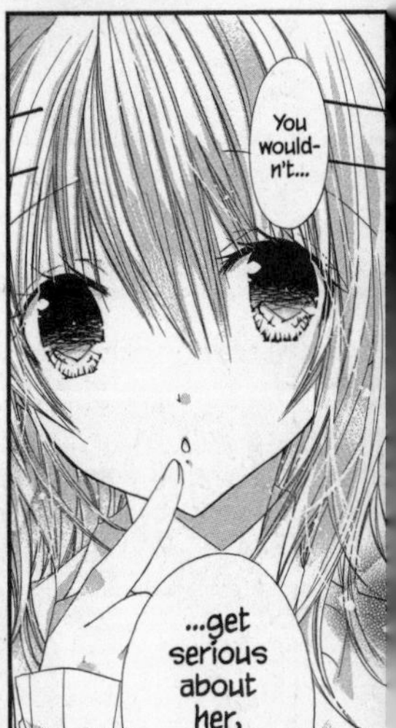
You wouldn't...
...get serious about her, would you?

For reasons known only to her, Mami Mizuno makes contact with Yukina. What is the true motive hidden behind her adorable smile?

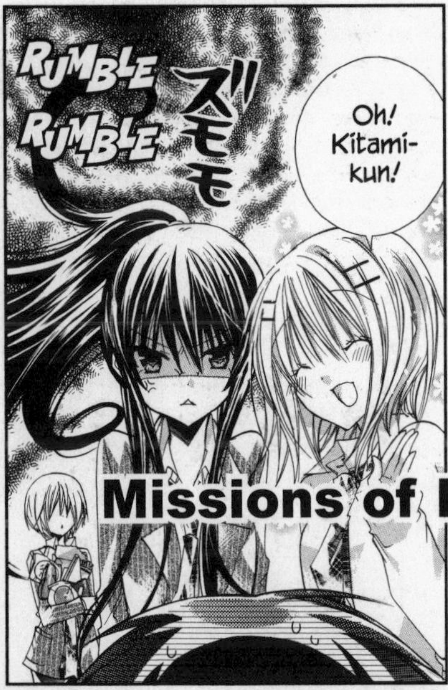
RUMBLE RUMBLE
ズモモ
Oh! Kitami-kun!

# Missions of Love volume four!

**Coming soon, but for now, enjoy this preview!**

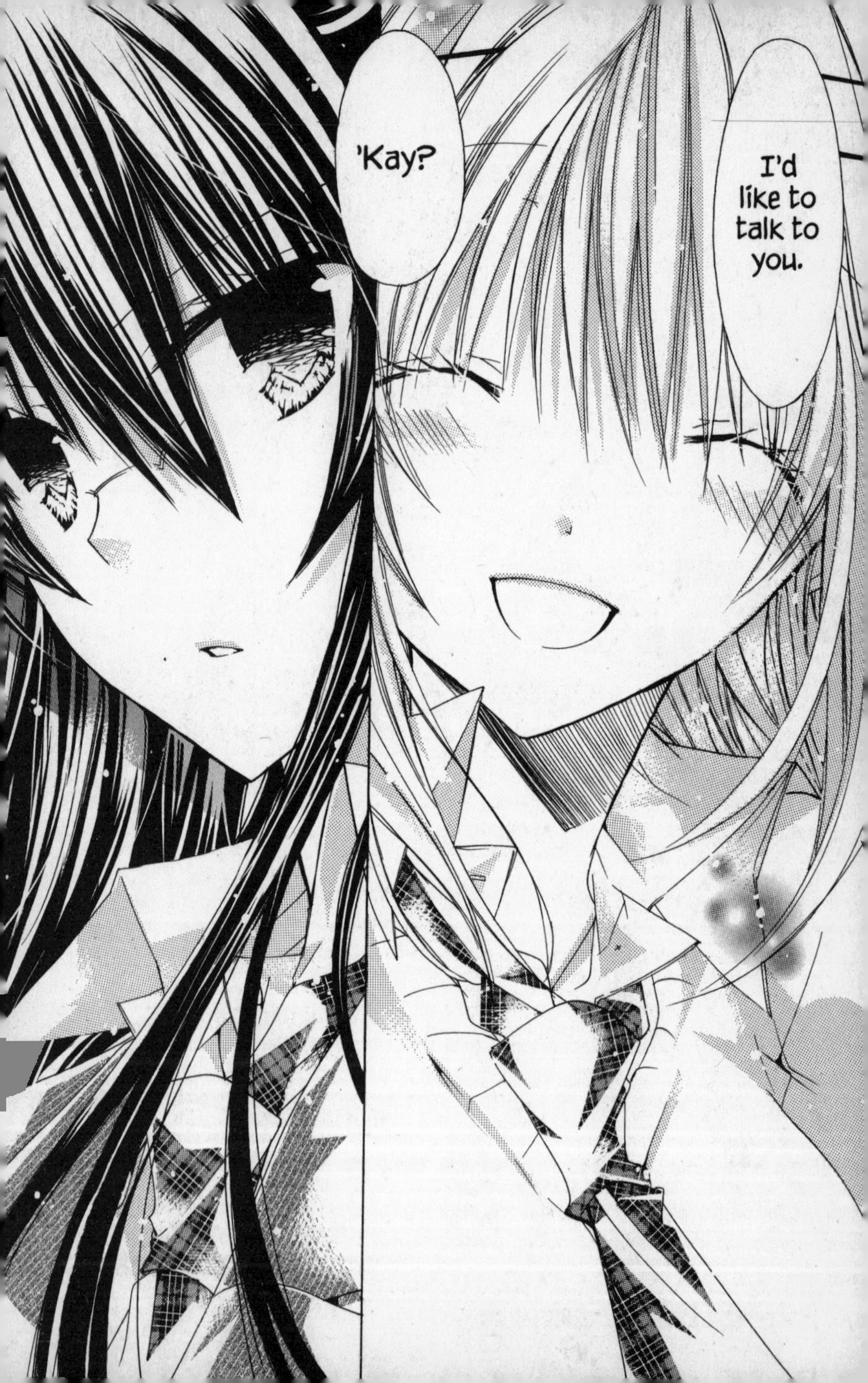
I'd like to talk to you.
'Kay?